ElasticSearch Cookbook

Second Edition

Over 130 advanced recipes to search, analyze, deploy, manage, and monitor data effectively with ElasticSearch

Alberto Paro

[PACKT] open source*
PUBLISHING
community experience distilled

BIRMINGHAM - MUMBAI

ElasticSearch Cookbook

Second Edition

First published: December 2013

Second edition: January 2015

Production reference: 1230115

Published by Packt Publishing Ltd.
Livery Place
35 Livery Street
Birmingham B3 2PB, UK.

ISBN 978-1-78355-483-6

www.packtpub.com

Credits

Author

Alberto Paro

Reviewers

Florian Hopf

Wenhan Lu

Suvda Myagmar

Dan Noble

Philip O'Toole

Acquisition Editor

Rebecca Youé

Content Development Editor

Amey Varangaonkar

Technical Editors

Prajakta Mhatre

Rohith Rajan

Copy Editors

Hiral Bhat

Dipti Kapadia

Neha Karnani

Shambhavi Pai

Laxmi Subramanian

Ashwati Thampi

Project Coordinator

Leena Purkait

Proofreaders

Ting Baker

Samuel Redman Birch

Stephen Copestake

Ameesha Green

Lauren E. Harkins

Indexer

Hemangini Bari

Graphics

Valentina D'silva

Production Coordinator

Manu Joseph

Cover Work

Manu Joseph

About the Author

Alberto Paro is an engineer, project manager, and software developer. He currently works as a CTO at Big Data Technologies and as a freelance consultant on software engineering for Big Data and NoSQL solutions. He loves to study emerging solutions and applications mainly related to Big Data processing, NoSQL, natural language processing, and neural networks. He began programming in BASIC on a Sinclair Spectrum when he was 8 years old, and to date, has collected a lot of experience using different operating systems, applications, and programming.

In 2000, he graduated in computer science engineering at Politecnico di Milano with a thesis on designing multiuser and multidevice web applications. He assisted professors at the university for about a year. He then came in contact with The Net Planet Company and loved their innovative ideas; he started working on knowledge management solutions and advanced data mining products. In summer 2014, his company was acquired by a Big Data technologies company, where he currently works mainly using Scala and Python on state-of-the-art big data software (Spark, Akka, Cassandra, and YARN). In 2013, he started freelancing as a consultant for Big Data, machine learning, and ElasticSearch.

In his spare time, when he is not playing with his children, he likes to work on open source projects. When he was in high school, he started contributing to projects related to the GNOME environment (gtkmm). One of his preferred programming languages is Python, and he wrote one of the first NoSQL backends on Django for MongoDB (Django-MongoDB-engine). In 2010, he began using ElasticSearch to provide search capabilities to some Django e-commerce sites and developed PyES (a Pythonic client for ElasticSearch), as well as the initial part of the ElasticSearch MongoDB river. He is the author of *ElasticSearch Cookbook* as well as a technical reviewer *Elasticsearch Server, Second Edition*, and the video course, *Building a Search Server with ElasticSearch*, all of which are published by Packt Publishing.

Acknowledgments

It would have been difficult for me to complete this book without the support of a large number of people.

First, I would like to thank my wife, my children, and the rest of my family for their valuable support.

On a more personal note, I'd like to thank my friend, Mauro Gallo, for his patience.

I'd like to express my gratitude to everyone at Packt Publishing who've been involved in the development and production of this book. I'd like to thank Amey Varangaonkar for guiding this book to completion, and Florian Hopf, Philip O'Toole, and Suvda Myagmar for patiently going through the first drafts and providing valuable feedback. Their professionalism, courtesy, good judgment, and passion for this book are much appreciated.

About the Reviewers

Florian Hopf works as a freelance software developer and consultant in Karlsruhe, Germany. He familiarized himself with Lucene-based search while working with different content management systems on the Java platform. He is responsible for small and large search systems, on both the Internet and intranet, for web content and application-specific data based on Lucene, Solr, and ElasticSearch. He helps to organize the local Java User Group as well as the Search Meetup in Karlsruhe, and he blogs at `http://blog.florian-hopf.de`.

Wenhan Lu is currently pursuing his master's degree in computer science at Carnegie Mellon University. He has worked for Amazon.com, Inc. as a software engineering intern. Wenhan has more than 7 years of experience in Java programming. Today, his interests include distributed systems, search engineering, and NoSQL databases.

Suvda Myagmar currently works as a technical lead at a San Francisco-based start-up called Expect Labs, where she builds developer APIs and tunes ranking algorithms for intelligent voice-driven, content-discovery applications. She is the co-founder of Piqora, a company that specializes in social media analytics and content management solutions for online retailers. Prior to working for start-ups, she worked as a software engineer at Yahoo! Search and Microsoft Bing.

Dan Noble is a software engineer from Washington, D.C. who has been a big fan of ElasticSearch since 2011. He's the author of the Python ElasticSearch driver called *rawes*, available at `https://github.com/humangeo/rawes`. Dan focuses his efforts on the development of web application design, data visualization, and geospatial applications.

Philip O'Toole has developed software and led software development teams for more than 15 years for a variety of applications, including embedded software, networking appliances, web services, and SaaS infrastructure. His most recent work with ElasticSearch includes leading infrastructure design and development of Loggly's log analytics SaaS platform, whose core component is ElasticSearch. He is based in the San Francisco Bay Area and can be found online at `http://www.philipotoole.com`.

www.PacktPub.com

Support files, eBooks, discount offers, and more

For support files and downloads related to your book, please visit www.PacktPub.com.

Did you know that Packt offers eBook versions of every book published, with PDF and ePub files available? You can upgrade to the eBook version at www.PacktPub.com, and as a print book customer, you are entitled to a discount on the eBook copy. Get in touch with us at service@packtpub.com for more details.

At www.PacktPub.com, you can also read a collection of free technical articles, sign up for a range of free newsletters, and receive exclusive discounts and offers on Packt books and eBooks.

https://www2.packtpub.com/books/subscription/packtlib

Do you need instant solutions to your IT questions? PacktLib is Packt's online digital book library. Here, you can search, access, and read Packt's entire library of books.

Why subscribe?

- ▶ Fully searchable across every book published by Packt
- ▶ Copy and paste, print, and bookmark content
- ▶ On demand and accessible via a web browser

Free access for Packt account holders

If you have an account with Packt at www.PacktPub.com, you can use this to access PacktLib today and view nine entirely free books. Simply use your login credentials for immediate access.

To Giulia and Andrea, my extraordinary children.

Table of Contents

Preface

One of the main requirements of today's applications is search capability. In the market, we can find a lot of solutions that answer this need, both in commercial as well as the open source world. One of the most used libraries for searching is Apache Lucene. This library is the base of a large number of search solutions such as Apache Solr, Indextank, and ElasticSearch.

ElasticSearch is written with both cloud and distributed computing in mind. Its main author, Shay Banon, who is famous for having developed Compass (http://www.compass-project.org), released the first version of ElasticSearch in March 2010.

Thus, the main scope of ElasticSearch is to be a search engine; it also provides a lot of features that allow you to use it as a data store and an analytic engine using aggregations.

ElasticSearch contains a lot of innovative features: it is JSON/REST-based, natively distributed in a Map/Reduce approach, easy to set up, and extensible with plugins. In this book, we will go into the details of these features and many others available in ElasticSearch.

Before ElasticSearch, only Apache Solr was able to provide some of these functionalities, but it was not designed for the cloud and does not use the JSON/REST API. In the last few years, this situation has changed a bit with the release of the SolrCloud in 2012. For users who want to more thoroughly compare these two products, I suggest you read posts by Rafał Kuć, available at http://blog.sematext.com/2012/08/23/solr-vs-elasticsearch-part-1-overview/.

ElasticSearch is a product that is in a state of continuous evolution, and new functionalities are released by both the ElasticSearch company (the company founded by Shay Banon to provide commercial support for ElasticSearch) and ElasticSearch users as plugins (mainly available on GitHub).

Founded in 2012, the ElasticSearch company has raised a total of USD 104 million in funding. ElasticSearch's success can best be described by the words of Steven Schuurman, the company's cofounder and CEO:

> *It's incredible to receive this kind of support from our investors over such a short period of time. This speaks to the importance of what we're doing: businesses are generating more and more data—both user- and machine-generated—and it has become a strategic imperative for them to get value out of these assets, whether they are starting a new data-focused project or trying to leverage their current Hadoop or other Big data investments.*

ElasticSearch has an impressive track record for its search product, powering customers such as Fourquare (which indexes over 50 million venues), the online music distribution platform SoundCloud, StumbleUpon, and the enterprise social network Xing, which has 14 million members. It also powers GitHub, which searches 20 terabytes of data and 1.3 billion files, and Loggly, which uses ElasticSearch as a key value store to index clusters of data for rapid analytics of logfiles.

In my opinion, ElasticSearch is probably one of the most powerful and easy-to-use search solutions on the market. Throughout this book and these recipes, the book's reviewers and I have sought to transmit our knowledge, passion, and best practices to help readers better manage ElasticSearch.

What this book covers

Chapter 1, Getting Started, gives you an overview of the basic concepts of ElasticSearch and the ways to communicate with it.

Chapter 2, Downloading and Setting Up, shows the basic steps to start using ElasticSearch, from the simple installation to running multiple nodes.

Chapter 3, Managing Mapping, covers the correct definition of data fields to improve both the indexing and search quality.

Chapter 4, Basic Operations, shows you the common operations that are required to both ingest and manage data in ElasticSearch.

Chapter 5, Search, Queries, and Filters, covers the core search functionalities in ElasticSearch. The search DSL is the only way to execute queries in ElasticSearch.

Chapter 6, Aggregations, covers another capability of ElasticSearch: the possibility to execute analytics on search results in order to improve the user experience and drill down the information.

Chapter 7, Scripting, shows you how to customize ElasticSearch with scripting in different programming languages.

Chapter 8, Rivers, extends ElasticSearch to give you the ability to pull data from different sources such as databases, NoSQL solutions, and data streams.

Chapter 9, Cluster and Node Monitoring, shows you how to analyze the behavior of a cluster/node to understand common pitfalls.

Chapter 10, Java Integration, describes how to integrate ElasticSearch in a Java application using both REST and native protocols.

Chapter 11, Python Integration, covers the usage of the official ElasticSearch Python client and the Pythonic PyES library.

Chapter 12, Plugin Development, describes how to create the different types of plugins: site and native plugins. Some examples show the plugin skeletons, the setup process, and their build.

What you need for this book

For this book, you will need a computer running a Windows OS, Macintosh OS, or Linux distribution. In terms of the additional software required, you don't have to worry, as all the components you will need are open source and available for every major OS platform.

For all the REST examples, the cURL software (`http://curl.haxx.se/`) will be used to simulate the command from the command line. It comes preinstalled on Linux and Mac OS X operating systems. For Windows, it can be downloaded from its site and added in a PATH that can be called from the command line.

Chapter 10, Java Integration, and *Chapter 12, Plugin Development*, require the Maven build tool (`http://maven.apache.org/`), which is a standard tool to manage builds, packaging, and deploying in Java. It is natively supported on most of the Java IDEs, such as Eclipse and IntelliJ IDEA.

Chapter 11, Python Integration, requires the Python Interpreter installed on your computer. It's available on Linux and Mac OS X by default. For Windows, it can be downloaded from the official Python website (`http://www.python.org`). The examples in this chapter have been tested using version 2.x.

Who this book is for

This book is for developers and users who want to begin using ElasticSearch or want to improve their knowledge of ElasticSearch. This book covers all the aspects of using ElasticSearch and provides solutions and hints for everyday usage. The recipes have reduced complexity so it is easy for readers to focus on the discussed ElasticSearch aspect and easily and fully understand the ElasticSearch functionalities.

The chapters toward the end of the book discuss ElasticSearch integration with Java and Python programming languages; this shows the users how to integrate the power of ElasticSearch into their Java- and Python-based applications.

Chapter 12, Plugin Development, talks about the advanced use of ElasticSearch and its core extensions, so you will need some prior Java knowledge to understand this chapter fully.

Sections

This book contains the following sections:

Getting ready

This section tells us what to expect in the recipe, and describes how to set up any software or any preliminary settings needed for the recipe.

How to do it...

This section characterizes the steps to be followed for "cooking" the recipe.

How it works...

This section usually consists of a brief and detailed explanation of what happened in the previous section.

There's more...

It consists of additional information about the recipe in order to make the reader more anxious about the recipe.

See also

This section may contain references to the recipe.

Conventions

In this book, you will find a number of styles of text that distinguish between different kinds of information. Here are some examples of these styles, and an explanation of their meaning.

Code words in text, database table names, folder names, filenames, file extensions, pathnames, dummy URLs, user input, and Twitter handles are shown as follows: "After the `name` and `type` parameters, usually a river requires an extra configuration that can be passed in the `_meta` property."

A block of code is set as follows:

```
cluster.name: elasticsearch
node.name: "My wonderful server"
network.host: 192.168.0.1
discovery.zen.ping.unicast.hosts: ["192.168.0.2","192.168.0.3[9300-
9400]"]
```

When we wish to draw your attention to a particular part of a code block, the relevant lines or items are set in bold:

```
cluster.name: elasticsearch
node.name: "My wonderful server"
network.host: 192.168.0.1
discovery.zen.ping.unicast.hosts: ["192.168.0.2","192.168.0.3[9300-
9400]"]
```

Any command-line input or output is written as follows:

```
curl -XDELETE 'http://127.0.0.1:9200/_river/my_river/'
```

New terms and **important words** are shown in bold. Words you see on the screen, in menus or dialog boxes, for example, appear in the text like this: "If you don't see the cluster statistics, put your node address to the left and click on the **connect** button."

[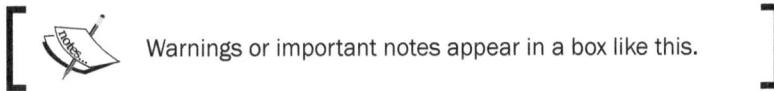 Warnings or important notes appear in a box like this.]

[ Tips and tricks appear like this.]

Reader feedback

Feedback from our readers is always welcome. Let us know what you think about this book—what you liked or may have disliked. Reader feedback is important for us to develop titles you really get the most out of.

To send us general feedback, simply send an e-mail to feedback@packtpub.com, and mention the book title via the subject of your message.

If there is a topic you have expertise in and you are interested in either writing or contributing to a book, see our author guide at www.packtpub.com/authors.

Customer support

Now that you are the proud owner of a Packt book, we have a number of things to help you get the most from your purchase.

Downloading the example code

You can download the example code files for all Packt books you have purchased from your account at http://www.packtpub.com. If you purchased this book elsewhere, you can visit http://www.packtpub.com/support and register to have the files e-mailed directly to you. The code bundle is also available on GitHub at https://github.com/aparo/elasticsearch-cookbook-second-edition.

Errata

Although we have taken every care to ensure the accuracy of our content, mistakes do happen. If you find a mistake in one of our books—maybe a mistake in the text or the code—we would be grateful if you could report this to us. By doing so, you can save other readers from frustration and help us improve subsequent versions of this book. If you find any errata, please report them by visiting http://www.packtpub.com/submit-errata, selecting your book, clicking on the **Errata Submission Form** link, and entering the details of your errata. Once your errata are verified, your submission will be accepted and the errata will be uploaded to our website or added to any list of existing errata under the **Errata** section of that title.

To view the previously submitted errata, go to https://www.packtpub.com/books/content/support and enter the name of the book in the search field. The required information will appear under the Errata section.

Piracy

Piracy of copyrighted material on the Internet is an ongoing problem across all media. At Packt, we take the protection of our copyright and licenses very seriously. If you come across any illegal copies of our works, in any form, on the Internet, please provide us with the location address or website name immediately so we can pursue a remedy.

Please contact us at copyright@packtpub.com with a link to the suspected pirated material.

We appreciate your help in protecting our authors, and our ability to bring you valuable content.

Questions

If you have a problem with any aspect of this book, you can contact us at questions@packtpub.com, and we will do our best to address the problem.

1
Getting Started

In this chapter, we will cover:

- ► Understanding nodes and clusters
- ► Understanding node services
- ► Managing your data
- ► Understanding clusters, replication, and sharding
- ► Communicating with ElasticSearch
- ► Using the HTTP protocol
- ► Using the native protocol
- ► Using the Thrift protocol

Introduction

To efficiently use **ElasticSearch**, it is very important to understand how it works.

The goal of this chapter is to give the readers an overview of the basic concepts of ElasticSearch and to be a quick reference for them. It's essential to understand the basics better so that you don't fall into the common pitfall about how ElasticSearch works and how to use it.

The key concepts that we will see in this chapter are: **node**, **index**, **shard**, **mapping/type**, **document**, and **field**.

ElasticSearch can be used both as a search engine as well as a data store.

A brief description of the ElasticSearch logic helps the user to improve performance, search quality, and decide when and how to optimize the infrastructure to improve scalability and availability.

Some details on data replications and base node communication processes are also explained.

At the end of this chapter, the protocols used to manage ElasticSearch are also discussed.

Understanding nodes and clusters

Every instance of ElasticSearch is called a **node**. Several nodes are grouped in a **cluster**. This is the base of the cloud nature of ElasticSearch.

Getting ready

To better understand the following sections, some basic knowledge about the concepts of the application node and cluster are required.

How it works...

One or more ElasticSearch nodes can be set up on a physical or a virtual server depending on the available resources such as RAM, CPU, and disk space.

A default node allows you to store data in it to process requests and responses. (In *Chapter 2, Downloading and Setting Up*, we'll see details about how to set up different nodes and cluster topologies).

When a node is started, several actions take place during its startup, such as:

- ▸ The configuration is read from the environment variables and the `elasticsearch.yml` configuration file

- ▸ A node name is set by the configuration file or is chosen from a list of built-in random names

- ▸ Internally, the ElasticSearch engine initializes all the modules and plugins that are available in the current installation

> **Downloading the example code**
>
> You can download the example code files for all Packt books you have purchased from your account at `http://www.packtpub.com`. If you purchased this book elsewhere, you can visit `http://www.packtpub.com/support` and register to have the files e-mailed directly to you.

After the node startup, the node searches for other cluster members and checks its index and shard status.

To join two or more nodes in a cluster, the following rules must be observed:

- ▶ The version of ElasticSearch must be the same (v0.20, v0.9, v1.4, and so on) or the join is rejected.
- ▶ The cluster name must be the same.
- ▶ The network must be configured to support broadcast discovery (it is configured to it by default) and they can communicate with each other. (See the *Setting up networking* recipe in *Chapter 2, Downloading and Setting Up.*)

A common approach in cluster management is to have a **master node**, which is the main reference for all cluster-level actions, and the other nodes, called **secondary nodes**, that replicate the master data and its actions.

To be consistent in the **write** operations, all the update actions are first committed in the master node and then replicated in the secondary nodes.

In a cluster with multiple nodes, if a master node dies, a **master-eligible** node is elected to be the new master node. This approach allows automatic failover to be set up in an ElasticSearch cluster.

There's more...

There are two important behaviors in an ElasticSearch node: the **non-data node** (or arbiter) and the data container behavior.

Non-data nodes are able to process **REST** responses and all other operations of search. During every action execution, ElasticSearch generally executes actions using a map/reduce approach: the non-data node is responsible for distributing the actions to the underlying shards (map) and collecting/aggregating the shard results (redux) to be able to send a final response. They may use a huge amount of RAM due to operations such as facets, aggregations, collecting hits and caching (such as scan/scroll queries).

Data nodes are able to store data in them. They contain the indices shards that store the indexed documents as **Lucene** (internal ElasticSearch engine) indices.

Using the standard configuration, a node is both an arbiter and a data container.

In big cluster architectures, having some nodes as simple arbiters with a lot of RAM, with no data, reduces the resources required by data nodes and improves performance in searches using the local memory cache of arbiters.

See also

- ▶ The *Setting up different node types* recipe in *Chapter 2, Downloading and Setting Up.*

Understanding node services

When a node is running, a lot of services are managed by its instance. These services provide additional functionalities to a node and they cover different behaviors such as networking, indexing, analyzing and so on.

Getting ready

Every ElasticSearch server that is running provides services.

How it works...

ElasticSearch natively provides a large set of functionalities that can be extended with additional plugins.

During a node startup, a lot of required services are automatically started. The most important are:

- **Cluster services**: These manage the cluster state, intra-node communication, and synchronization.

- **Indexing Service**: This manages all indexing operations, initializing all active indices and shards.

- **Mapping Service**: This manages the document types stored in the cluster (we'll discuss mapping in *Chapter 3*, *Managing Mapping*).

- **Network Services**: These are services such as **HTTP REST** services (default on port 9200), internal ES protocol (port 9300) and the **Thrift** server (port 9500), applicable only if the Thrift plugin is installed.

- **Plugin Service**: This enables us to enhance the basic ElasticSearch functionality in a customizable manner. (It's discussed in *Chapter 2*, *Downloading and Setting Up*, for installation and *Chapter 12*, *Plugin Development*, for detailed usage.)

- **River Service**: It is a pluggable service running within ElasticSearch cluster, pulling data (or being pushed with data) that is then indexed into the cluster. (We'll see it in *Chapter 8*, *Rivers*.)

- **Language Scripting Services**: They allow you to add new language scripting support to ElasticSearch.

> Throughout this book, we'll see recipes that interact with ElasticSearch services. Every base functionality or extended functionality is managed in ElasticSearch as a service.

Managing your data

If you are going to use ElasticSearch as a search engine or a distributed data store, it's important to understand concepts of how ElasticSearch stores and manages your data.

Getting ready

To work with ElasticSearch data, a user must have basic concepts of data management and **JSON** data format, which is the *lingua franca* to work with ElasticSearch data and services.

How it works...

Our main data container is called **index** (plural **indices**) and it can be considered as a database in the traditional **SQL** world. In an index, the data is grouped into data types called **mappings** in ElasticSearch. A mapping describes how the records are composed (**fields**).

Every record that must be stored in ElasticSearch must be a JSON object.

Natively, ElasticSearch is a schema-less data store; when you enter records in it during the **insert** process it processes the records, splits it into fields, and updates the schema to manage the inserted data.

To manage huge volumes of records, ElasticSearch uses the common approach to split an index into multiple shards so that they can be spread on several nodes. Shard management is transparent to the users; all common record operations are managed automatically in the ElasticSearch application layer.

Every record is stored in only a shard; the sharding algorithm is based on a record ID, so many operations that require loading and changing of records/objects, can be achieved without hitting all the shards, but only the shard (and its replica) that contains your object.

The following schema compares ElasticSearch structure with SQL and **MongoDB** ones:

ElasticSearch	SQL	MongoDB
Index (Indices)	Database	Database
Shard	Shard	Shard
Mapping/Type	Table	Collection
Field	Field	Field
Object (JSON Object)	Record (Tuples)	Record (BSON Object)

There's more...

To ensure safe operations on index/mapping/objects, ElasticSearch internally has rigid rules about how to execute operations.

In ElasticSearch, the operations are divided into:

- **Cluster/index operations**: All clusters/indices with active write are locked; first they are applied to the master node and then to the secondary one. The read operations are typically broadcasted to all the nodes.
- **Document operations**: All write actions are locked only for the single hit shard. The read operations are balanced on all the shard replicas.

When a record is saved in ElasticSearch, the destination shard is chosen based on:

- The id (unique identifier) of the record; if the id is missing, it is autogenerated by ElasticSearch
- If routing or parent (we'll see it in the parent/child mapping) parameters are defined, the correct shard is chosen by the hash of these parameters

Splitting an index in shard allows you to store your data in different nodes, because ElasticSearch tries to balance the shard distribution on all the available nodes.

Every shard can contain up to 2^32 records (about 4.9 billion), so the real limit to a shard size is its storage size.

Shards contain your data and during search process all the shards are used to calculate and retrieve results. So ElasticSearch performance in big data scales horizontally with the number of shards.

All native records operations (such as index, search, update, and delete) are managed in shards.

Shard management is completely transparent to the user. Only an advanced user tends to change the default shard routing and management to cover their custom scenarios. A common custom scenario is the requirement to put customer data in the same shard to speed up his operations (search/index/analytics).

Best practices

It's best practice not to have a shard too big in size (over 10 GB) to avoid poor performance in indexing due to continuous merging and resizing of index segments.

It is also not good to over-allocate the number of shards to avoid poor search performance due to native distributed search (it works as map and reduce). Having a huge number of empty shards in an index will consume memory and increase the search times due to an overhead on network and results aggregation phases.

See also

▸ Shard on Wikipedia
   `http://en.wikipedia.org/wiki/Shard_(database_architecture)`

Understanding clusters, replication, and sharding

Related to shard management, there is the key concept of **replication** and **cluster status**.

Getting ready

You need one or more nodes running to have a cluster. To test an effective cluster, you need at least two nodes (that can be on the same machine).

How it works...

An index can have one or more replicas; the shards are called **primary** if they are part of the primary replica, and **secondary** ones if they are part of replicas.

To maintain consistency in write operations, the following workflow is executed:

▸ The write operation is first executed in the primary shard

▸ If the primary write is successfully done, it is propagated simultaneously in all the secondary shards

▸ If a primary shard becomes unavailable, a secondary one is elected as primary (if available) and then the flow is re-executed

During search operations, if there are some replicas, a valid set of shards is chosen randomly between primary and secondary to improve its performance. ElasticSearch has several allocation algorithms to better distribute shards on nodes. For reliability, replicas are allocated in a way that if a single node becomes unavailable, there is always at least one replica of each shard that is still available on the remaining nodes.

The following figure shows some examples of possible shards and replica configuration:

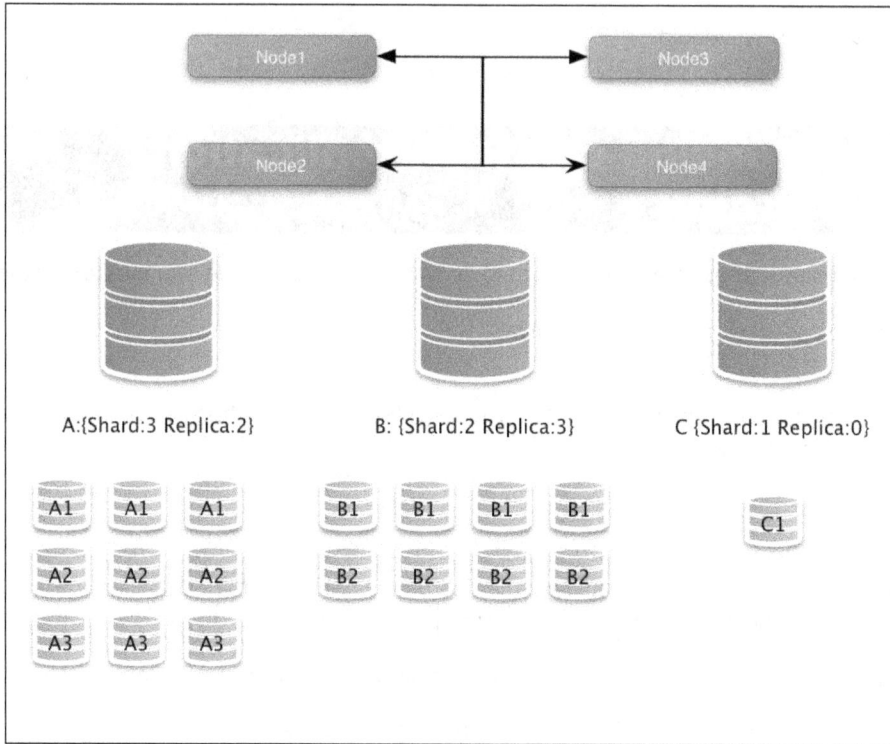

The replica has a cost in increasing the indexing time due to data node synchronization, which is the time spent to propagate the message to the slaves (mainly in an asynchronous way).

> To prevent data loss and to have high availability, it's good to have a least one replica; so your system can survive a node failure without downtime and without loss of data.

There's more...

Related to the concept of replication, there is the **cluster status** indicator that will show you information on the health of your cluster. It can cover three different states:

- ▸ Green: This shows that everything is okay
- ▸ Yellow: This means that some shards are missing but you can work on your cluster
- ▸ Red: This indicates a problem as some primary shards are missing

Solving the yellow status...

Mainly, yellow status is due to some shards that are not allocated.

If your cluster is in the *recovery* status (meaning that it's starting up and checking the shards before they are online), you need to wait until the shards' startup process ends.

After having finished the recovery, if your cluster is always in the yellow state, you may not have enough nodes to contain your replicas (for example, maybe the number of replicas is bigger than the number of your nodes). To prevent this, you can reduce the number of your replicas or add the required number of nodes. A good practice is to observe that the total number of nodes must not be lower than the maximum number of replicas present.

Solving the red status

This means you are experiencing lost data, the cause of which is that one or more shards are missing.

To fix this, you need to try to restore the node(s) that are missing. If your node restarts and the system goes back to the yellow or green status, then you are safe. Otherwise, you have obviously lost data and your cluster is not usable; the next action would be to delete the index/indices and restore them from backups or snapshots (if you have done them) or from other sources. To prevent data loss, I suggest having always a least two nodes and a replica set to 1 as good practice.

> Having one or more replicas on different nodes on different machines allows you to have a live backup of your data, which stays updated always.

See also

Setting up different node types in the next chapter.

Communicating with ElasticSearch

You can communicate with several protocols using your ElasticSearch server. In this recipe, we will take a look at the main protocols.

Getting ready

You will need a working instance of the ElasticSearch cluster.

How it works...

ElasticSearch is designed to be used as a RESTful server, so the main protocol is the HTTP, usually on port number 9200 and above. Thus, it allows using different protocols such as native and thrift ones.

Many others are available as extension plugins, but they are seldom used, such as `memcached`, `couchbase`, and `websocket`. (If you need to find more on the transport layer, simply type in `Elasticsearch transport` on the GitHub website to search.)

Every protocol has advantages and disadvantages. It's important to choose the correct one depending on the kind of applications you are developing. If you are in doubt, choose the **HTTP Protocol** layer that is the standard protocol and is easy to use.

Choosing the right protocol depends on several factors, mainly architectural and performance related. This schema factorizes advantages and disadvantages related to them. If you are using any of the protocols to communicate with ElasticSearch official clients, switching from a protocol to another is generally a simple setting in the client initialization.

Protocol	Advantages	Disadvantages	Type
HTTP	► Frequently used ► API is safe and has general compatibility for different versions of ES, although JSON is suggested	► HTTP overhead	► Text
Native	► Fast network layer ► Programmatic ► Best for massive indexing operations	► If the API changes, it can break the applications ► Requires the same version of the ES server ► Only on JVM	► Binary
Thrift	► Similar to HTTP	► Related to the Thrift plugin	► Binary

Using the HTTP protocol

This recipe shows us the usage of the HTTP protocol with an example.

Getting ready

You need a working instance of the ElasticSearch cluster. Using default configuration, ElasticSearch enables port number 9200 on your server to communicate in HTTP.

How to do it...

The standard RESTful protocol is easy to integrate.

We will see how easy it is to fetch the ElasticSearch greeting API on a running server on port 9200 using different programming languages:

▶ In BASH, the request will be:

```
curl -XGET http://127.0.0.1:9200
```

▶ In Python, the request will be:

```
import urllib
result = urllib.open("http://127.0.0.1:9200")
```

▶ In Java, the request will be:

```java
import java.io.BufferedReader;
import java.io.InputStream;
import java.io.InputStreamReader;
import java.net.URL;
… truncated…
  try{   // get URL content
    URL url = new URL("http://127.0.0.1:9200");
    URLConnection conn = url.openConnection();// open the
    stream and put it into BufferedReader
    BufferedReader br = new BufferedReader(new
    InputStreamReader(conn.getInputStream()));

    String inputLine;
    while ((inputLine = br.readLine()) != null){
    System.out.println(inputLine);
  }
  br.close();
  System.out.println("Done");
}
  Catch (MalformedURLException e) {
```

```
      e.printStackTrace();
    }
    catch (IOException e){
      e.printStackTrace();
    }
```

▸ In Scala, the request will be:

```
scala.io.Source.fromURL("http://127.0.0.1:9200",
"utf-8").getLines.mkString("\n")
```

For every language sample, the response will be the same:

```
{
  "ok" : true,
  "status" : 200,
  "name" : "Payge, Reeva",
  "version" : {
    "number" : "1.4.0",
    "snapshot_build" : false
  },
  "tagline" : "You Know, for Search"
}
```

How it works...

Every client creates a connection to the server index / and fetches the answer. The answer is a valid JSON object. You can invoke the ElasticSearch server from any language that you like.

The main advantages of this protocol are:

▸ **Portability**: This uses Web standards so that it can be integrated in different languages (Erlang, JavaScript, Python, Ruby, and so on) or called via a command-line application such as cURL.

▸ **Durability**: The REST APIs don't change often. They don't break for minor release changes as native protocol does.

▸ **Simple to use**: This has JSON-to-JSON interconnectivity.

▸ **Good support**: This has much more support than other protocols. Every plugin typically supports a REST endpoint on HTTP.

▸ **Easy cluster scaling**: You can simply put your cluster nodes behind an HTTP load balancer to balance the calls such as **HAProxy** or **NGinx**.

In this book, a lot of the examples are done by calling the HTTP API via the command-line cURL program. This approach is very fast and allows you to test functionalities very quickly.

There's more...

Every language provides drivers for best integration with ElasticSearch or RESTful web services.

The ElasticSearch community provides official drivers that support the most used programming languages.

Using the native protocol

ElasticSearch provides a native protocol, used mainly for low-level communication between nodes, but very useful for fast importing of huge data blocks. This protocol is available only for **Java Virtual Machine** (**JVM**) languages and commonly is used in Java, Groovy, and Scala.

Getting ready

You need a working instance of the ElasticSearch cluster; the standard port number for native protocol is 9300.

How to do it...

The following are the steps required to use the native protocol in a Java environment (we'll discuss this in depth in *Chapter 10, Java Integration*):

1. Before starting, we must be sure that **Maven** loads the `Elasticsearch.jar` file by adding the following code to the `pom.xml` file:

    ```
    <dependency>
      <groupId>org.elasticsearch</groupId>
      <artifactId>elasticsearch</artifactId>
      <version>1.4.1</version>
    </dependency>
    ```

2. Depending on the `Elasticsearch.jar` file, creating a Java client is quite easy:

    ```
    import org.elasticsearch.common.settings.ImmutableSettings;
    import org.elasticsearch.common.settings.Settings;
    import org.elasticsearch.client.Client;
    import org.elasticsearch.client.transport.TransportClient;
    ...
    Settings settings = ImmutableSettings.settingsBuilder()
    .put("client.transport.sniff", true).build();
      // we define a new settings
      // using sniff transport allows to autodetect other nodes
    Client client = new TransportClient(settings)
    ```

```
.addTransportAddress(new InetSocketTransportAddress("127.0.0.1",
9300));
// a client is created with the settings
```

How it works...

To initialize a native client, a settings object is required, which contains some configuration parameters. The most important ones are:

- ▸ `cluster.name`: This is the name of the cluster
- ▸ `client.transport.sniff`: This allows you to sniff out the rest of the cluster and add them into its list of machines to use

With the settings object, it's possible to initialize a new client by giving an IP address and port a number (default 9300).

There's more...

The native protocol is the internal one used in ElasticSearch. It's the fastest protocol that is available to communicate with ElasticSearch.

The native protocol is an optimized binary and works only for JVM languages; to use this protocol, you need to include the `elasticsearch.jar` in your JVM project. Because it depends on ElasticSearch implementation, it must be the same version of ElasticSearch cluster.

For this reason, every time you update ElasticSearch, you need to update the `elasticsearch.jar` file on which it depends and if there are internal API changes, you need to update your code.

To use this protocol, you need to study the internals of ElasticSearch, so it's not as easy to use as HTTP and Thrift protocol.

Native protocol is useful for massive data import. But as ElasticSearch is mainly thought as a REST HTTP server to communicate with, it lacks support for everything that is not standard in the ElasticSearch core, such as the plugin's entry points. So using this protocol, you are unable to call entry points made by external plugins.

> The native protocol seems the most easy to integrate in a Java/JVM project. However, due to its nature that follows the fast release cycles of ElasticSearch, it changes very often. Also, for minor release upgrades, your code is more likely to be broken. Thus, ElasticSearch developers wisely tries to fix them in the latest releases.

> ▸ The native protocol is the most used in the Java world and it will be deeply discussed in *Chapter 10, Java Integration* and *Chapter 12, Plugin Development*

> ▸ Further details on ElasticSearch Java API are available on the ElasticSearch website at `http://www.elasticsearch.org/guide/en/elasticsearch/client/java-api/current/index.html`

Using the Thrift protocol

Thrift is an interface definition language, initially developed by Facebook, used to define and create services. This protocol is now maintained by Apache Software Foundation.

Its usage is similar to HTTP, but it bypasses the limit of HTTP protocol (latency, handshake and so on) and it's faster.

Getting ready

You need a working instance of ElasticSearch cluster with the thrift plugin installed (`https://github.com/elasticsearch/elasticsearch-transport-thrift/`); the standard port for the Thrift protocol is 9500.

How to do it...

To use the Thrift protocol in a Java environment, perform the following steps:

1. We must be sure that Maven loads the thrift library adding to the `pom.xml` file; the code lines are:

```
<dependency>
  <groupId>org.apache.thrift</groupId>
  <artifactId>libthrift</artifactId>
  <version>0.9.1</version>
</dependency>
```

2. In Java, creating a client is quite easy using ElasticSearch generated classes:

```
import org.apache.thrift.protocol.TBinaryProtocol;
import org.apache.thrift.protocol.TProtocol;
import org.apache.thrift.transport.TSocket;
import org.apache.thrift.transport.TTransport;
import org.apache.thrift.transport.TTransportException;
import org.elasticsearch.thrift.*;
```

```
TTransport transport = new TSocket("127.0.0.1", 9500);
TProtocol protocol = new TBinaryProtocol(transport);
Rest.Client client = new Rest.Client(protocol);
transport.open();
```

3. To initialize a connection, first we need to open a socket transport. This is done with the `TSocket(host, port)` setting, using the ElasticSearch thrift standard port 9500.

4. Then the socket transport protocol must be encapsulated in a binary protocol, this is done with the `TBinaryProtocol(transport)` parameter.

5. Now, a client can be initialized by passing the protocol. The `Rest.Client` utility class and other utility classes are generated by `elasticsearch.thrift`. It resides in the `org.elasticsearch.thrift` namespace.

6. To have a fully working client, we must open the socket (`transport.open()`).

7. At the end of program, we should close the client connection (`transport.close()`).

There's more...

Some drivers, to connect to ElasticSearch, provide an easy-to-use API to interact with Thrift without the boulder that this protocol needs.

For advanced usage, I suggest the use of the Thrift protocol to bypass some problems related to HTTP limits, such as:

- ▸ The number of simultaneous connections required in HTTP; Thrift transport efficiently uses resources

- ▸ The network traffic is light weight because it is binary and is very compact

A big advantage of this protocol is that on the server side it wraps the REST entry points so that it can also be used with calls provided by external REST plugins.

See also

- ▸ For more details on Thrift visit its Wikipedia page at:
  `http://en.wikipedia.org/wiki/Apache_Thrift`

- ▸ For more complete reference on the Thrift ElasticSearch plugin, the official documentation is available at `https://github.com/elasticsearch/elasticsearch-transport-thrift/`

2
Downloading and Setting Up

In this chapter, we will cover the following topics:

- ► Downloading and installing ElasticSearch
- ► Setting up networking
- ► Setting up a node
- ► Setting up for Linux systems
- ► Setting up different node types
- ► Installing plugins in ElasticSearch
- ► Installing a plugin manually
- ► Removing a plugin
- ► Changing logging settings

Introduction

This chapter explains how to install and configure ElasticSearch, from a single developer machine to a big cluster, giving you hints on how to improve performance and skip misconfiguration errors.

There are different options to install ElasticSearch and set up a working environment for development and production.

When testing out ElasticSearch for a development cluster, the configuration tool does not require any configurations to be set in it. However, when moving to production, it is important to properly configure the cluster based on your data and use cases. The setup step is very important because a bad configuration can lead to bad results and poor performances, and it can even kill your server.

In this chapter, the management of ElasticSearch plugins is also discussed: installing, configuring, updating, and removing.

Downloading and installing ElasticSearch

ElasticSearch has an active community and the release cycles are very fast.

Because ElasticSearch depends on many common Java libraries (**Lucene**, **Guice**, and **Jackson** are the most famous), the ElasticSearch community tries to keep them updated and fixes bugs that are discovered in them and the ElasticSearch core. The large user base is also a source of new ideas and features to improve ElasticSearch use cases.

For these reasons, if it's possible, best practice is to use the latest available release (usually, the most stable release and with the least bugs).

Getting ready

You need an ElasticSearch supported operating system (Linux / Mac OS X / Windows) with JVM 1.7 or above installed. A web browser is required to download the ElasticSearch binary release.

How to do it...

In order to download and install an ElasticSearch server, we will perform the following steps:

1. Download ElasticSearch from the web. The latest version is always downloadable at `http://www.elasticsearch.org/download/`. Different versions are available for different operating systems:

    □   `elasticsearch-{version-number}.zip`: This is used for both Linux (or Mac OS X) and Windows operating systems

    □   `elasticsearch-{version-number}.tar.gz`: This is used for Linux and Mac operating systems

    □   `elasticsearch-{version-number}.deb`: This is used for a Debian-based Linux distribution (this also covers the Ubuntu family). It can be installed with the Debian command `dpkg -i elasticsearch-*.deb`.

- ❑ `elasticsearch-{version-number}.rpm`: This is used for Red Hat-based Linux distributions (this also covers the CentOS family). You can install this version with the command `rpm -i elasticsearch-{version number}.rpm`.

> These packages contain everything to start using ElasticSearch. At the time of writing this book, the latest and most stable version of ElasticSearch is 1.4.0. To check whether this is the latest available version, please visit `http://www.elasticsearch.org/download/`.

2. Extract the binary content:
    - ❑ After downloading the correct release for your platform, the installation consists of extracting the archive to a working directory.

> Choose a working directory that is safe for charset problems and does not have a long path name (path name) in order to prevent problems when ElasticSearch creates its directories to store index data.

   - ❑ For the Windows platform, a good directory can be `c:\es`, while on Unix and Mac OS X, you can use `/opt/es`.
   - ❑ To run ElasticSearch, you need a Java Virtual Machine version 1.7 or above installed. For better performance, I suggest that you use the latest Sun/Oracle 1.7 version.
   - ❑ If you are a Mac OS X user and you have installed Homebrew (`http://brew.sh/`), the first and second step is automatically managed by the `brew install elasticsearch` command.

3. Now, start the ElasticSearch executable to check whether everything is working. To start your ElasticSearch server, just navigate to the installation directory and type either of the following command lines depending on your platform:
    - ❑ For Linux and Mac OS X:

        ```
        # bin/elasticsearch
        ```

    - ❑ For Windows:

        ```
        # bin\elasticserch.bat
        ```

4. Your server should now start, as shown in the following screenshot:

```
➜ elasticsearch-1.4.0.Beta1 ls
LICENSE.txt    NOTICE.txt    README.textile bin        config      data      lib       logs
➜ elasticsearch-1.4.0.Beta1 bin/elasticsearch
[2014-10-12 11:11:50,180][INFO ][node         ] [ESCookBook] version[1.4.0.Beta1], pid[31025], build[1f25669/2014-10-01T14:58:15Z]
[2014-10-12 11:11:50,180][INFO ][node         ] [ESCookBook] initializing ...
[2014-10-12 11:11:50,183][INFO ][plugins      ] [ESCookBook] loaded [], sites []
[2014-10-12 11:11:52,157][INFO ][node         ] [ESCookBook] initialized
[2014-10-12 11:11:52,158][INFO ][node         ] [ESCookBook] starting ...
[2014-10-12 11:11:52,217][INFO ][transport    ] [ESCookBook] bound_address {inet[/0:0:0:0:0:0:0:0:9300]}, publish_address {inet[/192.168.1.19:93
00]}
[2014-10-12 11:11:52,233][INFO ][discovery    ] [ESCookBook] elasticsearch/t1Bcw-fbS4uaI4rhNOaTBw
[2014-10-12 11:11:55,260][INFO ][cluster.service] [ESCookBook] new_master [ESCookBook][t1Bcw-fbS4uaI4rhNOaTBw][Albertos-MacBook-Pro-2.local][inet[
/192.168.1.19:9300]], reason: zen-disco-join (elected_as_master)
[2014-10-12 11:11:55,277][INFO ][http         ] [ESCookBook] bound_address {inet[/0:0:0:0:0:0:0:0:9200]}, publish_address {inet[/192.168.1.19:92
00]}
[2014-10-12 11:11:55,277][INFO ][node         ] [ESCookBook] started
[2014-10-12 11:11:55,288][INFO ][gateway      ] [ESCookBook] recovered [0] indices into cluster_state
```

How it works...

The ElasticSearch package generally contains three directories:

▶ `bin`: This contains the script to start and manage ElasticSearch. The most important scripts are:

  ❑ `elasticsearch(.bat)`: This is the main script file to start the ElasticSearch server

  ❑ `plugin(.bat)`: This is a script to manage plugins

▶ `config`: This contains the ElasticSearch configurations. The most important files are:

  ❑ `elasticsearch.yml`: This is the main configuration file for ElasticSearch

  ❑ `logging.yml`: This is the logging configuration file

▶ `lib`: This contains all the libraries required to run ElasticSearch

Another directory that will be present in the future is the plugins directory. It's the one that stores the plugin code.

There's more...

During the ElasticSearch startup, there are a lot of events that occur:

▶ A node name is chosen automatically (such as `Robert Kelly`) if it is not provided in `elasticsearch.yml`. The name is randomly taken from an in-code embedded ElasticSearch text file (`src/main/resources/config/names.txt`).

▶ A node name hash is generated for this node (such as, `whqVp_4zQGCgMvJ1CXhcWQ`).

▶ If there are plugins (native or site), they are loaded. In this example, there are no plugins.

▶ If it is not configured automatically, ElasticSearch binds to all the network addresses, using two ports:

  ❑ Port 9300 is used for internal intranode communication

  ❑ Port 9200 is used for the HTTP REST API

▶ After the startup, if indices are available, they are restored.

If the given port numbers are already bound, ElasticSearch automatically increments the port number and tries to bind to them until a port is available (such as 9201, 9202, and so on). This feature is very useful when you want to fire up several nodes on the same machine for testing.

Many events are fired during ElasticSearch startup; we'll see them in detail in the upcoming recipes.

Setting up networking

Correctly setting up networking is very important for your nodes and cluster.

There are a lot of different installation scenarios and networking issues; we will cover two kinds of networking setups in this recipe:

▶ A standard installation with an autodiscovery working configuration

▶ A forced IP configuration, used if it is not possible to use autodiscovery

Getting ready

You need a working ElasticSearch installation, and you must know your current networking configuration (such as your IP addresses).

How to do it...

In order to configure networking, we will perform the following steps:

1. With your favorite text editor application, open the ElasticSearch configuration file. Using the standard ElasticSearch configuration file (`config/elasticsearch.yml`), your node is configured to bind to all your machine interfaces and does an autodiscovery of the broadcasting events, which means that it sends *signals* to every machine in the current LAN and waits for a response. If a node responds to this, it can join and be a part of a cluster. If another node is available in the same LAN, it can join the cluster too.

> Only nodes that run the same ElasticSearch version and cluster name (the `cluster.name` option in `elasticsearch.yml`) can join each other.

2. To customize the network preferences, you need to change some parameters in the `elasticsearch.yml` file, such as:

```
cluster.name: elasticsearch
node.name: "My wonderful server"
network.host: 192.168.0.1
discovery.zen.ping.unicast.hosts: ["192.168.0.2","192.168.0.3[9300-9400]"]
```

This configuration sets the cluster name to ElasticSearch, the node name, and the network address, it then tries to bind the node to the address given in the discovery section.

We can check the configuration when the node is being loaded. Now, start the server and check whether the networking is configured. The following code shows how it looks:

```
[...] [INFO ] [node             ] [ESCookBook] version[1.4.0.beta1],
pid[74304], build[f1585f0/2014-10-16T14:27:12Z]
[...] [INFO ] [node             ] [ESCookBook] initializing ...
[...] [INFO ] [plugins          ] [ESCookBook] loaded [transport-thrift,
river-twitter, mapper-attachments, lang-python, lang-javascript],
sites [head, HQ]
[...] [INFO ] [node             ] [ESCookBook] initialized
[...] [INFO ] [node             ] [ESCookBook] starting ...
[...] [INFO ] [thrift           ] [ESCookBook] bound on port [9500]
[...] [INFO ] [transport        ] [ESCookBook] bound_
address {inet[/0:0:0:0:0:0:0:0:9300]}, publish_address
{inet[/192.168.1.19:9300]}
[...] [INFO ] [cluster.service  ] [ESCookBook] new_master [ESCookBook]
[YDYjr0XRQeyQIWGcLzRiVQ] [MBPlocal] [inet[/192.168.1.19:9300]], reason:
zen-disco-join (elected_as_master)
[...] [INFO ] [discovery        ] [ESCookBook] elasticsearch-cookbook/
YDYjr0XRQeyQIWGcLzRiVQ
[...] [INFO ] [http             ] [ESCookBook] bound_
address {inet[/0:0:0:0:0:0:0:0:9200]}, publish_address
{inet[/192.168.1.19:9200]}
[...] [INFO ] [gateway          ] [ESCookBook] recovered [0] indices into
cluster_state
[...] [INFO ] [node             ] [ESCookBook] started
```

In this case, we see that:

- ▸ The transport layer binds to 0:0:0:0:0:0:0:0:9300 and 192.168.1.19:9300
- ▸ The REST HTTP interface binds to 0:0:0:0:0:0:0:0:9200 and 192.168.1.19:9200

How it works...

The following parameters are crucial for the node to start working:

- ▸ `cluster.name`: This sets up the name of the cluster. Only nodes with the same name can join together.
- ▸ `node.name`: If this field is not defined, it is automatically assigned by ElasticSearch. It allows you to define a name for the node. If you have a lot of nodes on different machines, it is useful to set this name to something meaningful in order to easily locate them. Using a valid name is easier to remember than a system-generated name, such as `whqVp_4zQGCgMvJ1CXhcWQ`. You must always set up a name for the `node.name` parameter if you need to monitor your server.
- ▸ `network.host`: This defines the IP address of the machine used to bind the node. If your server is on different LANs or you want to limit the bind to only a LAN, you must set this value to your server's IP address.
- ▸ `discovery.zen.ping.unicast.hosts` (this is optional if multicast is possible): This allows you to define a list of hosts (with ports or port ranges) to be used in order to discover other nodes to join the cluster. This setting allows you to use the node in a LAN where broadcasting is not allowed or autodiscovery is not working (such as packet-filtering routers). The referred port is the transport port, usually 9300. The addresses of the host list can be a mix of:
    - ❑ The hostname (such as, `myhost1`)
    - ❑ The IP address (such as, `192.168.1.2`)
    - ❑ The IP address or host name with the port, such as `myhost1:9300`, `192.168.168.1.2:9300`
    - ❑ The IP address or host name with a range of ports (such as, `myhost1:[9300-9400],192.168.168.1.2:[9300-9400]`)

Defining unicast hosts is generally required only if discovery is not working. The default configuration of ElasticSearch has autodiscovery on nodes in a LAN.

See also

- ▸ The *Setting up different node types* recipe in this chapter

Setting up a node

ElasticSearch allows you to customize several parameters in an installation. In this recipe, we'll see the most-used ones in order to define where to store data and improve performance in general.

Getting ready

You need a working ElasticSearch installation.

How to do it...

Perform the following steps to set up a simple node:

1. Open the `config/elasticsearch.yml` file with an editor of your choice.

2. Set up the directories that store your server data:

    ❑   For Linux or Mac OS X:

        ```
        path.conf: /opt/data/es/conf
        path.data: /opt/data/es/data1,/opt2/data/data2
        path.work: /opt/data/work
        path.logs: /opt/data/logs
        path.plugins: /opt/data/plugins
        ```

    ❑   For Windows:

        ```
        path.conf: c:\Elasticsearch\conf
        path.data: c:\Elasticsearch\data
        path.work: c:\Elasticsearch\work
        path.logs: c:\Elasticsearch\logs
        path.plugins: c:\Elasticsearch\plugins
        ```

3. Set up parameters to control the standard index creation. These parameters are:

    ```
    index.number_of_shards: 5
    index.number_of_replicas: 1
    ```

How it works...

The `path.conf` parameter defines the directory that contains your configuration: mainly `elasticsearch.yml` and `logging.yml`. This is the default `$ES_HOME/config` parameter with the `ES_HOME` directory you installed ElasticSearch in.

> It's useful to set up the `config` directory outside your application directory, so you don't need to copy configuration files every time you update the version or change the ElasticSearch installation directory.

The `path.data` parameter is the most important, as it allows you to define one or more directories where you can store your index data. When you define more than one directory, they are managed in a similar way as RAID 0, favoring locations with the most free space.

The `path.work` parameter is a location where ElasticSearch puts temporary files.

The `path.log` parameter is where logfiles are put. Logging is controlled in `logging.yml`.

The `path.plugins` parameter allows you to override the plugins path (the default is `$ES_HOME/plugins`). It's useful to use *system wide* plugins.

The main parameters used to control index and shards are `index.number_of_shards`, which controls the standard number of shards for a new created index, and `index.number_of_replicas`, which controls the initial number of replicas.

There's more...

There are a lot of other parameters that can be used to customize your ElasticSearch installation, and new ones are added with new releases. The most important parameters are described in this recipe and the *Setting up Linux systems* recipe in this chapter.

See also

- The *Setting up Linux systems* recipe in this chapter
- The official ElasticSearch documentation at `http://www.elasticsearch.org/guide/en/elasticsearch/reference/current/setup-configuration.html`

Setting up for Linux systems

If you are using a Linux system, you need to manage extra setup steps to improve performance or to resolve production problems with many indices.

This recipe covers two common errors that occur in production:

▸ *Too many open files*, which can corrupt your indices and data

▸ Slow performance when searching and indexing due to the garbage collector

> Other possible troubles arise when you run out of disk space. In this scenario, some files can get corrupted. To prevent your indices from corruption and possible data loss, a best practice is to monitor the storage space available.

Getting ready

You need a working ElasticSearch installation.

How to do it...

In order to improve performance on Linux systems, perform the following steps:

1. First, you need to change the current limit of the users that runs the ElasticSearch server. In our examples, we will call it *elasticsearch*.

2. To allow ElasticSearch to manage a large number of files, you need to increment the number of file descriptors (the number of files) that a user can manage. To do this, you must edit your `/etc/security/limits.conf` file and add these lines at the end, then a machine restart is required to ensure that changes are incorporated:

```
elasticsearch        -        nofile          299999
elasticsearch    ·   -        memlock         unlimited
```

3. In order to control memory swapping, you need to set up this parameter in `elasticsearch.yml`:

```
bootstrap.mlockall: true
```

4. To fix the memory usage size of the ElasticSearch server, you need to set up the `ES_MIN_MEM` and `ES_MAX_MEM` parameters to the same values as in `$ES_HOME/bin/ elasticsearch.in.sh` file. Otherwise, you can set up `ES_HEAP_SIZE` which automatically initializes the min and max values to the same.

How it works...

The standard limit of file descriptors (the maximum number of open files for a user) is typically 1,024. When you store a lot of records in several indices, you run out of file descriptors very quickly, so your ElasticSearch server becomes unresponsive and your indices might become corrupted, leading to a loss of data. If you change the limit to a very high number, your ElasticSearch server doesn't hit the maximum number of open files.

The other settings for memory restriction in ElasticSearch prevent memory swapping and give a performance boost in a production environment. This is required because during indexing and searching ElasticSearch creates and destroys a lot of objects in the memory. This large number of create/destroy actions fragments the memory, reducing performance: the memory becomes full of *holes*, and when the system needs to allocate more memory, it suffers an overhead to find *compacted* memory. If you don't set `bootstrap.mlockall: true`, then ElasticSearch dumps the memory onto a disk and defragments it back in the memory, which freezes the system. With this setting, the defragmentation step is done in the memory itself, providing a huge performance boost.

Setting up different node types

ElasticSearch is natively designed for the Cloud, so when you need to release a production environment with a huge number of records, and you need high availability and good performances, you need to aggregate more nodes in a cluster.

ElasticSearch allows you to define different type of node to balance and improve overall performance.

Getting ready

You need a working ElasticSearch installation.

How to do it...

For the advanced setup of a cluster, there are some parameters that must be configured to define different node types.

These parameters are in `config/elasticsearch.yml` and can be set by performing these steps:

1. Set up whether or not the node can be a master node:

   `node.master: true`

2. Set up whether or not a node must contain data:

   `node.data: true`

How it works...

The `node.master` parameter defines whether the node can become a master for the Cloud. The default value for this parameter is `true`.

A master node is an arbiter for the Cloud: it takes decisions about shard management, it keeps the cluster's status, and it's the main controller of every index action.

The optimal number of master nodes is given by the following equation:

$$Number\ of\ Master\ Nodes = \frac{Number\ of\ nodes}{2} + 1$$

`node.data` allows you to store data in the node. The default value for this parameter is `true`. This node will be a worker that indexes and searches data.

By mixing these two parameters, it's possible to have different node types:

node.master	node.data	Node description
true	true	This is the default node. It can be a master node and can contain data.
false	true	This node never becomes a master node, it only holds data. It can be defined as the *workhorse* of your cluster.
true	false	This node only serves as a master node, that is, it does not store any data and has free resources. This will be the *coordinator* of your cluster.
false	false	This node acts as a *search load balancer* (fetches data from nodes, aggregates results, and so on).

The most frequently used node type is the first one, but if you have a very big cluster or special needs, then you can differentiate the scope of your nodes to better serve searches and aggregations.

Installing plugins in ElasticSearch

One of the main features of ElasticSearch is the possibility to extend it with plugins. Plugins extend ElasticSearch features and functionality in several ways. There are two kinds of plugins:

- **Site plugins**: These are used to serve static content at their entry points. They are mainly used to create a management application for the monitoring and administration of a cluster. The most common site plugins are:
  - ElasticSearch head (`http://mobz.github.io/elasticsearch-head/`)
  - Elastic HQ (`http://www.elastichq.org/`)
  - Bigdesk (`http://bigdesk.org`)
- **Native plugins**: These are the `.jar` files that contain the application code. They are used for:
  - Rivers (plugins that allow you to import data from DBMS or other sources)
  - Scripting Language Engines (JavaScript, Python, Scala, and Ruby)
  - Custom analyzers, tokenizers, and scoring
  - REST entry points
  - Supporting new protocols (Thrift, memcache, and so on)
  - Supporting new storages (Hadoop)

Getting ready

You need a working ElasticSearch server installed.

How to do it...

ElasticSearch provides a script to automatically download and install plugins in the `bin/` directory called `plugin`.

The following steps are required to install a plugin:

1. Call the plugin and install it using the ElasticSearch command with the plugin name reference. To install an administrative interface for ElasticSearch, simply type the following command:
   - Linux / MacOSX:
   ```
   plugin -install mobz/elasticsearch-head
   ```

> ❑ Windows:
>
> ```
> plugin.bat -install mobz/elasticsearch-head
> ```

2. Start the node and check whether the plugin is correctly loaded.

The following screenshot shows the installation and the beginning of the ElasticSearch server with the installed plugin:

```
→ elasticsearch-1.4.0.Beta1  bin/plugin -install mobz/elasticsearch-head
-> Installing mobz/elasticsearch-head...
Trying https://github.com/mobz/elasticsearch-head/archive/master.zip...
Downloading .............................................................................................................
.............................................................................................................
...DONE
Installed mobz/elasticsearch-head into /Users/alberto/tmp/elasticsearch-1.4.0.Beta1/plugins/head
Identified as a _site plugin, moving to _site structure ...
→ elasticsearch-1.4.0.Beta1  bin/elasticsearch
[2014-10-12 14:32:33,180][INFO ][node              ] [ESCookBook] version[1.4.0.Beta1], pid[32240], build[1f25669/2014-10-01T14:58:15Z]
[2014-10-12 14:32:33,181][INFO ][node              ] [ESCookBook] initializing ...
[2014-10-12 14:32:33,186][INFO ][plugins           ] [ESCookBook] loaded [], sites [head]
[2014-10-12 14:32:35,861][INFO ][node              ] [ESCookBook] initialized
[2014-10-12 14:32:35,861][INFO ][node              ] [ESCookBook] starting ...
[2014-10-12 14:32:35,939][INFO ][transport         ] [ESCookBook] bound_address {inet[/0:0:0:0:0:0:0:0:9300]}, publish_address {inet[/192.168.1.19:93
00]}
[2014-10-12 14:32:35,959][INFO ][discovery         ] [ESCookBook] elasticsearch/U2E5RbBXTEqUgII8WRhuEA
[2014-10-12 14:32:38,982][INFO ][cluster.service   ] [ESCookBook] new_master [ESCookBook][U2E5RbBXTEqUgII8WRhuEA][Albertos-MacBook-Pro-2.local][inet[
/192.168.1.19:9300]], reason: zen-disco-join (elected_as_master)
[2014-10-12 14:32:39,003][INFO ][http              ] [ESCookBook] bound_address {inet[/0:0:0:0:0:0:0:0:9200]}, publish_address {inet[/192.168.1.19:92
00]}
[2014-10-12 14:32:39,003][INFO ][node              ] [ESCookBook] started
[2014-10-12 14:32:39,010][INFO ][gateway           ] [ESCookBook] recovered [0] indices into cluster_state
```

> Remember that a plugin installation requires an ElasticSearch server restart. For a site plugin, the restart is not mandatory.

How it works...

The plugin (`.bat`) script is a wrapper for ElasticSearch Plugin Manager. It can be used to install or remove a plugin with the `-remove` option.

To install a plugin, there are two methods:

- Passing the URL of the plugin (the `.zip` archive) with the `-url` parameter:

  ```
  bin/plugin -url http://mywoderfulserve.com/plugins/awesome-plugin.zip
  ```

- Using the `-install` parameter with the GitHub repository of the plugin

The install parameter, which must be provided, is formatted in this way:

```
<username>/<repo>[/<version>]
```

In the previous example the parameter settings were:

- `<username>` parameter as `mobz`
- `<repo>` parameter as `elasticsearch-head`
- `<version>` was not given, so the master/trunk was used

During the installation process, ElasticSearch Plugin Manager is able to do the following activities:

- Download the plugin
- Create a `plugins` directory in `ES_HOME` if it's missing
- Unzip the plugin's content in the plugin directory
- Remove temporary files

The installation process is completely automatic, and no further actions are required. The user must only pay attention to the fact that the process ends with an `Installed` message to be sure that the install process is completed correctly.

A server restart is always required to ensure that the plugin is correctly loaded by ElasticSearch.

There's more...

If your current ElasticSearch application depends on one or more plugins, a node can be configured to fire up only if these plugins are installed and available. To achieve this behavior, you can provide the `plugin.mandatory` directive in the `elasticsearch.yml` configuration file.

In the previous example (`elasticsearch-head`), this configuration line needs to be added:

```
plugin.mandatory: head
```

There are some points that you need to remember when installing plugins. The first and most important point is that the plugin must be certified for your current ElasticSearch version: some releases can break your plugins. Typically, the ElasticSearch versions supported by the plugin will be listed on the plugin developer page.

For example, if you take a look at the Python language plugin page (`https://github.com/elasticsearch/elasticsearch-lang-python`), you'll see a reference table similar to that shown in the following screenshot:

Python lang Plugin for Elasticsearch

The Python (jython) language plugin allows to have `python` as the language of scripts to execute.

In order to install the plugin, simply run:

```
bin/plugin -install elasticsearch/elasticsearch-lang-python/2.4.0
```

You need to install a version matching your Elasticsearch version:

elasticsearch	Python Lang Plugin	Docs
master	Build from source	See below
es-1.x	Build from source	2.5.0-SNAPSHOT
es-1.4	2.4.0	2.4.0
es-1.3	2.3.0	2.3.0
es-1.2	2.2.0	2.2.0
es-1.0	2.0.0	2.0.0
es-0.90	1.0.0	1.0.0

To build a SNAPSHOT version, you need to build it with Maven:

```
mvn clean install
plugin --install lang-python \
       --url file:target/releases/elasticsearch-lang-python-X.X.X-SNAPSHOT.zip
```

You must choose the version that works with your current ElasticSearch version.

Updating some plugins in a node environment can bring about malfunctions due to different plugin versions at different nodes. If you have a big cluster, for safety, it's better to check updates in a separate environment to prevent problems.

> Pay attention to the fact that updating an ElasticSearch server can also break your custom binary plugins due to some internal API changes.

See also

▸ On the ElasticSearch website, there is an updated list of the available plugins (`http://www.elasticsearch.org/guide/en/elasticsearch/reference/current/modules-plugins.html#_plugins`)

▸ The *Installing a plugin manually* recipe in this chapter to manually install a plugin

Installing a plugin manually

Sometimes, your plugin is not available online, or a standard installation fails, so you need to install your plugin manually.

Getting ready

You need an ElasticSearch server installed.

How to do it...

We assume that your plugin is named `awesome` and it's packed in a file called `awesome.zip`.

Perform the following steps to execute a manual installation:

1. Copy your ZIP file to the plugins directory of your ElasticSearch home installation.
2. If the directory named `plugins` doesn't exist, create it.
3. Unzip the contents of the plugin to the `plugins` directory.
4. Remove the zip archive to clean up unused files.

How it works...

Every ElasticSearch plugin is contained in a directory (usually, named as the plugin's name). If it is of the site plugin type, the plugin should contain a directory called `_site`, which contains the static files that must be served by the server. If the plugin is a binary one, the plugin directory should be filled with one or more `.jar` files.

When ElasticSearch starts, it scans the `plugins` directory and loads the plugins.

> If a plugin is corrupted or broken, the server won't start.

Removing a plugin

You have installed some plugins and now you need to remove a plugin because it's not required. Removing an ElasticSearch plugin is easy if everything goes right; otherwise you need to manually remove it.

This recipe covers both cases.

Getting ready

You need a working ElasticSearch Server installed, with an installed plugin, and you need to stop the ElasticSearch server in order to safely remove the plugin.

How to do it...

Perform the following steps to remove a plugin:

1. Stop your running node in order to prevent exceptions due to file removal.
2. Using the ElasticSearch Plugin Manager, which comes with its script wrapper (plugin), call the following commands:
   - For Linux/Mac OS X, call this:

     ```
     plugin -remove mobz/elasticsearch-head
     ```

     You can also use this command:

     ```
     plugin -remove head
     ```

   - On Windows, call the following:

     ```
     plugin.bat -remove mobz/elasticsearch-head
     ```

     You can also use the command shown here:

     ```
     plugin.bat -remove head
     ```

3. Restart the server.

How it works...

The Plugin Manager's -remove command tries to detect the correct name of the plugin and remove the directory of the installed plugin.

If there are undeletable files in your plugin directory (or a strange astronomical event that affects your server), the plugin script might fail; therefore, to manually remove a plugin, you need to follow these steps:

1. Go to the plugins directory.

2. Remove the directory with your plugin name.

Changing logging settings

Standard logging settings work very well for general usage.

Changing the log level can be useful when checking for bugs, or to understand malfunctions due to a bad configuration or strange plugin behavior. A verbose log can be used from the ElasticSearch community to cover problems.

If you need to debug your ElasticSearch server or change how the logging works (such as remotely sending events), you need to change the `logging.yml` parameters.

Getting ready

You need a working ElasticSearch Server installed.

How to do it...

In the `config` directory of your ElasticSearch installation directory, there is a `logging.yml` file that controls the work settings.

You need to perform the following steps to change the logging settings:

1. Omit every kind of logging that ElasticSearch has. Take for example the root level logging here:

   ```
   rootLogger: INFO, console, file
   ```

   Now, change the root level logging using this:

   ```
   rootLogger: DEBUG, console, file
   ```

2. Now, if you start ElasticSearch from the command line (with `bin/elasticsearch -f`), you should see a lot of garbage text that looks as follows:

   ```
   [...] [INFO ] [node] [ESCookBook] version[1.4.0.Beta1],
   pid[32363], build[1f25669/2014-10-01T14:58:15Z]
   ```

   ```
   [...] [INFO ] [node] [ESCookBook] initializing …
   ```

```
[…] [DEBUG] [node] [ESCookBook] using home [/opt/elasticsearch-
1.4.0.Beta1], config [/opt/elasticsearch-1.4.0.Beta1/config],
data [[/opt/elasticsearch-1.4.0.Beta1/data]], logs
[/opt/elasticsearch-1.4.0.Beta1/logs], work
[/opt/elasticsearch-1.4.0.Beta1/work], plugins
[/opt/elasticsearch-1.4.0.Beta1/plugins]

[…] [INFO ] [plugins              ] [ESCookBook] loaded [], sites
[head]

[…] [DEBUG] [common.compress.lzf] using encoder
[VanillaChunkDecoder] and decoder[{}]

[…] [DEBUG] [env         ] [ESCookBook] using node location
[[/opt/elasticsearch-1.4.0.Beta1/data/elasticsearch/nodes/0]],
local_node_id [0]

[…] [DEBUG] [threadpool] [ESCookBook] creating thread_pool
[generic], type [cached], keep_alive [30s]

[…] [DEBUG] [threadpool] [ESCookBook] creating thread_pool
[index], type [fixed], size [8], queue_size [200]

[…] [DEBUG] [threadpool] [ESCookBook] creating thread_pool
[bulk], type [fixed], size [8], queue_size [50]

… (truncated)…
```

How it works...

The ElasticSearch logging system is based on the **Log4j** library (http://logging.
apache.org/log4j/). Log4j is a powerful library that manages logging, so covering
all the functionalities of this library is outside the scope of this book. If a user needs
advanced usage, there are a lot of books and articles available on the Internet.

3
Managing Mapping

In this chapter, we will cover the following topics:

- Using explicit mapping creation
- Mapping base types
- Mapping arrays
- Mapping an object
- Mapping a document
- Using dynamic templates in document mapping
- Managing nested objects
- Managing a child document
- Adding a field with multiple mappings
- Mapping a geo point field
- Mapping a geo shape field
- Mapping an IP field
- Mapping an attachment field
- Adding metadata to a mapping
- Specifying a different analyzer
- Mapping a completion suggester

Introduction

Mapping is an important concept in ElasticSearch, as it defines how the search engine should process a document.

Search engines perform two main operations:

- **Indexing**: This is the action to receive a document and store/index/process it in an index

- **Searching**: This is the action to retrieve data from the index

These two operations are closely connected; an error in the indexing step can lead to unwanted or missing search results.

ElasticSearch has explicit mapping on an index/type level. When indexing, if a mapping is not provided, a default mapping is created by guessing the structure from the data fields that compose the document. Then, this new mapping is automatically propagated to all the cluster nodes.

The default type mapping has sensible default values, but when you want to change their behavior or customize several other aspects of indexing (storing, ignoring, completion, and so on), you need to provide a new mapping definition.

In this chapter, we'll see all the possible types that compose the mappings.

Using explicit mapping creation

If you consider an index as a database in the SQL world, a mapping is similar to the table definition.

ElasticSearch is able to understand the structure of the document that you are indexing (reflection) and creates the mapping definition automatically (explicit mapping creation).

Getting ready

You will need a working ElasticSearch cluster, an index named *test* (see the *Creating an index* recipe in *Chapter 4, Basic Operations*), and basic knowledge of JSON.

How to do it...

To create an explicit mapping, perform the following steps:

1. You can *explicitly* create *a mapping* by adding a new document in ElasticSearch:

   ❑ On a Linux shell:

   ```
   #create an index
   curl -XPUT http://127.0.0.1:9200/test
   #{acknowledged":true}

   #put a document
   curl -XPUT http://127.0.0.1:9200/test/mytype/1 -d
   '{"name":"Paul", "age":35}'
   # {"ok":true,"_index":"test","_type":"mytype","_id":"1","_
   version":1}

   #get the mapping and pretty print it
   curl -XGET http://127.0.0.1:9200/test/mytype/_
   mapping?pretty=true
   ```

2. This is how the resulting mapping, autocreated by ElasticSearch, should look:

   ```
   {
      "mytype" : {
        "properties" : {
          "age" : {
            "type" : "long"
          },
          "name" : {
            "type" : "string"
          }
        }
      }
   }
   ```

How it works...

The first command line creates an index named *test*, where you can configure the type/mapping and insert documents.

The second command line inserts a document into the index. (We'll take a look at index creation and record indexing in *Chapter 4, Basic Operations*.)

During the document's indexing phase, ElasticSearch checks whether the `mytype` type exists; if not, it creates the type dynamically.

ElasticSearch reads all the default properties for the field of the mapping and starts processing them:

> ▶ If the field is already present in the mapping, and the value of the field is valid (that is, if it matches the correct type), then ElasticSearch does not need to change the current mapping.

> ▶ If the field is already present in the mapping but the value of the field is of a different type, the type inference engine tries to upgrade the field type (such as from an integer to a long value). If the types are not compatible, then it throws an exception and the index process will fail.

> ▶ If the field is not present, it will try to autodetect the type of field; it will also update the mapping to a new field mapping.

There's more...

In ElasticSearch, the separation of documents in types is logical: the ElasticSearch core engine transparently manages it. Physically, all the document types go in the same **Lucene** index, so they are not fully separated. The concept of types is purely logical and is enforced by ElasticSearch. The user is not bothered about this internal management, but in some cases, with a huge amount of records, this has an impact on performance. This affects the reading and writing of records because all the records are stored in the same index file.

Every document has a unique identifier, called **UID**, for an index; it's stored in the special `_uid` field of the document. It's automatically calculated by adding the type of the document to the `_id` value. (In our example, the `_uid` value will be `mytype#1`.)

The `_id` value can be provided at the time of indexing, or it can be assigned automatically by ElasticSearch if it's missing.

When a mapping type is created or changed, ElasticSearch automatically propagates mapping changes to all the nodes in the cluster so that all the shards are aligned such that a particular type can be processed.

See also

> ▶ The *Creating an index* recipe in *Chapter 4, Basic Operations*
> ▶ The *Putting a mapping in an index* recipe in *Chapter 4, Basic Operations*

Mapping base types

Using explicit mapping allows you to be faster when you start inserting data using a schema-less approach, without being concerned about the field types. Therefore, in order to achieve better results and performance when indexing, it's necessary to manually define a mapping.

Fine-tuning the mapping has some advantages, as follows:

- ▸ Reduces the size of the index on disk (disabling functionalities for custom fields)
- ▸ Indexes only *interesting* fields (a general boost to performance)
- ▸ *Precooks* data for a fast search or real-time analytics (such as aggregations)
- ▸ Correctly defines whether a field must be analyzed in multiple tokens or whether it should be considered as a single token

ElasticSearch also allows you to use base fields with a wide range of configurations.

Getting ready

You need a working ElasticSearch cluster and an index named *test* (refer to the *Creating an index* recipe in *Chapter 4, Basic Operations*) where you can put the mappings.

How to do it...

Let's use a semi-*real-world* example of a shop order for our ebay-like shop.

Initially, we define the following order:

Name	Type	Description
id	Identifier	Order identifier
date	Date (time)	Date of order
customer_id	Id reference	Customer ID reference
name	String	Name of the item
quantity	Integer	Number of items
vat	Double	VAT for the item
sent	Boolean	Status, if the order was sent

Our order record must be converted to an ElasticSearch mapping definition:

```
{
  "order" : {
    "properties" : {
      "id" : {"type" : "string", "store" : "yes" ,
      "index":"not_analyzed"},
      "date" : {"type" : "date", "store" : "no" ,
      "index":"not_analyzed"},
      "customer_id" : {"type" : "string", "store" : "yes" ,
      "index":"not_analyzed"},
      "sent" : {"type" : "boolean", "index":"not_analyzed"},
      "name" : {"type" : "string",  "index":"analyzed"},
      "quantity" : {"type" : "integer", "index":"not_analyzed"},
      "vat" : {"type" : "double", "index":"no"}
    }
  }
}
```

Now the mapping is ready to be put in the index. We'll see how to do this in the *Putting a mapping in an index* recipe in *Chapter 4, Basic Operations*.

How it works...

The field type must be mapped to one of ElasticSearch's base types, adding options for how the field must be indexed.

The next table is a reference of the mapping types:

Type	ES type	Description
String, VarChar, Text	string	A text field: such as a `nice text` and `CODE0011`
Integer	integer	An integer (32 bit): such as 1, 2, 3, 4
Long	long	A long value (64 bit)
Float	float	A floating-point number (32 bit): such as 1, 2, 4, 5
Double	double	A floating-point number (64 bit)
Boolean	boolean	A Boolean value: such as `true`, `false`
Date/Datetime	date	A date or datetime value: such as `2013-12-25`, `2013-12-25T22:21:20`
Bytes/Binary	binary	This is used for binary data such as a file or stream of bytes.

Depending on the data type, it's possible to give explicit directives to ElasticSearch on processing the field for better management. The most-used options are:

- `store`: This marks the field to be stored in a separate index fragment for fast retrieval. Storing a field consumes disk space, but it reduces computation if you need to extract the field from a document (that is, in scripting and aggregations). The possible values for this option are `no` and `yes` (the default value is `no`).

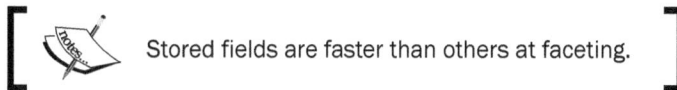

  > Stored fields are faster than others at faceting.

- `index`: This configures the field to be indexed (the default value is `analyzed`). The following are the possible values for this parameter:
  - `no`: This field is not indexed at all. It is useful to hold data that must not be searchable.
  - `analyzed`: This field is analyzed with the configured analyzer. It is generally lowercased and tokenized, using the default ElasticSearch configuration (`StandardAnalyzer`).
  - `not_analyzed`: This field is processed and indexed, but without being changed by an analyzer. The default ElasticSearch configuration uses the `KeywordAnalyzer` field, which processes the field as a single token.

- `null_value`: This defines a default value if the field is missing.

- `boost`: This is used to change the *importance* of a field (the default value is `1.0`).

- `index_analyzer`: This defines an analyzer to be used in order to process a field. If it is not defined, the analyzer of the parent object is used (the default value is `null`).

- `search_analyzer`: This defines an analyzer to be used during the search. If it is not defined, the analyzer of the parent object is used (the default value is `null`).

- `analyzer`: This sets both the `index_analyzer` and `search_analyzer` field to the defined value (the default value is `null`).

- `include_in_all`: This marks the current field to be indexed in the special `_all` field (a field that contains the concatenated text of all the fields). The default value is `true`.

- `index_name`: This is the name of the field to be stored in the Index. This property allows you to rename the field at the time of indexing. It can be used to manage data migration in time without breaking the application layer due to changes.

- `norms`: This controls the Lucene norms. This parameter is used to better score queries, if the field is used only for filtering. Its best practice to disable it in order to reduce the resource usage (the default value is `true` for analyzed fields and `false` for the `not_analyzed` ones).

There's more...

In this recipe, we saw the most-used options for the base types, but there are many other options that are useful for advanced usage.

An important parameter, available only for string mapping, is the `term_vector` field (the vector of the terms that compose a string; check out the Lucene documentation for further details at `http://lucene.apache.org/core/4_4_0/core/org/apache/lucene/index/Terms.html`) to define the details:

- ► `no`: This is the default value, which skips `term_vector` field
- ► `yes`: This stores the `term_vector` field
- ► `with_offsets`: This stores `term_vector` with a token offset (the start or end position in a block of characters)
- ► `with_positions`: This stores the position of the token in the `term_vector` field
- ► `with_positions_offsets`: This stores all the `term_vector` data

> Term vectors allow fast highlighting but consume a lot of disk space due to the storage of additional text information. It's best practice to activate them only in the fields that require highlighting, such as title or document content.

See also

- ► The ElasticSearch online documentation provides a full description of all the properties for the different mapping fields at `http://www.elasticsearch.org/guide/en/elasticsearch/reference/current/mapping-core-types.html`
- ► The *Specifying a different analyzer* recipe in this chapter shows alternative analyzers to the standard one.

Mapping arrays

An array or a multivalue field is very common in data models (such as multiple phone numbers, addresses, names, aliases, and so on), but it is not natively supported in traditional SQL solutions.

In SQL, multivalue fields require the creation of accessory tables that must be joined in order to gather all the values, leading to poor performance when the cardinality of records is huge.

ElasticSearch, which works natively in JSON, provides support for multivalue fields transparently.

Getting ready

You need a working ElasticSearch cluster.

How to do it...

Every field is automatically managed as an array. For example, in order to store *tags* for a document, this is how the mapping must be:

```
{
  "document" : {
    "properties" : {
      "name" : {"type" : "string",  "index":"analyzed"},
      "tag" : {"type" : "string", "store" : "yes" , "index":"not_
analyzed"},…
    …
    }
  }
}
```

This mapping is valid for indexing this document:

```
{"name": "document1", "tag": "awesome"}
```

It can also be used for the following document:

```
{"name": "document2", "tag": ["cool", "awesome", "amazing"]}
```

How it works...

ElasticSearch transparently manages the array; there is no difference whether you declare a single value or multiple values, due to its Lucene core nature.

Multiple values for a field are managed in Lucene by adding them to a document with the same field name (index_name in ES). If the index_name field is not defined in the mapping, it is taken from the name of the field. This can also be set to other values for custom behaviors, such as renaming a field at the indexing level or merging two or more JSON fields into a single Lucene field. Redefining the index_name field must be done with caution, as it impacts the search too. For people with a SQL background, this behavior might be strange, but this is a key point in the NoSQL world as it reduces the need for a join query and the need to create different tables to manage multiple values. An array of embedded objects has the same behavior as that of simple fields.

Mapping an object

The object is the base structure (analogous to a record in SQL). ElasticSearch extends the traditional use of objects, allowing the use of recursive embedded objects.

Getting ready

You need a working ElasticSearch cluster.

How to do it...

You can rewrite the mapping of the `order` type form of the *Mapping base types* recipe using an array of items:

```
{
  "order" : {
    "properties" : {
      "id" : {"type" : "string",
      "store" : "yes", "index":"not_analyzed"},
      "date" : {"type" : "date", "store" : "no",
      "index":"not_analyzed"},
      "customer_id" : {"type" : "string", "store" : "yes",
      "index":"not_analyzed"},
      "sent" : {"type" : "boolean", "store" : "no",
      "index":"not_analyzed"},
      "item" : {
        "type" : "object",
        "properties" : {
          "name" : {"type" : "string", "store" : "no",
          "index":"analyzed"},
          "quantity" : {"type" : "integer",
          "store" : "no",
          "index":"not_analyzed"},
          "vat" : {"type" : "double", "store" : "no",
          "index":"not_analyzed"}
        }
      }
    }
  }
}
```

How it works...

ElasticSearch speaks native JSON, so every complex JSON structure can be mapped into it.

When ElasticSearch is parsing an object type, it tries to extract fields and processes them as its defined mapping; otherwise it *learns* the structure of the object using reflection.

The following are the most important attributes for an object:

- ▶ `properties`: This is a collection of fields or objects (we consider them as columns in the SQL world).

- ▶ `enabled`: This is enabled if the object needs to be processed. If it's set to `false`, the data contained in the object is not indexed as it cannot be searched (the default value is `true`).

- ▶ `dynamic`: This allows ElasticSearch to add new field names to the object using reflection on the values of inserted data (the default value is `true`). If it's set to false, when you try to index an object containing a new field type, it'll be rejected silently. If it's set to `strict`, when a new field type is present in the object, an error is raised and the index process is skipped. Controlling the dynamic parameter allows you to be safe about changes in the document structure.

- ▶ `include_in_all`: This adds the object values (the default value is `true`) to the special `_all` field (used to aggregate the text of all the document fields).

The most-used attribute is `properties`, which allows you to map the fields of the object in ElasticSearch fields.

Disabling the indexing part of the document reduces the index size; however, the data cannot be searched. In other words, you end up with a smaller file on disk, but there is a cost incurred in functionality.

There's more...

There are other properties also which are also rarely used, such as `index_name` and `path`, which change *how* Lucene indexes the object, modifying the index's inner structure.

See also

Special objects, which are described in the *Mapping a document*, *Managing a child document*, and *Mapping a nested objects* recipes in this chapter.

Mapping a document

The document is also referred to as the root object. It has special parameters that control its behavior, which are mainly used internally to do special processing, such as routing or managing the **time-to-live** of documents.

In this recipe, we'll take a look at these special fields and learn how to use them.

Getting ready

You need a working ElasticSearch cluster.

How to do it...

You can extend the preceding order example by adding some special fields, as follows:

```
{
    "order": {
      "_id": {
        "path": "order_id"
      },
      "_type": {
        "store": "yes"
      },
      "_source": {
        "store": "yes"
      },
      "_all": {
        "enable": false
      },
      "_analyzer": {
        "path": "analyzer_field"
      },
      "_boost": {
        "null_value": 1.0
      },
      "_routing": {
        "path": "customer_id",
        "required": true
      },
      "_index": {
        "enabled": true
      },
```

```
    "_size": {
      "enabled": true,
      "store": "yes"
    },
    "_timestamp": {
      "enabled": true,
      "store": "yes",
      "path": "date"
    },
    "_ttl": {
      "enabled": true,
      "default": "3y"
    },
    "properties": {
... truncated ….
    }
  }
}
```

How it works...

Every special field has its own parameters and value options, as follows:

- ▶ _id (by default, it's not indexed or stored): This allows you to index only the ID part of the document. It can be associated with a path field that will be used to extract the id from the source of the document:

  ```
  "_id" : {
    "path" : "order_id"
  },
  ```

- ▶ _type (by default, it's indexed and not stored): This allows you to index the type of the document.

- ▶ _index (the default value is enabled=false): This controls whether the index must be stored as part of the document. It can be enabled by setting the parameter as enabled=true.

- ▶ _boost (the default value is null_value=1.0): This controls the boost (the value used to increment the score) level of the document. It can be overridden in the boost parameter for the field.

- ▶ _size (the default value is enabled=false): This controls the size if it stores the size of the source record.

- ▸ `_timestamp` (by default, `enabled=false`): This automatically enables the indexing of the document's timestamp. If given a `path` value, it can be extracted by the source of the document and used as a timestamp value. It can be queried as a standard datetime.

- ▸ `_ttl` (by default, `enabled=false`): The time-to-live parameter sets the expiration time of the document. When a document expires, it will be removed from the index. It allows you to define an optional parameter, `default`, to provide a default value for a type level.

- ▸ `_all` (the default is `enabled=true`): This controls the creation of the `_all` field (a special field that aggregates all the text of all the document fields). Because this functionality requires a lot of CPU and storage, if it is not required it is better to disable it.

- ▸ `_source` (by default, `enabled=true`): This controls the storage of the document source. Storing the source is very useful, but it's a storage overhead; so, if it is not required, it's better to turn it off.

- ▸ `_parent`: This defines the parent document (see the *Mapping a child document* recipe in this chapter).

- ▸ `_routing`: This controls in which shard the document is to be stored. It supports the following additional parameters:

  - ❑ `path`: This is used to provide a field to be used for routing (`customer_id` in the earlier example).

  - ❑ `required` (`true/false`): This is used to force the presence of the routing value, raising an exception if it is not provided

- ▸ `_analyzer`: This allows you to define a document field that contains the name of the analyzer to be used for fields that do not explicitly define an analyzer or an `index_analyzer`.

The power of control to index and process a document is very important and allows you to resolve issues related to complex data types.

Every special field has parameters to set a particular configuration, and some of their behaviors may change in different releases of ElasticSearch.

See also

- ▸ The *Using dynamic templates in document mapping* recipe in this chapter
- ▸ The *Putting a mapping in an index* recipe in *Chapter 4, Basic Operations*

Using dynamic templates in document mapping

In the *Using explicit mapping creation* recipe, we saw how ElasticSearch is able to guess the field type using reflection. In this recipe, we'll see how we can help it to improve its guessing capabilities via dynamic templates.

The dynamic template feature is very useful, for example, if you need to create several indices with similar types, because it allows you to remove the need to define mappings from coded initial routines to automatic index document creation. A typical use is to define types for logstash log indices.

Getting ready

You need a working ElasticSearch cluster.

How to do it...

You can extend the previous mapping by adding document-related settings:

```
{
   "order" : {
     "index_analyzer":"standard",
     "search_analyzer":"standard",
     "dynamic_date_formats":["yyyy-MM-dd", "dd-MM-yyyy"],
     "date_detection":true,
     "numeric_detection":true,
     "dynamic_templates":[
     {"template1":{
       "match":"*",
       "match_mapping_type":"long",
       "mapping":{"type":" {dynamic_type}",  "store":true}
     }}
     ],
     "properties" : {…}
   }
}
```

How it works...

The **Root** object (document) controls the behavior of its fields and all its child object fields.

In the document mapping, you can define the following fields:

▸ `index_analyzer`: This defines the analyzer to be used for indexing within this document. If an `index_analyzer` field is not defined in a field, then the field is taken as the default.

▸ `search_analyzer`: This defines the analyzer to be used for searching. If a field doesn't define an analyzer, the `search_analyzer` field of the document, if available, is taken.

> If you need to set the `index_analyzer` and `search_analyzer` field with the same value, you can use the analyzer property.

▸ `date_detection` (by default `true`): This enables the extraction of a date from a string.

▸ `dynamic_date_formats`: This is a list of valid date formats; it's used if `date_detection` is active.

▸ `numeric_detection` (by default `false`): This enables you to convert strings to numbers, if it is possible.

▸ `dynamic_templates`: This is a list of the templates used to change the explicit mapping, if one of these templates is matched. The rules defined in it are used to build the final mapping.

A dynamic template is composed of two parts: the matcher and the mapping.

In order to match a field to activate the template, several types of matchers are available:

▸ `match`: This allows you to define a match on the field name. The expression is a standard **glob** pattern (`http://en.wikipedia.org/wiki/Glob_(programming)`).

▸ `unmatch` (optional): This allows you to define the expression to be used to exclude matches.

▸ `match_mapping_type` (optional): This controls the types of the matched fields. For example, string, integer, and so on.

▸ `path_match` (optional): This allows you to match the dynamic template against the full dot notation of the field. For example, `obj1.*.value`.

▸ `path_unmatch` (optional): This does the opposite of `path_match`, that is, excluding the matched fields.

▶ `match_pattern` (optional): This allows you to switch the matchers to `regex` (regular expression); otherwise, the glob pattern match is used.

The dynamic template mapping part is standard, but with the ability to use special placeholders as follows:

▶ `{name}`:This will be replaced with the actual dynamic field name

▶ `{dynamic_type}`: This will be replaced with the type of the matched field

> The order of the dynamic templates is very important. Only the first one that matches is executed. It is a good practice to order the ones with stricter rules first, followed by the other templates.

There's more...

The dynamic template is very handy when you need to set a mapping configuration for all the fields. This action can be performed by adding a dynamic template similar to this one:

```
"dynamic_templates" : [
  {
    "store_generic" : {
      "match" : "*",
      "mapping" : {
        "store" : "yes"
      }
    }
  }
]
```

In this example, all the new fields, which will be added with the explicit mapping, will be stored.

See also

▶ The *Using explicit mapping creation* recipe in this chapter

▶ The *Mapping a document* recipe in this chapter

▶ The Glob pattern at `http://en.wikipedia.org/wiki/Glob_pattern`

Managing nested objects

There is a special type of embedded object: the nested object. This resolves problems related to Lucene indexing architecture, in which all the fields of the embedded objects are viewed as a single object. During a search in Lucene, it is not possible to distinguish between the values of different embedded objects in the same multivalued array.

If we consider the previous order example, it's not possible to distinguish between an item name and its quantity with the same query, as Lucene puts them in the same Lucene document object. We need to index them in different documents and to join them. This entire *trip* is managed by nested objects and nested queries.

Getting ready

You need a working ElasticSearch cluster.

How to do it...

A nested object is defined as a standard object with the type `nested`.

From the example in the *Mapping an object* recipe in this chapter, we can change the type from object to **nested** as follows:

```
{
  "order" : {
    "properties" : {
      "id" : {"type" : "string",
      "store" : "yes", "index":"not_analyzed"},
      "date" : {"type" : "date", "store" : "no",
      "index":"not_analyzed"},
      "customer_id" : {"type" : "string", "store" : "yes",
      "index":"not_analyzed"},
      "sent" : {"type" : "boolean", "store" : "no",
      "index":"not_analyzed"},
      "item" : {
        "type" : "nested",
        "properties" : {
          "name" : {"type" : "string", "store" : "no",
          "index":"analyzed"},
          "quantity" : {"type" : "integer", "store" : "no",
          "index":"not_analyzed"},
```

```
          "vat" : {"type" : "double", "store" : "no",
          "index":"not_analyzed"}
        }
      }
    }
  }
}
```

How it works...

When a document is indexed, if an embedded object is marked as nested, it's extracted by the original document and indexed in a new **external** document.

In the above example, we have reused the mapping of the previous recipe, *Mapping an Object*, but we have changed the type of the item from `object` to `nested`. No other action must be taken to convert an embedded objet to a nested one.

Nested objects are special Lucene documents that are saved in the same block of data as their parents — this approach allows faster joining with the parent document.

Nested objects are not searchable with standard queries, but only with nested ones. They are not shown in standard query results.

The lives of nested objects are related to their parents; deleting/updating a parent automatically deletes/updates all the nested children. Changing the parent means ElasticSearch will do the following:

- Mark old documents that are deleted
- Mark all nested documents that are deleted
- Index the new document's version
- Index all nested documents

There's more...

Sometimes, it is necessary to propagate information about nested objects to their parents or their root objects, mainly to build simpler queries about their parents. To achieve this goal, the following two special properties of nested objects can be used:

- `include_in_parent`: This allows you to automatically add the nested fields to the immediate parent
- `include_in_root`: This adds the nested objects' fields to the root object

These settings add to data redundancy, but they reduce the complexity of some queries, improving performance.

▸   The *Managing a child document* recipe in this chapter

Managing a child document

In the previous recipe, you saw how it's possible to manage relationships between objects with the nested object type. The disadvantage of using nested objects is their dependency on their parent. If you need to change the value of a nested object, you need to reindex the parent (this brings about a potential performance overhead if the nested objects change too quickly). To solve this problem, ElasticSearch allows you to define child documents.

Getting ready

You need a working ElasticSearch cluster.

How to do it...

You can modify the mapping of the `order` example from the *Mapping a document* recipe by indexing the items as separate child documents.

You need to extract the `item` object and create a new type of document item with the `_parent` property set:

```
{
    "order": {
        "properties": {
            "id": {
                "type": "string",
                "store": "yes",
                "index": "not_analyzed"
            },
            "date": {
                "type": "date",
                "store": "no",
                "index": "not_analyzed"
            },
            "customer_id": {
                "type": "string",
```

```
          "store": "yes",
          "index": "not_analyzed"
        },
        "sent": {
          "type": "boolean",
          "store": "no",
          "index": "not_analyzed"
        }
      }
    },
    "item": {
      "_parent": {
        "type": "order"
      },
      "properties": {
        "name": {
          "type": "string",
          "store": "no",
          "index": "analyzed"
        },
        "quantity": {
          "type": "integer",
          "store": "no",
          "index": "not_analyzed"
        },
        "vat": {
          "type": "double",
          "store": "no",
          "index": "not_analyzed"
        }
      }
    }
  }
}
```

The preceding mapping is similar to the mapping shown in the previous recipes. The `item` object is extracted from the order (in the previous example, it was nested) and added as a new mapping. The only difference is that `"type": "nested"` becomes `"type": "object"` (it can be omitted) and there is a new special field, `_parent`, which defines the parent-child relation.

How it works...

The child object is a standard root object (document) with an extra property defined, which is `_parent`.

The `type` property of `_parent` refers to the type of parent document.

The child document must be indexed in the same shard as the parent, so that when it is indexed, an extra parameter must be passed: `parent id`. (We'll see how to do this in later chapters.)

Child documents don't require you to reindex the parent document when you want to change their values, so they are faster for indexing, reindexing (updating), and deleting.

There's more...

In ElasticSearch, there are different ways in which you can manage relationships between objects:

- Embedding with `type=object`: This is implicitly managed by ElasticSearch, and it considers the embedded as part of the main document. It's fast but you need to reindex the main document to change a value of the embedded object.
- Nesting with `type=nested`: This allows a more accurate search and filtering of the parent, using a nested query on the children. Everything works as in the case of an embedded object, except for the query.
- External child documents: This is a document in which the children are external documents, with a `_parent` property to bind them to the parent. They must be indexed in the same shard as the parent. The join with the parent is a bit slower than with the nested one, because the nested objects are in the same data block as the parent in the Lucene index and they are loaded with the parent; otherwise the child documents require more read operations.

Choosing how to model the relationship between objects depends on your application scenario.

There is another approach that can be used, but only on big data documents, which brings poor performance as it's a decoupling join relation. You have to do the join query in two steps: first, you collect the ID of the children/other documents and then you search them in a field of their parent.

See also

- The *Using a has_child query/filter, Using a top_children query*, and *Using a has_parent query/filter* recipes in *Chapter 5, Search, Queries, and Filters*, for more information on child/parent queries.

Adding a field with multiple mappings

Often, a field must be processed with several core types or in different ways. For example, a string field must be processed as `analyzed` for search and as `not_analyzed` for sorting. To do this, you need to define a `multi_field` special property called `fields`.

> In the previous ElasticSearch versions (prior to 1.x), there was the `multi_field` type, but this has now deprecated and will be removed in favor of the `fields` property.

The `fields` property is a very powerful feature of mapping because it allows you to use the same field in different ways.

Getting ready

You need a working ElasticSearch cluster.

How to do it...

To define a multifields property, you need to:

1. Use field as a type – define the main field type, as we saw in the previous sections.

2. Define a dictionary that contains subfields called `fields`. The subfield with the same name as the parent field is the default one.

If you consider the item of your `order` example, you can index the name in this way:

```
"name": {
    "type": "string",
    "index": "not_analyzed",
    "fields": {
      "name": {
        "type": "string",
        "index": "not_analyzed"
      },
      "tk": {
        "type": "string",
        "index": "analyzed"
      },
      "code": {
        "type": "string",
```

```
        "index": "analyzed",
        "analyzer": "code_analyzer"
      }
    }
  },
```

If you already have a mapping stored in ElasticSearch and want to migrate the fields in a `fields` property, it's enough to save a new mapping with a different type, and ElasticSearch provides the merge automatically. New subfields in the `fields` property can be added without a problem at any moment, but the new subfields will be available only to new indexed documents.

How it works...

During indexing, when ElasticSearch processes a `fields` property, it reprocesses the same field for every subfield defined in the mapping.

To access the subfields of a multifield, we have a new `path` value built on the base field plus the subfield name. If you consider the earlier example, you have:

▶ `name`: This points to the default `field` subfield (the `not_analyzed` subfield)

▶ `name.tk`: This points to the standard analyzed (tokenized) field

▶ `name.code`: This points to a field analyzed with a code extractor analyzer

In the earlier example, we changed the analyzer to introduce a code extractor analyzer that allows you to extract the item code from a string.

Using the fields property, if you index a string such as `Good Item to buy - ABC1234` you'll have:

▶ `name = "Good Item to buy - ABC1234"` (useful for sorting)

▶ `name.tk=["good", "item", "to", "buy", "abc1234"]` (useful for searching)

▶ `name.code = ["ABC1234"]` (useful for searching and faceting)

There's more...

The `fields` property is very useful for data processing, because it allows you to define several ways to process a field's data.

For example, if you are working on a document content, you can define analyzers to extract names, places, date/time, geolocation, and so on as subfields.

The subfields of a multifield are standard core type fields; you can perform every process you want on them such as search, filter, facet, and scripting.

- ▶ The *Specifying a different analyzer* recipe in this chapter

Mapping a geo point field

ElasticSearch natively supports the use of geolocation types: special types that allow you to localize your document in geographic coordinates (latitude and longitude) around the world.

There are two main document types used in the geographic world: point and shape. In this recipe, we'll see **geo point**, the base element of geolocation.

Getting ready

You need a working ElasticSearch cluster.

How to do it...

The type of the field must be set to `geo_point` in order to define a geo point.

You can extend the earlier `order` example by adding a new field that stores the location of a customer. The following will be the result:

```
{
  "order": {
    "properties": {
      "id": {
        "type": "string",
        "store": "yes",
        "index": "not_analyzed"
      },
      "date": {
        "type": "date",
        "store": "no",
        "index": "not_analyzed"
      },
      "customer_id": {
        "type": "string",
        "store": "yes",
        "index": "not_analyzed"
      },
      "customer_ip": {
        "type": "ip",
        "store": "yes",
```

```
        "index": "not_analyzed"
    },
    "customer_location": {
        "type": "geo_point",
        "store": "yes"
    },
    "sent": {
        "type": "boolean",
        "store": "no",
        "index": "not_analyzed"
    }
  }
 }
}
```

How it works...

When ElasticSearch indexes a document with a geo point field (latitude, longitude), it processes the latitude and longitude coordinates and creates special accessory field data to quickly query these coordinates.

Depending on the properties, given a latitude and longitude it's possible to compute the geohash value (http://en.wikipedia.org/wiki/Geohash). The index process also optimizes these values for special computation, such as distance and ranges, and in a shape match.

Geo point has special parameters that allow you to store additional geographic data:

- ▶ lat_lon (by default, false): This allows you to store the latitude and longitude in the .lat and .lon fields. Storing these values improves performance in many memory algorithms used in distance and shape calculus.

> It makes sense to store values only if there is a single point value for a field, in multiple values.

- ▶ geohash (by default, false): This allows you to store the computed geohash value.
- ▶ geohash_precision (by default, 12): This defines the precision to be used in a geohash calculus. For example, given a geo point value [45.61752, 9.08363], it will store:
    - ❑ customer_location = "45.61752, 9.08363"
    - ❑ customer_location.lat = 45.61752
    - ❑ customer_location.lon = 9.08363
    - ❑ customer_location.geohash = "u0n7w8qmrfj"

There's more...

Geo point is a special type and can accept several formats as input:

- ▶ Latitude and longitude as properties:

```
"customer_location": {
    "lat": 45.61752,
    "lon": 9.08363
},
```

- ▶ Latitude and longitude as a string:

```
"customer_location": "45.61752,9.08363",
```

- ▶ Latitude and longitude as geohash string

- ▶ Latitude and longitude as a GeoJSON array (note that in this latitude and longitude are reversed):

```
"customer_location": [9.08363, 45.61752]
```

Mapping a geo shape field

An extension to the concept of point is shape. ElasticSearch provides a type that facilitates the management of arbitrary polygons: the geo shape.

Getting ready

You need a working ElasticSearch cluster with **Spatial4J** (v0.3) and **JTS** (v1.12) in the classpath to use this type.

How to do it...

In order to map a geo_shape type, a user must explicitly provide some parameters:

- ▶ tree (by default, geohash): This is the name of the prefix tree implementation called **geohash** for GeohashPrefixTree and **quadtree** for QuadPrefixTree.

- ▶ precision: This is used instead of tree_levels to provide a more human value to be used in the tree level. The precision number can be followed by the unit, such as 10 m, 10 km, 10 miles, and so on.

- ▶ tree_levels: This is the maximum number of layers to be used in the prefix tree.

- ▶ distance_error_pct (the default is 0,025% and the maximum value is 0,5%): This sets the maximum number of errors allowed in PrefixTree.

The `customer_location` mapping, which we have seen in the previous recipe using `geo_shape`, will be:

```
"customer_location": {
  "type": "geo_shape",
  "tree": "quadtree",
  "precision": "1m"
},
```

How it works...

When a shape is indexed or searched internally, a path tree is created and used.

A path tree is a list of terms that contain geographic information, computed to improve performance in evaluating geometric calculus.

The path tree also depends on the shape type, such as point, linestring, polygon, multipoint, and multipolygon.

See also

▶ To fully understand the logic behind geo shape, some good resources are the ElasticSearch page about geo shape and the sites of the libraries used for geographic calculus (`https://github.com/spatial4j/spatial4j` and `http://www.vividsolutions.com/jts/jtshome.htm`).

Mapping an IP field

ElasticSearch is used to collect and search logs in a lot of systems, such as Kibana (`http://www.elasticsearch.org/overview/kibana/` or `http://kibana.org/`) and logstash (`http://www.elasticsearch.org/overview/logstash/` or `http://logstash.net/`). To improve searching in these scenarios, it provides the IPv4 type that can be used to store IP addresses in an optimized way.

Getting ready

You need a working ElasticSearch cluster.

How to do it...

You need to define the type of the field that contains an IP address as `"ip"`.

Using the preceding `order` example, you can extend it by adding the customer IP:

```
"customer_ip": {
  "type": "ip",
  "store": "yes"
}
```

The IP must be in the standard point notation form, as shown in the following code:

```
"customer_ip":"19.18.200.201"
```

How it works...

When ElasticSearch is processing a document, if a field is an IP one, it tries to convert its value to a numerical form and generate tokens for fast value searching.

The IP has special properties:

- ▶ `index`: This defines whether the field should be indexed. Otherwise, no value must be set
- ▶ `precision_step` (by default, 4): This defines the number of terms that must be generated for its original value

The other properties (`store`, `boot`, `null_value`, and `include_in_all`) work as other base types.

The advantages of using IP fields over string fields are: faster speed in every range, improved filtering, and lower resource usage (disk and memory).

Mapping an attachment field

ElasticSearch allows you to extend its core types to cover new requirements with native plugins that provide new mapping types. The most-used custom field type is the attachment mapping type.

It allows you to index and search the contents of common documental files, such as Microsoft Office formats, open document formats, PDF, epub, and many others.

You need a working ElasticSearch cluster with the attachment plugin (`https://github.com/elasticsearch/elasticsearch-mapper-attachments`) installed.

It can be installed from the command line with the following command:

```
bin/plugin -install elasticsearch/elasticsearch-mapper-
attachments/1.9.0
```

The plugin version is related to the current ElasticSearch version; check the GitHub page for further details.

How to do it...

To map a field as an attachment, it's necessary to set the `type` field to `attachment`.

Internally, the attachment field defines the `fields` property as a multifield that takes some binary data (encoded base64) and extracts useful information such as author, content, title, date, and so on.

If you want to create a mapping for an e-mail storing attachment, it should be as follows:

```
{
  "email": {
    "properties": {
      "sender": {
        "type": "string",
        "store": "yes",
        "index": "not_analyzed"
      },
      "date": {
        "type": "date",
        "store": "no",
        "index": "not_analyzed"
      },
      "document": {
        "type": "attachment",
        "fields": {
          "file": {
            "store": "yes",
            "index": "analyzed"
          },
          "date": {
            "store": "yes"
```

```
            },
            "author": {
              "store": "yes"
            },
            "keywords": {
              "store": "yes"
            },
            "content_type": {
              "store": "yes"
            },
            "title": {
              "store": "yes"
            }
          }
        }
      }
    }
  }
}
```

How it works...

The attachment plugin uses **Apache Tika** internally, a library that specializes in text extraction from documents. The list of supported document types is available on the Apache Tika site (`http://tika.apache.org/1.5/formats.html`), but it covers all the common file types.

The attachment type field receives a base64 binary stream that is processed by Tika metadata and text extractor. The field can be seen as a multifield that stores different contents in its subfields:

- **file**: This stores the content of the file
- **date**: This stores the file creation data extracted by Tika metadata
- **author**: This stores the file's author extracted by Tika metadata
- **keywords**: This stores the file's keywords extracted by Tika metadata
- **content_type**: This stores the file's content type
- **title**: This stores the file's title extracted by Tika metadata

The default setting for an attachment plugin is to extract 100,000 characters. This value can be changed globally by setting the index settings to `index.mappings.attachment.indexed_chars` or by passing a value to the `_indexed_chars` property when indexing the element.

There's more...

The attachment type is an example of how it's possible to extend ElasticSearch with custom types.

The attachment plugin is very useful for indexing documents, e-mails, and all types of unstructured documents. A good example of an application that uses this plugin is ScrutMyDocs (`http://www.scrutmydocs.org/`).

See also

▸ The official attachment plugin page at `https://github.com/elasticsearch/elasticsearch-mapper-attachments`

▸ The Tika library page at `http://tika.apache.org`

▸ The ScrutMyDocs website at `http://www.scrutmydocs.org/`

Adding metadata to a mapping

Sometimes, when working with a mapping, you need to store some additional data to be used for display purposes, ORM facilities, and permissions, or you simply need to track them in the mapping.

ElasticSearch allows you to store any kind of JSON data you want in the mapping with the `_meta` special field.

Getting ready

You need a working ElasticSearch cluster.

How to do it...

The `_meta mapping` field can be populated with any data you want:

```
{
  "order": {
    "_meta": {
      "attr1": ["value1", "value2"],
      "attr2": {
        "attr3": "value3"
      }
    }
  }
}
```

How it works...

When ElasticSearch processes a mapping and finds a `_meta` field, it stores the field in the global mapping status and propagates the information to all the cluster nodes.

The `_meta` field is only used for storage purposes; it's not indexed or searchable. It can be used to do the following:

- Storing type metadata
- Storing ORM (Object Relational Mapping) related information
- Storing type permission information
- Storing extra type information (such as the icon or filename used to display the type)
- Storing template parts to render web interfaces

Specifying a different analyzer

In the previous recipes, we saw how to map different fields and objects in ElasticSearch and described how easy it is to change the standard analyzer with the `analyzer`, `index_analyzer`, and `search_analyzer` properties.

In this recipe, we will see several analyzers and how to use them in order to improve the quality of indexing and searching.

Getting ready

You need a working ElasticSearch cluster.

How to do it...

Every core type field allows you to specify a custom analyzer for indexing and searching as field parameters.

For example, if you want the name field to use a standard analyzer for indexing and a simple analyzer for searching, the mapping will be as follows:

```
{
  "name": {
    "type": "string",
    "index": "analyzed",
    "index_analyzer": "standard",
    "search_analyzer": "simple"
  }
}
```

How it works...

The concept of an analyzer comes from Lucene (the core of ElasticSearch). An analyzer is a Lucene element that is composed of a tokenizer, which splits a text into tokens, and one or more token filters, which perform token manipulation – such as lowercasing, normalization, removing stopwords, stemming, and so on.

During the indexing phase, when ElasticSearch processes a field that must be indexed, an analyzer is chosen by first checking whether it is defined in the field (`index_analyzer`), then in the document, and finally in the index.

Choosing the correct analyzer is essential to get good results during the query phase.

ElasticSearch provides several analyzers in its standard installation. In the following table, the most common analyzers are described:

Name	Description
standard	This divides text using a standard tokenizer, normalized tokens, and lowercase tokens, and also removes unwanted tokens
simple	This divides text and converts them to lowercase
whitespace	This divides text at spaces
stop	This processes the text with a standard analyzer and then applies custom stopwords
keyword	This considers all text as a token
pattern	This divides text using a regular expression
snowball	This works as a standard analyzer plus a stemming at the end of processing

For special language purposes, ElasticSearch supports a set of analyzers that are aimed at analyzing specific language text, such as Arabic, Armenian, Basque, Brazilian, Bulgarian, Catalan, Chinese, CKJ, Czech, Danish, Dutch, English, Finnish, French, Galician, German, Greek, Hindi, Hungarian, Indonesian, Italian, Norwegian, Persian, Portuguese, Romanian, Russian, Spanish, Swedish, Turkish, and Thai.

See also

There are several ElasticSearch plugins that extend the list of available analyzers. Checkout the plugins at GitHub. The following are the most famous ones:

> ▶ ICU analysis plugin (`https://github.com/elasticsearch/elasticsearch-analysis-icu`)

> ▶ Morphological Analysis Plugin (`https://github.com/imotov/elasticsearch-analysis-morphology`)

- ▶ Phonetic Analysis Plugin (`https://github.com/elasticsearch/elasticsearch-analysis-phonetic`)
- ▶ Smart Chinese Analysis Plugin (`https://github.com/elasticsearch/elasticsearch-analysis-smartcn`)
- ▶ Japanese (kuromoji) Analysis Plugin (`https://github.com/elasticsearch/elasticsearch-analysis-kuromoji`)

Mapping a completion suggester

In order to provide search functionalities for your user, one of the most common requirements is to provide text suggestions for your query.

ElasticSearch provides a helper to archive this functionality via a special type mapping called `completion`.

Getting ready

You need a working ElasticSearch cluster.

How to do it...

The definition of a completion field is similar to that of the previous core type fields. For example, to provide suggestions for a name with an alias, you can write a similar mapping:

```
{
    "name": {"type": "string", "copy_to":["suggest"]},
    "alias": {"type": "string", "copy_to":["suggest"]},
    "suggest": {
        "type": "complection",
        "payloads": true,
        "index_analyzer": "simple",
        "search_analyzer": "simple"
    }
}
```

In this example, we have defined two string fields, `name` and `alias`, and a `suggest` completer for them.

How it works...

There are several ways in which you can provide a suggestion in ElasticSearch. You can have the same functionality using some queries with wildcards or prefixes, but the completion fields are much faster due to the natively optimized structures used.

Internally, ElasticSearch builds a **Finite state transducer** (**FST**) structure to suggest terms. (The topic is described in great detail on its Wikipedia page at `http://en.wikipedia.org/wiki/Finite_state_transducer`.)

The following are the most important properties that can be configured to use the `completion` field:

- `index_analyzer` (by default, `simple`): This defines the analyzer to be used for indexing within the document. The default is simple, to keep stopwords, such as `at`, `the`, `of`, and `so`, in suggested terms.

- `search_analyzer` (by default, `simple`): This defines the analyzer to be used for searching.

- `preserve_separators` (by default, `true`): This controls how tokens are processed. If it is disabled, the *spaces* are trimmed in the suggestion, which allows it to match `fightc` as `fight club`.

- `max_input_length` (by default, `50`): This property reduces the characters in the input string to reduce the suggester size. The trial in suggesting the longest text is nonsense because it is against the usability.

- `payloads` (by default, `false`): This allows you to store payloads (additional items' values to be returned). For example, it can be used to return a product in an SKU:

```
curl -X PUT 'http://localhost:9200/myindex/mytype/1' -d '{
  "name" : "ElasticSearch Cookbook",
    "suggest" : {
      "input": ["ES", "ElasticSearch", "Elastic Search",
      "Elastic Search Cookbook" ],
      "output": "ElasticSearch Cookbook",
      "payload" : { "isbn" : "1782166629" },
      "weight" : 34
    }
}'
```

In the previous example, you can see the following functionalities that are available during indexing for the `completion` field:

- `input`: This manages a list of provided values that can be used for suggesting. If you are able to enrich your data, this can improve the quality of your suggester.

- `output` (optional): This is the result to be shown from the desired suggester.

- `payload` (optional): This is some extra data to be returned.

- `weight` (optional): This is a weight boost to be used to score the suggester.

At the start of the recipe, I showed a shortcut by using the `copy_to` field property to populate the completion field from several fields. The `copy_to` property simply copies the content of one field to one or more others fields.

See also

In this recipe, we only discussed the mapping and indexing functionality of completion; the search part will be discussed in the *Suggesting a correct query* recipe in *Chapter 5, Search, Queries, and Filters*.

4
Basic Operations

In this chapter, we will cover:

- ▶ Creating an index
- ▶ Deleting an index
- ▶ Opening/closing an index
- ▶ Putting a mapping in an index
- ▶ Getting a mapping
- ▶ Deleting a mapping
- ▶ Refreshing an index
- ▶ Flushing an index
- ▶ Optimizing an index
- ▶ Checking if an index or type exists
- ▶ Managing index settings
- ▶ Using index aliases
- ▶ Indexing a document
- ▶ Getting a document
- ▶ Deleting a document
- ▶ Updating a document
- ▶ Speeding up atomic operations (bulk operations)
- ▶ Speeding up GET operations (multi GET)

Introduction

Before starting with indexing and searching in ElasticSearch, we need to learn how to manage indices and perform operations on documents. In this chapter, we'll discuss different operations on indices such as **Create**, **Delete**, **Update**, **Read**, and **Open/Close**. These operations are very important because they allow us to better define the container (**index**) that will store your documents. The index Create/Delete actions are similar to the SQL's Create/Delete database commands.

After the indices management part, we'll learn how to manage mappings, which will complete the discussion that we started in the previous chapter, and to lay the foundation for the next chapter, which is mainly centered on **Search**.

A large portion of this chapter is dedicated to **CRUD** (**Create**, **Read**, **Update**, **Delete**) operations on records that are the *core* of records storage and management in ElasticSearch.

To improve indexing performance, it's also important to understand bulk operations and avoid their common pitfalls.

This chapter doesn't cover operations involving queries; these will be the main theme of *Chapter 5*, *Search, Queries, and Filters*. Likewise, the Cluster operations will be discussed in *Chapter 9*, *Cluster and Node Monitoring*, because they are mainly related to control and monitoring the Cluster.

Creating an index

The first operation before starting to Index data in ElasticSearch is to create an index—the main container of our data.

An Index is similar to Database concept in SQL, a container for types, such as tables in SQL, and documents, such as records in SQL.

Getting ready

You will need a working ElasticSearch cluster.

How to do it...

The HTTP method to create an index is PUT (POST also works); the REST URL contains the index name:

```
http://<server>/<index_name>
```

To create an index, we will perform the following steps:

1. Using the command line, we can execute a PUT call:

```
curl -XPUT http://127.0.0.1:9200/myindex -d '{
  "settings" : {
    "index" : {
      "number_of_shards" : 2,
      "number_of_replicas" : 1
    }
  }
}'
```

2. The result returned by ElasticSearch, if everything goes well, should be:

```
{"acknowledged":true}
```

3. If the index already exists, then a 400 error is returned:

```
{"error":"IndexAlreadyExistsException[[myindex] Already
exists]","status":400}
```

How it works...

There are some limitations to the Index name, due to accepted characters:

- ASCII letters (a-z)
- Numbers (0-9)
- Point ., minus -, ampersand &, and underscore _

> The index name will be mapped to a directory on your storage.

During index creation, the replication can be set with two parameters in the `settings/index` object:

- `number_of_shard`: This controls the number of shards that compose the index (every shard can store up to 2^32 documents).
- `number_of_replicas`: This controls the number of replicas (how many times your data is replicated in the cluster for high availability). A good practice is to set this value to at least to 1.

The API call initializes a new index, which means:

- The index is created in a primary node first and then its status is propagated to the cluster level
- A default mapping (empty) is created
- All the shards required by the index are initialized and ready to accept data

The index creation API allows us to define the mapping during creation time. The parameter required to define a mapping is `mapping` and it accepts multiple mappings. So, in a single call, it is possible to create an Index and insert the required mappings.

There's more...

The index creation command also allows us to pass the mappings section, which contains the mapping definitions. It is a shortcut to create an index with mappings, without executing an extra PUT mapping call.

A common example of this call, using the mapping from the *Putting a mapping in an index* recipe, is:

```
curl -XPOST localhost:9200/myindex -d '{
  "settings" : {
    "number_of_shards" : 2,
    "number_of_replicas" : 1
  },
  "mappings" : {
    "order" : {
      "properties" : {
        "id" : {"type" : "string", "store" : "yes" ,
        "index":"not_analyzed"},
        "date" : {"type" : "date", "store" : "no" ,
        "index":"not_analyzed"},
        "customer_id" : {"type" : "string", "store" : "yes" ,
        "index":"not_analyzed"},
        "sent" : {"type" : "boolean", "index":"not_analyzed"},
        "name" : {"type" : "string", "index":"analyzed"},
        "quantity" : {"type" : "integer", "index":"not_analyzed"},
        "vat" : {"type" : "double", "index":"no"}
      }
    }
  }
}'
```

See also

- ▶ The *Understanding clusters, replication, and sharding* recipe in *Chapter 1, Getting Started*
- ▶ The *Putting a mapping in an index* recipe in this chapter

Deleting an index

The counterpart of creating an index is deleting one.

Deleting an index means deleting its shards, mappings, and data. There are many common scenarios where we need to delete an index, such as the following:

- ▶ Removing the index to clean unwanted/obsolete data (for example, old **logstash** indices)
- ▶ Resetting an index for a scratch restart
- ▶ Deleting an index that has some missing shard, mainly due to some failure, to bring back the cluster to a valid state

Getting ready

You will need a working ElasticSearch cluster and the existing index created in the previous recipe.

How to do it...

The HTTP method used to delete an index is DELETE.

The URL contains only the index name:

```
http://<server>/<index_name>
```

To delete an index, we will perform the following steps:

1. From a command line, we can execute a DELETE call:

   ```
   curl -XDELETE http://127.0.0.1:9200/myindex
   ```

2. The result returned by ElasticSearch, if everything goes well, should be:

   ```
   {"acknowledged":true}
   ```

3. If the index doesn't exist, then a 404 error is returned:

   ```
   {"error":"IndexMissingException[[myindex] missing]","status":404}
   ```

How it works...

When an index is deleted, all the data related to the index is removed from the disk and is lost.

During the deletion process, at first, the cluster is updated when the shards are deleted from the storage. This operation is fast; in the traditional filesystem it is implemented as a recursive delete.

It's not possible to restore a deleted index if there is no backup.

Also, calling by using the special _all, index_name can be used to remove all the indices. In production, it is a good practice to disable the all indices deletion parameter by adding the following line to elasticsearch.yml:

```
action.destructive_requires_name:true
```

See also

> ▸ The *Creating an index* recipe in this chapter

Opening/closing an index

If you want to keep your data but save resources (memory/CPU), a good alternative to deleting an Index is to close it.

ElasticSearch allows you to open or close an index to put it in online/offline mode.

Getting ready

You will need a working ElasticSearch cluster and the index created in the *Creating an index* recipe in this chapter.

How to do it...

For opening/closing an index, we will perform the following steps:

1. From the command line, we can execute a POST call to close an index:
   ```
   curl -XPOST http://127.0.0.1:9200/myindex/_close
   ```

2. If the call is successful, the result returned by ElasticSearch should be:
   ```
   {,"acknowledged":true}
   ```

3. To open an index from the command line, enter:
   ```
   curl -XPOST http://127.0.0.1:9200/myindex/_open
   ```

4. If the call is successful, the result returned by ElasticSearch should be:

    ```
    {"acknowledged":true}
    ```

How it works...

When an index is closed, there is no overhead on the cluster (except for the metadata state); the index shards are turned off and don't use file descriptors, memory, or threads.

There are many use cases for closing an index, such as the following:

  ▶ Disabling date-based indices, for example, keeping an index for a week, month, or day, and when you want to keep several indices online (such as for 2 months) and some offline (such as from 2 to 6 months).

  ▶ When you do searches on all the active indices of a cluster but you don't want to search in some indices (in this case, using an alias is the best solution, but you can achieve the same alias concept with closed indices).

When an index is closed, calling on **open** restores its state.

See also

  ▶ The *Using index aliases* recipe in this chapter

Putting a mapping in an index

In the previous chapter, we saw how to build a mapping by indexing documents. This recipe shows how to put a type of mapping in an index. This kind of operation can be considered the ElasticSearch version of an SQL create table.

Getting ready

You will need a working ElasticSearch cluster and the index created in the *Creating an index* recipe in this chapter.

How to do it...

The HTTP method for puttting a mapping is PUT (POST also works).

The URL format for putting a mapping is:

```
http://<server>/<index_name>/<type_name>/_mapping
```

To put a mapping in an Index, we will perform the following steps:

1. If we consider the type order of the previous chapter, the call will be:

    ```
    curl -XPUT 'http://localhost:9200/myindex/order/_mapping' -d '{
      "order" : {
        "properties" : {
          "id" : {"type" : "string", "store" : "yes" ,
          "index":"not_analyzed"},
          "date" : {"type" : "date", "store" : "no" ,
          "index":"not_analyzed"},
          "customer_id" : {"type" : "string", "store" : "yes" ,
          "index":"not_analyzed"},
          "sent" : {"type" : "boolean",
          "index":"not_analyzed"},
          "name" : {"type" : "string", "index":"analyzed"},
          "quantity" : {"type" : "integer",
          "index":"not_analyzed"},
          "vat" : {"type" : "double", "index":"no"}
        }
      }
    }'
    ```

2. If successful, the result returned by ElasticSearch should be:

    ```
    {"acknowledged":true}
    ```

How it works...

This call checks if the index exists and then it creates one or more types of mapping as described in the definition. For the mapping description, see the previous chapter.

During mapping insertion, if there is an existing mapping for this type, it is merged with the new one. If there is a field with a different type and the type cannot be updated by expanding the `fields` property, an exception is raised. To prevent exception during the merging mapping phase, it's possible to specify the parameter `ignore_conflicts` to `true` (default is `false`).

The PUT mapping call allows us to set the type for several indices in one shot, listing the indices separated by comma or applying to all indexes using the `_all` alias.

See also

▸   The *Getting a mapping* recipe in this chapter (the following recipe.)

Getting a mapping

After having set our mappings for processing types, we sometimes need to control or analyze the mapping to prevent issues. The action to get the mapping for a type helps us to understand the record structure, or its evolution due to merging and implicit type guessing.

Getting ready

You will need a working ElasticSearch cluster and the mapping created in the previous recipe.

How to do it...

The HTTP method to get a mapping is GET.

The URL formats for getting a mapping are:

```
http://<server>/_mapping
http://<server>/<index_name>/_mapping
http://<server>/<index_name>/<type_name>/_mapping
```

To get a mapping from the type of an index, we will perform the following steps:

1. If we consider the type order of the previous chapter, the call will be:

    ```
    curl -XGET 'http://localhost:9200/myindex/order/_
    mapping?pretty=true'
    ```

    The `pretty` argument in the URL will `pretty` print the response output.

2. The result returned by ElasticSearch should be:

    ```
    {
      "myindex" : {
        "mappings" : {
          "order" : {
            "properties" : {
              "customer_id" : {
                "type" : "string",
                "index" : "not_analyzed",
                "store" : true
              },
    ... truncated
            }
          }
        }
      }
    }
    ```

How it works...

The mapping is stored at the cluster level in ElasticSearch. The call checks both index and type existence, and then returns the stored mapping.

> The returned mapping is in a reduced form, which means the default values for a field are not returned.

ElasticSearch stores only default field values to reduce network and memory consumption.

Querying the mapping is useful for several purposes:

- Debugging template level mapping
- Checking if implicit mapping was derivated correctly by guessing fields
- Retrieving the mapping metadata, which can be used to store type-related information
- Simply checking if the mapping is correct

If you need to fetch several mappings, it is better to do so at the index or cluster level in order to reduce the numbers of API calls.

See also

- The *Putting a mapping* recipe in this chapter
- The *Using dynamic templates in document mapping* recipe in *Chapter 3, Managing Mapping*

Deleting a mapping

The last **CRUD** (**Create, Read, Update, Delete**) operation related to mapping is the delete one.

Deleting a mapping is a destructive operation and must be done with care to prevent losing your data.

There are some use cases in which it's required to delete a mapping:

- Unused type: You delete it to clean the data.
- Wrong mapping: You might need to change the mapping, but you cannot upgrade it or remove some fields. You need to back up your data, create a new mapping, and reimport the data.

- Fast cleanup of a type: You can delete the mapping and recreate it (or you can execute a **Delete by query**, as explained in the *Deleting by query* recipe in *Chapter 5, Search, Queries, and Filters*.

Getting ready

You will need a working ElasticSearch cluster and the mapping created in the *Putting a mapping in an index* recipe in this chapter.

How to do it...

The HTTP method to delete a mapping is DELETE.

The URL formats for getting the mappings are:

```
http://<server>/<index_name>/<type_name>
http://<server>/<index_name>/<type_name>/_mapping
```

To delete a mapping from an index, we will perform the following steps:

1. If we consider the type order explained in the previous chapter, the call will be:

   ```
   curl -XDELETE 'http://localhost:9200/myindex/order/'
   ```

2. If the call is successful, the result returned by ElasticSearch should be an HTTP 200 status code with a similar message as the following:

   ```
   {"acknowledged":true}
   ```

3. If the mapping/type is missing, an exception is raised:

   ```
   {"error":"TypeMissingException[[myindex] type[order]
   missing]","status":404}
   ```

How it works...

ElasticSearch tries to find the mapping for an Index-type pair. If it's found, the mapping and all its related data are removed. If it is not found, an exception is raised.

> Deleting a mapping removes all the data associated with that mapping, so it's not possible to go back if there is no backup.

See also

- The *Putting a mapping in an index* recipe in this chapter

Refreshing an index

ElasticSearch allows the user to control the state of the searcher using forced refresh on an index. If not forced, the new indexed document will only be searchable after a fixed time interval (usually 1 second).

Getting ready

You will need a working ElasticSearch cluster and the index created in the *Creating an index* recipe in this chapter.

How to do it...

The URL formats for refreshing an index, are:

```
http://<server>/<index_name(s)>/_refresh
```

The URL format for refreshing all the indices in a cluster, is:

```
http://<server>/_refresh
```

The HTTP method used for both URLs is POST.

To refresh an index, we will perform the following steps:

1. If we consider the type order of the previous chapter, the call will be:

    ```
    curl -XPOST 'http://localhost:9200/myindex/_refresh'
    ```

2. The result returned by ElasticSearch should be:

    ```
    {"_shards":{"total":4,"successful":2,"failed":0}}
    ```

How it works...

Near Real-Time (**NRT**) capabilities are automatically managed by ElasticSearch, which automatically refreshes the indices every second if data is changed in them.

You can call the refresh on one or more indices (most indices are comma separated) or on all the indices.

ElasticSearch doesn't refresh the state of an index at every inserted document to prevent poor performance, due to excessive I/O required in closing and reopening file descriptors.

> You must force the refresh to have your last index data available for searching.

Generally, the best time to call the refresh is after having indexed a lot of data, to be sure that your records are searchable instantly.

See also

- ▶ The *Flushing an index* recipe in this chapter
- ▶ The *Optimizing an index* recipe in this chapter

Flushing an index

ElasticSearch, for performance reasons, stores some data in memory and on a transaction log. If we want to free memory, empty the transaction log, and be sure that our data is safely written on disk, we need to flush an index.

ElasticSearch automatically provides a periodic disk flush, but forcing a flush can be useful, for example:

- ▶ When we have to shutdown a node to prevent stale data
- ▶ To have all the data in a safe state (for example, after a big indexing operation to have all the data flushed and refreshed)

Getting ready

You will need a working ElasticSearch cluster and the index created in the *Creating an index* recipe in this chapter.

How to do it...

The HTTP method used for the URL operations is POST.

The URL format for flushing an index is:

```
http://<server>/<index_name(s)>/_flush[?refresh=True]
```

The URL format for flushing all the indices in a Cluster is:

```
http://<server>/_flush[?refresh=True]
```

To flush an index, we will perform the following steps:

1. If we consider the type order of the previous chapter, the call will be:

    ```
    curl -XPOST 'http://localhost:9200/myindex/_flush?refresh=True'
    ```

2. The result returned by ElasticSearch, if everything goes well, should be:

    ```
    {"_shards":{"total":4,"successful":2,"failed":0}}
    ```

The result contains the shard operation status.

How it works...

ElasticSearch tries not to put overhead in I/O operations caching some data in memory to reduce writes. In this way, it is able to improve performance.

To clean up memory and force this data on disk, the **flush** operation is required.

With the flush call, it is possible to make an extra request parameter, refresh, to also force the Index refresh.

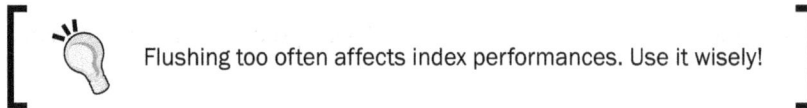

> Flushing too often affects index performances. Use it wisely!

See also

-   The *Refreshing an index* recipe in this chapter
-   The *Optimizing an index* recipe in this chapter

Optimizing an index

The core of ElasticSearch is based on Lucene, which stores the data in segments on the disk. During the life of an Index, a lot of segments are created and changed. With the increase of segment numbers, the speed of search decreases due to the time required to read all of them. The **optimize** operation allows us to consolidate the index for faster search performance, reducing segments.

Getting ready

You will need a working ElasticSearch cluster and the index created in the *Creating an index* recipe in this chapter.

How to do it...

The URL format to optimize one or more indices is:

```
http://<server>/<index_name(s)>/_optimize
```

The URL format to optimize all the indices in a cluster is:

```
http://<server>/_optimize
```

The HTTP method used is POST.

To optimize an index, we will perform the following steps:

1. If we consider the Index created in the *Creating an index recipe*, the call will be:

   ```
   curl -XPOST 'http://localhost:9200/myindex/_optimize'
   ```

2. The result returned by ElasticSearch should be:

   ```
   {"_shards":{"total":4,"successful":2,"failed":0}}
   ```

The result contains the shard operation status.

How it works...

Lucene stores your data in several segments on disk. These segments are created when you Index a new document/record or when you delete a document. Their number can be large (for this reason, in the setup, we have increased the file description number for the ElasticSearch process).

Internally, ElasticSearch has a merger, which tries to reduce the number of segments, but it's designed to improve the indexing performance rather than search performance. The optimize operation in Lucene tries to reduce the segments in an I/O intensive way, by removing unused ones, purging deleted documents, and rebuilding the Index with the minor number of segments.

The main advantages are:

▸ Reducing the file descriptors

▸ Freeing memory used by the segment readers

▸ Improving the search performance due to less segment management

> Optimization is a very I/O intensive operation. The index can be unresponsive during optimization. It is generally executed on indices that are rarely modified, such as consolidated date logstash indices.

There's more...

You can pass several additional parameters to the optimize call, such as:

- ► `max_num_segments` (by default `autodetect`): For full optimization, set this value to `1`.

- ► `only_expunge_deletes` (by default `false`): Lucene does not delete documents from segments, but it marks them as deleted. This flag merges only segments that have been deleted.

- ► `flush` (by default `true`): Using this parameter, ElasticSearch performs a flush after optimization.

- ► `wait_for_merge` (by default `true`): This parameter is used if the request needs to wait until the merge ends.

- ► `force` (default `false`): Using this parameter, ElasticSearch executes the optimization even if the index is already optimized.

See also

- ► The *Refreshing an index* recipe in this chapter
- ► The *Optimizing an index* recipe in this chapter

Checking if an index or type exists

A common pitfall error is to query for indices and types that don't exist. To prevent this issue, ElasticSearch gives the user the ability to check the index and type existence.

This check is often used during an application startup to create indices and types that are required for it to work correctly.

Getting ready

You will need a working ElasticSearch cluster and the mapping available in the index, as described in the previous recipes.

How to do it...

The HTTP method to check the existence is HEAD.

The URL format for checking an index is:

```
http://<server>/<index_name>/
```

The URL format for checking a type is:

```
http://<server>/<index_name>/<type>/
```

To check if an index exists, we will perform the following steps:

1. If we consider the index created in the *Creating an index* recipe in this chapter, the call will be:

   curl -i -XHEAD 'http://localhost:9200/myindex/'

   The `-i curl options` allows dumping the server headers.

2. If the index exists, an HTTP status code 200 is returned. If missing, then a 404 error is returned.

To check if a type exists, we will perform the following steps:

1. If we consider the mapping created in the putting a mapping in an index recipe (in this chapter), the call will be:

   curl -i -XHEAD 'http://localhost:9200/myindex/order/'

2. If the index exists, an HTTP status code 200 is returned. If missing, then a 404 error is returned.

How it works...

This is a typical HEAD REST call to check existence. It doesn't return a body response, only the status code.

> Before executing every action involved in indexing, generally upon application startup, it's good practice to check if an index or type exists to prevent future failures.

Managing index settings

Index settings are more important because they allow us to control several important ElasticSearch functionalities such as sharding/replica, caching, term management, routing, and analysis.

Getting ready

You will need a working ElasticSearch cluster and the index created in the *Creating an index* recipe in this chapter.

How to do it...

To manage the index settings, we will perform the steps given as follows:

1. To retrieve the settings of your current Index, the URL format is the following:

   ```
   http://<server>/<index_name>/_settings
   ```

2. We are reading information via REST API, so the method will be GET, and an example of a call using the index created in the *Creating an index* recipe, is:

   ```
   curl -XGET 'http://localhost:9200/myindex/_settings'
   ```

3. The response will be something similar to:

   ```
   {
     "myindex" : {
       "settings" : {
         "index" : {
           "uuid" : "pT65_cn_RHKmg1wPX7BGjw",
           "number_of_replicas" : "1",
           "number_of_shards" : "2",
           "version" : {
             "created" : "1020099"
           }
         }
       }
     }
   }
   ```

   The response attributes depend on the index settings. In this case, the response will be the number of replicas (1), and shard (2), and the index creation version (1020099). The UUID represents the unique ID of the index.

4. To modify the index settings, we need to use the PUT method. A typical settings change is to increase the replica number:

   ```
   curl -XPUT 'http://localhost:9200/myindex/_settings' -d '
   {"index":{ "number_of_replicas": "2"}}'
   ```

How it works...

ElasticSearch provides a lot of options to tune the index behavior, such as:

► Replica management:

   ❏ index.number_of_replica: This is the number of replicas each shard has

   ❏ index.auto_expand_replicas: This parameter allows us to define a dynamic number of replicas related to the number of shards

> Using `set index.auto_expand_replicas` to `0-all` allows us to create an index that is replicated in every node (very useful for settings or cluster propagated data such as language options/stopwords).

▶ Refresh interval (by default `1s`): In the previous recipe, *Refreshing an index*, we saw how to manually refresh an index. The index settings (`index.refresh_interval`) control the rate of automatic refresh.

▶ Cache management: These settings (`index.cache.*`) control the cache size and its life. It is not common to change them (refer to ElasticSearch documentation for all the available options at `http://www.elasticsearch.org/guide/en/ elasticsearch/reference/current/index-modules-cache.html`).

▶ Write management: ElasticSearch provides several settings to block read/write operations in an index and changing metadata. They live in `index.blocks` settings.

▶ Shard allocation management: These settings control how the shards must be allocated. They live in the `index.routing.allocation.*` namespace.

There are other index settings that can be configured for very specific needs. In every new version of ElasticSearch, the community extends these settings to cover new scenarios and requirements.

There is more...

The `refresh_interval` parameter provides several tricks to optimize the indexing speed. It controls the rate of refresh, and refreshing reduces the Index performances due to opening and closing of files. A good practice is to disable the refresh interval (set `-1`) during a big indexing bulk and restoring the default behavior after it. This can be done with the following steps:

1. Disabling the refresh:

    ```
    curl -XPOST 'http://localhost:9200/myindex/_settings' -d '
    {"index":{"index_refresh_interval": "-1"}}'
    ```

2. Bulk indexing some millions of documents

3. Restoring the refresh:

    ```
    curl -XPOST 'http://localhost:9200/myindex/_settings' -d '
    {"index":{"index_refresh_interval": "1s"}}'
    ```

4. Optionally, optimizing the index for search performances:

    ```
    curl -XPOST 'http://localhost:9200/myindex/_optimize'
    ```

See also

> ▸ The *Refreshing an index* recipe in this chapter
>
> ▸ The *Optimizing an index* recipe in this chapter

Using index aliases

Real world applications have a lot of indices and queries that span on more indices. This scenario requires defining all the indices names on which we need to perform queries; aliases allow grouping them by a common name.

Some common scenarios of this usage are:

> ▸ Log indices divided by date (such as `log_YYMMDD`) for which we want to create an alias for the *last week*, the *last month*, *today*, *yesterday*, and so on. This pattern is commonly used in log applications such as logstash (`http://logstash.net/`).
>
> ▸ Collecting website contents in several indices (*New York Times*, *The Guardian*, and so on) for those we want to refer to as an index aliases called *sites*.

Getting ready

You will need a working ElasticSearch cluster.

How to do it...

The URL format for control aliases are:

```
http://<server>/_aliases
http://<server>/<index>/_alias/<alias_name>
```

To manage the index aliases, we will perform the following steps:

1. We need to read the status of the aliases for all indices via the REST API, so the method will be GET, and an example of a call is:

   ```
   curl -XGET 'http://localhost:9200/_aliases'
   ```

2. It should give a response similar to this:

   ```
   {
     "myindex": {
       "aliases": {}
     },
   ```

```
    "test": {
      "aliases": {}
    }
}
```

Aliases can be changed with add and delete commands.

3. To read an alias for a single Index, we use the `_alias` endpoint:

   `curl -XGET 'http://localhost:9200/myindex/_alias'`

   The result should be:

   ```
   {
     "myindex" : {
       "aliases" : {
         "myalias1" : { }
       }
     }
   }
   ```

4. To add an alias:

   `curl -XPUT 'http://localhost:9200/myindex/_alias/myalias1'`

   The result should be:

   `{"acknowledged":true}`

   This action adds the `myindex` index to the `myalias1` alias.

5. To delete an alias:

   `curl -XDELETE 'http://localhost:9200/myindex/_alias/myalias1'`

   The result should be:

   `{"acknowledged":true}`

   The delete action has now removed `myindex` from the alias `myalias1`.

How it works...

During search operations, ElasticSearch automatically expands the alias, so the required indices are selected. The alias metadata is kept in the cluster state. When an alias is added/deleted, all the changes are propagated to all the cluster nodes. Aliases are mainly functional structures to simply manage indices when data is stored in multiple indices.

There's more...

An alias can also be used to define a filter and routing parameters.

Filters are automatically added to the query to filter out data. Routing via aliases allows us to control which shards to hit during searching and indexing.

An example of this call is:

```
curl -XPOST 'http://localhost:9200/myindex/_aliases/user1alias' -d '
{
  "filter" : {
    "term" : { "user" : "user_1" }
  },
  "search_routing" : "1,2",
  "index_routing" : "2"
}'
```

In this case, we add a new alias, `user1alias`, to an Index, `myindex`, adding:

- A filter to select only documents that match a field `user` with term `user_1`.
- A list of routing keys to select the shards to be used during the search.
- A routing key to be used during indexing. The routing value is used to modify the destination shard of the document.

> `search_routing` allows multi-value routing keys.
> `index_routing` is single value only.

Indexing a document

In ElasticSearch, there are two vital operations namely, **Indexing** and **Searching**.

Indexing means inserting one or more document in an index; this is similar to the `insert` command of a relational database.

In Lucene, the core engine of ElasticSearch, inserting or updating a document has the same cost. In Lucene and ElasticSearch, update means replace.

Getting ready

You will need a working ElasticSearch cluster and the mapping that was created in the *Putting a mapping in an index* recipe in this chapter.

How to do it...

To index a document, several REST entry points can be used:

Method	URL
POST	http://<server>/<index_name>/<type>
PUT/POST	http://<server>/<index_name>/<type> /<id>
PUT/POST	http://<server>/<index_name>/<type> /<id>/_create

We will perform the following steps:

1. If we consider the type order mentioned in earlier chapters, the call to index a document will be:

```
curl -XPOST 'http://localhost:9200/myindex/
order/2qLrAfPVQvCRMe7Ku8r0Tw' -d '{
  "id" : "1234",
  "date" : "2013-06-07T12:14:54",
  "customer_id" : "customer1",
  "sent" : true,
  "in_stock_items" : 0,
  "items":[
    {"name":"item1", "quantity":3, "vat":20.0},
    {"name":"item2", "quantity":2, "vat":20.0},
    {"name":"item3", "quantity":1, "vat":10.0}
  ]
}'
```

2. If the index operation is successful, the result returned by ElasticSearch should be:

```
{
  "_index":"myindex",
  "_type":"order",
  "_id":"2qLrAfPVQvCRMe7Ku8r0Tw",
  "_version":1,
  "created":true
}
```

Some additional information is returned from an indexing operation such as:

▶ An auto-generated ID, if not specified

▶ The version of the indexed document as per the Optimistic Concurrency Control

▶ Information if the record has been created

How it works...

One of the most used APIs in ElasticSearch is the index. Basically, indexing a JSON document consists of these steps:

- ▸ Routing the call to the correct shard based on the ID or routing/parent metadata. If the ID is not supplied by the client, a new one is created. (See *Chapter 1, Getting Started*, for more details).
- ▸ Validating the JSON which has been sent.
- ▸ Processing the JSON according to the mapping. If new fields are present in the document (the mapping can be updated), new fields are added in the mapping.
- ▸ Indexing the document in the shard. If the ID already exists, it is then updated.
- ▸ If it contains nested documents, it extracts them and processes them separately.
- ▸ Returns information about the saved document (ID and versioning).

It's important to choose the correct ID for indexing your data. If you don't provide an ID in ElasticSearch during the indexing phase, then it automatically associates a new ID to your document. To improve performance, the ID should generally be of the same character length to improve balancing of the data tree that holds them.

Due to the REST call nature, it's better to pay attention when not using ASCII characters because of URL encoding and decoding (or, be sure that the client framework you use correctly escapes them).

Depending on the mappings, other actions take place during the indexing phase, such as the propagation on replica, nested processing, and the percolator.

The document will be available for standard search calls after a refresh (forced with an API call or after the time slice of 1 second in near real time). Every GET API on the document doesn't require a refresh and can be instantly made available.

The refresh can also be forced by specifying the `refresh` parameter during indexing.

There's more...

ElasticSearch allows the passing of several query parameters in the index API URL for controlling how the document is indexed. The most commonly used ones are:

- ▸ `routing`: This controls the shard to be used for indexing, for example:

  ```
  curl -XPOST 'http://localhost:9200/myindex/order?routing=1'
  ```

- ▸ `parent`: This defines the parent of a child document and uses this value to apply routing. The parent object must be specified in the mappings, such as:

  ```
  curl -XPOST 'http://localhost:9200/myindex/order?parent=12'
  ```

- `timestamp`: This is the timestamp to be used in indexing the document. It must be activated in the mappings, such as in the following:

```
curl -XPOST 'http://localhost:9200/myindex/order?timestamp=
2013-01-25T19%3A22%3A22'
```

- `consistency` (one/quorum/all): By default, an index operation succeeds if set as a `quorum` (>replica/2+1) and if active shards are available. The write consistency value can be changed for indexing:

```
curl -XPOST 'http://localhost:9200/myindex/order?consistency=one'
```

- `replication` (sync/async): ElasticSearch returns replication from an index operation when all the shards of the current replication group have executed the operation. Setting the replication `async` allows us to execute the index synchronously only on the primary shard and asynchronously on other shards, returning from the call faster.

```
curl -XPOST 'http://localhost:9200/myindex/order?replication=async'
```

- `version`: This allows us to use the Optimistic Concurrency Control (http://en.wikipedia.org/wiki/Optimistic_concurrency_control). At first, in the indexing of a document, version is set as 1 by default. At every update, this value is incremented. Optimistic Concurrency Control is a way to manage concurrency in every insert or update operation. The already passed version value is the last seen version (usually returned by a GET or a search). The indexing happens only if the current index version value is equal to the passed one:

```
curl -XPOST 'http://localhost:9200/myindex/order?version=2'
```

- `op_type`: This can be used to force a `create` on a document. If a document with the same ID exists, the Index fails.

```
curl -XPOST 'http://localhost:9200/myindex/order?op_type=create'…
```

- `refresh`: This forces a refresh after having the document indexed. It allows us to have the documents ready for search after indexing them:

```
curl -XPOST 'http://localhost:9200/myindex/order?refresh=true'…
```

- `ttl`: This allows defining a *time to live* for a document. All documents in which the `ttl` has expired are deleted and purged from the index. This feature is very useful to define records with a fixed life. It only works if `ttl` is explicitly enabled in mapping. The value can be a date-time or a time value (a numeric value ending with s, m, h, d). The following is the command:

```
curl -XPOST 'http://localhost:9200/myindex/order?ttl=1d'
```

▶ `timeout`: This defines a time to wait for the primary shard to be available. Sometimes, the primary shard can be in an un-writable status (relocating or recovering from a gateway) and a timeout for the write operation is raised after 1 minute.

```
curl -XPOST 'http://localhost:9200/myindex/order?timeout=5m' …
```

See also

▶ The *Getting a document* recipe in this chapter

▶ The *Deleting a document* recipe in this chapter

▶ The *Updating a document* recipe in this chapter

▶ Optimistic Concurrency Control at `http://en.wikipedia.org/wiki/ Optimistic_concurrency_control`

Getting a document

After having indexed a document during your application life, it most likely will need to be retrieved.

The GET REST call allows us to get a document in real time without the need of a refresh.

Getting ready

You will need a working ElasticSearch cluster and the indexed document of the *Indexing a document* recipe.

How to do it...

The GET method allows us to return a document given its index, type and ID.

The REST API URL is:

```
http://<server>/<index_name>/<type_name>/<id>
```

To get a document, we will perform the following steps:

1. If we consider the document we indexed in the previous recipe, the call will be:

```
curl -XGET 'http://localhost:9200/myindex/order/2qLrAfPVQvCRMe7Ku8
r0Tw?pretty=true'
```

2. The result returned by ElasticSearch should be the indexed document:

```
{
"_index":"myindex","_type":"order","_
id":"2qLrAfPVQvCRMe7Ku8r0Tw","_version":1,"found":true, "_source"
: {
    "id" : "1234",
    "date" : "2013-06-07T12:14:54",
    "customer_id" : "customer1",
    "sent" : true,
    "items":[
        {"name":"item1", "quantity":3, "vat":20.0},
        {"name":"item2", "quantity":2, "vat":20.0},
        {"name":"item3", "quantity":1, "vat":10.0}
    ]
}}
```

Our indexed data is contained in the _source parameter, but other information is returned as well:

- ❑ _index: This is the index that stores the document
- ❑ _type: This denotes the type of the document
- ❑ _id: This denotes the ID of the document
- ❑ _version: This denotes the version of the document
- ❑ found: This denotes if the document has been found

3. If the record is missing, a 404 error is returned as the status code and the return JSON will be:

```
{
    "_id": "2qLrAfPVQvCRMe7Ku8r0Tw",
    "_index": "myindex",
    "_type": "order",
    "found": false
}
```

How it works...

ElasticSearch GET API doesn't require a refresh on the document. All the GET calls are in real time. This call is fast because ElasticSearch is implemented to search only on the shard that contains the record without other overhead. The IDs are often cached in memory for faster lookup.

The source of the document is only available if the _source field is stored (the default settings in ElasticSearch).

There are several additional parameters that can be used to control the GET call:

- ▶ `fields`: This allows us to retrieve only a subset of fields. This is very useful to reduce bandwidth or to retrieve calculated fields such as the attachment mapping ones:

  ```
  curl 'http://localhost:9200/myindex/order/2qLrAfPVQvCRMe7Ku8r0Tw?f
  ields=date,sent'
  ```

- ▶ `routing`: This allows us to specify the shard to be used for the GET operation. To retrieve a document with the routing used in indexing, the time taken must be the same as the search time:

  ```
  curl 'http://localhost:9200/myindex/order/2qLrAfPVQvCRMe7Ku8r0Tw?r
  outing=customer_id'
  ```

- ▶ `refresh`: This allows us to refresh the current shard before doing the GET operation. (It must be used with care because it slows down indexing and introduces some overhead):

  ```
  curl http://localhost:9200/myindex/order/2qLrAfPVQvCRMe7Ku8r0Tw?re
  fresh=true
  ```

- ▶ `preference`: This allows controlling which shard replica to choose to execute the GET operation. Generally, ElasticSearch chooses a random shard for the GET call. Possible values are:

  - ❑ `_primary`: This is used for the primary shard.
  - ❑ `_local`: This is used for trying first the local shard and then falling back to a random choice. Using the local shard reduces the bandwidth usage and should generally be used with auto—replicating shards (with the replica set to 0).
  - ❑ `custom value`: This is used for selecting shard-related values such as the `customer_id`, `username`, and so on.

There's more...

The GET API is fast, so a good practice for developing applications is to try to use it as much as possible. Choosing the correct ID during application development can lead to a big boost in performance.

If the shard that contains the document is not bound to an ID, then fetching the document requires a query with an ID filter (We will learn about it in *the Using an ID query/filter* recipe in *Chapter 5, Search, Queries, and Filters*).

If you don't need to fetch the record, but only need to check the existence, you can replace GET with HEAD and the response will be status code 200 if it exists, or 404 error, if missing.

The GET call has also a special endpoint, _source that allows fetching only the source of the document.

The GET Source REST API URL is:

```
http://<server>/<index_name>/<type_name>/<id>/_source
```

To fetch the source of the previous order, we will call:

```
curl -XGET
http://localhost:9200/myindex/order/2qLrAfPVQvCRMe7Ku8r0Tw/_source
```

See also

▸ The *Speeding up GET operation* recipe in this chapter

Deleting a document

Deleting documents in ElasticSearch is possible in two ways: by using the DELETE call or the DELETE BY QUERY call; we will learn about it in the next chapter.

Getting ready

You will need a working ElasticSearch cluster and the indexed document of the *Indexing a document* recipe in this chapter.

How to do it...

The REST API URL is the same as the GET calls, but the HTTP method is DELETE:

```
http://<server>/<index_name>/<type_name>/<id>
```

To delete a document, we will perform the following steps:

1. If we consider the `order` index in the *Indexing a document* recipe, the call to delete a document will be:

    ```
    curl -XDELETE
    'http://localhost:9200/myindex/order/2qLrAfPVQvCRMe7Ku8r0Tw'
    ```

2. The result returned by ElasticSearch should be:

    ```
    {
      "_id": "2qLrAfPVQvCRMe7Ku8r0Tw",
      "_index": "myindex",
      "_type": "order",
    ```

```
      "_version": 2,
      "found": true
   }
```

3. If the record is missing, a 404 error is returned as the status code and the return JSON will be:

```
{
   "_id": "2qLrAfPVQvCRMe7Ku8r0Tw",
   "_index": "myindex",
   "_type": "order",
   "_version": 2,
   "found": false
}
```

How it works...

Deleting a record only hits the shards that contain the document, so there is no overhead.

If the document is a child, the parent must be set to look for the correct shard.

There are several additional parameters that can be used to control the DELETE call. The most important ones are:

▶ routing: This allows us to specify the shard to be used for the DELETE operation

▶ version: This allows to define a version of the document to be deleted to prevent its modification

▶ parent: This is similar to routing, and is required if the document is a child one

> The DELETE operation doesn't have restore functionality. Every document that is deleted is lost forever.

Deleting a record is a fast operation, and is easy to use if the IDs of the documents to delete are available. Otherwise, we must use the DELETE BY QUERY call, which we will explore in the next chapter.

See also

▶ The *Deleting by query* recipe in *Chapter 5*, *Search, Queries, and Filters*

Updating a document

Documents stored in ElasticSearch can be updated at any time throughout their lives. There are two available solutions to perform this operation in ElasticSearch, namely by adding the new document, or by using the update call.

The update call works in two ways:

1. By providing a script (based on supported ElasticSearch scripting languages) which contains the code that must be executed to update the record
2. By providing a document that must be merged with the original one

The main advantage of an update versus an index is the reduction in networking.

Getting ready

You will need a working ElasticSearch cluster and the indexed document of the *Indexing a document* recipe in this chapter. To use the dynamic scripting languages, the dynamic scripting languages must be enabled (see *Chapter 7, Scripting*, to learn more).

How to do it...

As we are changing the state of the data, the HTTP method is POST and the REST URL is:

```
http://<server>/<index_name>/<type_name>/<id>/_update
```

To update a document, we will perform the following steps:

1. If we consider the type `order` of the previous recipe, the call to update a document will be:
   ```
   curl -XPOST 'http://localhost:9200/myindex/
   order/2qLrAfPVQvCRMe7Ku8r0Tw/_update' -d '{
   "script" : "ctx._source.in_stock_items += count",
   "params" : {
       "count" : 4
   }}'
   ```

2. If the request is successful, the result returned by ElasticSearch should be:
   ```
   {
     "_id": "2qLrAfPVQvCRMe7Ku8r0Tw",
     "_index": "myindex",
     "_type": "order",
     "_version": 3,
   ```

```
        "found": true,
        "ok": true
    }
```

3. The record will be:

```
    {
        "_id": "2qLrAfPVQvCRMe7Ku8r0Tw",
        "_index": "myindex",
        "_source": {
            "customer_id": "customer1",
            "date": "2013-06-07T12:14:54",
            "id": "1234",
            "in_stock_items": 4,
    ...
            "sent": true
        },
        "_type": "order",
        "_version": 3,
        "exists": true
    }
```

The visible changes are:

- The scripted field is changed

- The version is incremented

4. If you are using ElasticSearch (Version 1.2 or above) and you have disabled scripting support (default configuration), an error will be raised:

```
    {
        "error":"ElasticsearchIllegalArgumentException[failed to execute
    script]; nested: ScriptException[dynamic scripting disabled]; ",
        "status":400
    }
```

How it works...

The update operation applies changes to the document required in the script or in the update document, and it will reindex the changed document. In *Chapter 7, Scripting*, we will explore the scripting capabilities of ElasticSearch.

The standard language for scripting in ElasticSearch is **Groovy** (http://groovy.codehaus.org/), and is used in the examples.

The script can operate on the ctx._source, which is the source of the document (it must be stored to work), and can change the document in its place.

It's possible to pass parameters to a script by passing a JSON object. These parameters are available in the execution context.

A script can control the ElasticSearch behavior after the script execution by setting the `ctx.op` value of the context. Available values are:

- `ctx.op="delete"`: Using this, the document will be deleted after the script execution.
- `ctx.op="none"`: Using this, the document will skip the indexing process. A good practice to improve performance is to set the `ctx.op="none"` to prevent reindexing overhead if the script doesn't update the document.

In the `ctx`, it is possible to pass a `ttl` value to change the time of the life of an element by setting the `ctx._ttl` parameter.

The `ctx` parameter also manages the timestamp of the record in `ctx._timestamp`.

It's also possible to pass an additional object in the `upsert` property to be used if the document is not available in the `index`:

```
curl -XPOST 'http://localhost:9200/myindex/
order/2qLrAfPVQvCRMe7Ku8r0Tw/_update' -d '{
"script" : "ctx._source.in_stock_items += count",
"params" : {
     "count" : 4
},
"upsert" : {"in_stock_items":4}}'
```

If you need to replace some field values, a good solution is to not write a complex update script, but to use the special property `doc`, which allows to *overwrite* the values of an object. The document provided in the `doc` parameter will be merged with the original one. This approach is more easy to use, but it cannot set the `ctx.op`. So, if the update doesn't change the value of the original document, the next successive phase will always be executed:

```
curl -XPOST 'http://localhost:9200/myindex/
order/2qLrAfPVQvCRMe7Ku8r0Tw/_update' -d '{"doc" : {"in_stock_
items":10}}'
```

If the original document is missing, it is possible to use the provided `doc` for an `upsert` by providing the `doc_as_upsert` parameter:

```
curl -XPOST 'http://localhost:9200/myindex/order/2qLrAfPVQvCRMe7Ku8r0Tw/_
update' -d '{"doc" : {"in_stock_items":10}, "doc_as_upsert":true}'
```

Using MVEL, it is possible to apply advanced operations on field, such as:

- ▶ Removing a field:

  ```
  "script" : {"ctx._source.remove("myfield"}}
  ```

- ▶ Adding a new field:

  ```
  "script" : {"ctx._source.myfield=myvalue"}}
  ```

The update REST call is useful because it has some advantages:

- ▶ It reduces the bandwidth usage, as the update operation doesn't need a round-trip to the client holding the data.

- ▶ It's safer, because it automatically manages the Optimistic Concurrent Control. If a change happens during script execution, the script gets re-executed with the updated data.

- ▶ It can be bulk executed.

See also

- ▶ The *Speeding up atomic operations* recipe in this chapter (the next recipe)

Speeding up atomic operations (bulk operations)

When we are inserting, deleting, or updating a large number of documents, the HTTP overhead is significant. To speed up the process, ElasticSearch allow to execute bulk CRUD (Create, Read, Update, Delete) calls.

Getting ready

You will need a working ElastiSearch cluster.

How to do it...

As we are changing the state of the data, the HTTP method is POST and the REST URL is:

```
http://<server>/<index_name/_bulk
```

To execute a bulk action, we will perform the steps given as follows:

1. We need to collect the Create, Index, Delete, Update commands in a structure made of bulk JSON lines, composed by a line of action with metadata and another line with optional data related to the action. Every line must end with a newline, \n. The bulk data file should be, for example:

    ```
    { "index":{ "_index":"myindex", "_type":"order", "_id":"1"
    } }
    { "field1" : "value1",  "field2" : "value2"  }
    { "delete":{ "_index":"myindex", "_type":"order", "_id":"2"
    } }
    { "create":{ "_index":"myindex", "_type":"order", "_id":"3"
    } }
    { "field1" : "value1",  "field2" : "value2"  }
    { "update":{ "_index":"myindex", "_type":"order", "_id":"3"
    } }
    { "doc":{"field1" : "value1",  "field2" : "value2"  }}
    ```

2. This file can be sent with POST:

    ```
    curl -s -XPOST localhost:9200/_bulk --data-binary @bulkdata;
    ```

3. The result returned by ElasticSearch should collect all the responses of the actions.

How it works...

The bulk operation allows aggregating different calls as a single call. A header part with the action that is to be performed and a body for some operations such as Index, Create, and Update are present.

The header is composed by the action name and the object of parameters. Looking at the previous example for the, index, we have:

```
{ "index":{ "_index":"myindex", "_type":"order", "_id":"1" } }
```

For indexing and creating, an extra body is required with the data:

```
{ "field1" : "value1",  "field2" : "value2"  }
```

The delete action doesn't require optional data, so only the header composes it:

```
{ "delete":{ "_index":"myindex", "_type":"order", "_id":"1" } }
```

In the 0.90 or upper range, ElasticSearch allows to execute bulk update too:

```
{ "update":{ "_index":"myindex", "_type":"order", "_id":"3" } }
```

The header accepts all the common parameters of the update action, such as `doc`, `upsert`, `doc_as_upsert`, `lang`, `script`, and `params`. To control the number of retries in the case of concurrency, the bulk update defines the parameter `_retry_on_conflict`, set to the number of retries to be performed before raising an exception.

A possible body for the update is:

```
{ "doc":{"field1" : "value1",  "field2" : "value2"  }}
```

The bulk item can accept several parameters, such as:

- `routing`: To control the routing shard
- `parent`: To select a parent item shard, it is required if you are indexing some child documents
- `timestamp`: To set the index item timestamp
- `ttl`: To control the time to live of a document

Global bulk parameters that can be passed through query arguments are:

- `consistency` (one, quorum, all) (by default, `quorum`): This controls the number of active shards before executing write operations.
- `refresh`,(by default, `false`): This forces a refresh in the shards that are involved in bulk operations. The new indexed document will be available immediately without waiting for the standard refresh interval of 1s.

Usually, ElasticSearch client libraries that use ElasticSearch REST API automatically implements the serialization of bulk commands.

The correct number of commands to serialize in bulk is a user choice, but there are some hints to consider:

- In standard configuration, ElasticSearch limits the HTTP call to 100 megabytes in size. If the size is over the limit, the call is rejected.
- Multiple complex commands take a lot of time to be processed, so pay attention to client timeout.
- The small size of commands in bulk doesn't improve performance.

If the documents aren't big, 500 commands in bulk can be a good number to start with, and it can be tuned depending on data structures (number of fields, number of nested objects, complexity of fields, and so on).

See also

- Bulk API can also be used via UDP. See ElasticSearch documentation for more details at `http://www.elasticsearch.org/guide/en/elasticsearch/reference/current/docs-bulk-udp.html`.

Speeding up GET operations (multi GET)

The standard GET operation is very fast, but if you need to fetch a lot of documents by the ID, ElasticSearch provides multi GET operations.

Getting ready

You will need a working ElasticSearch Cluster and the document indexed from the *Indexing a document* recipe in this chapter.

How to do it...

The multi GET REST URLs are:

```
http://<server</_mget
http://<server>/<index_name>/_mget
http://<server>/<index_name>/<type_name>/_mget
```

To execute a multi GET action, we will perform the following steps:

1. The method is POST with a body that contains a list of document IDs and the Index/type if they are missing. As an example, using the first URL, we need to provide the Index, type, and ID:

```
curl -XPOST 'localhost:9200/_mget' -d '{
  "docs" : [
    {
      "_index" : "myindex",
      "_type" : "order",
      "_id" : "2qLrAfPVQvCRMe7Ku8r0Tw"
    },
    {
      "_index" : "myindex",
      "_type" : "order",
      "_id" : "2"
    }
  ]
}'
```

This kind of call allows fetching documents in several different indices and types.

2. If the Index and type are fixed, a call should also be in the form of:

```
curl 'localhost:9200/test/type/_mget' -d '{
  "ids" : ["1", "2"]
}'
```

The multi GET result is an array of documents.

How it works...

The multi GET call is a shortcut for executing many GET commands in one shot.

ElasticSearch internally spreads the GET in parallel on several shards and collects the results to return to the user.

The GET object can contain the following parameters:

- ▸ _index: The index that contains the document, it can be omitted if passed in the URL
- ▸ _type: The type of the document, it can be omitted if passed in the URL
- ▸ _id: The document ID
- ▸ fields (optional): A list of fields to retrieve
- ▸ routing (optional): The shard routing parameter

The advantages of the multi GET operation are:

- ▸ Reduced networking traffic both internally and externally in ElasticSearch
- ▸ Speeds up performace if used in an application, the time of processing a multi GET is quite similar to a standard GET.

See also...

- ▸ The *Getting a document* recipe in this chapter

5
Search, Queries, and Filters

In this chapter, we will cover the following recipes:

- ▶ Executing a search
- ▶ Sorting results
- ▶ Highlighting results
- ▶ Executing a scan query
- ▶ Suggesting a correct query
- ▶ Counting matched results
- ▶ Deleting by query
- ▶ Matching all the documents
- ▶ Querying/filtering for a single term
- ▶ Querying/filtering for a multiple term
- ▶ Using a prefix query/filter
- ▶ Using a Boolean query/filter
- ▶ Using a range query/filter
- ▶ Using span queries
- ▶ Using a match query
- ▶ Using an ID query/filter
- ▶ Using a has_child query/filter
- ▶ Using a top_children query

- ▸ Using a has_parent query/filter
- ▸ Using a regexp query/filter
- ▸ Using a function score query
- ▸ Using exists and missing filters
- ▸ Using and/or/not filters
- ▸ Using a geo bounding box filter
- ▸ Using a geo polygon filter
- ▸ Using a geo distance filter
- ▸ Using a query string query
- ▸ Using a template query

Introduction

After you have set the mappings and put the data in the indices, you can search. In this chapter, we will cover the different types of search queries and filters, validating queries, highlighting search results, and limiting fields. This chapter is the core of book: ultimately, everything in ElasticSearch is about serving the query and returning good quality results. To master the search, the user must understand the difference between a query and a filter, how to improve the quality, and how to speedily design more efficient queries. ElasticSearch allows you to use a rich **domain specific language** (**DSL**), a syntax language designed for searching, that covers all common needs, from a standard term query to complex Geoshape filtering.

This chapter is divided in two parts: the first part shows some API calls related to searches, and the second part covers the QueryDSL in detail.

All the recipes in this chapter require you to prepare and populate the required indices. In the code bundle available on the PacktPub website (`https://www.packtpub.com/big-data-and-business-intelligence/elasticsearch-cookbook`) or on GitHub (`https://github.com/aparo/elasticsearch-cookbook-second-edition`), there are scripts to initialize all the required data.

Executing a search

ElasticSearch was born as a search engine; its main work is to process queries and give results.

In this recipe, we'll see that a search in ElasticSearch is not just limited to matching documents but can also calculate additional information required to improve the search quality.

Getting ready

You need a working ElasticSearch cluster and an index populated with the script `chapter_05/populate_query.sh`, available in the code bundle for this book.

How to do it...

To execute a search and view the results, perform the following steps:

1. From the command line, execute a search, as follows:

   ```
   curl -XGET 'http://127.0.0.1:9200/test-index/test-
   type/_search' -d '{"query":{"match_all":{}}}'
   ```

   In this case, we have used a `match_all` query which means that *all* the documents are returned. We'll discuss this kind of query in the *Matching all documents* recipe in this chapter.

2. The command, if everything is all right, will return the following result:

   ```
   {
     "took" : 0,
     "timed_out" : false,
     "_shards" : {
       "total" : 5,
       "successful" : 5,
       "failed" : 0
     },
     "hits" : {
       "total" : 3,
       "max_score" : 1.0,
       "hits" : [ {
         "_index" : "test-index",
         "_type" : "test-type",
         "_id" : "1",
         "_score" : 1.0, "_source" : {"position": 1,
   "parsedtext": "Joe Testere nice guy", "name": "Joe Tester",
   "uuid": "11111"}
       }, {
         "_index" : "test-index",
         "_type" : "test-type",
         "_id" : "2",
         "_score" : 1.0, "_source" : {"position": 2,
   "parsedtext": "Bill Testere nice guy", "name": "Bill
   Baloney", "uuid": "22222"}
       }, {
         "_index" : "test-index",
   ```

```
        "_type" : "test-type",
        "_id" : "3",
        "_score" : 1.0, "_source" : {"position": 3, "parsedtext":
"Bill is not\n                    nice guy", "name": "Bill Clinton",
"uuid": "33333"}
    }]
  }
}
```

The result contains a lot of information, as follows:

- ▸ took: This is the time, in milliseconds, required to execute the query.

- ▸ time_out: This indicates whether a timeout has occurred during the search. This is related to the timeout parameter of the search. If a timeout occurred, you will get partial or no results.

- ▸ _shards: This is the status of the shards, which can be divided into the following:

  - ❏ total: This is the total number of shards.
  - ❏ successful: This is the number of shards in which the query was successful.
  - ❏ failed: This is the number of shards in which the query failed, because some error or exception occurred during the query.

- ▸ hits: This represents the results and is composed of the following:

  - ❏ total: This is the total number of documents that match the query.
  - ❏ max_score: This is the match score of the first document. Usually this is 1 if no match scoring was computed, for example in sorting or filtering.
  - ❏ hits: This is a list of the result documents.

The result document has a lot of fields that are always available and other fields that depend on the search parameters. The following are the most important fields:

- ▸ _index: This is the index that contains the document.
- ▸ _type: This is the type of the document.
- ▸ _id: This is the ID of the document.
- ▸ _source: This is the document's source (the default is returned, but it can be disabled).
- ▸ _score: This is the query score of the document.
- ▸ sort: These are the values that are used to sort, if the documents are sorted.
- ▸ highlight: These are the highlighted segments, if highlighting was requested.
- ▸ fields: This denotes some fields can be retrieved without the need to fetch all the source objects.

How it works...

The HTTP method used to execute a search is GET (but POST works too), and the REST URL is:

```
http://<server>/_search
http://<server>/<index_name(s)>/_search
http://<server>/<index_name(s)>/<type_name(s)>/_search
```

Multi-indices and types are comma separated. If an index or a type is defined, the search is limited to them only.

One or more aliases can be used as index names.

The core query is usually contained in the body of the GET/POST call, but a lot of options can also be expressed as URI query parameters, as follows:

- q: This is the query string used to perform simple string queries:

  ```
  curl -XGET 'http://127.0.0.1:9200/test-index/test-
  type/_search?q=uuid:11111'
  ```

- df: This is the default field to be used within the query:

  ```
  curl -XGET 'http://127.0.0.1:9200/test-index/test-type/_
  search?df=uuid&q=11111'
  ```

- from (by default, 0): This is the start index of the hits.

- size (by default, 10): This is the number of hits to be returned.

- analyzer: This is the default analyzer to be used.

- default_operator (default, OR): This can be set to AND or OR.

- explain: This allows the user to return information on how the score is calculated:

  ```
  curl -XGET 'http://127.0.0.1:9200/test-index/test-type/_search?q=p
  arsedtext:joe&explain=true'
  ```

- fields: This allows you to define fields that must be returned:

  ```
  curl -XGET 'http://127.0.0.1:9200/test-index/test-type/_search?q=p
  arsedtext:joe&fields=name'
  ```

- sort (by default, score): This allows you to change the order of the documents. Sort is ascendant by default; if you need to change the order, add desc to the field:

  ```
  curl -XGET 'http://127.0.0.1:9200/test-index/test-type/_
  search?sort=name:desc'
  ```

- timeout (not active by default): This defines the timeout for the search. ElasticSearch tries to collect results until the timeout. If a timeout is fired, all the hits accumulated are returned.

- ▶ `search_type`: This defines the search strategy. A reference is available in the online ElasticSearch documentation at `http://www.elasticsearch.org/guide/en/ elasticsearch/reference/current/search-request-search-type.html`.

- ▶ `track_scores` (by default, `false`): If this is `true`, it tracks the score and allows it to be returned with the hits. It's used in conjunction with `sort`, because sorting by default prevents a match score being returned.

- ▶ `pretty` (by default, `false`): If this is `true`, the results will be *pretty* printed.

Generally, the query is contained in the body of the search, a JSON object. The body of the search is the core of ElasticSearch's search functionalities; and the list of search capabilities extends with every release. For the current version (1.4.x) of ElasticSearch, the following parameters are available:

- ▶ `query`: This contains the query to be executed. Later in this chapter, we will see how to create different kinds of queries in order to cover several scenarios.

- ▶ `from` (by default, `0`) and `size` (by default, `10`): These allow you to control pagination. `from` defines the start position of the hits to be returned.

> Pagination is applied to the currently returned search results. Firing the same query can lead to different results if a lot of records have the same score or if new document are ingested. If you need to process all the result documents without repetition, you need to execute scan or scroll queries.

- ▶ `sort`: This allows you to change the order of the matched documents. This option is fully covered in the next recipe, *Sorting a result*.

- ▶ `post_filter` (optional): This allows you to filter out the query results without affecting the facet count. It's usually used to filter by facets values.

- ▶ `_source` (optional): This allows you to control the returned source. It can be disabled (`false`), partially returned (`obj.*`), or multiple exclude/include rules. This functionality can be used instead of fields to return values (for a complete coverage, take a look at the ElasticSearch reference at `http://www.elasticsearch.org/ guide/en/elasticsearch/reference/current/search-request-source-filtering.html`).

- ▶ `fielddata_fields` (optional): This allows you to return the field data representation of your field.

- ▶ `fields` (optional): This controls the fields to be returned.

> Returning only the required fields reduces network and memory usage, improving performance.

▸ `facets` (optional): This controls the aggregated data that must be computed on the results. Using facets improves the user experience on a search. Facets are deprecated and will be removed from the future versions of ElasticSearch. The aggregation layer covers the functionalities previously managed by facets.

▸ `aggregations` or `aggs` (optional): This controls the aggregation layer for analytics. It will be discussed in *Chapter 6, Aggregations*.

▸ `index_boost` (optional): This allows you to define the per-index boost value. It is used to increase/decrease the score of the results in the boosted indices.

▸ `highlighting` (optional): This allows you to define the fields and settings that will be used to calculate a query abstract. (Take a look at the *Highlighting results* recipe in this chapter.)

▸ `version` (by default, `false`): This adds the version of a document to the results.

▸ `rescore` (optional): This allows you to define an extra query to be used in the score to improve the quality of results. The `rescore` query is executed on the hits that match the first query and the filter.

▸ `min_score` (optional): If this is given/set, all the resulting documents that have a score lower than the set value are rejected.

▸ `explain` (optional): This parameter returns information on how the TD/IF score is calculated for a particular document.

▸ `script_fields` (optional): This defines a script to compute extra fields to be returned with a hit. We'll see ElasticSearch scripting in *Chapter 7, Scripting*.

▸ `suggest` (optional): If this is set, a query and a field returns the most significant terms related to this query. This parameter allows you to implement the Google search-like *did you mean* functionality. (see the *Suggesting a correct query* recipe of this chapter)

▸ `search_type` (optional): This defines how ElasticSearch should process a query. We'll see the **scan query** in the *Executing a scan query* recipe of this chapter.

▸ `scroll` (optional): This controls scrolling in the scroll/scan queries. The `scroll` allows you to have an ElasticSearch equivalent of a DBMS cursor.

There's more...

If you are using `sort`, pay attention to the tokenized fields. The sort order depends on the lower order token if it is ascendant and on the higher order token if it is descendent. For the preceding example, the results are as follows:

```
...
"hits" : [ {
        "_index" : "test-index",
        "_type" : "test-type",
```

```
      "_id" : "1",
      "_score" : null, "_source" : {"position": 1, "parsedtext":
      "Joe Testere nice guy", "name": "Joe Tester", "uuid":
      "11111"},
      "sort" : [ "tester" ]
    }, {
      "_index" : "test-index",
      "_type" : "test-type",
      "_id" : "3",
      "_score" : null, "_source" : {"position": 3, "parsedtext":
      "Bill is not\n                    nice guy", "name": "Bill
      Clinton", "uuid": "33333"},
      "sort" : [ "clinton" ]
    }, {
      "_index" : "test-index",
      "_type" : "test-type",
      "_id" : "2",
      "_score" : null, "_source" : {"position": 2, "parsedtext":
      "Bill Testere nice guy", "name": "Bill Baloney", "uuid":
      "22222"},
      "sort" : [ "bill" ]
    }
```

> Two main concepts are important in a search: **query** and **filter**.
> A query means that the matched results are scored using an
> internal Lucene-scoring algorithm; in a filter, the results are
> only matched, without scoring. Because a filter doesn't need to
> compute the score, it is generally faster and can be cached.

To improve the quality of the resulting score, ElasticSearch provides the **rescore** functionality.
This capability allows you to reorder a top number of documents with another query, so it's
generally much more expensive, for example, if the query contains a lot of matched queries
or scripting. This approach allows you to execute the `rescore` query only on a small subset
of results, reducing the overall computation time and resources.

Rescore, as with every query, is executed at the shard level, so it's automatically distributed.

> The best candidates to be executed in a rescore query are
> complex queries with a lot of nested options and everything that
> uses scripting (due to a massive overhead of scripting languages).

The following example will show you how to execute a fast query (Boolean) in the first phase and then rescore it with a match query in the rescore section:

```
curl -s -XPOST 'localhost:9200/_search' -d '{
    "query" : {
        "match" : {
            "parsedtext" : {
                "operator" : "or",
                "query" : "nice guy joe",
                "type" : "boolean"
            }
        }
    },
    "rescore" : {
        "window_size" : 100,
        "query" : {
            "rescore_query" : {
                "match" : {
                    "parsedtext" : {
                        "query" : "joe nice guy",
                        "type" : "phrase",
                        "slop" : 2
                    }
                }
            },
            "query_weight" : 0.8,
            "rescore_query_weight" : 1.5
        }
    }
}'
```

The following are the rescore parameters:

- window_size: This controls how many results per shard must be considered in the rescore functionality.

- query_weight (by default, 1.0) and rescore_query_weight (by default, 1.0): These are used to compute the final score using the following formula:

  final_score=query_score*query_weight + rescore_score*rescore_query_weight

> If a user wants to only keep the rescore score, he/she can set the query_weight parameter to 0.

- ▸ The *Executing an aggregation* recipe in the next chapter
- ▸ The *Highlighting results* recipe in this chapter
- ▸ The *Executing a scan query* recipe in this chapter
- ▸ The *Suggesting terms for a query* recipe in this chapter

Sorting results

When searching for results, the most common criteria for sorting in ElasticSearch is the relevance to a text query. Sometimes, real-world applications need to control the sorting criteria in typical scenarios, as follows:

- ▸ Sorting a user by their last name and first name
- ▸ Sorting items by stock symbols and price (ascending and descending)
- ▸ Sorting documents by size, file type, source, and so on

Getting ready

You need a working ElasticSearch cluster and an index populated with the script `chapter_05/populate_query.sh`, available in the code bundle for this book.

How to do it...

In order to sort the results, perform the following steps:

1. Add a `sort` section to your query, as follows:

   ```
   curl -XGET 'http://127.0.0.1:9200/test-index/test-type/_
   search?pretty=true' -d '{"query":{"match_all":{}},
     "sort" : [
        {"price" : {"order" : "asc", "mode" : "avg", "ignore_
   unmapped":true, "missing":"_last"}},
     "_score"
        ]
   }'
   ```

2. The returned result will be similar to this:

   ```
   ...,
      "hits" : {
        "total" : 3,
        "max_score" : null,
   ```

```
"hits" : [ {
  "_index" : "test-index",
  "_type" : "test-type",
  "_id" : "1",
  "_score" : null, "_source" :{ … "price":4.0},
  "sort" : [ 4.0 ]
}, {
…
```

The sorting result is very special: the `_score` parameter is not computed and an extra field, `sort`, is created to collect the value used for sorting.

How it works...

The `sort` parameter can be defined as a list that can contain both simple strings and JSON objects.

The sort string is the name of the field (such as `field1`, `field2`, `field3`, and `fields4`) that is used to sort, similar to SQL's **order by** statement.

The JSON object allows you to use the following extra parameters:

▶ `order` (asc/desc): This defines whether the order must be considered in the ascending format (which is the default) or the descending format.

▶ `ignore_unmapped` (true/false): This allows you to ignore the fields that do not have mappings in them. This option prevents errors during a search due to missing mappings.

▶ `unmapped_type`: This defines the type of the sort parameter, if it is missing.

▶ `missing` (_last/_first): This defines how to manage a missing value: we can put them at the end (_last) of the results or at the start (_first).

▶ `mode`: This defines how to manage multiple value fields. The following are the possible values:

  ❑ `min`: This is the minimum value that is chosen (in the case of multiple prices for an item, it chooses the lower value to be used for the comparison).

  ❑ `max`: This is the maximum value that is chosen.

  ❑ `sum`: Using this, the sort value will be computed as the sum of all the values. This mode is only available on numeric fields.

  ❑ `avg`: This sets the sort value, with which the sort result will be an average of all the values. This mode is only available on numeric fields.

> If you want to add the match score value to the sort list, you must use the special sort field: `_score`.

If we want to use sorting for a nested object, there are two extra parameters that can be used:

- nested_path: This defines the nested object to be used for sorting. The field defined for sorting will be related to the nested_path parameter. If it is not defined, the sorting field will be related to the document root. For example, if we have an address object nested in a person document, we can sort for the city.name values and use:
  - address.city.name: This is used if you want to sort without defining the nested_path.
  - city.name: Using this defines a nested_path address.

- nested_filter: This defines a filter that can be used to remove non-matching nested documents from the sorting value extraction. This filter allows a better selection of values to be used for sorting.

> The sorting process requires the sorting fields of all the matched query documents to be fetched in order to be compared. To prevent high memory usage, it's better to sort on numeric fields, and in the case of string sorting, select short text fields processed with an analyzer that don't tokenize the text.

There's more...

There are two special sorting types: **geo distance** and **scripting**.

Geo distance sorting uses the distance from a geopoint (location) as a metric to compute the ordering. Check out the following example of sorting:

```
...
"sort" : [
        {
            "_geo_distance" : {
                "pin.location" : [-70, 40],
                "order" : "asc",
                "unit" : "km"
            }
        }
    ],
...
```

The earlier example accepts special parameters as follows:

- unit: This defines the unit system (metric in the earlier example) to be used in order to compute the distance.
- distance_type (sloppy_arc/arc/plane): This defines the type of distance to be computed.

The `_geo_distance` name for the field is mandatory.

The point of reference for the sorting can be defined in several ways, as we already discussed in the *Mapping a geo point field* recipe in *Chapter 3, Managing Mapping*.

How to use scripting to sort will be discussed in the *Sorting data using scripts* recipe in *Chapter 7, Scripting*, after we introduce the scripting capabilities of ElasticSearch.

See also

▸ The *Mapping a geo point field* recipe in *Chapter 3, Managing Mapping*

▸ The *Sorting data using scripts* recipe in *Chapter 7, Scripting*

Highlighting results

ElasticSearch does a good job of finding matching results in large text documents too. Searching text in very large blocks is very useful, but to improve user experience, it is sometimes necessary to show the abstract to the users, which is a small portion of the text that matches the query. The abstract is a common way to help users understand how the matched document is relevant to them. The highlight functionality in ElasticSearch is designed to do this.

Getting ready

You need a working ElasticSearch cluster and an index populated with the script `chapter_05/populate_query.sh`, available in the code bundle for this book.

How to do it...

In order to search and highlight the results, perform the following steps:

1. From the command line, execute a search with a `highlight` parameter:

```
curl -XGET 'http://127.0.0.1:9200/test-index/_search?pretty=true&from=0&size=10' -d '
{
  "query": {"query_string": {"query": "joe"}},
  "highlight": {
    "pre_tags": ["<b>"],
    "fields": {
      "parsedtext": {"order": "score"},
      "name": {"order": "score"}},
```

```
            "post_tags": ["</b>"]
        }
    }
}'
```

2. If everything works all right, the command will return the following result:

```
{
    ... truncated ...
    "hits" : {
        "total" : 1,
        "max_score" : 0.44194174,
        "hits" : [ {
            "_index" : "test-index",
            "_type" : "test-type",
            "_id" : "1",
            "_score" : 0.44194174, "_source" : {"position": 1,
            "parsedtext": "Joe Testere nice guy", "name": "Joe
            Tester", "uuid": "11111"},
            "highlight" : {
                "name" : [ "<b>Joe</b> Tester" ],
                "parsedtext" : [ "<b>Joe</b> Testere nice guy" ]
            }
        }]
    }
}
```

As you can see, in the results, there is a new field called `highlight`, which contains the highlighted fields along with an array of fragments.

How it works...

When the `highlight` parameter is passed to the search object, ElasticSearch tries to execute it on the document's results.

The highlighting phase, which is after the document fetching phase, tries to extract the highlight by following these steps:

1. It collects the terms available in the query.

2. It initializes the highlighter with the parameters passed during the query.

3. It extracts the fields we are interested in and tries to load them if they are stored; otherwise they are taken from the source.

4. It executes the query on a single field in order to detect the more relevant parts.

5. It adds the highlighted fragments that are found in the resulting hit.

Using the highlighting functionality is easy, but there are some important factors that you need to pay attention to:

▶ The field that must be highlighted should be available in one of the forms explained earlier. It must be stored in the source or the term vector.

> The ElasticSearch highlighter checks the presence of the data field first as a term vector (the fastest way to execute the highlighting). If the field has no term vectors, it tries to load the field value from the stored fields. If the field is not stored, it loads the JSON source, interprets it, and extracts the data value if it is available. Obviously, the last approach is the slowest and resource-intensive approach.

▶ If a special analyzer is used in the search, it should be passed to the highlighter as well (this is often managed automatically).

There are several parameters that can be passed to the highlighted object to control the highlighting process, given as follows:

▶ `number_of_fragments` (by default, 5): This parameter controls how many fragments are returned. It can be configured globally or for a field.

▶ `fragment_size` (by default, 100): This specifies the number of characters that the fragments must contain. It can be configured globally or for a field.

▶ `pre_tags/post_tags`: These are a list of tags that can be used to mark the highlighted text.

▶ `tags_schema="styled"`: This allows you to define the tag schema that marks highlights with different tags in order of importance. This is a helper to reduce the definition of a lot of `pre_tags/post_tags`.

See also

▶ The *Executing a search* recipe in this chapter

Executing a scan query

Every time a query is executed, the results are calculated and returned to the user. In ElasticSearch, there is no deterministic order for the records; pagination on a big block of values can result in inconsistency between the results due to documents being added and deleted, and also between documents with the same score. The scan query tries to resolve these kinds of problems by providing a special cursor that allows you to uniquely iterate all the documents. It's often used to back up documents or reindex them.

Getting ready

You need a working ElasticSearch cluster and an index populated with the script
(`chapter_05/populate_query.sh`) available in the code bundle for this book.

How to do it...

In order to execute a scan query, perform the following steps:

1. From the command line, execute a search of the type scan:

   ```
   curl -XGET 'http://127.0.0.1:9200/test-index/test-
   type/_search?pretty=true&search_type=scan&scroll=10m&size=50' -d
   '{"query":{"match_all":{}}}'
   ```

2. If everything works all right, the command will return a result, as follows:

   ```
   {
       "_scroll_id" : "c2Nhbjs1OzQ1Mzp4d1FtcngONlNCYUpVOXh4cOZiYll3OzQ
   1Njp4d1FtcngONlNCYUpVOXh4cOZiYll3OzQ1Nzp4d1FtcngONlNCYUpVOXh4cOZi
   Yll3OzQ1NDp4d1FtcngONlNCYUpVOXh4cOZiYll3OzQ1NTp4d1FtcngONlNCYUpVO
   Xh4cOZiYll3OzE7dG90YWxfaGl0czozOw==",
       "took" : 1,
       "timed_out" : false,
       "_shards" : {
         "total" : 5,
         "successful" : 5,
         "failed" : 0
       },
       "hits" : {
         "total" : 3,
         "max_score" : 0.0,
         "hits" : [ ]
   }
   ```

   The result is composed of the following parameters:

   - ❑ `scroll_id`: This is the value to be used to scroll records.
   - ❑ `took`: This is the time required to execute the query.
   - ❑ `timed_out`: This is used to notify whether the query, if any query has, timed out.
   - ❑ `_shards`: This gives information about the status of shards during the query.
   - ❑ `hits`: This gives the total hits. The hits other than the total are available when you scroll.

- ► Using the `scroll_id` parameter, you can use the scroll IDs to get the results:

```
curl -XGET 'localhost:9200/_search/scroll?scroll=10m' -d 'c2Nhbjs
10zQ2Mzp4d1Ftcng0N1NCYUpVOXh4c0ZiY1130zQ2Njp4d1Ftcng0N1NCYUpVOXh4
c0ZiY1130zQ2Nzp4d1Ftcng0N1NCYUpVOXh4c0ZiY1130zQ2NDp4d1Ftcng0N1NCY
UpVOXh4c0ZiY1130zQ2NTp4d1Ftcng0N1NCYUpVOXh4c0ZiY1130zE7dG90YWxfaG
10czozOw=='
```

3. The result should be similar to this:

```
{
    "_scroll_id" : "c2NhbjswOzE7dG90YWxfaGl0czozOw==",
    "took" : 20,
    "timed_out" : false,
    "_shards" : {
      "total" : 5,
      "successful" : 0,
      "failed" : 5
    },
    "hits" : {
      "total" : 3,
      "max_score" : 0.0,
  ...}
```

How it works...

The scan query is interpreted as a standard search. This kind of search is designed to iterate on a large set of results, so the score and the order are not computed.

During the query phase, every shard stores the state of the IDs in the memory until a timeout.

A scan query can be processed in two steps, as follows:

1. The first part of the preceding example code executes a query and returns a `scroll_id` value, which can be used to fetch the results.

2. The second part of the preceding example code executes the document scrolling. You iterate the second step, getting the new `scroll_id` value, in order to fetch other documents.

> If you need to iterate on a big set of records, a scan query must be used; otherwise you might have duplicated results.

A scan query is similar to every executed standard query, but there are two special parameters that must be passed in the query string:

 ▸ `search_type=scan`: This informs ElasticSearch to execute a scan query.

 ▸ `scroll=(your timeout)`: This allows you to define how long the hits should live. The time can be expressed in seconds using the `s` postfix (such as, `5s`, `10s`, and `15s`) or in minutes using the `m` postfix (that is `5m`, `10m`). If you are using a long timeout, you must ensure that your nodes have a lot of RAM in order to keep the resulting ID live. This parameter is mandatory.

> Size is also special as it is treated *per shard*, meaning that if you have a size equal to 10 and 5 shards, each scroll will return 50 documents.

See also

 ▸ The *Executing a Search* recipe in this chapter

Suggesting a correct query

It's very common for users to commit typing errors or to require suggestions for the words they are writing. These issues are solved by ElasticSearch with the suggest functionality.

Getting ready

You need a working ElasticSearch cluster and an index populated with the script `chapter_05/populate_query.sh`, available in the code bundle for this book.

How to do it...

In order to suggest relevant terms by query, perform the following steps:

1. From the command line, execute a `suggest` call:

```
curl -XGET 'http://127.0.0.1:9200/test-index/_suggest?pretty=true'
-d ' {
  "suggest1" : {
    "text" : "we find tester",
    "term" : {
      "field" : "parsedtext"
    }
  }
}'
```

2. This result will be returned by ElasticSearch if everything works all right:

```json
{
  "_shards": {
      "failed": 0,
      "successful": 5,
      "total": 5
  },
  "suggest1": [
    {
      "length": 2,
      "offset": 0,
      "options": [],
      "text": "we"
    },
    {
      "length": 4,
      "offset": 3,
      "options": [],
      "text": "find"
    },
    {
      "length": 6,
      "offset": 8,
      "options": [
        {
          "freq": 2,
          "score": 0.8333333,
          "text": "testere"
        }
      ],
      "text": "tester"
    }
  ]
}
```

The preceding result is composed of the following:

- The shard's status at the time of the query.
- The list of tokens with their available candidates.

How it works...

The **suggest** API call works by collecting term statistics on all the index shards. Using Lucene field statistics, it is possible to detect the correct or complete term.

The HTTP method used to execute a suggestion is GET (but POST also works). The URLs for the REST endpoints are:

```
http://<server>/_suggest
http://<server>/<index_name(s)>/_suggest
```

> This call can be also embedded in the standard search API call.

There are two types of suggesters: the term suggester and the phrase suggester.

The terms suggester is the simpler form of suggester. It only requires the text and the field to work. It also allows you to set a lot of parameters, for example: the minimum size for a word, how to sort results, the suggester strategy, and so on. A complete reference is available on the ElasticSearch website.

The phrase suggester is able to keep relationships between terms that it needs to suggest. The phrase suggester is less efficient than the term suggester, but it provides better results.

The suggest API is a new feature, so parameters and options can change between releases; New suggesters can also be added via plugins.

See also

- The *Executing a Search* recipe in this chapter

- The phrase suggester's online documentation at
  http://www.elasticsearch.org/guide/en/elasticsearch/reference/current/search-suggesters-phrase.html

- The completion suggester's online documentation at
  http://www.elasticsearch.org/guide/en/elasticsearch/reference/current/search-suggesters-completion.html

- The context suggester's online documentation at
  http://www.elasticsearch.org/guide/en/elasticsearch/reference/current/suggester-context.html

Counting matched results

It is often required to return only the count of the matched results and not the results themselves. The advantages of using a count request is the performance it offers and reduced resource usage, as a standard search call also returns hits count.

A lot of scenarios involve counting, as follows:

▸ To return the number of, for example, posts for a blog or comments for a post.

▸ To validate that some items are available. Are there posts? Are there comments?

Getting ready

You need a working ElasticSearch cluster and an index populated with the script `chapter_05/populate_query.sh`, available in the code bundle for this book.

How to do it...

In order to execute a counting query, perform the following steps:

1. From the command line, execute a count query:

```
curl -XGET 'http://127.0.0.1:9200/test-index/test-type/_
count?pretty=true' -d '{"query":{"match_all":{}}}'
```

2. The following result should be returned by ElasticSearch if everything works all right:

```
{
  "count" : 3,
  "_shards" : {
    "total" : 5,
    "successful" : 5,
    "failed" : 0
  }
}
```

The result is composed of the count result (a long type value) and the shard's status at the time of the query.

How it works...

The query is interpreted as it is done for searching. The count is processed and distributed in all the shards, in which it's mapped in a low-level Lucene count call. With every hit, a shard returns a count that is aggregated and returned to the user.

> In ElasticSearch, it is faster to count than search. If results are not required, it's good practice to use it.

The HTTP method to execute a count is GET (but POST works too). The URL examples for the REST endpoints are:

```
http://<server>/_count
http://<server>/<index_name(s)>/_count
http://<server>/<index_name(s)>/<type_name(s)>/_count
```

Multi-indices and types are comma separated. If an index or a type is defined, the search is limited to them only. An alias can be used as the index name.

Typically, a body is used to express a query, but for a simple query, q (the query argument) can be used. Take the following code as an example:

```
curl -XGET 'http://127.0.0.1:9200/test-index/test-
type/_count?q=uuid:11111'
```

> Counts can also be requested from a normal search call by configuring the search_type parameter to count. More details are available in the ElasticSearch documentation at http://www.elasticsearch.org/guide/en/elasticsearch/reference/current/search-request-search-type.html.

See also

▸ The *Executing a search* recipe in this chapter

Deleting by query

In the *Deleting a document* recipe from *Chapter 4, Basic Operations*, we saw how to delete a document(). A document can be deleted very quickly, but it requires you to know the document ID.

ElasticSearch provides a call to delete all the documents that match a query.

Getting ready

You need a working ElasticSearch cluster and an index populated with the script (chapter_05/populate_query.sh) available in the code bundle for this book.

How to do it...

In order to execute a DELETE by query, perform the following steps:

1. Using the command line, execute a query, as follows:

```
curl -XDELETE 'http://127.0.0.1:9200/test-index/test-type/_
query?pretty=true' -d '{"query":{"match_all":{}}}'
```

2. The following result should be returned by ElasticSearch, if everything works all right:

```
{
  "_indices" : {
    "test-index" : {
      "_shards" : {
        "total" : 5,
        "successful" : 5,
        "failed" : 0
      }
    }
  }
}
```

3. The result is composed of the shard's status at the time of the DELETE query.

How it works...

The query is interpreted in the same way as it is done for searching. The DELETE query is processed and distributed to all the shards.

> When you want to remove all the documents without deleting the mapping, using a DELETE query along with a match all query allows you to clean your mapping of all the documents. This call is analogous to the truncate table syntax of the SQL language.

The HTTP method to execute a DELETE query is DELETE, and the URL examples for the REST endpoints are:

```
http://<server>/_query
http://<server>/<index_name(s)>/_query
http://<server>/<index_name(s)>/<type_name(s)>/_query
```

Multiple indices and types are comma separated. If an index or a type is defined, the search is limited only to them. An alias can be used as the index name.

Typically, a body is used to express a query, but for a simple query, q (the query argument) can be used, as follows:

```
curl -XDELETE 'http://127.0.0.1:9200/test-index/test-type/_
query?q=uuid:11111'
```

See also

▸ The *Executing a Search* recipe in this chapter

Matching all the documents

One of the most used queries, usually in conjunction with a filter, is the match all query. This kind of query allows you to return all the documents.

Getting ready

You need a working ElasticSearch cluster and an index populated with the script chapter_05/populate_query.sh, available in the code bundle for this book.

How to do it...

In order to execute a match_all query, perform the following steps:

1. From the command line, execute the query:

   ```
   curl -XPOST 'http://127.0.0.1:9200/test-index/test-
   type/_search?pretty=true' -d '{"query":{"match_all":{}}}'
   ```

2. The following result should be returned by ElasticSearch if everything works all right:

   ```
   {
     "took" : 52,
     "timed_out" : false,
     "_shards" : {
       "total" : 5,
       "successful" : 5,
       "failed" : 0
     },
     "hits" : {
       "total" : 3,
       "max_score" : 1.0,
       "hits" : [{
         "_index" : "test-index",
         "_type" : "test-type",
   ```

```
        "_id" : "1",
        "_score" : 1.0, "_source" : {"position": 1,
        "parsedtext": "Joe Testere nice guy", "name": "Joe
        Tester", "uuid": "11111"}
      }, {
        "_index" : "test-index",
        "_type" : "test-type",
        "_id" : "2",
        "_score" : 1.0, "_source" : {"position": 2,
        "parsedtext": "Bill Testere nice guy", "name": "Bill
        Baloney", "uuid": "22222"}
      }, {
        "_index" : "test-index",
        "_type" : "test-type",
        "_id" : "3",
        "_score" : 1.0, "_source" : {"position": 3,
        "parsedtext": "Bill is not\n nice
        guy", "name": "Bill Clinton", "uuid": "33333"}
      }]
    }
  }
```

The result is a standard query result, as we have seen in the *Executing a Search* recipe in this chapter.

How it works...

The match_all query is one of the most commonly used query types. It's fast because it doesn't require the score calculus (it's wrapped in a Lucene ConstantScoreQuery query).

The match_all query is often used in conjunction with a filter in a filter query, as follows:

```
curl -XPOST "http://localhost:9200/test-index/test-type/_search" -d'
{
  "query": {
    "filtered": {
      "query": {
        "match_all": {}
      },
      "filter": {
        "term": {
          "myfield": "myterm"
        }
      }
    }
  }
}'
```

> If no query is defined in the search object, the default query will be a `match_query` query.

See also

▸ The *Executing a search* recipe in this chapter

Querying/filtering for a single term

Searching or filtering for a particular term is frequently done. A term query and filter work with exact values and are generally very fast.

The term query/filter can be compared to the equals "=" query in the SQL world (for the fields that are not tokenized).

Getting ready

You need a working ElasticSearch cluster and an index populated with the script `chapter_05/populate_query.sh`, available in the code bundle for this book.

How to do it...

In order to execute a term query/filter, perform the following steps:

1. Execute a term query from the command line:

```
curl -XPOST 'http://127.0.0.1:9200/test-index/test-type/_
search?pretty=true' -d '{
  "query": {
    "term": {
      "uuid": "33333"
    }
  }
}'
```

2. The following result should be returned by ElasticSearch if everything works all right:

```
{
  "took" : 58,
  "timed_out" : false,
  "_shards" : {
    "total" : 5,
    "successful" : 5,
```

```
      "failed" : 0
    },
    "hits" : {
      "total" : 1,
      "max_score" : 0.30685282,
      "hits" : [ {
        "_index" : "test-index",
        "_type" : "test-type",
        "_id" : "3",
        "_score" : 0.30685282, "_source" : {"position": 3,
"parsedtext": "Bill is not\n                    nice guy", "name":
"Bill Clinton", "uuid": "33333"}
      } ]
    }
  }
}
```

The result is a standard query result, as we have seen in the *Executing a Search* recipe in this chapter.

3. Execute a term filter from the command line:

```
curl -XPOST 'http://127.0.0.1:9200/test-index/test-type/_
search?pretty=true' -d '{
    "query": {
        "filtered": {
            "filter": {
                "term": {
                    "uuid": "33333"
                }
            },
            "query": {
                "match_all": {}
            }
        }
    }
}'
```

4. This is the result:

```
{
  "took" : 4,
  "timed_out" : false,
  "_shards" : {
    "total" : 5,
    "successful" : 5,
    "failed" : 0
  },
```

```
        "hits" : {
          "total" : 1,
          "max_score" : 1.0,
          "hits" : [ {
            "_index" : "test-index",
            "_type" : "test-type",
            "_id" : "3",
            "_score" : 1.0, "_source" : {"position": 3, "parsedtext":
    "Bill is not\n                nice guy", "name": "Bill Clinton",
    "uuid": "33333"}
          } ]
        }
      }
```

How it works...

Lucene, due to its inverted index, is one of the fastest engines to search for a term/value in a field.

Every field that is indexed in Lucene is converted in a fast search structure for its particular type:

- ▶ The text is split into tokens if it is analyzed or saved as a single token
- ▶ Numeric fields are converted into their fastest binary representations
- ▶ Date and Date-time fields are converted into binary forms

In ElasticSearch, all these conversions are automatically managed. The search for a term, independent of the value, is archived by ElasticSearch using the correct format for the field.

Internally, during a term query execution, all the documents matching the term are collected and then sorted by their scores (the scoring depends on the Lucene similarity algorithm chosen). The term filter follows the same approach, but because it doesn't require the score step, it's much faster.

If we take a look at the results of the previous searches, for the term query, the hit has 0.30685282 as the score and the filter has 1.0. The time required to score a sample if it is very small is not so relevant, but if you have thousands or millions of documents, it takes a lot more time.

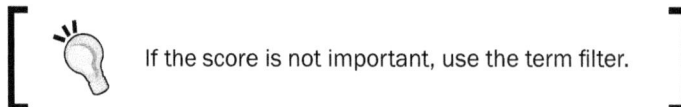

> If the score is not important, use the term filter.

A filter is preferred to query when the score is not important, for example, in the following scenarios:

▸ Filtering permissions

▸ Filtering numerical values

▸ Filtering ranges

> In a filtered query, the filter is applied first, narrowing down the number of documents to be matched against the query, and then the query is applied.

There's more...

Matching a term is the basic function of Lucene and ElasticSearch. In order to correctly use a query/filter, you need to pay attention to how the field is indexed.

As we saw in *Chapter 3, Managing Mapping*, the terms of an indexed field depend on the analyzer that is used to index it. In order to better understand this concept, in the following table, there is a representation of a phrase that depends on several analyzers. Take the phrase: `Peter's house is big`, as an example:

Mapping index	Analyzer	Tokens
`no`	(No index)	(No tokens)
`not_analyzed`	`KeywordAnalyzer`	`[Peter's house is big]`
`analyzed`	`StandardAnalyzer`	`[peter, s, house, is, big]`

The common pitfalls in searching are related to misunderstanding the analyzer/mapping configuration.

The `KeywordAnalyzer` analyzer, which is used as a default for the `not_analyzed` field, saves the text without any changes as a single token.

The `StandardAnalyzer` analyzer, the default for the `analyzed` field, tokenizes on whitespaces and punctuation; and every token is converted to lowercase. You should use the same analyzer that is used in indexing to analyze the query (the default settings). In the preceding example, if the phrase is analyzed with the `StandardAnalyzer` analyzer, you cannot search for the term `Peter`, but you have to search for `peter`, because the `StandardAnalyzer` analyzer executes a lowercasing on the terms.

> When the same field requires one or more search strategies, you need to use the `fields` property using the different analyzers that you need.

▶ The *Executing a search* recipe in this chapter

Querying/filtering for multiple terms

The previous type of search works very well if you need to search for a single term. If you want to search for multiple terms, you can do that in two ways: using an AND/OR filter or using the multiple term query.

Getting ready

You need a working ElasticSearch cluster and an index populated with the script chapter_05/populate_query.sh, available in the code bundle for this book.

How to do it...

In order to execute a terms query/filter, perform the following steps:

1. Execute a terms query from the command line:

```
curl -XPOST 'http://127.0.0.1:9200/test-index/test-type/_
search?pretty=true' -d '{
  "query": {
    "terms": {
      "uuid": ["33333", "32222"]
    }
  }
}'
```

The result returned by ElasticSearch is the same as in the previous recipe.

2. If you want to use the terms query in a filter, this is how the query should look:

```
curl -XPOST 'http://127.0.0.1:9200/test-index/test-type/_
search?pretty=true' -d '{
  "query": {
    "filtered": {
      "filter": {
        "terms": {
          "uuid": ["33333", "32222"]
        }
      },
      "query": {
```

```
          "match_all": {}
        }
      }
    }
  }'
```

How it works...

The terms query/filter is related to the preceding type of query. It extends the term query to support multiple values.

This call is very useful because the concept of filtering on multiple values is very common. In traditional SQL, this operation is achieved with the `in` keyword in the `where` clause:

```
Select * from *** where color in ("red", "green")
```

In the preceding examples, the query searches for `uuid` with the values `33333` or `22222`.

The terms query/filter is not merely a helper for the term matching function, but it also allows you to define extra parameters in order to control the query behavior:

- ▸ `minimum_match`/`minimum_should_match`: This parameter controls the number of matched terms that are required to validate the query. For example, the following query matches all the documents where the color fields have at least two values from a list of `red`, `blue`, and `white`:

```
"terms": {
  "color": ["red", "blue", "white"],
  "minimum_should_match":2
}
```

- ▸ `disable_coord`: With this parameter, a Boolean function indicates whether the `coord` query must be enabled or disabled. The `coord` query is a query option that is used for better scoring by overlapping the match in Lucene. For more details, visit `http://lucene.apache.org/core/4_0_0/core/org/apache/lucene/search/similarities/Similarity.html`.

- ▸ `boost`: This parameter is the standard query boost value used to modify the query weight.

The term filter is very powerful, as it allows you to define the strategy that must be used in order to filter terms. The strategies are passed in the `execution` parameter, and the following parameters are currently available:

- ▸ `plain` (default): This parameter works as a terms query. It generates a bit set with the terms, and is evaluated. This strategy cannot be automatically cached.

- ▶ `bool`: This parameter generates a term query for every term and then creates a Boolean filter to be used in order to filter terms. This approach allows you to reuse the term filters required for the Boolean filtering, which increases the performance if the subterm filters are reused.

- ▶ `and`: This parameter is similar to the `bool` parameter, but the term filter's subqueries are wrapped in an AND filter.

- ▶ `or`: This parameter is also similar to the `bool` parameter, but the term filter's subqueries are wrapped in an OR filter.

There's more...

Because term filtering is very powerful, in order to increase performance the terms can be fetched by other documents during the query. This is a very common scenario. Take, for example, a user that contains a list of the groups it is associated with, and you want to filter the documents that can only be seen by *some* groups. This is how the pseudo code should be:

```
curl -XGET localhost:9200/my-index/document/_search?pretty=true -d
'{
  "query" : {
    "filtered" : {
      "query":{"match_all":{}},
      "filter" : {
        "terms" : {
          "can_see_groups" : {
            "index" : "my-index",
            "type" : "user",
            "id" : "1bw71LaxSzSp_zV6NB_YGg",
            "path" : "groups"
          }
        }
      }
    }
  }
}'
```

In the preceding example, the list of groups is fetched at runtime from a document (which is always identified by an index, type, and ID) and the path (`field`) that contains the values to be put in it. This pattern is similar to the one used in SQL:

```
select * from xxx where can_see_group in (select groups from user
where user_id='1bw71LaxSzSp_zV6NB_YGg')
```

Generally, **NoSQL** data stores do not support joins, so the data must be optimized to search using de-normalization or other techniques. ElasticSearch does not provide the join as in SQL, but it provides similar alternatives, as follows:

- ▶ Child/parent queries
- ▶ Nested queries
- ▶ Term filter with external document term fetching

See also

- ▶ The *Executing a search* recipe in this chapter
- ▶ The *Querying/filtering for term* recipe in this chapter
- ▶ The *Using a Boolean query/filter* recipe in this chapter
- ▶ The *Using and/or/not filters* recipe in this chapter

Using a prefix query/filter

The prefix query/filter is used when only the starting part of a term is known. It allows you to complete truncated or partial terms.

Getting ready

You need a working ElasticSearch cluster and an index populated with the script `chapter_05/populate_query.sh`, available in the code bundle for this book.

How to do it...

In order to execute a prefix query/filter, perform the following steps:

1. Execute a prefix query from the command line:

```
curl -XPOST 'http://127.0.0.1:9200/test-index/test-type/_
search?pretty=true' -d '{
  "query": {
    "prefix": {
      "uuid": "333"
    }
  }
}'
```

2. The result returned by ElasticSearch is the same as in the previous recipe.

3. If you want to use the prefix query in a filter, this is how the query should look:

```
curl -XPOST 'http://127.0.0.1:9200/test-index/test-type/_
search?pretty=true' -d '{
  "query": {
    "filtered": {
      "filter": {
        "prefix": {
          "uuid": "333"
        }
      },
      "query": {
        "match_all": {}
      }
    }
  }
}'
```

How it works...

When a prefix query/filter is executed, Lucene has a special method to skip to terms that start with a common prefix, so the execution of a prefix query is very fast.

The prefix query/filter is used, in general, in scenarios where term completion is required, as follows:

- Name completion
- Code completion
- On-type completion

When designing a tree structure in ElasticSearch, if the ID of the item is designed to contain the hierarchic relation, it can speed up application filtering a lot. The following table, for example, shows the ID and the corresponding elements:

ID	Element
001	Fruit
00102	Apple
0010201	Green apple
0010202	Red apple
00103	Melon
0010301	White melon
002	Vegetables

In the preceding example, we have structured IDs that contain information about the tree structure, which allows you to create queries, as follows:

- Filter by all fruit:

  ```
  "prefix": {"fruit_id": "001" }
  ```

- Filter by all apple types:

  ```
  "prefix": {"fruit_id": "001002" }
  ```

- Filter by all vegetables:

  ```
  "prefix": {"fruit_id": "002" }
  ```

If the preceding structure is compared to a standard SQL `parent_id` table in a very large dataset, the reduction in join and the fast search performance of Lucene can filter the results in a few milliseconds, compared to a few seconds/minutes.

> Structuring the data in the correct way can provide an impressive performance boost!

See also

- The _Querying/filtering for terms_ recipe in this chapter

Using a Boolean query/filter

Every person who uses a search engine has at some point in time used the syntax with minus (-) and plus (+) to include or exclude some query terms. The Boolean query/filter allows you to programmatically define a query to include, exclude, or optionally include terms (`should`) in the query.

This kind of query/filter is one of the most important ones, because it allows you to aggregate a lot of simple queries/filters, which we will see in this chapter, to build a big complex query.

Getting ready

You need a working ElasticSearch cluster and an index populated with the script `chapter_05/populate_query.sh`, available in the code bundle for this book.

How to do it...

In order to execute a Boolean query/filter, perform the following steps:

1. Execute a Boolean query using the command line:

```
curl -XPOST 'http://127.0.0.1:9200/test-index/test-type/_
search?pretty=true' -d '{
  "query": {
    "bool" : {
      "must" : {
        "term" : { "parsedtext" : "joe" }
      },
      "must_not" : {
        "range" : {
          "position" : { "from" : 10, "to" : 20 }
        }
      },
      "should" : [
        {
          "term" : { "uuid" : "11111" }
        },
        {
          "term" : { "uuid" : "22222" }
        }
      ],
      "minimum_number_should_match" : 1,
      "boost" : 1.0
    }
  }
}'
```

2. The result returned by ElasticSearch is similar to the result from the previous recipes, but in this case, it should return just one record (ID: 1).

3. If you want to use a Boolean filter, use the following query:

```
curl -XPOST 'http://127.0.0.1:9200/test-index/test-type/_
search?pretty=true' -d '{
  "query": {
    "filtered": {
      "filter": {
        "bool" : {
          "must" : {
            "term" : { "parsedtext" : "joe" }
          },
```

```
            "must_not" : {
              "range" : {
                "position" : { "from" : 10, "to" : 20 }
              }
            },
            "should" : [
              {
                "term" : { "uuid" : "11111" }
              },
              {
                "term" : { "uuid" : "22222" }
              }
            ]
          }
        },
        "query": {
          "match_all": {}
        }
      }
    }
  }'
```

How it works...

The Boolean query/filter is often one of the more frequently used ones because it allows you to compose a big query using a lot of simple ones. It must have one of these three parts:

- must: This is a list of the queries/filters that *must* be satisfied. All the must queries must be verified to return hits. It can be seen as an AND filter with all its subqueries.

- must_not: This is a list of the queries/filters that must not be matched. It can be seen as a NOT filter of an AND query.

- should: This is a list of the queries that can be verified. The value of the minimum number of queries that must be verified is controlled by the minimum_number_should_match parameter (by default, 1).

> The Boolean filter is faster than a group of AND/OR/NOT queries because it is optimized to execute fast Boolean bitwise operations on a document's bitmap results.

See also

- The *Querying/filtering for Terms* recipe in this chapter

Using a range query/filter

Searching/filtering by range is a very common scenario in a real-world application. The following are a few standard cases:

▶ Filtering by a numeric value range (such as price, size, age, and so on)

▶ Filtering by date (for example, the events of 03/07/12 can be a range query, from 03/07/12 00:00:00 and 03/07/12 24:59:59)

▶ Filtering by term range (for example, terms from A to D)

Getting ready

You need a working ElasticSearch cluster, an index named *test* (see *Chapter 4*, *Basic Operations*, to create an index named *test*), and basic knowledge of JSON.

How to do it...

In order to execute a range query/filter, perform the following steps:

▶ Consider the previous example's data, which contains a `position` integer field. This can be used to execute a query in order to filter positions between 3 and 5, as follows:

```
curl -XPOST 'http://127.0.0.1:9200/test-index/test-type/_
search?pretty=true' -d '{
  "query": {
    "filtered": {
      "filter": {
        "range" : {
          "position" : {
            "from" : 3,
            "to" : 4,
            "include_lower" : true,
            "include_upper" : false
          }
        }
      },
      "query": {
        "match_all": {}
      }
    }
  }
}'
```

How it works...

A range query is used because scoring results can cover several interesting scenarios, as follows:

▶ Items with high availability in stocks should be presented first

▶ New items should be highlighted

▶ Most bought item should be highlighted

The range filter is very useful for numeric values, as the earlier example shows. The parameters that a range query/filter will accept are:

▶ `from` (optional): This is the start value for the range

▶ `to` (optional): This is the end value for the range

▶ `include_in_lower` (optional, by default `true`): This parameter includes the start value in the range

▶ `include_in_upper` (optional, by default `true`): This parameter includes the end value in the range

In a range filter, other helper parameters are available to simplify a search:

▶ `gt` (greater than): This parameter has the same functionality as the `from` parameter and the `include_in_lower` field when set to `false`

▶ `gte` (greater than or equal to): This parameter has the same functionality to set the `from` parameter and the `include_in_lower` field to `true`

▶ `lt` (lesser than): This parameter has the same functionality to set the `to` parameter and the `include_in_lower` field to `false`

▶ `lte` (lesser than or equal to): This parameter has the same functionality to set the `to` parameter and the `include_in_lower` field to `false`

There's more...

In ElasticSearch, a range query/filter covers several types of SQL queries, such as <, <=, >, and >= on numeric values.

In ElasticSearch, because date-time fields are managed internally as numeric fields, it's possible to use range queries/filters for date values. If the field is a `date` field, every value in the range query is automatically converted to a numeric value. For example, if you need to filter the documents of this year, this is how the range fragment will be:

```
"range" : {
  "timestamp" : {
    "from" : "2014-01-01",
```

```
      "to" : "2015-01-01",
      "include_lower" : true,
      "include_upper" : false
   }
}
```

Using span queries

The big difference between standard databases (SQL as well as many NoSQL databases, such as MongoDB, Riak, or CouchDB) and ElasticSearch is the number of facilities to express text queries.

The SpanQuery family is a group of queries that control a sequence of text tokens via their positions. Standard queries and filters don't take into account the positional presence of text tokens.

Span queries allow you to define several kinds of queries:

▸ The exact phrase query

▸ The exact fragment query (such as, `Take off`, `give up`)

▸ A partial exact phrase with a *slop*, that is, other tokens between the searched terms (such as `the man` with slop 2 can also match `the strong man`, `the old wise man`, and so on)

Getting ready

You need a working ElasticSearch cluster and an index populated with the script `chapter_05/populate_query.sh`, available in the code bundle for this book.

How to do it...

In order to execute span queries, perform the following steps:

1. The main element in span queries is the `span_term` term whose usage is similar to the term of a standard query. One or more `span_term` can be aggregated to formulate a span query. The `span_first` query defines a query in which the `span_term` must match in the first token or ones near it. Take the following code as an example:

```
curl -XPOST 'http://127.0.0.1:9200/test-index/test-type/_
search?pretty=true' -d '{
  "query": {
    "span_first" : {
      "match" : {
```

```
            "span_term" : { "parsedtext" : "joe" }
          },
          "end" : 5
        }
      }
    }'
```

2. The `span_or` query is used to define multiple values in a span query. This is very handy for a simple synonym search:

```
curl -XPOST 'http://127.0.0.1:9200/test-index/test-type/_
search?pretty=true' -d '{
  "query": {
    "span_or" : {
      "clauses" : [
          { "span_term" : { "parsedtext" : "nice" } },
          { "span_term" : { "parsedtext" : "cool" } },
          { "span_term" : { "parsedtext" : "wonderful"}
      ]
    }
  }
}'
```

The list of clauses is the core of the `span_or` query, because it contains the span terms that should match.

3. Similar to the `span_or` query, there is a `span_multi` query, which wraps multiple term queries such as prefixes and wildcards, as follows:

```
curl -XPOST 'http://127.0.0.1:9200/test-index/test-type/_
search?pretty=true' -d '{
  "query": {
    "span_multi":{
      "match":{
        "prefix" : { "parsedtext" :  { "value" : "jo" } }
      }
    }
  }
}'
```

4. All these kinds of queries can be used to create the `span_near` query that allows you to control the token sequence of the query:

```
curl -XPOST 'http://127.0.0.1:9200/test-index/test-type/_
search?pretty=true' -d '{
  "query": {
    "span_near" : {
      "clauses" : [
```

```
                { "span_term" : { "parsedtext" : "nice" } },
                { "span_term" : { "parsedtext" : "joe" } },
                { "span_term" : { "parsedtext" : "guy" } }
            ],
            "slop" : 3,
            "in_order" : false,
            "collect_payloads" : false
        }
      }
    }'
```

How it works...

Lucene provides the span queries available in ElasticSearch. The base span query is `span_term`, which works exactly the same as the term query. The goal of this span query is to match an exact term (field plus text). It's possible to compose and formulate the other kind of span queries.

> The main use of a span query is for a proximity search: to search terms that are close to each other.

A `span_first` function is used in a `span_term` query to match a term that must be in the first position. If the *end* parameter (integer) is defined, it extends the first token that matches the passed value.

One of the most powerful span queries is the `span_or` query, which allows you to define multiple terms in the same position. It covers several scenarios, as follows:

- Multiple names
- Synonyms
- Several verbal forms

The `span_or` query does not have the counterpart `span_and` query function, as it does not have any meaning, because span queries are merely positional.

If the number of terms that must be passed to a `span_or` query function is huge, it can sometimes be reduced with a `span_multi` query using a prefix or wildcard. This approach allows you to make matches. For example, for the terms `play`, `playing`, `plays`, `player`, `players` and so on, a prefix query with `play` must be used.

The other most powerful span query is `span_near`, which allows you to define whether a list of span queries (clauses) needs to be matched in a sequence or not. The following parameters can be passed to this span query:

- `in_order` (by default, `true`): This parameter defines that the term that is matched in the clauses must be executed in an order. If you define two `span_near` queries with two span terms to match `joe` and `black`, you will not be able to match the text `black joe` if the `in_order` parameter is true.

- `slop` (by default, `0`): This parameter defines the distance between the terms that must match the clauses.

> By setting slop to `0` and the `in_order` parameter to true, you will be creating an *exact phrase* match.

A span near (`span_near`) query and slop can be used to create a phrase match that can have some terms that are not known. For example, consider matching an expression such as `the house`. If you need to execute an exact match, you need to write a similar query:

```
{
    "query": {
        "span_near" : {
            "clauses" : [
                { "span_term" : { "parsedtext" : "the" } },
                { "span_term" : { "parsedtext" : "house" } }
            ],
            "slop" : 0,
            "in_order" : true
        }
    }
}
```

Now, if you have, for example, an adjective between the article and `house` (such as `the wonderful house`, *the big house*, and so on), the previous query will never match them. To achieve this goal, slop must be set to `1`.

Usually, slop is set to `1`, `2`, or `3`. High values have no meaning.

See also

- The *Using a match query* recipe in this chapter

Using a match query

ElasticSearch provides a helper to build complex span queries that depend on simple preconfigured settings. This helper is called a **match query**.

Getting ready

You need a working ElasticSearch cluster and an index populated with the script `chapter_05/populate_query.sh`, available in the code bundle for this book.

How to do it...

In order to execute a match query, perform the following steps:

1. The standard usage of a match query simply requires the field name and the query text:

```
curl -XPOST 'http://127.0.0.1:9200/test-index/test-type/_
search?pretty=true' -d '{
  "query": {
    "match" : {
      "parsedtext" : {
        "field": "nice guy",
        "operator": "and"
      }
    }
  }
}'
```

2. If you need to execute the same query as a phrase query, the type of match changes in the `match_phrase` function:

```
curl -XPOST 'http://127.0.0.1:9200/test-index/test-type/_
search?pretty=true' -d '{
  "query": {
    "match_phrase" : {
      "parsedtext" : "nice guy"
    }
  }
}'
```

3. An extension of the previous query used in text completion or the *search as you type* functionality is the `match_phrase_prefix` function:

```
curl -XPOST 'http://127.0.0.1:9200/test-index/test-type/_
search?pretty=true' -d '{
```

```
  "query": {
    "match_phrase_prefix" : {
      "parsedtext" : "nice gu"
    }
  }
}'
```

How it works...

The match query aggregates several frequently used query types that cover standard query scenarios. The standard match query creates a Boolean query that can be controlled by these parameters:

- ▶ `operator` (by default, `OR`): This parameter defines how to store and process terms. If it's set to `OR`, all the terms are converted to a Boolean query with all the terms in `should` clauses. If it's set to `AND`, the terms will build a list of `must` clauses.

- ▶ `analyzer` (by default, it is based on mapping or it is set in the search setup): This parameter allows you to override the default analyzer of the field.

- ▶ `fuzziness`: This parameter allows you to define fuzzy term searches (see the *Using QueryString query* recipe in this chapter). In relation to this parameter, the `prefix_length` and `max_expansion` parameters are available.

- ▶ `zero_terms_query` (can be none/all, but by default, it is `none`): This parameter allows you to define a tokenizer filter that removes all the terms from the query. The default behavior is to return nothing or all of the documents. This is the case when you build an English query search for the `the` or a terms that could match all the documents.

- ▶ `cutoff_frequency`: This parameter allows you to handle dynamic stopwords (very common terms in text) at runtime. During query execution, terms over the `cutoff_frequency` value are considered to be stopwords. This approach is very useful because it allows you to convert a general query to a domain-specific query, because the terms to skip depend on the text statistic. The correct value must be defined empirically.

The Boolean query created from the match query is very handy, but it suffers some of the common problems related to Boolean queries, such as term position. If the term position matters, you need to use another family of match queries, such as the `match_phrase` query. The `match_phrase` type in a match query builds long span queries from the query text. The parameters that can be used to improve the quality of the phrase query are the analyzers for text processing, and the slop parameter controls the distance between terms (see the *Using Span queries* recipe in this chapter).

If the last term is partially complete and you want to provide your users with the *query while writing* functionality, the phrase type can be set to `match_phrase_prefix`. This type builds a `span near` query in which the last clause is a span prefix term. This functionality is often used for **typeahead** widgets, as shown in the following screenshot:

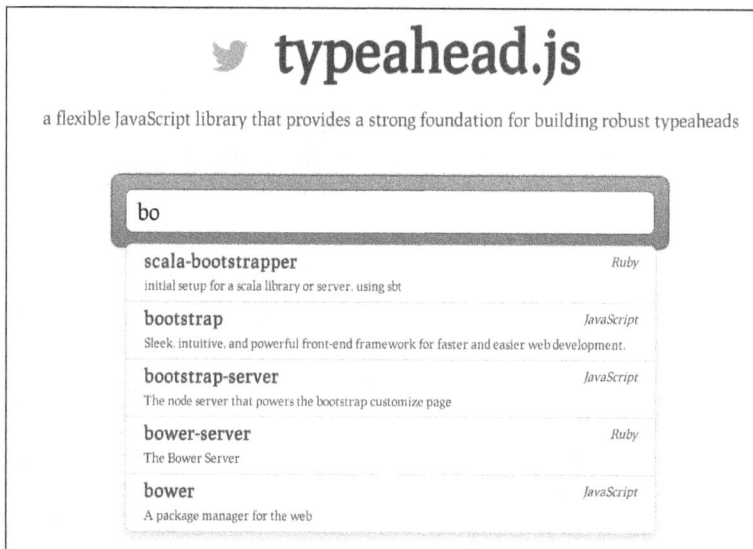

The match query is a very useful query type or, as I have previously defined, it helps to build several common queries internally.

See also

▸ The *Using Span queries* recipe in this chapter

▸ The *Using Boolean query/filter* recipe in this chapter

▸ The *Using Prefix query/filter* recipe in this chapter

Using an ID query/filter

The ID query/filter allows you to match documents by their IDs.

Getting ready

You need a working ElasticSearch cluster and an index populated with the script `chapter_05/populate_query.sh`, available in the code bundle for this book.

How to do it...

In order to execute ID queries/filters, perform the following steps:

1. The ID query to fetch IDs 1, 2, 3 of the type `test-type` is in this form:

```
curl -XPOST 'http://127.0.0.1:9200/test-index/test-type/_
search?pretty=true' -d '{
  "query": {
    "ids" : {
      "type" : "test-type",
      "values" : ["1", "2", "3"]
    }
  }
}'
```

2. The same query can be converted to a filter query, similar to this one:

```
curl -XPOST 'http://127.0.0.1:9200/test-index/test-type/_
search?pretty=true' -d '{
  "query": {
    "filtered": {
      "filter": {
        "ids" : {
          "type" : "test-type",
          "values" : ["1", "2", "3"]
        }
      },
      "query": {
        "match_all": {}
      }
    }
  }
}'
```

How it works...

Querying/filtering by ID is a fast operation because IDs are often cached in-memory for a fast lookup.

The following parameters are used in this query/filter:

▶ `ids` (required): This parameter is a list of the IDs that must be matched.

▶ `type` (optional): This parameter is a string or a list of strings that defines the types in which to search. If it is not defined, then the type is taken from the URL of the call.

> ElasticSearch internally stores the ID of a document in a special field called the _uid field composed of the type#id parameter. A _uid field is unique to an index.

Usually, the standard way to use an ID query/filter is to select documents. This query allows you to fetch documents without knowing the shard that contains the documents.

Documents are stored in shards based on a hash on their IDs. If a parent ID or a routing is defined, they are used to choose other shards. In these cases, the only way to fetch the document by knowing its ID is to use the ID query/filter.

If you need to fetch multiple IDs and there are no routing changes (due to the parent_id or routing parameter at index time), it's better not to use this kind of query, but to use the GET/Multi-GET API calls in order to get documents, as they are much faster and also work in real time.

See also

▸ The *Getting a document* recipe in *Chapter 4, Basic Operations*

▸ The *Speeding up GET operations (multi GET)* recipe in *Chapter 4, Basic Operations*

Using a has_child query/filter

ElasticSearch does not only support simple documents, but it also lets you define a hierarchy based on parent and children. The has_child query allows you to query for the parent documents of which children match some queries.

Getting ready

You need a working ElasticSearch cluster and an index populated with the script chapter_05/populate_query.sh, available in the code bundle for this book.

How to do it...

In order to execute the has_child queries/filters, perform the following steps:

1. Search for the parents, test-type, for which the children, test-type2, have a term in the field value as value1. We can create this kind of query as follows:

```
curl -XPOST 'http://127.0.0.1:9200/test-index/test-type/_
search?pretty=true' -d '{
  "query": {
    "has_child" : {
```

```
        "type" : "test-type2",
        "query" : {
          "term" : {
            "value" : "value1"
          }
        }
      }
    }
  }
}'
```

2. If scoring is not important for performances, it's better to reformulate the query as a filter in this way:

```
curl -XPOST 'http://127.0.0.1:9200/test-index/test-type/_
search?pretty=true' -d '{
  "query": {
    "filtered": {
      "filter": {
        "has_child" : {
          "type" : "test-type2",
          "query" : {
            "term" : {
              "value" : "value1"
            }
          }
        }
      },
      "query": {
        "match_all": {}
      }
    }
  }
}'
```

How it works...

This kind of query works by returning parent documents whose children match the query. The query executed on children can be of any type. The prerequisite for this kind of query is that the children must be correctly indexed in the shard of their parent.

Internally, this kind of query is a query executed on the children, and all the IDs of the children are used to filter the parent. A system must have enough memory to store the child IDs.

The parameters that are used to control this process are:

▶ `type`: This is the type of the children, which is part of the same index as the parent.

▶ `query`: This is the query that can be executed for selecting the children. For achieving this any kind of query can be used.

▶ `score_mode` (by default, `none`; the available values are `max`, `sum`, `avg`, and `none`): This parameter, if defined, allows you to aggregate the children's scores with the parent scores.

▶ `min_children` and `max_children` (optional): This is the minimum/maximum number of children required to match the parent document.

In ElasticSearch, a document must have only one parent, because the parent ID is used to choose the shard to put the children in.

> When working with child documents, it is important to remember that they *must* be stored in the same shard as their parents. So, special precautions must be taken to fetch, modify, and delete them if the parent (ID) is unknown. It's a good practice to store the `parent_id` parameter as a field of the child.

As the parent-child relationship can be considered similar to a foreign key of standard SQL, there are some limitations due the distributed nature of ElasticSearch, as follows:

▶ There must be a parent for the type.

▶ The *join* part of child/parent is done in a shard and not distributed on all the clusters, in order to reduce networking and increase its performance.

See also

▶ The *Indexing a document* recipe in *Chapter 4, Basic Operations*

Using a top_children query

In the previous recipe, the `has_child` query consumes a huge amount of memory because it requires you to fetch all child IDs. To bypass this limitation in huge data contexts, the `top_children` query allows you to fetch only the top child results. This scenario is very common: think of a blog with the latest 10 comments.

Getting ready

You need a working ElasticSearch cluster and an index populated with the script `chapter_05/populate_query.sh`, available in the code bundle for this book.

How to do it...

In order to execute the `top_children` query, perform the following steps:

▶ Search the `test-type` parent of which the `test-type2` top child has a term in the field value as `value1`. We can create a query, as follows:

```
curl -XPOST 'http://127.0.0.1:9200/test-index/test-type/_
search?pretty=true' -d '{
  "query": {
    "top_children" : {
      "type" : "test-type2",
      "query" : {
        "term" : {
          "value" : "value1"
        }
      },
      "score" : "max",
      "factor" : 5,
      "incremental_factor" : 2
    }
  }
}'
```

How it works...

This kind of query works by returning parent documents whose children match the query. The query executed on the children can be of any type.

Internally, this kind of query is a query executed on the children, and then the top IDs of the children are used to filter the parent. If the number of child IDs is not enough, other IDs are fetched.

The following parameters are used to control this process:

▶ `type`: This parameter denotes the type of the children. This type is a part of the same index as the parent.

▶ `query`: This parameter is a query that can be executed in order to select the children. Any kind of query can be used.

▶ `score` (max/ sum/ avg): This parameter allows you to control the chosen score in order to select the children.

- ▶ `factor` (by default, 5): This parameter is the multiplicative factor used to fetch the children. Because one parent can have a lot of children and the `parent_id` ID required for a query is a set of the returned children, you need to fetch more `parent_id` IDs from the children to be sure that you have the correct number of resulting hits. With a factor of 5 and 10 result hits required, about 50 child IDs must be fetched.

- ▶ `incremental_factor`: (by default, 2): This parameter is the multiplicative factor to be used if there are not enough child documents fetched by the first query. The equation that controls the number of fetched children is:

  `desired_hits * factor * incremental_factor`

See also

- ▶ The *Indexing a document* recipe in *Chapter 4, Basic Operations*
- ▶ The *Using a has_child query/filter* recipe in this chapter

Using a has_parent query/filter

In the previous recipes, we have seen the `has_child` query. ElasticSearch provides a query to search child documents based on the parent query: the `has_parent` query.

Getting ready

You need a working ElasticSearch cluster and an index populated with the script `chapter_05/populate_query.sh`, available in the code bundle for this book.

How to do it...

In order to execute the `has_parent` query/filter, perform the following steps:

1. Search for the `test-type2` children of which the `test-type` parents have a term `joe` in the `parsedtext` field. Create the query as follows:

```
curl -XPOST 'http://127.0.0.1:9200/test-index/test-
type2/_search?pretty=true' -d '{
  "query": {
    "has_parent" : {
      "type" : "test-type",
      "query" : {
        "term" : {
          "parsedtext" : "joe"
        }
```

```
            }
          }
        }
      }'
```

2. If scoring is not important, then it's better to reformulate the query as a filter in this way:

```
curl -XPOST 'http://127.0.0.1:9200/test-index/test-
type2/_search?pretty=true' -d '{
  "query": {
    "filtered": {
      "filter": {
        "has_parent" : {
          "type" : "test-type",
          "query" : {
            "term" : {
              "parsedtext" : "joe"
            }
          }
        }
      },
      "query": {
        "match_all": {}
      }
    }
  }'
```

How it works...

This kind of query works by returning child documents whose parent matches the parent query.

Internally, this subquery is executed on the parents, and all the IDs of the matching parents are used to filter the children. A system must have enough memory to store all the parent IDs.

The following parameters are used to control this process:

- ▶ `type`: This parameter suggests the type of the parent.
- ▶ `query`: This is the query that can be executed to select the parents. Any kind of query can be used.
- ▶ `score_type` (by default, `none`; the available values are `none` and `score`): Using this parameter with the default configuration `none`, ElasticSearch ignores the scores for the parent document, which reduces memory usage and increases performance. If it's set to `score`, the parent's query score is aggregated with the children's score.

See also

- ▶ The *Indexing a document* recipe in *Chapter 4, Basic Operations*

Using a regexp query/filter

In the previous recipes, we saw different term queries (terms, fuzzy, and prefix). Another powerful terms query is the `regexp` (regular expression) query.

Getting ready

You will need a working ElasticSearch cluster and an index populated with the script `chapter_05/populate_query.sh`, available in the code bundle for this book.

How to do it...

In order to execute a `regexp` query/filter, perform the following steps:

1. Execute a `regexp` term query from the command line:

```
curl -XPOST 'http://127.0.0.1:9200/test-index/test-
type/_search?pretty=true' -d '{
  "query": {
    = "regexp": {
      "parsedtext": {
        "value": "j.*",
        "flags" : "INTERSECTION|COMPLEMENT|EMPTY"
      }
    }
  }
}'
```

2. If scoring is not important, it's better to reformulate the query as a filter in this way:

```
curl -XPOST 'http://127.0.0.1:9200/test-index/test-
type/_search?pretty=true' -d '{
  "query": {
    "filtered": {
      "filter": {
        "regexp": {
          "parsedtext": "j.*"
        }
      },
      "query": {
        "match_all": {}
      }
    }
  }
}'
```

How it works...

The `regexp` query/filter executes the regular expression against all the terms of the documents. Internally, Lucene compiles the regular expression in an **automaton** to improve performance, so, the performance of this query/filter is generally not very fast, as the performance depends on the regular expression used.

To speed up the `regexp` query/filter, a good approach is to have a regular expression that doesn't start with a wildcard.

The following parameters are used to control this process:

- `boost` (by default, `1.0`): These are the values used to boost the score for the `regexp` query.
- `flags`: This is a list of one or more flags pipe (`|`) delimited. These flags are available:
  - ALL: This flag enables all optional `regexp` syntax
  - ANYSTRING: This flag enables any string (`@`)
  - AUTOMATON: This flag enables the named automata (`<identifier>`)
  - COMPLEMENT: This flag enables the complement (`~`)
  - EMPTY: This flag enables an empty language (`#`)
  - INTERSECTION: This flag enables intersection (`&`)
  - INTERVAL: This flag enables numerical intervals (`<n-m>`)
  - NONE: This flag enables no optional `regexp` syntax

> To avoid poor performance in a search, don't execute `regex` starting with `.*`.

See also

- Read the official documentation for Regexp queries at `http://www.elasticsearch.org/guide/en/elasticsearch/reference/current/query-dsl-regexp-query.html`
- The *Querying/filtering for terms* recipe in this chapter

Using a function score query

This kind of query is one of the most powerful queries available, because it allows extensive customization. The function score query allows you to define a function that controls the score of the documents that are returned by a query.

Generally, these functions are CPU-intensive and executing them on a large dataset requires a lot of memory, but computing them in a small subset can significantly improve the search quality.

These are the common scenarios used for this query:

- ▸ Creating a custom score function (for example with the decay function)
- ▸ Creating a custom boost factor, for example, based on another field (such as boosting a document by its distance from a point)
- ▸ Creating a custom filter score function, for example based on scripting ElasticSearch capabilities
- ▸ Ordering the documents randomly

Getting ready

You need a working ElasticSearch cluster and an index populated with the script (`chapter_05/populate_query.sh`) available in the code bundle for this book.

How to do it...

In order to execute a function score query, perform the following steps:

1. Execute a function score query using the following command line:

```
curl -XPOST 'localhost:9200/_search?pretty' -d '{
  "query": {
    "function_score": {
      "query": {
        "query_string": {
          "query": "bill"
        }
      },
      "functions": [{
        "linear": {
          "position": {
            "origin": "0",
            "scale": "20"
```

```
            }
        }
        }],
        "score_mode": "multiply"
        }
    }
}'
```

We execute a query to search for `bill`, and we score the result with the `linear` function on the `position` field.

2. This is how the result should look:

```
{
  ...truncated...
  "hits" : {
    "total" : 2,
    "max_score" : 0.41984466,
    "hits" : [ {
      "_index" : "test-index",
      "_type" : "test-type",
      "_id" : "2",
      "_score" : 0.41984466,
      "_source":{"position": 2, ...truncated...}
    }, {
      "_index" : "test-index",
      "_type" : "test-type",
      "_id" : "3",
      "_score" : 0.12544023,
      "_source":{"position": 3, ...truncated... }
    } ]
  }
}
```

How it works...

The function score query is probably the most complex query type to master due to the natural complexity of the mathematical algorithm involved in the scoring.

The following is the generic full form of the function score query:

```
"function_score": {
  "(query|filter)": {},
  "boost": "boost for the whole query",
  "functions": [
```

```
    {
      "filter": {},
      "FUNCTION": {}
    },
    {
      "FUNCTION": {}
    }
  ],
  "max_boost": number,
  "boost_mode": "(multiply|replace|)",
  "score_mode": "(multiply|max|)",
  "script_score": {},
  "random_score": {"seed ": number}
}
```

These are the parameters that exist in the preceding code:

- ▸ query or filter (optional, by default the match_all query): This is the query/filter used to match the required documents.

- ▸ boost (by default, 1.0): This is the boost that is to be applied to the whole query.

- ▸ functions: This is a list of the functions used to score the queries. In a simple case, use only one function. In the function object, a filter can be provided to apply the function only to a subset of documents, because the filter is applied first.

- ▸ max_boost (by default, java FLT_MAX): This sets the maximum allowed value for the boost score.

- ▸ boost_mode (by default, multiply): This parameter defines how the function score is combined with the query score. These are the possible values:

  - ❏ multiply (default): The query score and function score is multiplied using this parameter

  - ❏ replace: By using this value, only the function score is used, while the query score is ignored

  - ❏ sum: Using this, the query score and function score are added

  - ❏ avg: This value is the average between the query score and the function score

  - ❏ max: This is the maximum value of the query score and the function score

  - ❏ min: This is the minimum value of the query score and the function score

- ▸ score_mode (by default, multiply): This parameter defines how the resulting function scores (when multiple functions are defined) are combined. These are the possible values:

  - ❏ multiply: The scores are multiplied

  - ❏ sum: The scores are added together

- ❏ `avg`: The scores are averaged
- ❏ `first`: The filter is applied to the first function that has a match
- ❏ `max`: The maximum score is used
- ❏ `min`: The minimum score is used

- ▶ `script_score` (optional): This parameter allows you to define a script score function that is to be used in order to compute the score (ElasticSearch scripting will be discussed in *Chapter 7, Scripting*). This parameter is very useful to implement simple script algorithms. The original score value is in the `_score` function scope. This allows you to define similar algorithms, as follows:

```
"script_score": {
  "params": {
    "param1": 2,
    "param2": 3.1
  },
  "script": "_score * doc['my_numeric_field'].value / pow(param1, param2)"
}
```

- ▶ `random_score` (optional): This parameter allows you to randomly score the documents. It is very useful to retrieve records randomly.

ElasticSearch provides native support for the most common scoring decay distribution algorithms, as follows:

- ▶ **Linear**: This algorithm is used to linearly distribute the scores based on a distance from a value
- ▶ **Exponential** (exp): This algorithm is used for the exponential decay function
- ▶ **Gaussian** (gauss): This algorithm is used for the Gaussian decay function

Choosing the correct function distribution depends on the context and data distribution.

See also

- ▶ *Chapter 7, Scripting,* to learn more about scripting
- ▶ The official ElasticSearch documentation at `http://www.elasticsearch.org/guide/en/elasticsearch/reference/current/query-dsl-function-score-query.html`
- ▶ Blog posts at `http://jontai.me/blog/2013/01/advanced-scoring-in-elasticsearch/` and `https://www.found.no/foundation/function-scoring/`

Using exists and missing filters

One of the main characteristics of ElasticSearch is its schema-less indexing capability. Records in ElasticSearch can have missing values. To manage them, two kinds of filters are supported:

▸ **Exists filter**: This checks whether a field exists in a document

▸ **Missing filter**: This checks whether a field is missing

Getting ready

You need a working ElasticSearch cluster and an index populated with the script `chapter_05/populate_query.sh`, available in the code bundle for this book.

How to do it...

In order to execute existing and missing filters, perform the following steps:

1. To search all the test-type documents that have a field called `parsedtext`, this will be the query:

```
curl -XPOST 'http://127.0.0.1:9200/test-index/test-type/_
search?pretty=true' -d '{
  "query": {
    "filtered": {
      "filter": {
        "exists": {
          "field":"parsedtext"
        }
      },
      "query": {
        "match_all": {}
      }
    }
  }
}'
```

2. To search all the `test-type` documents that do not have a field called `parsedtext`, this is how the query should look:

```
curl -XPOST 'http://127.0.0.1:9200/test-index/test-type/_
search?pretty=true' -d '{
  "query": {
    "filtered": {
```

```
      "filter": {
        "missing": {
          "field":"parsedtext"
        }
      },
      "query": {
        "match_all": {}
      }
    }
  }
}'
```

How it works...

The exists and missing filters take only a `field` parameter, which contains the name of the field to be checked.

If you use simple fields, there are no pitfalls, but if you are using a single embedded object or a list of these objects, you need to use a subobject field, due to the way in which ElasticSearch/Lucene works.

The following example helps you understand how ElasticSearch maps JSON objects to Lucene documents internally. Take the example of the following JSON document:

```
{
  "name":"Paul",
  "address":{
    "city":"Sydney",
    "street":"Opera House Road",
    "number":"44"
  }
}
```

ElasticSearch will internally index the document, as shown here:

```
name:paul
address.city:Sydney
address.street:Opera House Road
address.number:44
```

As you can see, there is no indexed field named `address`, so the existing filter on the term `address` fails. To match documents with an address, you must search for a subfield (such as, `address.city`).

Using and/or/not filters

When building complex queries, some typical Boolean operation filters are required, as they allow you to construct complex filter relations as in the traditional relational database world.

Any query DSL cannot be completed if there is no and, or, or not filter.

Getting ready

You need a working ElasticSearch cluster and an index populated with the script chapter_05/populate_query.sh, available in the code bundle for this book.

How to do it...

In order to execute and/or/not filters, perform the following steps:

1. Search for documents with parsedtext equal to joe and uuid equal to 11111 in this way:

```
curl -XPOST 'http://127.0.0.1:9200/test-index/test-type/_
search?pretty=true' -d '{
  "query": {
    "filtered": {
      "filter": {
        "and": [
          {
            "term": {
              "parsedtext":"joe"
            }
          },
          {
            "term": {
              "uuid":"11111"
            }
          }
        ]
      },
      "query": {
        "match_all": {}
      }
    }
  }
}'
```

2. Search for documents with uuid equal to 11111 or 22222 with a similar query:

```
curl -XPOST 'http://127.0.0.1:9200/test-index/test-type/_
search?pretty=true' -d '{
  "query": {
    "filtered": {
      "filter": {
        "or": [
          {
            "term": {
              "uuid":"11111"
            }
          },
          {
            "term": {
              "uuid":"22222"
            }
          }
        ]
      },
      "query": {
        "match_all": {}
      }
    }
  }
}'
```

3. Search for documents with uuid *not* equal to 11111 using this query:

```
curl -XPOST 'http://127.0.0.1:9200/test-index/test-type/_search'
-d '{
  "query": {
    "filtered": {
      "filter": {
        "not": {
          "term": {
            "uuid":"11111"
          }
        }
      },
      "query": {
        "match_all": {}
      }
    }
  }
}'
```

How it works...

The Boolean operator filters are the simplest filters available in ElasticSearch. The and and or queries accept a list of subfilters that can be used. This kind of Boolean operator filters are very fast, as in Lucene they are converted to very efficient bitwise operations on document IDs.

Also, the not filter is as fast as the Boolean operators, but it requires only a single filter to be negated.

From a user's point of view, you can consider these fields as traditional numerical group operations, as follows:

 ▶ and: In this operation, the documents that match all the subfilters are returned

 ▶ or: In this operation, the documents that match a least one of the subfields are returned

 ▶ not: In this operation, the documents that don't match the subfield are returned

> For performance reasons, a Boolean filter is faster than a bulk of and/or/not filters.

Using a geo bounding box filter

One of the most common operations in geolocalization is searching for a box (square).

Getting ready

You need a working ElasticSearch cluster and an index populated with the GeoScript chapter_05/geo/populate_geo.sh, available in the code bundle for this book.

How to do it...

A search to filter documents related to a bounding box (40.03, 72.0) and (40.717, 70.99) can be done with a similar query:

```
curl -XGET http://127.0.0.1:9200/test-mindex/_search?pretty -d '{
  "query": {
    "filtered": {
      "filter": {
        "geo_bounding_box": {
          "pin.location": {
            "bottom_right": {
```

```
          "lat": 40.03,
          "lon": 72.0
        },
        "top_left": {
          "lat": 40.717,
          "lon": 70.99
        }
      }
    }
  },
  "query": {
    "match_all": {}
  }
}
}
}'
```

How it works...

ElasticSearch has a lot of optimization options to search for a box shape. The latitude and longitude are indexed for a fast range check, so this kind of filter is executed really quickly.

The parameters required to execute a `geo_bounding_box` filter are the `top_left` and `bottom_right` geo-points.

It's possible to use several representations of a geo-point, as described in the *Mapping a geo point field* recipe in *Chapter 3, Managing Mapping*.

See also

▶ The *Mapping a geo point field* recipe in *Chapter 3, Managing Mapping*

Using a geo polygon filter

The previous recipe, *Using a geo bounding box filter*, shows you how to filter on a square section, which is the most common case. ElasticSearch provides a way to filter user-defined polygonal shapes via the `geo_polygon` filter. This filter is useful if the filter is based on a country/region/district shape.

Getting ready

You need a working ElasticSearch cluster and an index populated with the GeoScript `chapter_05/geo/populate_geo.sh`, available in the code bundle for this book.

How to do it...

Search for documents in which `pin.location` is part of a triangle (a shape made up of three geopoints), as follows:

```
curl -XGET http://127.0.0.1:9200/test-mindex/_search?pretty -d '{
  "query": {
    "filtered": {
      "filter": {
        "geo_polygon" {
          "pin.location": {
            "points": [
              {
                "lat": 50,
                "lon": -30
              },
              {
                "lat": 30,
                "lon": -80
              },
              {
                "lat": 80,
                "lon": -90
              }
            ]
          }
        }
      },
      "query": {
        "match_all": {}
      }
    }
  }
}'
```

How it works...

The geo polygon filter allows you to define your own shape with a list of geo-points so that ElasticSearch can filter the documents that are in the polygon.

It can be considered an extension of the geo bounding box for a generic polygonal form.

See also

▸ The *Mapping a geo point field* recipe in *Chapter 3, Managing Mapping*

▸ The *Using a geo bounding box filter* recipe in this chapter

Using geo distance filter

When you are working with geolocations, one of the most common tasks is to filter results based on their distance from a location. This scenario covers the following common site requirements:

- Finding the nearest restaurant in a 20 km distance
- Finding your nearest friends in a 10 km range

The `geo_distance` filter is used to achieve this goal.

Getting ready

You need a working ElasticSearch cluster and an index populated with the GeoScript `chapter_05/geo/populate_geo.sh`, available in the code bundle for this book.

How to do it...

Search for documents in which the `pin.location` is 200 km away from latitude 40, longitude 70, as follows:

```
curl -XGET 'http://127.0.0.1:9200/test-mindex/_search?pretty' -d '{
  "query": {
    "filtered": {
      "filter": {
        "geo_distance": {
          "pin.location": {
            "lat": 40,
            "lon": 70
          },
          "distance": "200km",
          "optimize_bbox": "memory"
        }
      },
      "query": {
        "match_all": {}
      }
    }
  }
}'
```

How it works...

As discussed in the *Mapping a geo point Field* recipe in *Chapter 3, Managing Mapping*, there are several ways to define a geo point, and it is internally saved in an optimized way so that it can be searched.

The distance filter executes a distance calculation between a given geo-point and the points in the documents, returning hits that satisfy the distance requirement.

These parameters control the distance filter:

- ▶ The field and the point of reference to be used in order to calculate the distance. In the preceding example, we have `pin.location` and (40,70).
- ▶ `distance`: This parameter defines the distance to be considered. It is usually expressed as a string by a number plus a unit.
- ▶ `unit` (optional): This parameter can be the unit of the distance value if the distance is defined as a number. These are the valid values:
    - ❑ `in` or `inch`
    - ❑ `yd` or `yards`
    - ❑ `m` or `miles`
    - ❑ `km` or `kilometers`
    - ❑ `m` or `meters`
    - ❑ `mm` or `millimeters`
    - ❑ `cm` or `centimeters`
- ▶ `distance_type` (by default, `sloppy_arc`; the valid choices are `arc/sloppy_arc/ plane`): This parameter defines the type of algorithm used to calculate the distance.
- ▶ `optimize_bbox`: This parameter defines that you first need to filter with a bounding box in order to improve performance. This kind of optimization removes a lot of document evaluations, limiting the check to values that match a square. These are the valid values for this parameter:
    - ❑ `memory` (default): This parameter does the memory check.
    - ❑ `indexed`: This parameter checks using the indexing values. It only works if the latitude and longitude are indexed.
    - ❑ `none`: This parameter disables bounding box optimization.

There's more...

There's a range version of this filter too that allows you to filter by range. The `geo_distance_range` filter works as a standard range filter (see the *Using a range query/filter* recipe in this chapter), in which the range is defined in the `from` and `to` parameters. For example, the preceding code can be converted into a range without the `from` part, as follows:

```
curl -XGET 'http://127.0.0.1:9200/test-mindex/_search?pretty' -d '{
  "query": {
    "filtered": {
      "filter": {
        "geo_distance_range": {
          "pin.location": {
            "lat": 40,
            "lon": 70
          },
          "to": "200km",
          "optimize_bbox": "memory"
        }
      },
      "query": {
        "match_all": {}
      }
    }
  }
}'
```

See also

- ▶ The *Mapping a geo point field* recipe in *Chapter 3, Managing Mapping*
- ▶ The *Using a range query/filter* in this chapter

Using a QueryString query

In the previous recipes, we saw several types of query that use text to match the results. The QueryString query is a special type of query that allows you to define complex queries by mixing field rules.

It uses the Lucene query parser in order to parse text to complex queries.

Getting ready

You need a working ElasticSearch cluster and an index populated with the GeoScript `chapter_05/populate_query.sh`, available in the code bundle for this book.

How to do it...

We want to retrieve all the documents that match `parsedtext`, `joe`, or `bill`, with a `price` between `4` and `6`.

To execute this QueryString query, this is how the code will look:

```
curl -XPOST 'http://127.0.0.1:9200/test-index/test-type/_
search?pretty=true' -d ' {
  "query": {
    "query_string": {
      "default_field": "parsedtext",
      "query": "(bill OR joe) AND price:[4 TO 6]"
    }
  }
}'
```

The search will return three results.

How it works...

The QueryString query is one of the most powerful types of queries. The only required field is `query`, which contains the query that must be parsed with the Lucene query parser (`http://lucene.apache.org/core/4_10_2/queryparser/org/apache/lucene/queryparser/classic/package-summary.html`).

The Lucene query parser is able to analyze complex query syntax and convert it to many of the query types that we have seen in the previous recipes.

These are the optional parameters that can be passed to the QueryString query:

- ▶ `default_field` (by default, `_all`): This defines the default field to be used for querying. It can also be set at the index level, defining the `index.query.default_field` index property.

- ▶ `fields`: This defines a list of fields to be used during querying and replaces the `default_field` field. The `fields` parameter also allows you to use wildcards as values (such as, `city.*`).

- ▶ `default_operator` (by default, `OR`; the available values are `AND` and `OR`): This is the default operator to be used for text in a `query` parameter.

- ▶ `analyzer`: This is the analyzer that must be used for the query string.

- ▶ `allow_leading_wildcard` (by default, `true`): This parameter allows the use of the `*` and `?` wildcards as the first character. Using similar wildcards leads to performance penalties.

- ▶ lowercase_expanded_terms (by default, true): This controls whether all expansion terms (generated by fuzzy, range, wildcard, and prefix) must be lowercased.

- ▶ enable_position_increments (by default, true): This enables the position increment in queries. For every query token, the positional value is incremented by 1.

- ▶ fuzzy_max_expansions (by default, 50): This controls the number of terms to be used in a fuzzy term expansion.

- ▶ fuzziness (by default, AUTO): This sets the fuzziness value for fuzzy queries.

- ▶ fuzzy_prefix_length (by default, 0): This sets the prefix length for fuzzy queries.

- ▶ phrase_slop (by default, 0): This sets the default slop (the number of optional terms that can be present in the middle of given terms) for phrases. If it is set to zero, the query will be an exact phrase match.

- ▶ boost (by default, 1.0): This defines the boost value of the query.

- ▶ analyze_wildcard (by default, false): This enables the processing of the wildcard terms in the query.

- ▶ auto_generate_phrase_queries (by default, false): This enables the autogeneration of phrase queries from the query string.

- ▶ minimum_should_match: This controls how many should clauses should be verified to match the result. The value can be an integer (such as, 3), a percentage (such as, 40%), or a combination of both.

- ▶ lenient (by default, false): If set to true, the parser will ignore all format-based failures (such as date conversion from text to number).

- ▶ locale (by default, ROOT): This is the locale used for string conversion.

There's more...

The query parser is very powerful and can support a wide range of complex queries. These are the most common cases:

- ▶ field:text: This parameter is used to match a field that contains some text. It's mapped on a term query/filter.

- ▶ field:(term1 OR term2): This parameter is used to match some terms in OR. It's mapped on a term query/filter.

- ▶ field:"text": This parameter is used for a exact text match. It's mapped on a match query.

- ▶ _exists_:field: This parameter is used to match documents that have a field. It's mapped on an exists filter.

- ▶ _missing_:field: This parameter is used to match documents that don't have a field. It's mapped on a missing filter.

- ► `field:[start TO end]`: This parameter is used to match a range from the `start` value to the `end` value. The `start` and `end` values can be terms, numbers, or valid date-time values. The `start` and `end` values are included in the range. If you want to exclude a range, you must replace the `[]` delimiters with `{ }`.

- ► `field:/regex/`: This parameter is used to match regular expressions.

The query parser also supports a text modifier, which is used to manipulate the text functionalities. These are the most commonly used text modifiers:

- ► Fuzziness using the `text~` form: The default fuzziness value is 2, which allows the **Damerau–Levenshtein** edit-distance algorithm to be used (`http://en.wikipedia.org/wiki/Damerau%E2%80%93Levenshtein_distance`).

- ► Wildcards with `?`: This replaces a single character or `*` to replace zero or more characters (such as `b?ll` or `bi*` to match bill).

- ► Proximity search `"term1 term2"~3`: This allows you to match phrase terms with a defined slop (such as, `"my umbrella"~3` matches `"my green umbrella"`, `"my new umbrella"`, and so on).

See also

- ► The Lucene official query parser syntax reference at `http://lucene.apache.org/core/4_10_2/queryparser/org/apache/lucene/queryparser/classic/package-summary.html`.

- ► The official ElasticSearch documentation about the query string query at `http://www.elasticsearch.org/guide/en/elasticsearch/reference/current/query-dsl-query-string-query.html`.

Using a template query

ElasticSearch provides the capability to provide a template and some parameters to fill it. This functionality is very useful because it allows you to manage query templates stored in the server's filesystem or in the `.scripts` index, allowing you to change them without changing your application code.

Getting ready

You need a working ElasticSearch cluster and an index populated with the GeoScript `chapter_05/populate_query.sh`, available in the code bundle for this book.

How to do it...

The Template query is composed of two components: the query and the parameters that must be filled in. We can execute a template query in several ways.

To execute an embedded template query, use the following code:

```
curl -XPOST 'http://127.0.0.1:9200/test-index/test-type/_
search?pretty=true' -d '{
  "query": {
    "template": {
      "query": {
        "term": {
          "uuid": "{{value}}"
        }
      },
      "params": {
        "value": "22222"
      }
    }
  }
}'
```

If you want to use an indexed stored template, perform the following steps:

1. Store the template in the `.scripts` index:

   ```
   curl -XPOST 'http://127.0.0.1:9200/_search/template/myTemplate' -d
   '
   {
     "template": {
       "query": {
         "term": {
           "uuid": "{{value}}"
         }
       }
     }
   }'
   ```

2. Now, call the template with the following code:

   ```
   curl -XPOST 'http://127.0.0.1:9200/test-index/test-type/_search/
   template?pretty=true' -d '{
     "template": {
       "id": "myTemplate"
     },
   ```

```
    "params": {
      "value": "22222"
    }
  }'
```

How it works...

A template query is composed of two components:

> ▸ A template, that can be any query object that is supported by ElasticSearch. The template uses the `mustache` (`http://mustache.github.io/`) syntax, a very common syntax to express templates.

> ▸ An optional dictionary of parameters to be used in order to fill the template.

When the search query is called, the template is loaded, populated with the parameter data, and executed as a normal query.

The template query is a shortcut to use the same query with different values.

Typically, the template is generated by executing the query in the standard way and then adding parameters, if required, when *templating* it. The template query also allows you to define the template as a string, but the user must pay attention to escaping it (see the official documentation at `http://www.elasticsearch.org/guide/en/elasticsearch/reference/current/query-dsl-template-query.html` for escaping templates). It allows you to remove the query execution from the application code and put it in the filesystem or indices.

There's more...

The template query can retrieve a previously stored template from the disk (it must be stored in the `config/scripts` directory with the `.mustache` extension) or from the `.scripts` special index.

The search template can be managed in ElasticSearch via the special end points, `/_search/template`. These are the special endpoints:

> ▸ To store a template:
>
> ```
> curl -XPOST 'http://127.0.0.1:9200/_search/template/<template_name>' -d
> <template_body>
> ```

> ▸ To retrieve a template:
>
> ```
> curl -XGET 'http://127.0.0.1:9200/_search/template/<template_name>'
> ```

▶ To delete a template:

```
curl -XDELETE 'http://127.0.0.1:9200/_search/template/<template_
name>'
```

> The indexed templates and scripts are stored in the `.script` index. This is a normal index and can be managed as a standard data index.

See also

▶ The official mustache documentation at `http://mustache.github.io/`

▶ The official ElasticSearch documentation about search templates at `http://www.elasticsearch.org/guide/en/elasticsearch/reference/current/search-template.html`

▶ The official ElasticSearch documentation about query templates at `http://www.elasticsearch.org/guide/en/elasticsearch/reference/current/query-dsl-template-query.html`

6
Aggregations

In this chapter, we will cover the following topics:

- ▶ Executing an aggregation
- ▶ Executing the stats aggregation
- ▶ Executing the terms aggregation
- ▶ Executing the range aggregation
- ▶ Executing the histogram aggregation
- ▶ Executing the date histogram aggregation
- ▶ Executing the filter aggregation
- ▶ Executing the global aggregation
- ▶ Executing the geo distance aggregation
- ▶ Executing the nested aggregation
- ▶ Executing the top hit aggregation

Introduction

In developing search solutions, not only are results important, but they also help us to improve quality and search focus.

ElasticSearch provides a powerful tool to achieve these goals: **aggregations**.

The main usage of aggregations is to provide additional data to the search results to improve their quality or to augment them with additional information. For example, in searching for news articles, facets that can be interesting for calculation are the articles written by authors and the date histogram of their publishing date.

Thus, aggregations are used not only to improve results, but also to provide an insight into stored data (Analytics); for this, we have a lot of tools, and one of which is called **Kibana** (http://www.elasticsearch.org/overview/kibana/).

Generally, the aggregations are displayed to the end user with graphs or a group of filtering options (for example, a list of categories for the search results).

The actual aggregation framework is an evolution of the previous ElasticSearch functionality called **facets**. Facets were helpful and powerful, but had a lot of limitations in their design. The ElasticSearch team decided to evolve them into the aggregation framework (facets are already deprecated in ElasticSearch 1.x, and they will be removed from the next ElasticSearch major release also). For a complete coverage of facets, take a look at *ElasticSearch Cookbook*, *Packt Publishing*, at http://www.packtpub.com/elasticsearch-cookbook/book.

Since the ElasticSearch aggregation framework provides scripting functionalities, it is able to cover a wide spectrum of scenarios. In this chapter, some simple scripting functionalities are shown related to aggregations, but we will cover in-depth scripting in the next chapter.

The aggregation framework is also the base for advanced analytics as shown in software such as Kibana (http://www.elasticsearch.org/overview/kibana/), or similar software. It's very important to understand how the various types of aggregations work and when to choose them.

Executing an aggregation

ElasticSearch provides several functionalities other than search; it allows executing statistics and real-time analytics on searches via aggregations.

Getting ready

You need a working ElasticSearch cluster and an index populated with the script, which is available at https://github.com/aparo/elasticsearch-cookbook-second-edition.

How to do it...

To execute an aggregation, we will perform the steps given as follows:

1. From the command line, we can execute a query with aggregations:

```
curl -XGET 'http://127.0.0.1:9200/test-index/test-
type/_search?pretty=true&size=0' -d '{
  "query": {
    "match_all": {}
  },
```

```
      "aggregations": {
        "tag": {
          "terms": {
            "field": "tag",
            "size": 10
          }
        }
      }
    }
  }'
```

In this case, we have used a `match_all` query plus a terms aggregation that is used to count terms.

2. The result returned by ElasticSearch, if everything is all right, should be:

```
{
  "took" : 3,
  "timed_out" : false,
  "_shards" : {… truncated …},
  "hits" : {
    "total" : 1000,
    "max_score" : 0.0,
    "hits" : [ ]
  },
  "aggregations" : {
    "tag" : {
      "buckets" : [ {
        "key" : "laborum",
        "doc_count" : 25
      }, {
        "key" : "quidem",
        "doc_count" : 15
      }, {
        "key" : "maiores",
        "doc_count" : 14
      }, {
…. Truncated ….
      }, {
        "key" : "praesentium",
        "doc_count" : 9
      } ]
    }
  }
}
```

The results are not returned because we have fixed the result size to 0. The aggregation result is contained in the `aggregation` field. Each type of aggregation has its own result format (the explanation of this kind of result is in the *Executing terms aggregation* recipe in this chapter).

> It's possible to execute an aggregation calculation without returning search results to reduce bandwidth by passing the search `size` parameter set to 0.

How it works...

Every search can return an aggregation calculation, computed on the query results; the aggregation phase is an additional step in query postprocessing—for example, highlighting the results. To activate the aggregation phase, an aggregation must be defined using the `aggs` or `aggregations` keyword.

There are several types of aggregation that can be used in ElasticSearch.

In this chapter, we'll cover all standard aggregations available; additional aggregation types can be provided with a plugin and scripting.

Aggregations are the bases for real-time analytics. They allow us to execute:

- ▶ Counting
- ▶ Histograms
- ▶ The range aggregation
- ▶ Statistics
- ▶ The geo distance aggregation

The following shows the executed query results using a histogram:

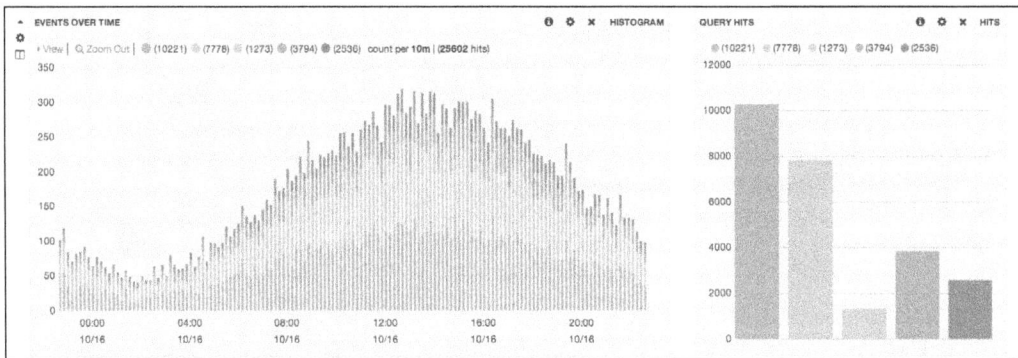

Aggregations are always executed on search hits; they are usually computed in a Map/Reduce way. The map step is distributed in shards, but the reduce step is done in the *called* node.

As aggregation computation requires a lot of data to be kept in memory; it can be very memory-intensive. For example, to execute a terms aggregation, it requires that all unique terms in the field, which is used for aggregating, be kept in memory. Executing this operation on million of documents requires storing a large number of values in memory.

The aggregation framework was introduced in ElasticSearch 1.x as an evolution of the facets feature. Its main difference from facets is the possibility of executing the analytics with several nesting levels of subaggregations; facets were plain and were limited to a single-level aggregation. Aggregations keep information of documents that go into an aggregation bucket, and an aggregation output can be the input of the next aggregation.

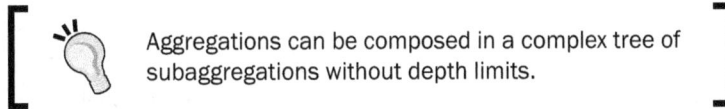

> Aggregations can be composed in a complex tree of subaggregations without depth limits.

The generic form for an aggregation is as follows:

```
"aggregations" : {
  "<aggregation_name>" : {
    "<aggregation_type>" : {
      <aggregation_body>
    }
    [,"aggregations" : { [<sub_aggregation>]+ } ]?
  }
  [,"<aggregation_name_2>" : { ... } ]*
}
```

Aggregation nesting allows us to cover very advanced scenarios in executing analytics such as aggregating data by country, by region, or by people's ages, where age groups are ordered in the descending order. There are no more limits in mastering analytics.

The following schema summarizes the main difference between the deprecated facets system and the aggregation framework:

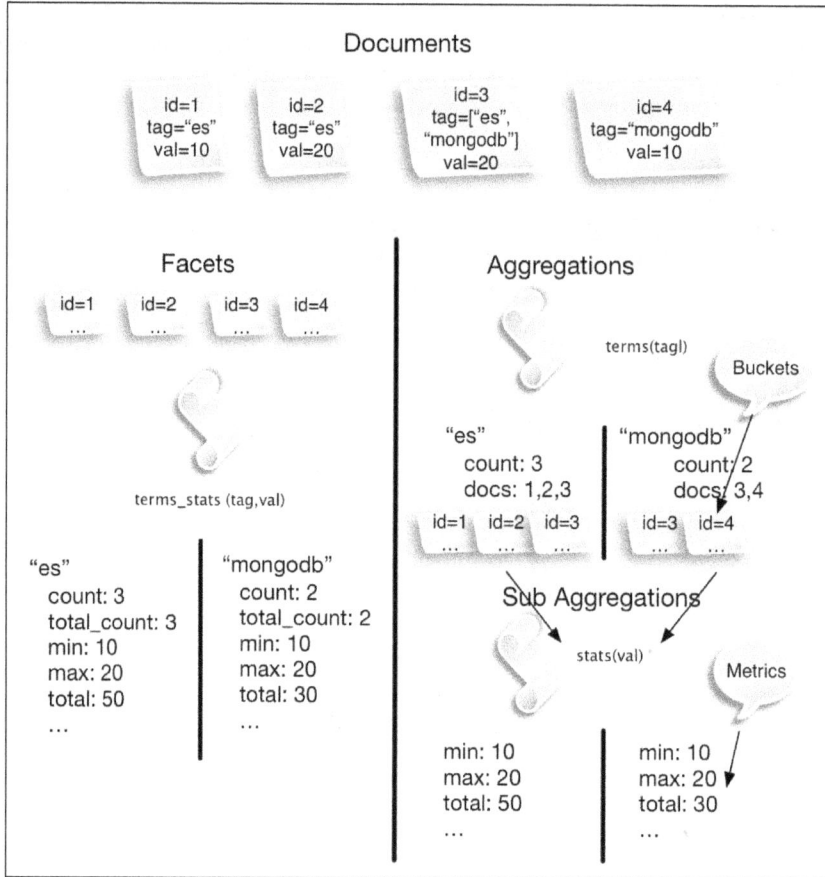

As you can see in the preceding figure, there are two kinds of aggregators:

  ▸ **Bucketing aggregators**: They produce buckets, where a bucket has an associated value and a set of documents (for example, the terms aggregator produces a bucket per term for the field it's aggregating on). A document can end up in multiple buckets if the document has multiple values for the field being aggregated on (in our example, the document with id=3). If a bucket aggregator has one or more *downstream* (such as, child) aggregators, these are run on each generated bucket.

  ▸ **Metric aggregators**: They receive a set of documents as input and produce statistical results computed for the specified field. The output of metric aggregators does not include any information linked to individual documents; it contains just the statistical data.

Generally, the order of buckets depends on the bucket aggregator used—for example, when using the terms aggregator, the buckets are, by default, ordered by count. The aggregation framework allows us to order by subaggregation metrics (for example, the preceding example can be ordered by the `stats.avg` value).

See also

▶ Refer to the *Executing the terms aggregation* recipe in this chapter for a more detailed explanation of aggregation

Executing the stats aggregation

The most commonly used metric aggregations are **stats aggregations**. They are generally used as terminal aggregation steps to compute a value to be used directly or for sorting.

Getting ready

You need a working ElasticSearch cluster and an index populated with the script (`chapter_06/ executing_stat_aggregations.sh`) available at `https://github.com/aparo/ elasticsearch-cookbook-second-edition`.

How to do it...

To execute a stats aggregation, we will perform the steps given as follows:

1. We want to calculate all statistical values of a matched query in the `age` field. The REST call should be as follows:

```
curl -XPOST "http://127.0.0.1:9200/test-index/_search?size=0" -d '
{
  "query": {
    "match_all": {}
  },
  "aggs": {
    "age_stats": {
      "extended_stats": {
        "field": "age"
      }
    }
  }
}'
```

2. The result, if everything is fine, should be:

```
{
  "took" : 2,
  "timed_out" : false,
  "_shards" : { ...truncated...},
  "hits" : {
    "total" : 1000,
    "max_score" : 0.0,
    "hits" : [ ]
  },
  "aggregations" : {
    "age_stats" : {
      "count" : 1000,
      "min" : 1.0,
      "max" : 100.0,
      "avg" : 53.243,
      "sum" : 53243.0,
      "sum_of_squares" : 3653701.0,
      "variance" : 818.8839509999999,
      "std_deviation" : 28.616148430562767
    }
  }
}
```

In the answer, under the `aggregations` field, we have the statistical results of our aggregation under the defined field `age_stats`.

How it works...

After the search phase, if any aggregations are defined, they are computed.

In this case, we have requested an `extended_stats` aggregation labeled `age_stats` and that computes a lot of statistical indicators.

The available statistical aggregators are:

▶ `min`: This computes the minimum value for a group of buckets.

▶ `max`: This computes the maximum value for a group of buckets.

▶ `avg`: This computes the average value for a group of buckets.

▶ `sum`: This computes the sum of all buckets.

▶ `value_count`: This computes the count of values in the bucket.

▶ `stats`: This computes all the base metrics such as `min`, `max`, `avg`, `count`, and `sum`.

- ▸ `extended_stats`: This computes the `stats` metric plus `variance`, the standard deviation (`std_deviation`), and the sum of squares (`sum_of_squares`).

- ▸ `percentiles`: This computes `percentiles` (the point at which a certain percentage of observed values occurs) of some values. (Visit Wikipedia at `http://en.wikipedia.org/wiki/Percentile` for more information about percentiles.)

- ▸ `percentile_ranks`: This computes the rank of values that hits a percentile range.

- ▸ `cardinality`: This computes an approximate count of distinct values in a field.

- ▸ `geo_bounds`: A metric aggregation that computes the bounding box containing all geo point values for a field.

Every metric value requires different computational needs, so it is a good practice to limit the indicators to the required one so that CPU time and memory are not wasted; this increases performance.

In the earlier listing, I cited only the most used, natively available aggregators in ElasticSearch; other metric types can be provided via plugins.

See also

- ▸ Official ElasticSearch documentation about stats aggregation at `http://www.elasticsearch.org/guide/en/elasticsearch/reference/current/search-aggregations-metrics-stats-aggregation.html`

- ▸ Extended stats aggregation at `http://www.elasticsearch.org/guide/en/elasticsearch/reference/current/search-aggregations-metrics-extendedstats-aggregation.html`

Executing the terms aggregation

Terms aggregation is one of the most commonly used aggregations. It groups documents in buckets based on a single term value. This aggregation is often used to narrow down a search.

Getting ready

You need a working ElasticSearch cluster and an index populated with the script (`chapter_06/executing_terms_aggregation.sh`) available at `https://github.com/aparo/elasticsearch-cookbook-second-edition`.

How to do it...

To execute a terms aggregation, we will perform the steps given as follows:

1. We want to calculate the top-10 tags of all the documents; for this the REST call should be as follows:

```
curl -XGET 'http://127.0.0.1:9200/test-index/test-type/_
search?pretty=true&size=0' -d '{
  "query": {
    "match_all": {}
  },
  "aggs": {
    "tag": {
      "terms": {
        "field": "tag",
        "size": 10
      }
    }
  }
}'
```

   In this example, we need to match all the items, so the match_all query is used.

2. The result returned by ElasticSearch, if everything is all right, should be:

```
{
  "took" : 63,
  "timed_out" : false,
  "_shards" : { ...truncated...  },
  "hits" : {
    "total" : 1000,
    "max_score" : 0.0,
    "hits" : [ ]
  },
  "aggregations" : {
    "tag" : {
      "buckets" : [ {
        "key" : "laborum",
        "doc_count" : 25
      }, {
        "key" : "quidem",
        "doc_count" : 15
      }, {
        ....truncated ...
      }, {
```

```
        "key" : "praesentium",
        "doc_count" : 9
      } ]
    }
  }
}
```

The aggregation result is composed of several buckets with two parameters:

▸ `key`: This is the term used to populate the bucket

▸ `doc_count`: This is the number of results with the `key` term

How it works...

During a search, there are a lot of phases that ElasticSearch will execute. After query execution, the aggregations are calculated and returned along with the results.

In this recipe, we see that the terms aggregation require the following as parameters:

▸ `field`: This is the field to be used to extract the facets data. The field value can be a single string (shown as `tag` in the preceding example) or a list of fields (such as `["field1", "field2", …]`).

▸ `size` (by default `10`): This controls the number of facets value that is to be returned.

▸ `min_doc_count` (optional): This returns the terms that have a minimum number of documents count.

▸ `include` (optional): This defines the valid value to be aggregated via a regular expression. This is evaluated before `exclude`. Regular expressions are controlled by the `flags` parameter. Consider the following example:

```
"include" : {
  "pattern" : ".*labor.*",
  "flags" : "CANON_EQ|CASE_INSENSITIVE"
},
```

▸ `exclude` (optional): This parameter removes terms that are contained in the `exclude` list from the results. Regular expressions are controlled by the `flags` parameter.

▸ `order` (optional; by default this is `doc_count`): This parameter controls the calculation of the top *n* bucket values that are to be returned. The `order` parameter can be one of these types:

  ❑ `_count` (default): This parameter returns the aggregation values ordered by count

❑ `_term`: This parameter returns the aggregation values ordered by the term value (such as `"order"` : `{ "_term" : "asc" })`

❑ A subaggregation name; consider the following as an example:

```
{
  "aggs" : {
    "genders" : {
      "terms" : {
        "field" : "tag",
        "order" : { "avg_val" : "desc" }
      },
      "aggs" : {
        "avg_age" : { "avg" : { "field" : "age" } }
      }
    }
  }
}
```

Terms aggregation are very useful for representing an overview of values used for further filtering. In a graph, they are often shown as a bar chart, as follows:

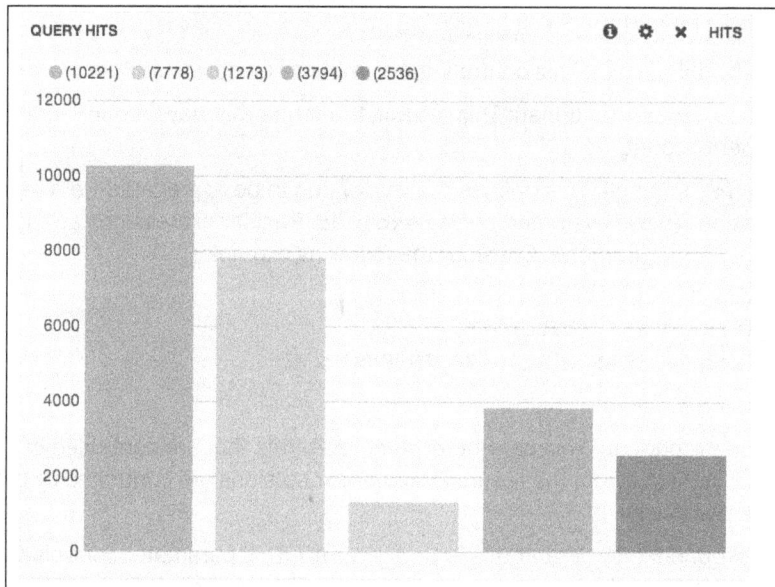

There's more...

Sometimes, we need to have much more control over terms aggregation; this can be achieved by adding an ElasticSearch script in the `script` field.

With scripting, it is possible to modify the term used for the aggregation to generate a new value that can be used. A simple example, in which we append the `123` value to all the terms, is as follows:

```
{
    "query" : {
        "match_all" : {   }
    },
    "aggs" : {
        "tag" : {
            "terms" : {
                "field" : "tag",
                "script" : "_value + '123'"
            }
        }
    }
}
```

Scripting can also be used to control the inclusion/exclusion of some terms. In this case, the returned value from the script must be a Boolean (true/false). If we want an aggregation with terms that start with the `a` character, we can use a similar aggregation:

```
{
    "query" : {
        "match_all" : {   }
    },
    "aggs" : {
        "tag" : {
            "terms" : {
                "field" : "tag",
                "script" : "_value.startsWith('a')"
            }
        }
    }
}
```

In the previous terms aggregation examples, we provided the `field` or `fields` parameter to select the field that is to be used to compute the aggregation. It's also possible to pass a `script` parameter that replaces `field` and `fields` in order to define the field to be used to extract the data. The `script` can fetch from the `doc` variable in the given context.

In the case of `doc`, the earlier example can be rewritten as:

```
...  "tag": {
            "terms": {
                "script": "doc['tag'].value",
```

```
            "size": 10
          }
        }
   ...
```

See also

▶   *Chapter 7, Scripting*, to know more about scripting

Executing the range aggregation

The previous recipe describes an aggregation type that can be very useful if a bucket must be computed on terms or on a limited number of items. Otherwise, it's often required to return the buckets that are aggregated in ranges—the **range aggregation** answers this requirement. The commons scenarios in which this aggregation can be used are:

▶   Price ranges (used in shops)

▶   Size ranges

▶   Alphabetical ranges

Getting ready

You need a working ElasticSearch cluster and an index populated with the script (chapter_06/ executing_range_aggregations.sh) available at https://github.com/aparo/ elasticsearch-cookbook-second-edition.

How to do it...

To execute range aggregations, we will perform the steps given as follows:

1.   We want to provide three types of aggregation ranges, as follows:

   ❑   Price aggregation: This method aggregates the price of the items in a range

   ❑   Age aggregation: This method aggregates the age contained in a document in four ranges of 25 years

   ❑   Date aggregation: This method aggregates the ranges of 6 months of the previous year and all months this year

2.   To obtain this result, we need to execute a query, as follows:

```
curl -XGET 'http://127.0.0.1:9200/test-index/test-type/_
search?pretty=true&size=0' -d ' {
  "query": {
```

```
        "match_all": {}
    },
    "aggs": {
      "prices": {
        "range": {
          "field": "price",
          "ranges": [
            {"to": 10},
            {"from": 10,"to": 20},
            {"from": 20,"to": 100},
            {"from": 100}
          ]
        }
      },
      "ages": {
        "range": {
          "field": "age",
          "ranges": [
            {"to": 25},
            {"from": 25,"to": 50},
            {"from": 50,"to": 75},
            {"from": 75}
          ]
        }
      },
      "range": {
        "range": {
          "field": "date",
          "ranges": [
            {"from": "2012-01-01","to": "2012-07-01"},
            {"from": "2012-07-01","to": "2012-12-31"},
            {"from": "2013-01-01","to": "2013-12-31"}
          ]
        }
      }
    }
  }'
```

3. The results will be something like the following:

```
{
  "took" : 7,
  "timed_out" : false,
  "_shards" : {…truncated…},
  "hits" : {…truncated…},
```

```
            "aggregations" : {
              "range" : {
                "buckets" : [ {
                  "key" : "20120101-01-01T00:00:00.000Z-20120631-01-
                  01T00:00:00.000Z",
                  "from" : 6.348668943168E17,
                  "from_as_string" : "20120101-01-01T00:00:00.000Z",
                  "to" : 6.34883619456E17,
                  "to_as_string" : "20120631-01-01T00:00:00.000Z",
                  "doc_count" : 0
                }, ...truncated... ]
              },
              "prices" : {
                "buckets" : [ {
                  "key" : "*-10.0",
                  "to" : 10.0,
                  "to_as_string" : "10.0",
                  "doc_count" : 105
                }, ...truncated...]
              },
              "ages" : {
                "buckets" : [ {
                  "key" : "*-25.0",
                  "to" : 25.0,
                  "to_as_string" : "25.0",
                  "doc_count" : 210
                }, ...truncated...]
              }
            }
          }
```

Every aggregation result has the following fields:

- The to, to_string, from, and from_string fields that define the original range of the aggregation
- doc_count: This gives the number of results in this range
- key: This is a string representation of the range

How it works...

This kind of aggregation is generally executed on numerical data types (integer, float, long, and dates). It can be considered as a list of range filters executed on the result of the query.

Date/date-time values, when used in a filter/query, must be expressed in string format; the valid string formats are yyyy-MM-dd'T'HH:mm:ss and yyyy-MM-dd.

Each range is computed independently; thus, in their definition, they can overlap.

There's more...

There are two special range aggregations used to target date and IPv4 ranges.

They are similar to the range aggregation, but they provide special functionalities to control date and IP address ranges.

The date range aggregation (`date_range`) defines the `from` and `to` fields in **Date Math** expressions. For example, to execute an aggregation of hits of before and after a 6-month period, the aggregation will be as follows:

```
{
  "aggs": {
    "range": {
      "date_range": {
        "field": "date",
        "format": "MM-yyyy",
        "ranges": [
          { "to": "now-6M/M" },
          { "from": "now-6M/M" }
        ]
      }
    }
  }
}
```

In the preceding example, the buckets will be formatted in the form of *month-year* (MM-YYYY) in two ranges. The `now` parameter defines the actual date-time, `-6M` means minus 6 months, and `/M` is a shortcut for division using the `month` value. (A complete reference on Date Math expressions and code is available at `http://www.elasticsearch.org/guide/en/elasticsearch/reference/current/search-aggregations-bucket-daterange-aggregation.html`.)

The IPv4 range aggregation (`ip_range`) defines the ranges in the following formats:

- The IP range form:
  ```
  {
    "aggs" : {
      "ip_ranges" : {
        "ip_range" : {
          "field" : "ip",
          "ranges" : [
            { "to" : "192.168.1.1" },
            { "from" : "192.168.2.255" }
          ]
  ```

```
            }
          }
        }
      }
```

 ▸ CIDR masks:

```
{
  "aggs" : {
    "ip_ranges" : {
      "ip_range" : {
        "field" : "ip",
        "ranges" : [
          { "mask" : "192.168.1.0/25" },
          { "mask" : "192.168.1.127/25" }
        ]
      }
    }
  }
}
```

See also

 ▸ The *Using a range query/filter* recipe in *Chapter 5, Search, Queries, and Filters*

Executing the histogram aggregation

ElasticSearch numerical values can be used to process histogram data. The histogram representation is a very powerful way to show data to end users.

Getting ready

You need a working ElasticSearch cluster and an index populated with the script (chapter_06/executing_histogram_aggregations.sh) available at https://github.com/aparo/elasticsearch-cookbook-second-edition.

How to do it...

Using the items populated with the script, we want to calculate aggregations on:

 ▸ Age with an interval of 5 years
 ▸ Price with an interval of 10$
 ▸ Date with an interval of 6 months

To execute histogram aggregations, we will perform the steps given as follows:

1. The query will be as follows:

```
curl -XGET 'http://127.0.0.1:9200/test-index/test-type/_
search?pretty=true&size=0' -d '{
  "query": {
    "match_all": {}
  },
  "aggregations": {
    "age" : {
      "histogram" : {
        "field" : "age",
        "interval" : 5
      }
    },
    "price" : {
      "histogram" : {
        "field" : "price",
        "interval" : 10.0
      }
    }
  }
}'
```

2. The result (stripped) will be:

```
{
  "took" : 23,
  "timed_out" : false,
  "_shards" : {…truncated…},
  "hits" : {…truncated…},
  "aggregations" : {
    "price" : {
      "buckets" : [ {
        "key_as_string" : "0",
        "key" : 0,
        "doc_count" : 105
      }, {
        "key_as_string" : "10",
        "key" : 10,
        "doc_count" : 107
      …truncated…       } ]
    },
    "age" : {
      "buckets" : [ {
        "key_as_string" : "0",
        "key" : 0,
        "doc_count" : 34
      }, {
```

```
            "key_as_string" : "5",
            "key" : 5,
            "doc_count" : 41
        }, {...truncated...      } ]
    }
  }
}
```

The aggregation result is composed of `buckets`: a list of aggregation results. These results are composed of the following:

▸ `key`: This is the value that is always on the *x* axis on the histogram graph

▸ `key_as_string`: This is a string representation of the key value

▸ `doc_count`: This denotes the document bucket size

How it works...

This kind of aggregation is calculated in a distributed manner, in each shard with search results, and then the aggregation results are aggregated in the search node server (arbiter), which is then returned to the user.

The histogram aggregation works only on numerical fields (Boolean, Integer, long Integer, float) and date/date-time fields (that are internally represented as long). To control histogram generation on a defined `field`, the `interval` parameter is required, which is used to generate an interval to aggregate the hits.

For numerical fields, this value is a number (in the preceding example, we have done numerical calculation on age and price).

The general representation of a histogram can be a bar chart, similar to the following:

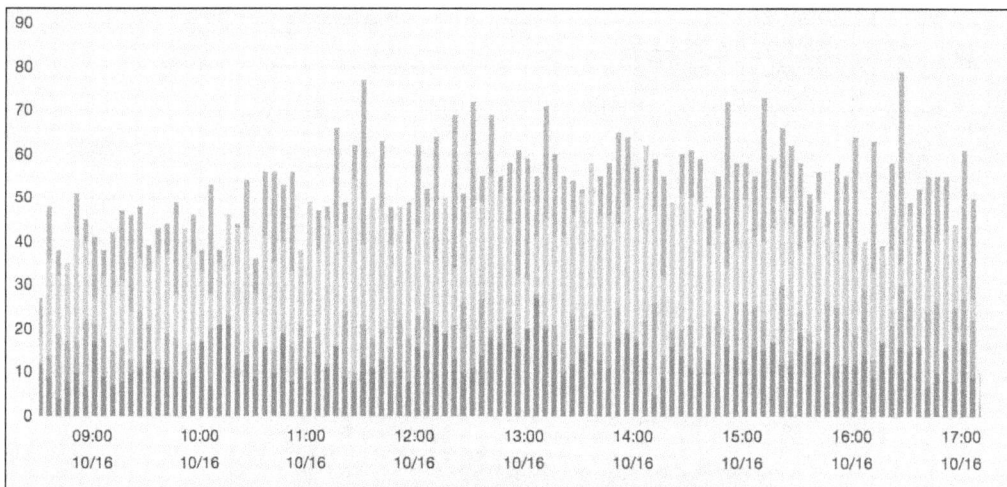

There's more...

Histogram aggregations can be also improved using ElasticSearch scripting functionalities. It is possible to script using _value if a field is stored or via the doc variable.

An example of a scripted aggregation histogram using _value is as follows:

```
curl -XGET 'http://127.0.0.1:9200/test-index/test-
type/_search?&pretty=true&size=0' -d '{
  "query": {
    "match_all": {}
  },
  "aggs": {
    "age" : {
      "histogram" : {
        "field" : "age",
        "script": "_value*3",
        "interval" : 5
      }
    }
  }
}'
```

An example of a scripted aggregation histogram using _doc is as follows:

```
curl -XGET 'http://127.0.0.1:9200/test-index/test-
type/_search?&pretty=true&size=0' -d '{
  "query": {
    "match_all": {}
  },
  "aggs": {
    "age" : {
      "histogram" : {
        "script": "doc['age'].value",
        "interval" : 5
      }
    }
  }
}'
```

See also

▶ The *Executing the date histogram aggregation* recipe

Executing the date histogram aggregation

The previous recipe works mainly on numeric fields; ElasticSearch provides a custom date histogram aggregation to operate on date/date-time values. This aggregation is required because date values need more customization to solve problems such as time zone conversion and special time intervals.

Getting ready

You need a working ElasticSearch cluster and an index populated with the script (chapter_06/executing_date_histogram_aggregations.sh) available at https://github.com/aparo/elasticsearch-cookbook-second-edition.

How to do it...

We need two different date/time aggregations that are:

▶ An annual aggregation

▶ A quarter aggregation, but with time zone +1:00

To execute date histogram aggregations, we will perform the steps given as follows:

1. The query will be as follows:

```
curl -XGET 'http://127.0.0.1:9200/test-index/test-
type/_search? pretty=true' -d '
{
  "query": {
    "match_all": {}
  },
  "aggs": {
    "date_year": {
      "date_histogram": {
        "field": "date",
        "interval": "year"
      }
    },
    "date_quarter": {
      "date_histogram": {
        "field": "date",
        "interval": "quarter" ,
        "time_zone": "+01:00"
      }
    }
  }
}'
```

2. The corresponding results are as follows:

```
{
  "took" : 29,
  "timed_out" : false,
  "_shards" : {…truncated…},
  "hits" : {…truncated…},
  "aggregations" : {
    "date_year" : {
      "buckets" : [ {
        "key_as_string" : "2010-01-01T00:00:00.000Z",
        "key" : 1262304000000,
        "doc_count" : 40
      }, {
        "key_as_string" : "2011-01-01T00:00:00.000Z",
        "key" : 1293840000000,
        "doc_count" : 182
      }, …truncated…]
    },
    "date_quarter" : {
      "buckets" : [ {
        "key_as_string" : "2010-10-01T00:00:00.000Z",
        "key" : 1285891200000,
        "doc_count" : 40
      }, {
        "key_as_string" : "2011-01-01T00:00:00.000Z",
        "key" : 1293840000000,
        "doc_count" : 42
      }, …truncated…]
    }
  }
}
```

The aggregation result is composed of `buckets`: a list of aggregation results. These results are composed of the following:

- ▶ key: This is the value that is always on the *x* axis on the histogram graph
- ▶ key_as_string: This is a string representation of the key value
- ▶ doc_count: This denotes the document bucket size

How it works...

The main difference in the preceding histogram recipe is that the interval is not numerical, but generally date intervals are defined time constants. The `interval` parameter allows us to use several values such as:

- ▶ Year
- ▶ Quarter
- ▶ Month
- ▶ Week
- ▶ Day
- ▶ Hour
- ▶ Minute

When working with date values, it's important to use the correct time zones to prevent query errors. By default, ElasticSearch uses the UTC milliseconds, from epoch, to store date-time values. To better handle the correct timestamp, there are some parameters that can be used such as:

- ▶ `time_zone` (or `pre_zone`, in which case it's is optional): This parameter allows defining a time zone offset to be used in value calculation. This value is used to preprocess the date-time value for the aggregation. The value can be expressed in numeric form (such as `-3`) if specifying hours or minutes, then it must be defined in the time zone. A string representation can be used (such as `+07:30`).
- ▶ `post_zone` (optional): This parameter takes the result and applies the time zone offset to that result.
- ▶ `pre_zone_adjust_large_interval` (by default, this is `false` and is optional): This parameter applies the hour interval also for `day` or above intervals.

See also

- ▶ Visit the official ElasticSearch documentation on date histogram aggregation at `www.elasticsearch.org/guide/en/elasticsearch/reference/current/search-aggregations-bucket-datehistogram-aggregation.html` for more details on managing time zone issues

Executing the filter aggregation

Sometimes, we need to reduce the number of hits in our aggregation to satisfy a particular filter. To obtain this result, the filter aggregation is used.

Getting ready

You need a working ElasticSearch cluster and an index populated with the script (chapter_06/test_filter_aggregation.sh) available at https://github.com/aparo/elasticsearch-cookbook-second-edition.

How to do it...

We need to compute two different filter aggregations that are:

- The count of documents that have ullam as tag
- The count of documents that have age equal to 37

To execute filter aggregations, we will perform the steps given as follows:

1. The query to execute these aggregations is as follows:

```
curl -XGET 'http://127.0.0.1:9200/test-index/test-
type/_search?size=0&pretty=true' -d '
{
  "query": {
    "match_all": {}
  },
  "aggregations": {
    "ullam_docs": {
      "filter" : {
        "term" : { "tag" : "ullam" }
      }
    },
    "age37_docs": {
      "filter" : {
        "term" : { "age" : 37 }
      }
    }
  }
}'
```

In this case, we have used simple filters, but they can be more complex if needed.

2. The results of the preceding query with aggregations will be as follows:

```
{
  "took" : 5,
  "timed_out" : false,
  "_shards" : {
    "total" : 5,
    "successful" : 5,
    "failed" : 0
  },
  "hits" : {
    "total" : 1000,
    "max_score" : 0.0,
    "hits" : [ ]
  },
  "aggregations" : {
    "age37_docs" : {
      "doc_count" : 6
    },
    "ullam_docs" : {
      "doc_count" : 17
    }
  }
}
```

How it works...

Filter aggregation is very simple; it executes a count on a filter in a matched element. You can consider this aggregation as a count query on the results. As we can see from the preceding result, the aggregation contains one value doc_count, which is the count result.

It can be seen as a very simple aggregation; generally, users tend not to use it as they prefer statistical aggregations, which also provide a count; alternatively, in the worst cases, they execute another search that generates more server workload.

The big advantage of this kind of aggregation is that the count, whenever possible, is executed via a filter, which is way faster than iterating all the results.

Another important advantage is that the filter can be composed of every possible valid Query DSL element.

There's more...

It's often required to have a document count that doesn't match a filter or generally doesn't have a particular field (or is null). For this kind of scenario, there is a special aggregation type: missing.

For example, to count the number of documents missing the `code` field, the query will be as follows:

```
curl -XGET 'http://127.0.0.1:9200/test-index/test-
type/_search?size=0&pretty' -d '
{
  "query": {
    "match_all": {}
  },
  "aggs": {
    "missing_code": {
      "missing" : {
        "field" : "code"
      }
    }
  }
}'
```

The result will be as follows:

```
{
  ... truncated ...
  "aggregations" : {
    "missin_code" : {
      "doc_count" : 1000
    }
  }
}
```

See also

▸ The *Counting matched results* recipe in *Chapter 5, Search, Queries, and Filters*

▸ The *Executing a scan query* recipe in *Chapter 5, Search, Queries, and Filters*

Executing the global aggregation

Aggregations are generally executed on query search results, ElasticSearch provides a special aggregation—`global`—that is executed globally on all the documents without being influenced by the query.

Getting ready

You need a working ElasticSearch cluster and an index populated with the script (`executing_global_aggregations.sh`) available at `https://github.com/aparo/elasticsearch-cookbook-second-edition`.

How to do it...

To execute global aggregations, we will perform the steps given as follows:

1. If we want to compare a global average with a query one, the call will be something like this:

```
curl -XGET 'http://127.0.0.1:9200/test-index/test-
type/_search?size=0&pretty=true' -d '
{
  "query": {
    "term" : { "tag" : "ullam" }
  },
  "aggregations": {
    "query_age_avg": {
      "avg" : {
        "field" :  "age"
      }
    },
    "all_persons":{
      "global": {},
      "aggs":{
        "age_global_avg": {
          "avg" : {
            "field" :  "age"
          }
        }
      }
    }
  }
}'
```

2. The result will be as follows:

```
{
  "took" : 133,
  "timed_out" : false,
  "_shards" : {...truncated...},
  "hits" : {
    "total" : 17,
    "max_score" : 0.0,
    "hits" : [ ]
  },
  "aggregations" : {
    "all_persons" : {
```

```
        "doc_count" : 1000,
        "age_global_avg" : {
          "value" : 53.243
        }
      },
      "query_age_avg" : {
        "value" : 53.470588235294116
      }
    }
  }
}
```

In the example, the `query_age_avg` function is computed on the query and the `age_global_avg` function on all the documents.

How it works...

This kind of aggregation is mainly used as *top* aggregation—that is, as a start point for other subaggregations. The body of the global aggregations is empty; it doesn't have any optional parameters. The most frequently used cases are comparative aggregations executed on filters with those without aggregation, as in the preceding example.

Executing the geo distance aggregation

Among the other standard types that we have seen in previous aggregations, ElasticSearch allows executing aggregations against a geo point: geo distance aggregations. This is an evolution of the previously discussed range aggregations built to work on geo locations.

Getting ready

You need a working ElasticSearch cluster and an index populated with the script (`executing_geo_distance_aggregations.sh`) available at `https://github.com/aparo/elasticsearch-cookbook-second-edition`.

How to do it...

Using the position field available in documents, we will aggregate the other documents in four ranges:

► Fewer than 10 kilometers

► From 10 to 20 kilometers

► From 20 to 50 kilometers

- From 50 to 100 kilometers
- Above 100 kilometers

To execute geo distance aggregations, we will perform the steps given as follows:

1. To achieve these goals, we will create a geo distance aggregation with a code similar to this one:

```
curl -XGET 'http://127.0.0.1:9200/test-index/test-
type/_search?pretty=true&size=0' -d ' {
  "query" : {
    "match_all" : {}
  },
  "aggs" : {
    "position" : {
      "geo_distance" : {
        "field":"position",
        "origin" : {
          "lat": 83.76,
          "lon": -81.20
        },
        "ranges" : [
          { "to" : 10 },
          { "from" : 10, "to" : 20 },
          { "from" : 20, "to" : 50 },
          { "from" : 50, "to" : 100 },
          { "from" : 100 }
        ]
      }
    }
  }
}'
```

2. The result will be as follows:

```
{
  "took" : 177,
  "timed_out" : false,
  "_shards" : {…truncated…},
  "hits" : {…truncated…},
  "aggregations" : {
    "position" : {
      "buckets" : [ {
        "key" : "*-10.0",
        "from" : 0.0,
        "to" : 10.0,
```

```
        "doc_count" : 0
    }, {
      "key" : "10.0-20.0",
      "from" : 10.0,
      "to" : 20.0,
      "doc_count" : 0
    }, {
      "key" : "20.0-50.0",
      "from" : 20.0,
      "to" : 50.0,
      "doc_count" : 0
    }, {
      "key" : "50.0-100.0",
      "from" : 50.0,
      "to" : 100.0,
      "doc_count" : 0
    }, {
      "key" : "100.0-*",
      "from" : 100.0,
      "doc_count" : 1000
    } ]
  }
}
}
```

How it works...

The geo range aggregation is an extension of the range aggregations that work on geo localizations. It works only if a field is mapped as a `geo_point`. The field can contain a single or multivalue geo point.

This aggregation requires at least three parameters:

- ▶ `field`: This is the field of the geo point to work on
- ▶ `origin`: This is the geo point to be used to compute the distances
- ▶ `ranges`: This is a list of ranges to collect documents based on their distance from the target point

The geo point can be defined in one of these accepted formats:

- ▶ Latitude and longitude as properties, such as `{"lat": 83.76, "lon": -81.20 }`
- ▶ Longitude and latitude as an array, such as `[-81.20, 83.76]`
- ▶ Latitude and longitude as a string, such as `"83.76, -81.20"`
- ▶ Geohash, for example, `fnyk80`

The ranges are defined as a couple of `from/to` values. If one of them is missing, they are considered as unbound. The metric system used for the range is by default set to kilometers—but by using the property `unit`, it's possible to set it to:

- `mi` or `miles`
- `in` or `inch`
- `yd` or `yard`
- `km` or `kilometers`
- `m` or `meters`
- `cm` or `centimeter`
- `mm` or `millimeters`

It's also possible to set how the distance is computed with the `distance_type` parameter. Valid values for this parameter are:

- `arc`: This uses the Arc Length formula. It is the most precise. (See `http://en.wikipedia.org/wiki/Arc_length` for more details on the arc length algorithm.)
- `sloppy_arc` (default): It's a faster implementation of the Arc Length formula, but is less precise.
- `plane`: This uses the plane distance formula. It is the most fastest of all and CPU-intensive, but it too is less precise.

As for the range filter, the range values are treated independently, so overlapping ranges are allowed.

When the results are returned, this aggregation provides a lot of information in its fields:

- `from/to`: This defines the analyzed range
- `Key`: This defines the string representation of the range
- `doc_count`: This defines the number of documents in the bucket that match the range

See also

- The *Executing the range aggregation* recipe in this chapter
- The *Mapping a geo point field* recipe in *Chapter 3, Managing Mapping*
- The geohash grid aggregation at `http://www.elasticsearch.org/guide/en/elasticsearch/reference/current/search-aggregations-bucket-geohashgrid-aggregation.html`

Executing nested aggregation

Nested aggregations allow us to execute analysis on nested documents. When working with complex structures, nested objects are very common.

Getting ready

You need a working ElasticSearch cluster and an index populated with the script available at `https://github.com/aparo/elasticsearch-cookbook-second-edition`.

How to do it...

To execute nested aggregations, we will perform the steps given as follows:

1. We must index documents with a nested type, as discussed in the *Managing nested objects* recipe in *Chapter 3, Managing Mapping*:

```
{
  "product" : {
    "properties" : {
      "resellers" : {
        "type" : "nested"
        "properties" : {
          "username" : { "type" : "string", "index" :
          "not_analyzed" },
          "price" : { "type" : "double" }
        }
      },
      "tags" : { "type" : "string", "index":"not_analyzed"}
    }
  }
}
```

2. To return the minimum price the products can be purchased at, we create a nested aggregation with code similar to this one:

```
curl -XGET 'http://127.0.0.1:9200/test-
index/product/_search?pretty=true&size=0' -d ' {
  "query" : {
    "match" : { "name" : "my product" }
  },
  "aggs" : {
    "resellers" : {
      "nested" : {
```

```
                    "path" : "resellers"
                },
                "aggs" : {
                  "min_price" : { "min" : { "field" : "resellers.price" } }
                }
            }
        }
    }
}'
```

3. The result will be as follows:

```
{
    "took" : 7,
    "timed_out" : false,
    "_shards" : {...truncated...},
    "hits" : {...truncated...},
    "aggregations": {
        "resellers": {
            "min_price": {
                "value" : 130
            }
        }
    }
}
```

In this case, the resulting aggregation is a simple `min` metric that we have already seen in the second recipe of this chapter.

How it works...

The nested aggregation requires only the `path` data of the field, which is relative to the parent and contains the nested documents.

After having defined the nested aggregation, all the other kinds of aggregations can be used in the subaggregations.

There's more...

ElasticSearch provides a way to aggregate values from nested documents to their parent; this aggregation is called `reverse_nested`.

In the preceding example, we can aggregate the top tags for the reseller with a similar query:

```
curl -XGET 'http://127.0.0.1:9200/test-
index/product/_search?pretty=true&size=0' -d ' {
  "query" : {
```

```
      "match" : { "name" : "my product" }
  }
  "aggs" : {
    "resellers" : {
      "nested" : {
        "path" : "resellers"
      },
      "aggs" : {
        "top_resellers" : {
          "terms" : {
            "field" : "resellers.username"
          }
        },
        "aggs" : {
          "resellers_to_product" : {
            "reverse_nested" : {},
            "aggs" : {
              "top_tags_per_reseller" : {
                "terms" : { "field" : "tags" }
              }
            }
          }
        }
      }
    }
  }
}'
```

In this example, there are several steps:

1. We aggregate initially for nested resellers data.

2. Having activated the nested resellers documents, we are able to term-aggregate by its username field (`resellers.username`).

3. From the top resellers aggregation, we go back to aggregate on the parent via `"reverse_nested"`.

4. Now, we can aggregate `tags` of the parent document.

The response of the query is similar to this one:

```
{
   "took" : 93,
   "timed_out" : false,
   "_shards" : {…truncated…},
   "hits" : {…truncated…},
```

```
      "aggregations": {
        "resellers": {
          "top_usernames": {
            "buckets" : [
              {
                "key" : "username_1",
                "doc_count" : 17,
                "resellers_to_product" : {
                  "top_tags_per_reseller" : {
                    "buckets" : [
                      {
                        "key" : "tag1",
                        "doc_count" : 9
                      },…
                    ]
                  }
                },…
              }
            ]
          }
        }
      }
    }
```

Executing the top hit aggregation

The top hit aggregation is different from the other aggregation types. All the previous aggregations have metric (simple values) or bucket values; the top hit aggregation returns buckets of search hits.

Generally, the top hit aggregation is used as a subaggregation so that the top matching documents can be aggregated in buckets.

Getting ready

You need a working ElasticSearch cluster and an index populated with the script (chapter_06/executing_top_hit_aggregations.sh) available at https://github.com/aparo/elasticsearch-cookbook-second-edition.

How to do it...

To execute a top hit aggregation, we will perform the steps given as follows:

1. We want to aggregate the documents hits by tag (`tags`) and return only the `name` field of documents with a maximum age (`top_tag_hits`). We'll execute the search and aggregation with the following command:

```
curl -XGET 'http://127.0.0.1:9200/test-index/test-
type/_search' -d '{
  "query": {
    "match_all": {}
  },
  "size": 0,
  "aggs": {
    "tags": {
      "terms": {
        "field": "tag",
        "size": 2
      },
      "aggs": {
        "top_tag_hits": {
          "top_hits": {
            "sort": [
              {
                "age": {
                  "order": "desc"
                }
              }
            ],
            "_source": {
              "include": [
                "name"
              ]
            },
            "size": 1
          }
        }
      }
    }
  }
}'
```

2. The result will be as follows:

```
{
  "took" : 5,
  "timed_out" : false,
  "_shards" : ...truncated...,
  "hits" : ...truncated...,
  "aggregations" : {
    "tags" : {
      "buckets" : [ {
        "key" : "laborum",
        "doc_count" : 18,
        "top_tag_hits" : {
          "hits" : {
            "total" : 18,
            "max_score" : null,
            "hits" : [ {
              "_index" : "test-index",
              "_type" : "test-type",
              "_id" : "730",
              "_score" : null,
              "_source":{"name":"Gladiator"},
              "sort" : [ 90 ]
            } ]
          }
        }
      }, {
        "key" : "sit",
        "doc_count" : 10,
        "top_tag_hits" : {
          "hits" : {
            "total" : 10,
            "max_score" : null,
            "hits" : [ {
              "_index" : "test-index",
              "_type" : "test-type",
              "_id" : "732",
              "_score" : null,
              "_source":{"name":"Masked Marvel"},
              "sort" : [ 96 ]
            } ]
          }
        }
      } ]
    }
  }
}
```

How it works...

The top hit aggregation allows collecting buckets of hits from another aggregation. It provides optional parameters to control the result's slicing. These are as follows:

- ▶ `from` (by default 0): This is the starting position of the hits in the bucket.
- ▶ `size` (by default, set to the parent bucket size): This is the hit bucket size.
- ▶ `sort` (by default `score`): This allows us to sort for different values. Its definition is similar to the search sort in *Chapter 5, Search, Queries, and Filters*.

To control the returned hits, it is possible to use the same parameters as used for a search:

- ▶ `_source`: This allows us to control the returned source. It can be disabled (`false`), partially returned (`obj.*`), or can have multiple exclude/include rules. In the earlier example, we have returned only the name field:

```
"_source": {
  "include": [
    "name"
  ]
},
```

- ▶ `highlighting`: This allows us to define fields and settings to be used to calculate a query abstract.
- ▶ `fielddata_fields`: This allows us to return field data representation of your field.
- ▶ `explain`: This returns information on how the score is calculated for a particular document.
- ▶ `version` (by default `false`): This adds the version of a document in the results.

> Top hit aggregation can be used to implement a *field collapsing* feature; this is done by using first a terms aggregation on the field that we want to collapse and then collecting the documents with a top hit aggregation.

See Also

- ▶ The *Executing a search* recipe in *Chapter 5, Search, Queries, and Filters*
- ▶ The *Executing the terms aggregation* recipe in this chapter

7
Scripting

In this chapter, we will cover the following recipes:

- ▶ Installing additional script plugins
- ▶ Managing scripts
- ▶ Sorting data using scripts
- ▶ Computing return fields with scripting
- ▶ Filtering a search via scripting
- ▶ Updating a document using scripts

Introduction

ElasticSearch has a powerful way of extending its capabilities with custom scripts, which can be written in several programming languages. The most common ones are **Groovy**, **MVEL**, **JavaScript**, and **Python**.

We already had a taste of ElasticSearch's scripting capabilities in the previous chapter, where we used scripting for aggregations. In this chapter, we will see how it's possible to create custom scoring algorithms, special processed return fields, custom sorting, and complex update operations on records.

The scripting concept of ElasticSearch can be seen as an advanced stored procedures system in the NoSQL world; so, for an advanced usage of ElasticSearch, it is very important to master it.

Installing additional script plugins

ElasticSearch provides native scripting (a Java code compiled in JAR) and Groovy, but a lot of interesting languages are also available, such as JavaScript and Python. In older ElasticSearch releases, prior to version 1.4, the official scripting language was MVEL, but due to the fact that it was not well-maintained by MVEL developers, in addition to the impossibility to sandbox it and prevent security issues, MVEL was replaced with Groovy. Groovy scripting is now provided by default in ElasticSearch. The other scripting languages can be installed as plugins.

Getting ready

You will need a working ElasticSearch cluster.

How to do it...

In order to install JavaScript language support for ElasticSearch (1.3.x), perform the following steps:

1. From the command line, simply enter the following command:

   ```
   bin/plugin --install elasticsearch/elasticsearch-lang-
   javascript/2.3.0
   ```

2. This will print the following result:

   ```
   -> Installing elasticsearch/elasticsearch-lang-javascript/2.3.0...
   Trying http://download.elasticsearch.org/elasticsearch/
   elasticsearch-lang-javascript/elasticsearch-lang-javascript-
   2.3.0.zip...
   Downloading ....DONE
   Installed lang-javascript
   ```

   > If the installation is successful, the output will end with `Installed`; otherwise, an error is returned.

3. To install Python language support for ElasticSearch, just enter the following command:

   ```
   bin/plugin -install elasticsearch/elasticsearch-lang-python/2.3.0
   ```

   > The version number depends on the ElasticSearch version. Take a look at the plugin's web page to choose the correct version.

How it works...

Language plugins allow you to extend the number of supported languages to be used in scripting.

During the ElasticSearch startup, an internal ElasticSearch service called PluginService loads all the installed language plugins.

> In order to install or upgrade a plugin, you need to restart the node.

The ElasticSearch community provides common scripting languages (a list of the supported scripting languages is available on the ElasticSearch site plugin page at `http://www.elasticsearch.org/guide/en/elasticsearch/reference/current/modules-plugins.html`), and others are available in GitHub repositories (a simple search on GitHub allows you to find them).

The following are the most commonly used languages for scripting:

* **Groovy** (`http://groovy.codehaus.org/`): This language is embedded in ElasticSearch by default. It is a simple language that provides scripting functionalities. This is one of the fastest available language extensions. Groovy is a dynamic, object-oriented programming language with features similar to those of Python, **Ruby**, **Perl**, and **Smalltalk**. It also provides support to write a functional code.

* **JavaScript** (`https://github.com/elasticsearch/elasticsearch-lang-javascript`): This is available as an external plugin. The JavaScript implementation is based on Java Rhino (`https://developer.mozilla.org/en-US/docs/Rhino`) and is really fast.

* **Python** (`https://github.com/elasticsearch/elasticsearch-lang-python`): This is available as an external plugin, based on **Jython** (`http://jython.org`). It allows Python to be used as a script engine. Considering several benchmark results, it's slower than other languages.

There's more...

Groovy is preferred if the script is not too complex; otherwise, a native plugin provides a better environment to implement complex logic and data management.

> The performance of every language is different; the fastest one is the native Java. In the case of dynamic scripting languages, Groovy is faster, as compared to JavaScript and Python.

In order to access document properties in Groovy scripts, the same approach will work as in other scripting languages:

- ▶ `doc.score`: This stores the document's score.
- ▶ `doc['field_name'].value`: This extracts the value of the `field_name` field from the document. If the value is an array or if you want to extract the value as an array, you can use `doc['field_name'].values`.
- ▶ `doc['field_name'].empty`: This returns `true` if the `field_name` field has no value in the document.
- ▶ `doc['field_name'].multivalue`: This returns `true` if the `field_name` field contains multiple values.

If the field contains a geopoint value, additional methods are available, as follows:

- ▶ `doc['field_name'].lat`: This returns the latitude of a geopoint. If you need the value as an array, you can use the `doc['field_name'].lats` method.
- ▶ `doc['field_name'].lon`: This returns the longitude of a geopoint. If you need the value as an array, you can use the `doc['field_name'].lons` method.
- ▶ `doc['field_name'].distance(lat,lon)`: This returns the plane distance, in miles, from a latitude/longitude point. If you need to calculate the distance in kilometers, you should use the `doc['field_name'].distanceInKm(lat,lon)` method.
- ▶ `doc['field_name'].arcDistance(lat,lon)`: This returns the arc distance, in miles, from a latitude/longitude point. If you need to calculate the distance in kilometers, you should use the `doc['field_name'].arcDistanceInKm(lat,lon)` method.
- ▶ `doc['field_name'].geohashDistance(geohash)`: This returns the distance, in miles, from a geohash value. If you need to calculate the same distance in kilometers, you should use `doc['field_name']` and the `geohashDistanceInKm(lat,lon)` method.

By using these helper methods, it is possible to create advanced scripts in order to boost a document by a distance that can be very handy in developing geolocalized centered applications.

Managing scripts

Depending on your scripting usage, there are several ways to customize ElasticSearch to use your script extensions.

In this recipe, we will see how to provide scripts to ElasticSearch via files, indexes, or inline.

Getting ready

You will need a working ElasticSearch cluster populated with the `populate` script (`chapter_06/populate_aggregations.sh`) used in *Chapter 6*, *Aggregations*, available at `https://github.com/aparo/elasticsearch-cookbook-second-edition`.

How to do it...

To manage scripting, perform the following steps:

1. Dynamic scripting is disabled by default for security reasons; we need to activate it in order to use dynamic scripting languages such as JavaScript or Python. To do this, we need to turn off the disable flag (`script.disable_dynamic: false`) in the ElasticSearch configuration file (`config/elasticseach.yml`) and restart the cluster.

2. To increase security, ElasticSearch does not allow you to specify scripts for non-sandbox languages. Scripts can be placed in the `scripts` directory inside the `configuration` directory. To provide a script in a file, we'll put a `my_script.groovy` script in the `config/scripts` location with the following code content:

   ```
   doc["price"].value * factor
   ```

3. If the dynamic script is enabled (as done in the first step), ElasticSearch allows you to store the scripts in a special index, `.scripts`. To put `my_script` in the index, execute the following command in the command terminal:

   ```
   curl -XPOST localhost:9200/_scripts/groovy/my_script -d '{
     "script":"doc[\"price\"].value * factor"
   }'
   ```

4. The script can be used by simply referencing it in the `script_id` field; use the following command:

   ```
   curl -XGET 'http://127.0.0.1:9200/test-index/test-type/_
   search?&pretty=true&size=3' -d '{
     "query": {
       "match_all": {}
     },
     "sort": {
       "_script" : {
         "script_id" : "my_script",
         "lang" : "groovy",
         "type" : "number",
         "ignore_unmapped" : true,
         "params" : {
           "factor" : 1.1
   ```

```
        },
        "order" : "asc"
      }
    }
  }'
```

How it works...

ElasticSearch allows you to load your script in different ways; each one of these methods has their pros and cons.

The most secure way to load or import scripts is to provide them as files in the `config/scripts` directory. This directory is continuously scanned for new files (by default, every 60 seconds). The scripting language is automatically detected by the file extension, and the script name depends on the filename.

If the file is put in subdirectories, the directory path becomes part of the filename; for example, if it is `config/scripts/mysub1/mysub2/my_script.groovy`, the script name will be `mysub1_mysub2_my_script`. If the script is provided via a filesystem, it can be referenced in the code via the `"script": "script_name"` parameter.

Scripts can also be available in the special `.script` index. These are the REST end points:

  ▶ To retrieve a script, use the following code:

    `GET http://<server>/_scripts/<language>/<id>`

  ▶ To store a script use the following code:

    `PUT http://<server>/_scripts/<language>/<id>`

  ▶ To delete a script use the following code:

    `DELETE http://<server>/_scripts/<language>/<id>`

The indexed script can be referenced in the code via the `"script_id": "id_of_the_script"` parameter. The recipes that follow will use inline scripting because it's easier to use it during the development and testing phases.

> Generally, a good practice is to develop using the inline dynamic scripting in a request, because it's faster to prototype. Once the script is ready and no changes are needed, it can be stored in the index since it is simpler to call and manage. In production, a best practice is to disable dynamic scripting and store the script on the disk (generally, dumping the indexed script to disk).

▸ The scripting page on the ElasticSearch website at `http://www.elasticsearch.org/guide/en/elasticsearch/reference/current/modules-scripting.html`

Sorting data using script

ElasticSearch provides scripting support for the sorting functionality. In real world applications, there is often a need to modify the default sort by the match score using an algorithm that depends on the context and some external variables. Some common scenarios are given as follows:

▸ Sorting places near a point

▸ Sorting by most-read articles

▸ Sorting items by custom user logic

▸ Sorting items by revenue

Getting ready

You will need a working ElasticSearch cluster and an index populated with the script used in *Chapter 6, Aggregations*, which is available at `https://github.com/aparo/elasticsearch-cookbook-second-edition`.

How to do it...

In order to sort using scripting, perform the following steps:

1. If you want to order your documents by the `price` field multiplied by a `factor` parameter (that is, sales tax), the search will be as shown in the following code:

```
curl -XGET 'http://127.0.0.1:9200/test-index/test-type/_
search?&pretty=true&size=3' -d '{
  "query": {
    "match_all": {}
  },
  "sort": {
    "_script" : {
      "script" : "doc[\"price\"].value * factor",
      "lang" : "groovy",
      "type" : "number",
      "ignore_unmapped" : true,
```

```
        "params" : {
          "factor" : 1.1
        },
            "order" : "asc"
          }
      }
}'
```

In this case, we have used a `match_all` query and a `sort` script.

2. If everything is correct, the result returned by ElasticSearch should be as shown in the following code:

```
{
  "took" : 7,
  "timed_out" : false,
  "_shards" : {
    "total" : 5,
    "successful" : 5,
    "failed" : 0
  },
  "hits" : {
    "total" : 1000,
    "max_score" : null,
    "hits" : [ {
      "_index" : "test-index",
      "_type" : "test-type",
      "_id" : "161",
      "_score" : null, "_source" : … truncated …,
      "sort" : [ 0.0278578661440021 ]
    }, {
      "_index" : "test-index",
      "_type" : "test-type",
      "_id" : "634",
      "_score" : null, "_source" : … truncated …,
      "sort" : [ 0.08131364254827411 ]
    }, {
      "_index" : "test-index",
      "_type" : "test-type",
      "_id" : "465",
      "_score" : null, "_source" : … truncated …,
      "sort" : [ 0.1094966959069832 ]
    } ]
  }
}
```

How it works...

The `sort` parameter, which we discussed in *Chapter 5, Search, Queries, and Filters*, can be extended with the help of scripting.

The `sort` scripting allows you to define several parameters, as follows:

- ▶ `order` (default `"asc"`) (`"asc"` or `"desc"`): This determines whether the order must be ascending or descending.
- ▶ `script`: This contains the code to be executed.
- ▶ `type`: This defines the type to convert the value.
- ▶ `params` (optional, a JSON object): This defines the parameters that need to be passed.
- ▶ `lang` (by default, `groovy`): This defines the scripting language to be used.
- ▶ `ignore_unmapped` (optional): This ignores unmapped fields in a sort. This flag allows you to avoid errors due to missing fields in shards.

Extending the sort with scripting allows the use of a broader approach to score your hits.

> ElasticSearch scripting permits the use of every code that you want. You can create custom complex algorithms to score your documents.

There's more...

Groovy provides a lot of built-in functions (mainly taken from Java's Math class) that can be used in scripts, as shown in the following table:

Function	Description
`time()`	The current time in milliseconds
`sin(a)`	Returns the trigonometric sine of an angle
`cos(a)`	Returns the trigonometric cosine of an angle
`tan(a)`	Returns the trigonometric tangent of an angle
`asin(a)`	Returns the arc sine of a value
`acos(a)`	Returns the arc cosine of a value
`atan(a)`	Returns the arc tangent of a value
`toRadians(angdeg)`	Converts an angle measured in degrees to an approximately equivalent angle measured in radians
`toDegrees(angrad)`	Converts an angle measured in radians to an approximately equivalent angle measured in degrees

Function	Description
`exp(a)`	Returns Euler's number raised to the power of a value
`log(a)`	Returns the natural logarithm (base e) of a value
`log10(a)`	Returns the base 10 logarithm of a value
`sqrt(a)`	Returns the correctly rounded positive square root of a value
`cbrt(a)`	Returns the cube root of a double value
`IEEEremainder(f1, f2)`	Computes the remainder operation on two arguments, as prescribed by the IEEE 754 standard
`ceil(a)`	Returns the smallest (closest to negative infinity) value that is greater than or equal to the argument and is equal to a mathematical integer
`floor(a)`	Returns the largest (closest to positive infinity) value that is less than or equal to the argument and is equal to a mathematical integer
`rint(a)`	Returns the value that is closest in value to the argument and is equal to a mathematical integer
`atan2(y, x)`	Returns the angle theta from the conversion of rectangular coordinates $(x, y\_)$ to polar coordinates $(r, \_theta)$
`pow(a, b)`	Returns the value of the first argument raised to the power of the second argument
`round(a)`	Returns the closest integer to the argument
`random()`	Returns a random double value
`abs(a)`	Returns the absolute value of a value
`max(a, b)`	Returns the greater of the two values
`min(a, b)`	Returns the smaller of the two values
`ulp(d)`	Returns the size of the unit in the last place of the argument
`signum(d)`	Returns the `signum` function of the argument
`sinh(x)`	Returns the hyperbolic sine of a value
`cosh(x)`	Returns the hyperbolic cosine of a value
`tanh(x)`	Returns the hyperbolic tangent of a value
`hypot(x,y)`	Returns `sqrt(x^2+y^2)` without an intermediate overflow or underflow
`acos(a)`	Returns the arc cosine of a value
`atan(a)`	Returns the arc tangent of a value

If you want to retrieve records in a random order, you can use a script with a random method, as shown in the following code:

```
curl -XGET 'http://127.0.0.1:9200/test-index/test-type/_
search?&pretty=true&size=3' -d '{
  "query": {
    "match_all": {}
  },
  "sort": {
    "_script" : {
      "script" : "Math.random()",
      "lang" : "groovy",
      "type" : "number",
      "params" : {}
    }
  }
}'
```

In this example, for every hit, the new sort value is computed by executing the Math. random() scripting function.

See also

► The official ElasticSearch documentation at http://www.elasticsearch.org/ guide/en/elasticsearch/reference/current/modules-scripting.html

Computing return fields with scripting

ElasticSearch allows you to define complex expressions that can be used to return a new calculated field value. These special fields are called script_fields, and they can be expressed with a script in every available ElasticSearch scripting language.

Getting ready

You will need a working ElasticSearch cluster and an index populated with the script (chapter_06/populate_aggregations.sh) used in *Chapter 6, Aggregations*, which is available at https://github.com/aparo/elasticsearch-cookbook-second-edition.

How to do it...

In order to compute return fields with scripting, perform the following steps:

1. Return the following script fields:

   ❏ `"my_calc_field"`: This concatenates the text of the `"name"` and `"description"` fields

   ❏ `"my_calc_field2"`: This multiplies the `"price"` value by the `"discount"` parameter

2. From the command line, execute the following code:

```
curl -XGET 'http://127.0.0.1:9200/test-index/test-type/_
search?&pretty=true&size=3' -d '{
  "query": {
    "match_all": {}
  },
  "script_fields" : {
    "my_calc_field" : {
      "script" : "doc[\"name\"].value + \" -- \" +
doc[\"description\"].value"
    },
    "my_calc_field2" : {
      "script" : "doc[\"price\"].value * discount",
      "params" : {
        "discount"  : 0.8
      }
    }
  }
}'
```

3. If everything works all right, this is how the result returned by ElasticSearch should be:

```
{
  "took" : 4,
  "timed_out" : false,
  "_shards" : {
    "total" : 5,
    "successful" : 5,
    "failed" : 0
  },
  "hits" : {
    "total" : 1000,
    "max_score" : 1.0,
    "hits" : [ {
```

```
            "_index" : "test-index",
            "_type" : "test-type",
            "_id" : "4",
            "_score" : 1.0,
            "fields" : {
              "my_calc_field" : "entropic -- accusantium",
              "my_calc_field2" : 5.480038242170081
            }
        }, {
            "_index" : "test-index",
            "_type" : "test-type",
            "_id" : "9",
            "_score" : 1.0,
            "fields" : {
              "my_calc_field" : "frankie -- accusantium",
              "my_calc_field2" : 34.79852410178313
            }
        }, {
            "_index" : "test-index",
            "_type" : "test-type",
            "_id" : "11",
            "_score" : 1.0,
            "fields" : {
              "my_calc_field" : "johansson -- accusamus",
              "my_calc_field2" : 11.824173084636591
            }
        } ]
    }
}
```

How it works...

The scripting fields are similar to executing an SQL function on a field during a select operation.

In ElasticSearch, after a search phase is executed and the hits to be returned are calculated, if some fields (standard or script) are defined, they are calculated and returned.

The script field, which can be defined with all the supported languages, is processed by passing a value to the source of the document and, if some other parameters are defined in the script (in the discount factor example), they are passed to the script function.

The script function is a code snippet; it can contain everything that the language allows you to write, but it must be evaluated to a value (or a list of values).

See also

▶ The *Installing additional script plugins* recipe in this chapter to install additional languages for scripting

▶ The *Sorting using script* recipe to have a reference of the extra built-in functions in Groovy scripts

Filtering a search via scripting

In *Chapter 5*, *Search, Queries, and Filters*, we have learnt about filters. ElasticSearch scripting allows you to extend the traditional filter with custom scripts.

Using scripting to create a custom filter is a convenient way to write scripting rules that are not provided by Lucene or ElasticSearch, and to implement business logic that is not available in the query DSL.

Getting ready

You will need a working ElasticSearch cluster and an index populated with the (chapter_06/ populate_aggregations.sh) script used in *Chapter 6*, *Aggregations*, which is available at https://github.com/aparo/elasticsearch-cookbook-second-edition.

How to do it...

In order to filter a search using a script, perform the following steps:

1. Write a search with a filter that filters out a document with the value of age less than the parameter value:

```
curl -XGET 'http://127.0.0.1:9200/test-index/test-type/_
search?&pretty=true&size=3' -d '{
  "query": {
    "filtered": {
      "filter": {
        "script": {
          "script": "doc[\"age\"].value > param1",
          "params" : {
            "param1" : 80
          }
        }
      },
      "query": {
        "match_all": {}
      }
```

```
                }
             }
        }'
```

> In this example, all the documents in which the value of age is greater than `param1` are qualified to be returned.

2. If everything works correctly, the result returned by ElasticSearch should be as shown here:

```
{
  "took" : 30,
  "timed_out" : false,
  "_shards" : {
    "total" : 5,
    "successful" : 5,
    "failed" : 0
  },
  "hits" : {
    "total" : 237,
    "max_score" : 1.0,
    "hits" : [ {
      "_index" : "test-index",
      "_type" : "test-type",
      "_id" : "9",
      "_score" : 1.0, "_source" :{ … "age": 83, … }
    }, {
      "_index" : "test-index",
      "_type" : "test-type",
      "_id" : "23",
      "_score" : 1.0, "_source" : { … "age": 87, … }
    }, {
      "_index" : "test-index",
      "_type" : "test-type",
      "_id" : "47",
      "_score" : 1.0, "_source" : {…. "age": 98, …}
    } ]
  }
}
```

How it works...

The script filter is a language script that returns a Boolean value (`true`/`false`). For every hit, the script is evaluated, and if it returns `true`, the hit passes the filter. This type of scripting can only be used as Lucene filters, not as queries, because it doesn't affect the search (the exceptions are `constant_score` and `custom_filters_score`).

These are the scripting fields:

- `script`: This contains the code to be executed
- `params`: These are optional parameters to be passed to the script
- `lang` (defaults to `groovy`): This defines the language of the script

The script code can be any code in your preferred and supported scripting language that returns a Boolean value.

There's more...

Other languages are used in the same way as Groovy.

For the current example, I have chosen a standard comparison that works in several languages. To execute the same script using the JavaScript language, use the following code:

```
curl -XGET 'http://127.0.0.1:9200/test-index/test-type/_
search?&pretty=true&size=3' -d '{
  "query": {
    "filtered": {
      "filter": {
        "script": {
          "script": "doc[\"age\"].value > param1",
          "lang":"javascript",
          "params" : {
            "param1" : 80
          }
        }
      },
      "query": {
        "match_all": {}
      }
    }
  }
}'
```

For Python, use the following code:

```
curl -XGET 'http://127.0.0.1:9200/test-index/test-type/_
search?&pretty=true&size=3' -d '{
  "query": {
    "filtered": {
      "filter": {
        "script": {
          "script": "doc[\"age\"].value > param1",
          "lang":"python",
          "params" : {
            "param1" : 80
          }
        }
      },
      "query": {
        "match_all": {}
      }
    }
  }
}'
```

See also

▸ The *Installing additional script plugins* recipe in this chapter to install additional languages for scripting

▸ The *Sorting data using script* recipe in this chapter to get a reference of the extra built-in functions in Groovy scripts

Updating a document using scripts

ElasticSearch allows you to update a document in its place.

Updating a document via scripting reduces the network traffic (otherwise, you would need to fetch the document, change the field, and send it back) and improves performance when you need to process huge amounts of documents.

Getting ready

You will need a working ElasticSearch cluster and an index populated with the script used in *Chapter 6, Aggregations*, which is available at `https://github.com/aparo/elasticsearch-cookbook-second-edition`.

How to do it...

In order to update a document using scripting, perform the following steps:

1. Write an update action that adds a tag value to a list of tags available in the source of a document. This is how the code should look:

    ```
    curl -XPOST 'http://127.0.0.1:9200/test-index/test-type/9/_
    update?&pretty=true' -d '{
      "script" : "ctx._source.tag += tag",
      "params" : {
        "tag" : "cool"
      }
    }'
    ```

2. If everything works correctly, this is how the result returned by ElasticSearch should look:

    ```
    {
      "ok" : true,
      "_index" : "test-index",
      "_type" : "test-type",
      "_id" : "9",
      "_version" : 2
    }
    ```

3. If you retrieve the document now, this is what you will have:

    ```
    {
      "_index" : "test-index",
      "_type" : "test-type",
      "_id" : "9",
      "_version" : 2,
      "found" : true,
      "_source":{
          "in_stock": true,
          "tag": ["alias", "sit", "cool"],
          "name": "Frankie Raye", ...truncated...
          }
    }
    ```

    From the result, you can also see that the version number increases by one.

How it works...

The REST HTTP method that is used to update a document is **POST**.

The URL contains only the index name, type, document ID, and action, as follows:

```
http://<server>/<index_name>/<type>/<document_id>/_update
```

The update action is composed of the following three steps:

1. **Get operation** (very fast): This operation works on real-time data (no need to refresh) and retrieves the record
2. **Script execution**: The script is executed on the document, and if required, it is updated
3. **Saving the document**: The document, if needed, is saved

The script execution follows the workflow in the following manner:

▸ The script is compiled and the result is cached to improve re-execution. The compilation depends on the scripting language; it detects errors in the script, such as typographical, syntax, and language-related errors. The compilation step can be CPU-bound, so ElasticSearch caches the compilation results for further execution.

▸ The document is executed in the script context. The document data is available in the `ctx` variable in the script.

The update script can set several parameters in the `ctx` variable. These are the most important parameters:

▸ `ctx._source`: This contains the source of the document.

▸ `ctx._timestamp`: If it's defined, this value is set to the document's timestamp.

▸ `ctx.op`: This defines the main operation type to be executed. There are several available values, as follows:

  ❑ `index` (the default value): The record is reindexed with the update values.

  ❑ `delete`: The document is deleted after the update.

  ❑ `none`: The document is skipped without reindexing the document.

> If you need to execute a large number of update operations, it's better to perform them in bulk in order to improve your application's performance.

There's more...

The previous example can be rewritten using JavaScript language, and looks as shown in the following command:

```
curl -XPOST 'http://127.0.0.1:9200/test-index/test-type/9/_
update?&pretty=true' -d '{
  "script" : "ctx._source.tag += tag",
```

```
  "lang":"js",
  "params" : {
    "tag" : "cool"
  }
}'
```

The previous example can be written using the Python language, as follows:

```
curl -XPOST 'http://127.0.0.1:9200/test-index/test-type/9/_
update?&pretty=true' -d '{
  "script" : "ctx[\"_source\"][\"tag\"] =
  list(ctx[\"_source\"][\"tag\"]) + [tag]",
  "lang":"python",
    "params" : {
    "tag" : "cool"
  }
}'
```

In the Python example, the Java list must be converted into a Python list to allow the addition of elements; the back conversion is automatically done.

> To improve performance, if a field is not changed, it's a good practice to set the `ctx._op` variable equal to none in order to disable the indexing of the unchanged document.

In the following example, we will execute an update that adds new "tags" and "labels" values to an object, but we will mark the document for indexing only if the tags or labels values are changed:

```
curl -XPOST 'http://127.0.0.1:9200/test-index/test-type/9/_
update?&pretty=true' -d '{
  "script" : "ctx.op = \"none\";
  if(ctx._source.containsValue(\"tags\")){
    foreach(item:new_tags){
      if(!ctx._source.tags.contains(item)){
        ctx._source.tags += item;
        ctx.op = \"index\";
      }
    }
  }else{
    ctx._source.tags=new_tags;
    ctx.op = \"index\";
  };
  if(ctx._source.containsValue(\"labels\")){
    foreach(item:new_labels){
```

```
      if(!ctx._source.labels.contains(item)){
        ctx._source.labels += item;
        ctx.op = \"index\";
      }
    }
  }else{
    ctx._source.labels=new_labels;
    ctx.op = \"index\";
  };",
  "params" : {
    "new_tags" : ["cool", "nice"],
    "new_labels" : ["red", "blue", "green"]
  }
}'
```

The preceding code is `pretty` printed. When saving your script, the newline should be coded as an \n character.

The preceding script uses the following steps:

1. It marks the operation to the `none` value to prevent indexing, if in the following steps the original source is not changed.

2. It checks whether the `tags` field is available in the source object.

3. If the `tags` field is available in the source object, it iterates all the values of the `new_tags` list. If the value is not available in the current `tags` list, it adds the value and updates the operation to index.

4. If the `tags` field doesn't exist in the source object, it simply adds it to the source and marks the operation to index.

5. The steps from 2 to 4 are repeated for the `labels` value. The repetition is present in this example to show the ElasticSearch user how it is possible to update multiple values in a single update operation.

This script can be quite complex, but it shows the powerful capabilities of scripting in ElasticSearch.

8
Rivers

In this chapter, we will cover the following recipes:

- ▶ Managing a river
- ▶ Using the CouchDB river
- ▶ Using the MongoDB river
- ▶ Using the RabbitMQ river
- ▶ Using the JDBC river
- ▶ Using the Twitter river

Introduction

There are two ways to put your data into ElasticSearch. As you have seen in previous chapters, one way is to use the index API, which allows you to store documents in ElasticSearch via the PUT/POST API or the bulk API. The other way is to use a service that fetches the data from an external source (at one time or periodically) and puts it in the cluster.

ElasticSearch calls these services **rivers**, and the ElasticSearch community provides several rivers to connect to different data sources, as follows:

- ▶ CouchDB
- ▶ MongoDB
- ▶ RabbitMQ
- ▶ SQL DBMS (Oracle, MySQL, PostgreSQL, and so on)
- ▶ Redis
- ▶ Twitter
- ▶ Wikipedia

Rivers are available as external plugins at `http://www.elasticsearch.org/guide/en/elasticsearch/reference/current/modules-plugins.html#river`, which provides an updated list of the available ElasticSearch rivers. In this chapter, we'll discuss how to manage a river (create, check, and delete) and how to configure the most common ones.

A river is a very handy tool to ingest data in ElasticSearch, but it has its advantages and disadvantages.

These are the main advantages of rivers:

- A built-in main functionality in the ElasticSearch core (although in the future, it might be removed)
- Autorestart is managed by ElasticSearch in the event of a cluster startup or migration to another node in case of a node failure
- Easily deployable as an ElasticSearch plugin

These are the main disadvantages of rivers:

- Failures or a malfunction in a river can cause the node or cluster to hang
- There is no river balancer, so some nodes can have a high overhead due to the execution of a river, reducing overall performance
- An update to a river requires a cluster restart
- It's very difficult to debug a river in a multiple node environment

The river system is a good tool to use for prototyping functionalities, but due to its issues, it can lead to cluster instability. A best practice is to execute data ingestion in a separate application. This approach is used, for example, in logstash, the log data ingestion system of ElasticSearch (`http://www.elasticsearch.org/overview/logstash` and `http://logstash.net/`).

Managing a river

In ElasticSearch, there are two main action-related river setups: creating a river and deleting a river.

Getting ready

You will need a working ElasticSearch cluster.

How to do it...

A river is uniquely defined by a name and type. The river type is the type name defined in the loaded river plugins. After the `name` and `type` parameters, a river usually requires an extra configuration that can be passed in the `_meta` property.

In order to manage a river, perform the following steps:

1. To create a river (`my_river`), the HTTP method used is `PUT` (`POST` will work, too), as shown here:

    ```
    curl -XPUT 'http://127.0.0.1:9200/_river/my_river/_meta' -d '{
      "type" : "dummy"
    }'
    ```

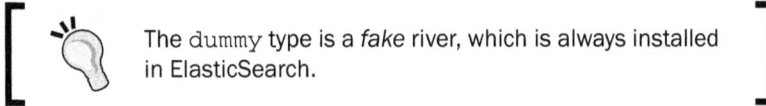

    > The `dummy` type is a *fake* river, which is always installed in ElasticSearch.

2. This is how the result will look:

    ```
    {"created":true,"_index":"_river","_type":"my_river","_id":
    "_meta","_version":1}
    ```

3. If you take a look at the ElasticSearch logs, you'll see some new lines, as shown here:

    ```
    [2014-07-27 12:20:55,518][INFO ][cluster.metadata        ]
    [White Pilgrim] [_river] creating index, cause [auto(index
    api)], shards [1]/[1], mappings []
    [2014-07-27 12:20:55,557][INFO ][cluster.metadata        ]
    [White Pilgrim] [_river] update_mapping [my_river]
    (dynamic)
    [2014-07-27 12:20:56,569][INFO ][river.dummy             ]
    [White Pilgrim] [dummy][my_river] create
    [2014-07-27 12:20:56,569][INFO ][river.dummy             ]
    [White Pilgrim] [dummy][my_river] start
    [2014-07-27 12:20:56,582][INFO ][cluster.metadata        ]
    [White Pilgrim] [_river] update_mapping [my_river]
    (dynamic)
    ```

4. To remove a river, use the `DELETE` HTTP method. If you consider the previously created river, this should be the REST call:

    ```
    curl -XDELETE 'http://127.0.0.1:9200/_river/my_river/'
    ```

    The following will be the result:

    ```
    {"acknowledged":true}
    ```

5. If you take a look at the ElasticSearch logs, you'll see some new lines, as follows:

    ```
    [2014-07-27 12:22:04,464][INFO ][cluster.metadata        ]
    [White Pilgrim] [[_river]] remove_mapping [[my_river]]
    [2014-07-27 12:22:04,466][INFO ][river.dummy             ]
    [White Pilgrim] [dummy][my_river] close
    ```

How it works...

During an ElasticSearch node startup, the river service is automatically activated.

Depending on the river implementation, there are two different usages: **one shot** and **periodically**. In one shot usage, the river is created with some parameters. It executes its process and then it removes itself once the process is complete. This approach is mainly used to process files, dumps, and every source that needs to be processed only once, as the data in it does not change. In periodical usage, the river waits for a time interval after it has processed all the data and then restarts processing new data, if available. This case is typical of data sources that are updated frequently such as DBMS, MongoDB, **RabbitMQ**, and **Redis**.

Rivers are stored in a special index, `_river` (In ElasticSearch, all special indices start with the `_` character.). The document type, `name`, becomes the river name, and the `_meta` document is located at the place where the river configuration is stored.

The `_river` index is automatically replicated in every cluster node.

When ElasticSearch receives a `create` river call, it creates the new river mapping and starts the river. Generally, the river is composed of the following components:

 ► **Producer threads**: These collect the documents to be indexed and send them to a consumer (thread)
 ► **Consumer threads**: These execute the bulk insertion of documents sent by the producer

When the river is started, these threads are also started, and the data is processed and sent to the cluster.

In our example, we can see that a river is started by taking a look at the ElasticSearch logfiles.

When you want to remove a river, the `DELETE` call removes it from the execution. At the server level, ElasticSearch stops the river, flushes the stale data, and removes it from the `_river` index.

ElasticSearch always guarantees that a single river instance is running in the cluster (singleton). If the river is executed on a node and if this node should die, the river is rescheduled to work on another cluster node. It's the application logic of the river that keeps track of the river status and does not reprocess the same data.

There's more...

When a river is executing, a special document `_status` is available under the river name. This is a standard ElasticSearch document that can be fetched with the GET API.

For the preceding example, it's possible to check the status with this code:

```
curl -XGET 'http://127.0.0.1:9200/_river/my_river/_status'
```

The answer will be similar to the following:

```
{
    "_id": "_status",
    "_index": "_river",
    "_source": {
      "node": {
        "id": "I_mWzO-tRHWG-DpQOFuw4w",
        "name": " White Pilgrim",
        "transport_address": "inet[/127.0.0.1:9300]"
      }
    },
    "_type": "my_river",
    "_version": 1,
    "found": true
}
```

In the _source function, the node attribute defines in which node the river is in execution. The status can also contain special river fields, describing the current river position in the process (for example, the number of documents processed, the last river cycle, and so on).

See also

 ▶ The *Installing a plugin manually* recipe in *Chapter 2, Downloading and Setting Up*

Using the CouchDB river

CouchDB is a NoSQL data store that stores data in the JSON format, similar to ElasticSearch. It can be queried with the map/reduce task and provides the REST API, so every operation can be done via HTTP API calls.

Using ElasticSearch to index and search CouchDB data is very handy, as it extends the CouchDB data store with Lucene's search capabilities.

Getting ready

You will need a working ElasticSearch cluster and a working CouchDB server to connect to.

How to do it...

In order to use the CouchDB river, perform the following steps:

1. First, you need to install the CouchDB river plugin, which is available on GitHub
   (`https://github.com/elasticsearch/elasticsearch-river-couchdb`),
   and is maintained by the ElasticSearch company. You can install the river plugin in
   the usual way:

   ```
   bin/plugin -install elasticsearch/elasticsearch-river-
   couchdb/2.0.0
   ```

   > Internally, the CouchDB river plugin uses the attachment plugin and
   > JavaScript plugins, and it is a good practice to install them.

2. After a node restart, you can create a configuration (`config.json`) for your
   CouchDB river:

   ```
   {
       "type": "couchdb",
       "couchdb": {
           "host": "localhost",
           "port": 5984,
           "db": "my_db",
           "filter": null
       },
       "index": {
           "index": "my_db",
           "type": "my_db",
           "bulk_size": "100",
           "bulk_timeout": "10ms"
       }
   }
   ```

3. Now, create the river with this configuration:

   ```
   curl -XPUT 'http://127.0.0.1:9200/_river/couchriver/_meta'
   -d @config.json
   ```

4. This is how the result will look:

   ```
   {"_index":"_river","_type":" couchriver
   ","_id":"_meta","_version":1, "created":true }
   ```

How it works...

The CouchDB river is designed to be fast at detecting changes and propagating them from CouchDB to ElasticSearch. It is designed to hook the `_changes` feed of CouchDB so that it does not create any overhead in polling the server and consumes as less resources as possible.

This approach prevents the execution of a lot of map/reduce queries on CouchDB to retrieve the new or changed documents.

To create a CouchDB river, the type must be set to `couchdb`. The following parameters must be passed to the `couchdb` object:

- `protocol` (by default, `http`; the valid values are `http` and `https`): This parameter defines the protocol to be used.
- `no_verify` (by default, `false`): If this parameter is set to `true`, the river will skip the HTTPS certificate validation.
- `host` (by default, `localhost`): This parameter defines the host server to be used.
- `port` (by default, `5984`) : This parameter defines the CouchDB port number.
- `heartbeat` (by default, `10s`) and `read_timeout` (by default, `30s`): These parameters are used to control the HTTP connection timeouts.
- `db` (by default, the river name): This parameter defines the name of the database that is to be monitored.
- `filter`: This parameter defines some filters that can be applied to remove unwanted documents.
- `filter_params`: This parameter defines a list of keys/values used to filter out documents.
- `ignore_attachments` (by default, `false`): If this parameter is `true`, the document that contains the attachment will be skipped. It requires the **Attachment** plugin installed.
- `user` and `password`: These parameters, if defined, are used to authenticate the user to CouchDB.
- `script`: This is an optional script to be executed on documents.

The CouchDB river also provides a good tuning on indexing by letting the user configure several index parameters in the `index` object, as follows:

- `index`: This parameter is the index name to be used
- `type`: This parameter is the type to be used
- `bulk_size` (by default, `100`): This parameter is the number of bulk items to be collected before sending them as bulk

- ▸ `bulk_timeout` (by default, `10` milliseconds): If changes are detected within the `bulk_timeout` time, they are packed up to `bulk_size` before being sent

- ▸ `max_concurrent_bulk` (by default, `1`): This parameter controls the count of the concurrent bulk requests that are to be executed

When the river starts, it initializes two threads:

- ▸ **Slurper thread**: This manages the connection between ElasticSearch and the CouchDB server. It continuously fetches the changes in CouchDB and puts them in a queue to be read by the indexer. Generally, this thread is called a **producer**.

- ▸ **Indexer thread**: This collects items from the queue and prepares the bulk to be indexed. It is often referred to as a **consumer**.

There's more...

The CouchDB river is very fast and well-designed. It has two important tools to improve the quality of your ingested documents: filter and script.

The filter, if applicable, allows you to filter documents in CouchDB's `_change` stream, reducing the bandwidth and the documents that must be indexed. The filter can also be used to partition your CouchDB database. For example, it allows you to create rivers that use one index per user to store documents.

The script allows document manipulation before indexing them. Typical scenarios cover adding/cloning/editing/joining fields, but other document manipulations are available, which are limited only by the capabilities of the chosen scripting language.

See also

- ▸ The CouchDB river plugin's home page at
  `https://github.com/elasticsearch/elasticsearch-river-couchdb`

Using the MongoDB river

MongoDB is a very common NoSQL data storage system used all over the world. One of the main things that it lacks is that it was not designed for text searching.

Although the latest MongoDB version provides full-text search, its completeness and functionality are, by far, more limited than the current ElasticSearch version. So, it's quite common to use MongoDB as the data store and ElasticSearch to search. The MongoDB river, initially developed by me and now maintained by Richard Louapre, helps to create a bridge between these two applications.

Getting ready

You will need a working ElasticSearch cluster and a working MongoDB instance installed on the same machine as ElasticSearch, with replica sets enabled (`http://docs.mongodb.org/manual/tutorial/deploy-replica-set/` and `http://docs.mongodb.org/manual/tutorial/convert-standalone-to-replica-set/`). You need to restore the sample data available in `mongodb/data` with the following command:

```
mongorestore -d escookbook escookbook
```

How to do it...

To use the MongoDB river, perform the following steps:

1. First, install the MongoDB river plugin, which is available on GitHub (`https://github.com/richardwilly98/elasticsearch-river-mongodb`). You can install the river plugin in the usual way:

   ```
   bin/plugin -install richardwilly98/elasticsearch-river-mongodb
   ```

   > As the internal MongoDB river plugin uses the ElasticSearch attachment plugin (if you need to import documents from GridFS) and sometimes the JavaScript scripting language (if you want to use filtering), it is a good practice to install these scripting languages.

2. Restart your ElasticSearch node to make sure the river plugin is loaded. In the log, this is what you should see:

   ```
   [2014-08-04 15:39:29,705][INFO ][plugins                  ]
   [Dirtnap] loaded [river-twitter, transport-thrift, river-
   mongodb, mapper-attachments, lang-python, lang-javascript],
   sites [bigdesk, head]
   ```

3. You need to create a `config.json` file to be used to configure the river. In our case, we define a database and a collection to fetch the data:

   ```
   {
     "type" : "mongodb",
     "mongodb" : {
      "servers" : [
       { "host" : "localhost", "port" : 27017 }
      ],
      "db" : "escookbook",
      "collection" : "items"
     },
     "index" : {
   ```

```
      "name" : "items"
    }
  }
}
```

4. Now, create the river with the current configuration:

   ```
   curl -XPUT 'http://127.0.0.1:9200/_river/mongodbriver/_meta' -
   d @config.json
   ```

5. This is how the result will look:

   ```
   {"_index":"_river","_type":"mongodbriver","_id":"_meta","_v
   ersion":1, "created":true}
   ```

How it works...

MongoDB fetches data from a MongoDB instance and puts it in the current cluster. It's important that the MongoDB instance be correctly configured in the replica set, as the river works on the `oplog` collection. The `oplog` (operations log) collection is a special collection that is used to keep track of every MongoDB change. The river interprets the log actions and replicates them in ElasticSearch. Using this approach, it's not necessary to continue polling the MongoDB cluster and searches that can significantly reduce the performance are not required.

> The actual implementation of the MongoDB river is also compatible with TokuMX (`https://github.com/Tokutek/mongo`), a high performance distribution of MongoDB.

The ElasticSearch configuration used in the preceding example is quite simple. There are two main sections in the configuration:

▸ Mongodb: This contains the MongoDB-related parameters. These are the most important ones:

   ❑ `servers`: This is a list of hosts and ports to connect to.

   ❑ `credentials`: This is a list of database credentials (db, user, and password). Take the following code as an example:

   ```
   {"db":"mydatabase", "user":"username",
   "password":"myseceret"}
   ```

   ❑ db: This defines the database to be monitored.

   ❑ `collection`: This defines the collection to be monitored.

   ❑ `gridfs`: This defines a Boolean that indicates whether the collection is GridFS.

   ❑ `filter`: This defines an extra filter to filter out records.

- ❑ `index`: This defines the index where the documents have to be stored in ElasticSearch. The most important parameters that can be passed are as follows:

    `name`: This is the index name to be used

    `type`: This is the type to be used

If no mappings are defined, the river will autodetect the format from the MongoDB document.

> One of the main advantages of using this plugin is that because it works on `oplog`, it always keeps the data updated without the MongoDB overhead.

See also

- ▶ The MongoDB river plugin's home page at `https://github.com/richardwilly98/elasticsearch-river-mongodb`

Using the RabbitMQ river

RabbitMQ is a fast message broker that can handle thousands of messages per second. It can be very handy to use in conjunction with ElasticSearch in order to bulk index the records.

The RabbitMQ river plugin is designed for waiting messages that contain a list of bulk operations. When a new message is delivered to RabbitMQ, it's delivered to ElasticSearch via the plugin to be executed.

Getting ready

You will need a working ElasticSearch cluster and a working RabbitMQ instance installed on the same machine as ElasticSearch.

How to do it...

In order to use the RabbitMQ river, perform the following steps:

1. First, you need to install the RabbitMQ river plugin, which is available on GitHub (`https://github.com/elasticsearch/elasticsearch-river-rabbitmq`). You can install the river plugin in the usual way:

    ```
    bin/plugin -install elasticsearch/elasticsearch-river-
    rabbitmq/2.3.0
    ```

2. This is how the result should look:

```
-> Installing elasticsearch/elasticsearch-river-
rabbitmq/2.3.0...
Trying http://download.elasticsearch.org/elasticsearch/elasticsear
ch-river-rabbitmq/elasticsearch-river-rabbitmq-2.3.0.zip...
Downloading ..................DONE
Installed river-rabbitmq
```

3. Restart your ElasticSearch node to ensure that the river plugin is loaded. In the log, you should see the following code:

```
[2013-10-14 23:08:43,639][INFO ][plugins                    ]
[Fault Zone] loaded [river-rabbitmq, river-twitter,
transport-thrift, river-mongodb, mapper-attachments, lang-
python, river-couchdb, lang-javascript], sites [bigdesk,
head]
```

4. You need to create a configuration file (.json) to be used to configure the river:

```
{
  "type" : "rabbitmq",
  "rabbitmq" : {
    "host" : "localhost",
    "port" : 5672,
    "user" : "guest",
    "pass" : "guest",
    "vhost" : "/",
    "queue" : "elasticsearch",
    "exchange" : "elasticsearch",
    "routing_key" : "elasticsearch",
    "exchange_declare" : true,
    "exchange_type" : "direct",
    "exchange_durable" : true,
    "queue_declare" : true,
    "queue_bind" : true,
    "queue_durable" : true,
    "queue_auto_delete" : false,
    "heartbeat" : "30m",
    "nack_errors" : "true"
  },
  "index" : {
    "bulk_size" : 100,
    "bulk_timeout" : "10ms",
    "ordered" : false,
    "replication" : "default"
  }
}
```

5. Now, create the river with the current configuration:

```
curl -XPUT 'http://127.0.0.1:9200/_river/rabbitriver/_meta'
-d @config.json
```

6. This will be the result:

```
{"_index":"_river","_type":" rabbitriver
","_id":"_meta","_version":1, "created":true }
```

How it works...

The RabbitMQ river instantiates a connection to the RabbitMQ server and waits for the messages to finish processing. The only kind of messages that the plugin is able to process are bulk operation messages.

> Every bulk operation must terminate with a new line \n; otherwise, the last operation is of little depth.

Typically, the connection between RabbitMQ and ElasticSearch is a direct connection, which means that as the message is sent to the RabbitMQ server, it is redirected to ElasticSearch.

The river type is `rabbitmq`, and all client configurations live on the `rabbitmq` object. These are the most common parameters for the RabbitMQ river:

- `host` (by default, `localhost`): This defines the RabbitMQ server's address.
- `port` (by default, `5672`): This defines the RabbitMQ server's port.
- `user` and `pass`: These define the user and password credentials required to access the RabbitMQ server, respectively.
- `vhost` (by default, `/`): This defines the RabbitMQ virtual host to be used.
- `exchange_declare` (false/true) and `exchange` (by default, `elasticsearch`): These control whether the exchange must be bound and the exchange object name, respectively.
- `exchange_type` (by default, `direct`): This defines the type of exchange to be used.
- `exchange_durable` (by default, `true`): This defines a durable exchange that can survive if the RabbitMQ broker restarts; otherwise it is transient.
- `queue_declare` (false/true) and `queue` (by default, `elasticsearch`): These control whether a queue must be bound and the queue name, respectively.
- `queue_durable` (by default, `true`): This defines a durable queue that can survive if the RabbitMQ broker restarts; otherwise, it is transient.
- `queue_auto_delete` (by default, `false`): This defines a queue where consumers finish (no messages remaining), in which all the messages need to be automatically deleted.

- ▸ `heartbeat`: This controls the heartbeat delay in the connection. It's used to prevent connection dropping if there is network inactivity.

- ▸ `nack_errors` (by default, `false`): If it is true, there can be failures in bulk action which need to be skipped; otherwise, they are marked as rejected and reprocessed.

Sometimes, the RabbitMQ server is configured in cluster mode for high availability. In this configuration, there is no single host, but a list of multiple hosts. They can be defined in a list of addresses in this way:

```
{
    "rabbitmq" : {
      "addresses" : [
        {
            "host" : "host1",
            "port" : 5672
        },
        {
            "host" : "host2",
            "port" : 5672
        }
      ]
    }
    ...
}
```

There's more...

The RabbitMQ river plugin, along with scripting, allows you to control two important aspects of bulk processing: the global bulk with the `bulk_scripting_filter` function and every single document with `script_filter` that must be indexed or created. The definition of these two script filters is accepted as a standard for every filter.

The following are the parameters:

- ▸ `script`: This is the code of the script
- ▸ `script_lang`: This is the language to be used to interpret the code
- ▸ `script_params`: This is a dictionary/map/key-value containing the additional parameter to be passed to the script

The `bulk_script_filter` function will receive a block of text (body) that is the text of a list of actions. The script must return another block of text to be processed by ElasticSearch. If the script returns null, the bulk is skipped.

The following is an example of the `bulk_script_filter` declaration:

```
{
   "type" : "rabbitmq",
     "rabbitmq" : {
         ...
     },
     "index" : {
         ...
     },
     "bulk_script_filter" : {
         "script" : "myscript",
         "script_lang" : "native",
         "script_params" : {
             "param1" : "val1",
             "param2" : "val2"
             ...
         }
     }
}
```

If a `script_filter` function is defined, a `ctx` context is passed to the script for every document, which must be indexed or created.

The following is an example of the `script_filter` declaration:

```
{
     "type" : "rabbitmq",
     "rabbitmq" : {
         ...
     },
     "index" : {
         ...
     },
     "script_filter" : {
         "script" : "ctx.type1.field1 += param1",
         "script_lang" : "groovy",
         "script_params" : {
             "param1" : 1
         }
     }
}
```

The RabbitMQ broker is a very powerful tool that supports high load and balancing, moving the peak load on the RabbitMQ message queue. The performance of a message queue in RabbitMQ is by far faster than that of ElasticSearch in processing `insert` because a message queue system doesn't require you to index the data. So, it can be a good frontend to resolve ElasticSearch index peaks and also to allow the execution of delayed bulk if an ElasticSearch node is down.

See also

> ▸ The RabbitMQ river documentation at
>   `https://github.com/elasticsearch/elasticsearch-river-rabbitmq`
> ▸ The *Managing a river* recipe in this chapter

Using the JDBC river

Generally, application data is stored in a DBMS of some kind (Oracle, MySQL, PostgreSql, a Microsoft SQL server, and SQLite, among others). To power up a traditional application with the advanced search capabilities of ElasticSearch and Lucene, all this data must be imported to ElasticSearch. The JDBC river by Jörg Prante allows you to connect to the DBMS, executing queries and indexing the results.

This plugin can work both as a standard river or as a standalone feeder, so the ingestion part can be executed independently of ElasticSearch.

Getting ready

You will need a working ElasticSearch cluster.

How to do it...

In order to use the JDBC river, perform the following steps:

1. First, you need to install the JDBC river plugin, which is available on GitHub
   (`https://github.com/jprante/elasticsearch-river-jdbc`). You can
   install the river plugin using the following code:

   ```
   bin/plugin -url http://xbib.org/repository/org/xbib/elasticsearch/
   plugin/elasticsearch-river-jdbc/1.3.4.4/elasticsearch-river-jdbc-
   1.3.4.4-plugin.zip -install river-jdbc
   ```

2. This is how the result should look:

```
-> Installing river-jdbc...
Trying http://xbib.org/repository/org/xbib/elasticsearch/plugin/el
asticsearch-river-jdbc/1.3.4.4/elasticsearch-river-jdbc-
1.3.4.4-plugin.zip...
Downloading … .....DONE
Installed river-jdbc into …/elasticsearch/plugins/river-
jdbc
```

> The JDBC river plugin does not bundle the DBMS drivers, so you need to download them and put them in the plugin directory (typically, `$ES_HOME/plugins/river-jdbc`).

3. If you need to use PostgreSQL, you need to download the driver from `http://jdbc.postgresql.org/download.html`. The direct link to the current driver is available at `http://jdbc.postgresql.org/download/postgresql-9.2-1003.jdbc4.jar`.

4. If you need to use MySQL, you need to download the driver from `http://dev.mysql.com`. The direct link to the current driver is available at `http://dev.mysql.com/get/Downloads/Connector-J/mysql-connector-java-5.1.26.zip/from/http://cdn.mysql.com/`.

5. Restart your ElasticSearch node to ensure that the river plugin is loaded. In the log, you should see the following lines:

```
…
[2014-10-18 14:59:10,143][INFO ][node                       ]
[Fight-Man] initializing ...
[2014-10-18 14:59:10,163][INFO ][plugins                    ]
[Fight-Man] loaded [river-twitter, transport-thrift, jdbc-
1.3.4.4], sites []
```

6. You need to create a configuration file (`.json`) to configure the river. In our case, we define a PostgreSQL database, `items`, and an `items` table to fetch the data:

```
{
  "type" : "jdbc",
  "jdbc" :{
    "strategy" : "oneshot",
    "driver" : "org.postgresql.Driver",
    "url" : "jdbc:postgresql://localhost:5432/items",
    "user" : "username",
    "password" : "password",
    "sql" : "select * from items",
    "schedule" : "1h",
    "scale" : 0,
```

```
        "autocommit" : false,
        "fetchsize" : 100,
        "max_rows" : 0,
        "max_retries" : 3,
        "max_retries_wait" : "10s",
        "locale" : "it",
        "digesting" : true
    },
    "index" : {
        "index" : "jdbc",
        "type" : "jdbc",
        "max_bulk_actions" : 1000,
        "max_concurrrent_bulk_requests" : 10,
        "versioning" : false,
        "acknowledge" : false
    }
}
```

7. Now, create the river with the current configuration:

```
curl -XPUT 'http://127.0.0.1:9200/_river/jdbcriver/_meta' -d
@config.json
```

8. The following result will be obtained:

```
{"_index":"_river","_type":"jdbcriver","_id":"_meta","_vers
ion":1, "created":true}
```

How it works...

The JDBC river is a very versatile river that has a lot of options and covers a large number of common scenarios related to database issues. Since it works with every database system, it provides JDBC drivers, as it is available without built-in drivers. They must be separately installed, usually in the river directory.

The common flow to use the JDBC river is to provide a connection and an SQL query to fetch SQL records that will be converted to ElasticSearch records.

The river type is jdbc and all the client configurations live on the jdbc object. These are the most common parameters:

▶   strategy (by default, simple): This is the strategy that is used by the JDBC river; currently, the following strategies can be implemented:

   ❑   simple: This fetches data with the SQL query, indexes the data in ElasticSearch, waits for the next poll interval, and then restarts the cycle.

   ❑   column: This fetches all the records of a table without using SQL.

- ► `driver`: This is the JDBC driver class. Every JDBC driver defines its own class:
    - ❑ MySQL: `com.mysql.jdbc.Driver`
    - ❑ PostgreSQL: `org.postgresql.Driver`
    - ❑ Oracle: `oracle.jdbc.OracleDriver`
    - ❑ SQL server: `com.microsoft.sqlserver.jdbc.SQLServerDriver`
- ► `url`: This defines the JDBC URL for the driver.
- ► `user`: This defines the database user's name.
- ► `password`: This defines the database user's password.
- ► `sql`: This is the SQL statement (either a string or a list of statement objects). Typically, this is a `select` statement. If it ends with `.sql`, the statement is looked up in the ElasticSearch server's filesystem. A statement object is usually composed of the following:
    - ❑ `statement`: This is usually the SQL `select` statement that queries the records
    - ❑ `parameter` (an optional list of strings): This binds parameters to the SQL statement (in order)
    - ❑ `Callable` (by default, `false`): If this is `true`, the SQL statement is interpreted as a JDBC `CallableStatement` object
- ► `locale` (optional; by default, it is set to the server locale value): This is the default locale that is used to parse numeric and monetary values.
- ► `timezone`: This is the timezone for the JDBC `setTimestamp()` calls when binding parameters with timestamp values.
- ► `rounding`: This determines the rounding mode for numeric values such as `ceiling`, `down`, `floor`, `halfdown`, `halfeven`, `halfup`, `unnecessary`, and `up`.
- ► `scale`: This gives precision in the numeric values.
- ► `ignore_null_values` (by default, `false`): If this is enabled, it ignores the `NULL` values when constructing the JSON document.
- ► `autocommit` (by default, `false`): This is true if each statement is automatically executed. If it is false, they are committed in block.
- ► `fetchsize`: This is the fetch size for large result sets; most drivers implement `fetchsize` to control the amount of rows in the buffer while iterating through the result set.
- ► `max_rows`: This limits the number of row fetches by a statement; the rest of the rows are ignored.

- ► `max_retries`: This defines the number of retries to connect/reconnect to a database. This is often used when there are problems with the DBMS to automatically reconnect if the connection is dropped.

- ► `max_retries_wait` (by default, `"30s"`): This is the specified wait time between retries.

- ► `schedule`: This is either a single one or a list of Cron expressions used for a scheduled execution. Visit the JDBC river plugin home page (`https://github.com/jprante/elasticsearch-river-jdbc`) for more information.

- ► `cronpoolsize` (by default, `4`): This is the thread pool size of the Cron job executions for a scheduled parameter. If this is set to `1`, jobs will be executed serially.

The JDBC river also provides a good tuning on indexing, letting the user set several index parameters in the `index` object, which are given as follows:

- ► `index`: This defines the ElasticSearch index used to index the data from JDBC.

- ► `type`: This defines the ElasticSearch type of the index used to index the data from JDBC.

- ► `max_bulk_actions`: This defines the length of each bulk index request submitted.

- ► `max_concurrent_bulk_requests`: This defines the maximum number of concurrent bulk requests. This setting controls the rate of bulk operations to prevent a DBMS or ElasticSearch overhead for very high fetches and index cycles.

- ► `index_settings`: This defines the optional settings for the ElasticSearch index.

- ► `type_mapping`: This defines an optional mapping for the ElasticSearch index type.

The JDBC river plugin has a lot of options, whereby selecting the correct one depends on a particular scenario.

It's a very handy tool to import data from traditional relational databases without too much effort. If complex data manipulation on databases is required, it's better to implement custom river plugins to do the job.

There's more...

The JDBC river can be used as a standalone feeder for ElasticSearch. The feeder interface and the river interface share the same code and functionalities.

The river approach is a *pull* approach (it grabs the data from a location and puts it in ElasticSearch), while the feeder is of the *push* approach type (it sends the data to the ElasticSearch cluster, for example, logstash). In the `bin/jdbc` directory of the river, there are samples of JDBC feeder invocations.

It shares the same JDBC section of the river and also includes some other parameters that control the ElasticSearch client.

- ▸ `elasticsearch`: This is the ElasticSearch server to connect to. Generally, it's defined with the address (`ip`, `port`) and cluster name
- ▸ `client` (by default, `bulk`; the available values are `bulk` and `node`): This is the type of client that can be used
- ▸ `concurrency` (by default, `1`): This is the number of concurrent pipelines to be executed

The following is an example of a feeder invocation script for a bash shell:

```
#!/bin/sh
java="/usr/bin/java"
echo '
{
  "concurrency" : 1,
  "elasticsearch" :
  "es://localhost:9300?es.cluster.name=elasticsearch",
  "client" : "bulk",
  "jdbc" : {
    ...truncated...
  }
}
' | ${java} \
-cp $(pwd):$(pwd)/\*:$(pwd)/../../lib/\* \
org.xbib.elasticsearch.plugin.feeder.Runner \
org.xbib.elasticsearch.plugin.feeder.jdbc.JDBCFeeder
```

The `jdbc` section is the same between the river and the feeder; it's mandatory to define the ElasticSearch server that must be used to index documents.

The main feeder entry point is the `org.xbib.elasticsearch.plugin.feeder.Runner` runner function that requires a feeder to instantiate (`org.xbib.elasticsearch.plugin.feeder.jdbc.JDBCFeeder`), and the configuration is read by the standard input.

See also

- ▸ The JDBC river plugin's home page and documentation at `https://github.com/jprante/elasticsearch-river-jdbc`
- ▸ The *Managing a river* recipe in this chapter

Using the Twitter river

In the previous recipes, you saw rivers that fetch data from data stores such as SQL and NoSQL. In this recipe, we'll discuss how to use the **Twitter river** in order to collect tweets from Twitter and store them in ElasticSearch.

Getting ready

You will need a working ElasticSearch cluster and an OAuth Twitter token. To obtain the Twitter token, you need to log in to the Twitter developer account at `https://dev.twitter.com/apps/` and create a new app, `https://dev.twitter.com/apps/new`.

How to do it...

In order to use the Twitter river, perform the following steps:

1. First, you need to install the Twitter river plugin, which is available on GitHub (`https://github.com/elasticsearch/elasticsearch-river-twitter`). You can install the river plugin using the following command:

   bin/plugin -install elasticsearch/elasticsearch-river-twitter/2.4.0

2. The following result will be obtained:

   ```
   -> Installing elasticsearch/elasticsearch-river-twitter/2.4.0...
   Trying http://download.elasticsearch.org/elasticsearch/
   elasticsearch-river-twitter/elasticsearch-river-twitter-
   2.4.0.zip...
   Downloading …..…DONE
   Installed river-twitter into …/elasticsearch/plugins/river-twitter
   ```

3. Restart your ElasticSearch node to ensure that the river plugin is loaded. In the log, you should see the following lines:

   ```
   ...
   [2014-10-18 14:59:10,143][INFO ][node                        ]
   [Fight-Man] initializing ...
   [2014-10-18 14:59:10,163][INFO ][plugins                     ]
   [Fight-Man] loaded [river-twitter, transport-thrift, jdbc-river],
   sites []
   ```

4. You need to create a configuration file (`.json`) that can be used to configure the river, as follows:

   ```
   {
     "type" : "twitter",
   ```

```
  "twitter" : {
    "oauth" : {
      "consumer_key" : "*** YOUR Consumer key HERE ***",
      "consumer_secret" : "*** YOUR Consumer secret HERE
***",
      "access_token" : "*** YOUR Access token HERE ***",
      "access_token_secret" : "*** YOUR Access token secret
      HERE ***"
    },
    "type" : "sample",
    "ignore_retweet" : true
  },
  "index" : {
    "index" : "my_twitter_river",
    "type" : "status",
    "bulk_size" : 100
  }
}
```

5. Now, create the river with the current configuration:

```
curl -XPUT 'http://127.0.0.1:9200/_river/twitterriver/_meta' -d @
config.json
```

6. This is how the result will look:

```
{"_index":"_river","_type":"twitterriver",
"_id":"_meta","_version":1, "created":true}
```

How it works...

The Twitter river, after authenticating with the Twitter API, starts collecting tweets and sending them in bulk to ElasticSearch.

The river type is `twitter` and all client configurations live on the Twitter object. These are the most common parameters:

▶ `oauth`: This is an object that contains the four keys to access the Twitter API. These are generated when you create a Twitter application:

- ❏ `consumer_key`
- ❏ `consumer_secret`
- ❏ `access_token`
- ❏ `access_token_secret`

- ▸ `type`: This will be of one of the four types allowed by the Twitter API:
    - ❏ `sample`: This type takes samples from public tweets
    - ❏ `user`: This type listens to tweets in the authenticated user's timeline
    - ❏ `filter`: This type allows you to filter tweets based on a criteria (check out https://dev.twitter.com/docs/api/1.1/post/statuses/filter)
    - ❏ `firehose`: This type grabs all the public tweets

- ▸ `raw` (by default, `false`): If this is `true`, the tweets are indexed in ElasticSearch without any change. Otherwise, they are processed and cleaned by the ElasticSearch river. Take a look at https://github.com/elasticsearch/elasticsearch-river-twitter/blob/master/src/main/java/org/elasticsearch/river/twitter/Twitterriver.java (around line number 560) for more details.

- ▸ `ignore_retweet` (by default, `false`): If this is `true`, retweets are skipped.

There's more...

To control the Twitter flow, it's possible to define an additional `filter` object.

Defining a filter automatically switches the type to `filter`. The Twitter filter API allows you to define additional parameters to `filter`, as follows:

- ▸ `tracks`: This is a list of the keywords to be tracked

- ▸ `follow`: These are the IDs of Twitter users to be followed

- ▸ `locations`: These are a set of bounding boxes in the GeoJSON format (longitude, latitude) to track geographic sections

- ▸ `language`: This is a list of language codes to filter on

These are all the filter capabilities allowed by Twitter, in order to reduce the number of tweets sent to you and to focus the search to a particular segment.

This is how a filter river configuration will look:

```
{
  "type" : "twitter",
  "twitter" : {
    "oauth" : {
      "consumer_key" : "*** YOUR Consumer key HERE ***",
      "consumer_secret" : "*** YOUR Consumer secret HERE ***",
      "access_token" : "*** YOUR Access token HERE ***",
      "access_token_secret" : "*** YOUR Access token secret HERE ***"
    },
    "filter" : {
```

```
        "tracks" : ["elasticsearch", "cookbook", "packtpub"],
      }
    }
  }
```

See also

- ▶ The Twitter river plugin's home page and documentation at
  `https://github.com/elasticsearch/elasticsearch-river-twitter`
- ▶ The *Managing a river* recipe in this chapter

9
Cluster and Node Monitoring

In this chapter we will cover:

- ▶ Controlling cluster health via the API
- ▶ Controlling cluster state via the API
- ▶ Getting cluster node information via the API
- ▶ Getting node statistics via the API
- ▶ Managing repositories
- ▶ Executing a snapshot
- ▶ Restoring a snapshot
- ▶ Installing and using BigDesk
- ▶ Installing and using ElasticSearch Head
- ▶ Installing and using SemaText SPM
- ▶ Installing and using Marvel

Introduction

In the ElasticSearch ecosystem, it can be immensely useful to monitor nodes and clusters to manage and improve their performance and state. There are several issues that might arise at the cluster level, such as the following:

- ▶ Node overheads: Some nodes might have too many shards allocated and become bottlenecks for the entire cluster

- ▶ Node shutdown: This can happen due to many reasons—for example, full disks, hardware failures, and power problems

- ▶ Shard relocation: Problems or corruptions related to shard relocation, due to which some shards are unable to get an online status

- ▶ Very large shards: If a shard is too big, the index performance decreases due to the Lucene massive segments merging

- ▶ Empty indices and shards: They waste memory and resources but, because every shard has a lot of active thread, if there is a huge number of unused indices and shards, general cluster performance is degraded

Detecting malfunction or bad performances can be done via the API or via some front-end plugins that can be activated in ElasticSearch.

Some of the plugins introduced in this chapter allow readers to have a working web dashboard on their ElasticSearch data, monitor cluster health, back up/restore their data, and allow testing queries before implementing them in the code.

Controlling cluster health via the API

In the *Understanding clusters, replication, and sharding* recipe in *Chapter 1, Getting Started*, we discussed the ElasticSearch cluster and how to manage red and yellow states.

ElasticSearch provides a convenient way to manage cluster state, which is one of the first things to check in case of problems.

Getting ready

You need a working ElasticSearch cluster.

How to do it...

To control cluster health, we will perform the following steps:

1. To view cluster health, the HTTP method is GET and the curl command is:

   ```
   curl -XGET 'http://localhost:9200/_cluster/health?pretty'
   ```

2. The result will be:

   ```
   {
     "cluster_name" : "elasticsearch",
     "status" : "green",
     "timed_out" : false,
   ```

```
    "number_of_nodes" : 2,
    "number_of_data_nodes" : 2,
    "active_primary_shards" : 5,
    "active_shards" : 10,
    "relocating_shards" : 0,
    "initializing_shards" : 0,
    "unassigned_shards" : 0
}
```

How it works...

Every ElasticSearch node keeps the cluster status. The status can be of three types:

- green: This means everything is ok.
- yellow: This means that some nodes or shards are missing, but they don't compromise the cluster functionality. Mainly, some replicas are missing (a node is down or there aren't enough nodes for replicas), but there is at least one copy of each active shard. It also indicates that read and write functions are working.
- red: This indicates that some primary shards are missing. You cannot write to the indices whose status is red; results might either not be complete or only partial results might be returned. Generally, you need to restart the node that is down and possibly create some replicas.

> The yellow/red state could be transient if some nodes are in recovery mode. In this case, just wait until recovery completes.

However, cluster health has a lot of more information:

- cluster_name: This is the name of the cluster.
- timeout: This is a Boolean value indicating whether the REST API hits the timeout set in the call.
- number_of_nodes: This indicates the number of nodes that are in the cluster.
- number_of_data_nodes: This shows the number of nodes that can store data. For different types of nodes, refer to the Setting up different node types recipe in *Chapter 2, Downloading and Setting Up*.
- active_primary_shards: This shows the number of active primary shards. The primary shards are the masters for writing operations.
- active_shards: This shows the number of active shards. These shards can be used for searching.
- relocating_shards: This shows the number of shards that are relocating—that is, migrating from one node to another. This is mainly due to cluster node balancing.

- ▶ `initializing_shards`: This shows the number of shards that are in the initializing state. The initializing process is done at shard startup. It's a transient state before becoming active and it's made up of several steps. The most important ones are as follows:

    - ❏ Copy shard data, if it's a replica of another one
    - ❏ Check Lucene indices
    - ❏ Process transaction log as needed

- ▶ `unassigned_shards`: This shows the number of shards that are not assigned to a node mainly due to having set a replica number larger than the number of nodes. During startup, shards that are not initialized already or in the process of initializing will be counted here.

Installed plugins can play an important role in shard initialization. If you use a mapping type provided by a native plugin and you remove the plugin (or the plugin cannot be initialized due to API changes), the shard initialization will fail. These issues can easily be detected by reading the ElasticSearch log file.

> While upgrading your cluster to a new ElasticSearch release, ensure that you upgrade your mapping plugins or that they can work with the new ElasticSearch release; otherwise your shards will fail to initialize, thus giving a red status to your cluster.

There's more...

This API call is very useful; it's possible to execute it against one or more indices to obtain their health in the cluster. This approach allows the isolation of indices with problems. The API call to execute this is as follows:

```
curl -XGET 'http://localhost:9200/_cluster/health/index1,index2,indexN'
```

The previous calls also have additional request parameters to control the health of the cluster. These parameters are as follows:

- ▶ `level`: This controls the level of the health information returned. This parameter accepts only `cluster`, `index`, and `shards`.

- ▶ `timeout` (by default, `30s`): This is the waiting time of a `wait_for_*` parameter.

- ▶ `wait_for_status`: This waits for the server to provide the status (green, yellow, or red) until timeout.

- ▶ `wait_for_relocating_shards` (0 by default): This allows the server to wait to reach the provided number of relocating shards or the timeout period.

- ▶ `wait_for_nodes`: This waits until the defined number of nodes is available in the cluster. The value for this parameter can also be an expression such as >N, >=N, <N, <=N, ge(N), gt(N), le(N), or lt(N).

See also

- ▶ The *Understanding clusters, replication, and sharding* recipe in *Chapter 1, Getting Started*
- ▶ The *Setting up different node types* recipe in *Chapter 2, Downloading and Setting Up*

Controlling cluster state via the API

The previous recipe returns information only about the health of the cluster. If you need more details about your cluster, you need to query its state.

Getting ready

You need a working ElasticSearch cluster.

How to do it...

To check the cluster state, we will perform the steps given as follows:

1. To view the cluster state, the HTTP method is GET and the curl command is:

   ```
   curl -XGET 'http://localhost:9200/_cluster/state'
   ```

2. The result will contain the following data sections:

   - ❏ General cluster information:

     ```
     {
         "cluster_name" : "es-cookbook",
         "version" : 13,
         "master_node" : "R3Gwu0a6Q9GTHPQ6cg95ZA",
         "blocks" : { },
         Node address information:
         "nodes" : {
           "R3Gwu0a6Q9GTHPQ6cg95ZA" : {
             "name" : "Man-Ape",
             "transport_address" : "inet[/192.168.1.13:9300]",
             "attributes" : { }
           },
           "68PBx8g5TZKRxTMii9_EFw" : {
             "name" : "Azazel",
     ```

```
        "transport_address" : "inet[/192.168.1.13:9301]",
        "attributes" : { }
      }
    },
```

❑ Cluster metadata information (templates, indices with mappings, and alias):

```
"metadata" : {
  "templates" : { },
  "indices" : {
    "test-index" : {
      "state" : "open",
      "settings" : {
        "index" : {
          "number_of_shards" : "5",
            "number_of_replicas" : "1",
              "version" : {
              "created" : "1030199"
            },
            "uuid" : "psw_W6YXQNy60_KbfD10_Q"
          }
        },
        "mappings" : {…truncated…}
      },
      "aliases" : [ "my-cool-alias" ]
    }
  }
},
```

❑ Routing tables to find the shards:

```
"routing_table" : {
  "indices" : {
    "test-index" : {
      "shards" : {
        "2" : [ {
          "state" : "STARTED",
          "primary" : true,
          "node" : "68PBx8g5TZKRxTMii9_EFw",
          "relocating_node" : null,
          "shard" : 2,
          "index" : "test-index"
          ….truncated…
        }
      }
    }
  }
},
```

❑ Routing nodes:

```
"routing_nodes" : {
  "unassigned" : [ ],
    "nodes" : {
      "68PBx8g5TZKRxTMii9_EFw" : [ {
        "state" : "STARTED",
        "primary" : true,
        "node" : "68PBx8g5TZKRxTMii9_EFw",
        "relocating_node" : null,
        "shard" : 2,
        "index" : "test-index"
      ...truncated... ]
    }
  },
  "allocations" : [ ]
}
```

How it works...

The cluster state contains information about the whole cluster; it's normal that its output is very large.

The call output contains common fields, as follows:

▶ `cluster_name`: This is the name of the cluster.

▶ `master_node`: This is the identifier of the master node. The master node is the primary node for cluster management.

The call output also contains several sections such as the following:

▶ `blocks`: This section shows the active blocks in a cluster.

▶ `nodes`: This shows the list of nodes in the cluster. For every node we have the following:

 ❑ id: This is the hash used to identify the node in ElasticSearch (for example, `pyGyXwh1ScqmnDw5etNS0w`)

 ❑ name: This is the name of the node

 ❑ `transport_address`: This is the IP address and the port number used to connect to this node

 ❑ `attributes`: These are additional node attributes

▶ `metadata`: This is the definition of the indices; they relate to the mappings.

▶ `routing_table`: These are the index/shard routing tables that are used to select the primary and secondary shards as well as their nodes.

▶ `routing_nodes`: This is the routing for the nodes.

The metadata section is the most used one because it contains all the information related to the indices and their mappings. This is a convenient way to gather all the indices mappings in one go; otherwise you need to call the get mapping for every type.

The metadata section is composed of several sections that are as follows:

- ▸ `templates`: These are templates that control the dynamic mapping for created indices
- ▸ `indices`: These are the indices that exist in the cluster

The indices subsection returns a full representation of all the metadata descriptions for every index. It contains the following:

- ▸ `state` (open/closed): This returns whether an index is open (that is, it can be searched and it can index data) or closed. See the *Opening/closing an index* recipe in *Chapter 4, Basic Operations*).
- ▸ `settings`: These are the index settings. They include the following:
  - ❑ `index.number_of_replicas`: This indicates the number of replicas of an index; it can be changed with an update index settings call
  - ❑ `index.number_of_shards`: This indicates the number of shards in an index; this value cannot be changed in an index
  - ❑ `index.version.created`: This denotes the index version
- ▸ `mappings`: These are defined in the index. This section is similar to getting a mapping response. See the *Getting a mapping* recipe in *Chapter 4, Basic Operations*.
- ▸ `alias`: This is a list of index aliases that allow you to aggregate indices with a single name or to define alternative names for an index.

The routing records for indices and shards have similar fields. They are as follows:

- ▸ `state` (UNASSIGNED, INITIALITING, STARTED, RELOCATING): This shows the state of the shard or an index
- ▸ `primary` (true/false): This shows whether the shard or node is primary
- ▸ `node`: This shows the ID of the node
- ▸ `relocating_node`: This field, if validated, shows the node ID in which the shard is relocated
- ▸ `shard`: This shows the number of the shard
- ▸ `index`: This shows the name of the index in which the shard is contained

There's more...

The cluster state call returns a lot of information; it's possible to filter out the different section parts. The parameters are as follows:

- `filter_blocks` (`true/false`): This is used to filter out the blocks section of the response

- `filter_nodes` (`true/false`): This is used to filter out the node section of the response

- `filter_metadata` (`true/false`): This is used to filter out the metadata section of the response

- `filter_routing_table` (`true/false`): This is used to filter out the `routing_table` section of the response

- `filter_indices`: This is a list of index names to be include in the metadata

- `filter_index_templates` (`true/false`): This is used to filter out the templates section of the index metadata response

See also

- The *Understanding clusters, replication, and sharding* recipe in *Chapter 1, Getting Started*

- The *Opening/closing an index* recipe in *Chapter 4, Basic Operations*

- The *Getting a mapping* recipe in *Chapter 4, Basic Operations*

Getting cluster node information via the API

The earlier recipes allow us to return information to a cluster level; ElasticSearch provides calls to gather information at a node level.

Getting ready

You need a working ElasticSearch cluster.

How to do it...

To get information on nodes, we will perform the following steps:

1. To retrieve node information, the HTTP method is GET and the curl command is:

```
curl -XGET 'http://localhost:9200/_nodes?all=true'
curl -XGET 'http://localhost:9200/_nodes/<nodeId1>,<nodeId2>?all=true'
```

2. The result will be as follows:

```
{
  "cluster_name" : "es-cookbook",
  "nodes" : {
    "R3Gwu0a6Q9GTHPQ6cg95ZA" : {
      "name" : "Man-Ape",
      "transport_address" : "inet[/192.168.1.13:9300]",
      "host" : "Albertos-MacBook-Pro-2.local",
      "ip" : "192.168.1.13",
      "version" : "1.3.1",
      "build" : "2de6dc5",
      "thrift_address" : "/192.168.1.13:9500",
      "http_address" : "inet[/192.168.1.13:9200]",
      "settings" : {
        "name" : "Man-Ape",
        "path" : {...truncated...          },
        "foreground" : "yes"
      },
      "os" : {
        "refresh_interval_in_millis" : 1000,
        "available_processors" : 8,
        "cpu" : {
          "vendor" : "Intel",
          "model" : "MacBookPro10,1",
          "mhz" : 2700,
          "total_cores" : 8,
          "total_sockets" : 8,
          "cores_per_socket" : 16,
          "cache_size_in_bytes" : 256
        },
        "mem" : {
          "total_in_bytes" : 17179869184
        },
        "swap" : {
          "total_in_bytes" : 6442450944
        }
      },
```

```
      "process" : {
        "refresh_interval_in_millis" : 1000,
        "id" : 71849,
        "max_file_descriptors" : 10240,
        "mlockall" : false
      },
      "jvm" : {
        "pid" : 71849,
        "version" : "1.8.0_05",
        "vm_name" : "Java HotSpot(TM) 64-Bit Server VM",
        "vm_version" : "25.5-b02",
        "vm_vendor" : "Oracle Corporation",
        "start_time_in_millis" : 1406963548972,
        "mem" : {
          "heap_init_in_bytes" : 268435456,
          "heap_max_in_bytes" : 1037959168,
          "non_heap_init_in_bytes" : 2555904,
          "non_heap_max_in_bytes" : 0,
          "direct_max_in_bytes" : 1037959168
        },
        "gc_collectors" : [ "ParNew", "ConcurrentMarkSweep" ],
        "memory_pools" : [ "Code Cache", "Metaspace", "Compressed
Class Space", "Par Eden Space", "Par Survivor Space", "CMS Old
Gen" ]
      },
      "thread_pool" : {
        "percolate" : {
          "type" : "fixed",
          "min" : 8,
          "max" : 8,
          "queue_size" : "1k"
        … truncated…
      },
      "network" : {
        "refresh_interval_in_millis" : 5000,
        "primary_interface" : {
          "address" : "192.168.1.13",
          "name" : "en0",
          "mac_address" : "28:CF:E9:17:61:AB"
        }
      },
      "transport" : {
        "bound_address" : "inet[/0:0:0:0:0:0:0:0:9300]",
        "publish_address" : "inet[/192.168.1.13:9300]"
      },
      "http" : {
        "bound_address" : "inet[/0:0:0:0:0:0:0:0:9200]",
```

```
      "publish_address" : "inet[/192.168.1.13:9200]",
      "max_content_length_in_bytes" : 104857600
    },
    "plugins" : [ {
      "name" : "lang-javascript",
      "version" : "2.3.0",
      "description" : "JavaScript plugin allowing to add
      javascript scripting support",
      "jvm" : true,
      "site" : false
    }, ... truncated... ]
  }
 }
}
```

How it works...

The node information call provides an overview of the node's configuration; it covers a lot of information. The most important sections are the following:

- ▶ hostname: This is the name of the host.
- ▶ http: This section gives information about HTTP configuration, such as the following:
  - ❑ bound_address: This is the address bound by ElasticSearch.
  - ❑ max_content_lenght (100 mb by default): This is the maximum size of any HTTP content that ElasticSearch receives. HTTP payloads bigger than this size are rejected.

> The default 100 MB HTTP limit can be changed in the elasticsearch.yml configuration file. It can lead to malfunction due to big payloads (often in conjunction with the attachment mapper plugin), so it's important to keep the limit in mind while conducting bulk actions or working with an attachment.

  - ❑ publish_address: This is the address used to publish the ElasticSearch node.

- ▶ http_address: This is the address exposed to use HTTP REST API. When creating HTTP clients, this section can be used to implement an auto-discovery functionality.

- ▶ jvm: This section contains information about the node JVM: version, vendor, name, pid, and memory (heap and non heap).

> It's *highly* recommended that you run all the nodes on the same JVM version and type.

► `Network`: This section contains information about the network interfaces used by the node—such as address, MAC address, and name.

► `Osos`: This section provides operating system information about the node that is running ElasticSearch—for example, processor information, memory, and swap.

► `plugins`: This section provides a list of every plugin installed in the node; this information includes the following:

   ❑ `name`: This is the plugin name

   ❑ `description`: This is the plugin description

   ❑ `version`: This is the plugin version

> All the nodes must have the same plugin version. A difference in the plugin version in a node leads to unexpected failures.

   ❑ `jvm`: This shows whether the plugin is a JAR type

   ❑ `site`: This shows whether the plugin is a site type

► `process`: This section contains information about the currently running ElasticSearch processes and includes the following:

   ❑ `id`: This is the ID of the process

   ❑ `max_file_descriptors`: This denotes the max file descriptor number

► `settings`: This section contains information about the current cluster and the path of the ElasticSearch node. The most important fields are the following:

   ❑ `cluster_name`: This is the name of the cluster

   ❑ `name`: This is the name of the node

   ❑ `path.*`: This is the configured path of an ElasticSearch instance

► `thread_pool`: This section contains information about the several types of thread pools running in a node.

► `thrift_address`: This is the address of the Thrift protocol (it is available only if the Thrift plugin is installed).

▶ `transport`: This section contains information about the transport protocol, used for intracluster communication or by the native client to communicate with a cluster. The response format is similar to the HTTP type; it consists of the following:

   ❑ `bound_address`: If a specific IP is not set, then it is set in the configuration file

   ❑ `publish_address`: This is the address used to publish the native transport protocol

▶ `transport_address`: This is the address of the transport protocol.

▶ `version`: This is the current ElasticSearch version.

There's more...

The API call allows for the filtering of the section that must be returned. In our example, we have set the `all=true` parameters to return all the sections. Otherwise, we can select one or more of the following sections:

▶ `http`

▶ `jvm`

▶ `network`

▶ `os`

▶ `process`

▶ `plugins`

▶ `settings`

▶ `thread_pool`

▶ `transport`

For example, if you need only the `os` and `plugins` information, the call will be as follows:

```
curl -XGET 'http://localhost:9200/_nodes/os,plugins'
```

See also

▶ The *Using the native protocol*, *Using the HTTP protocol*, and *Using the Thrift protocol* recipes in *Chapter 1, Getting Started*

▶ The *Setting up networking* recipe in *Chapter 2, Downloading and Setting Up*

▶

Getting node statistics via the API

The node statistics call API is used to collect real-time data of your node, such as memory usage, threads usage, the number of indexes, and searches.

Getting ready

You need a working ElasticSearch cluster.

How to do it...

To get nodes statistics, we will perform the following steps:

1. To retrieve the node statistics, the HTTP method is GET and the curl command is:

```
curl -XGET 'http://localhost:9200/_nodes/stats?all=true'
curl -XGET 'http://localhost:9200/_nodes/<nodeId1>,<nodeId2>/
stats?all=true'
```

2. The result will be a long list of all the node statistics. The result is composed of the following:

   ❑ A header describing the cluster name and the nodes section:

   ```
   {
     "cluster_name" : "es-cookbook",
     "nodes" : {
       "R3Gwu0a6Q9GTHPQ6cg95ZA" : {
         "timestamp" : 1406986967655,
         "name" : "Man-Ape",
         "transport_address" : "inet[/192.168.1.13:9300]",
         "host" : "Albertos-MacBook-Pro-2.local",
         "ip" : [ "inet[/192.168.1.13:9300]", "NONE" ],
   ```

   ❑ Statistics related to indices:

   ```
           "indices" : {
             "docs" : {
               "count" : 1000,
               "deleted" : 0
             },
             "store" : {
               "size_in_bytes" : 1075946,
               "throttle_time_in_millis" : 0
             },
             ... truncated ...
           },
   ```

❑ Statistics related to the operating system:

```
"os" : {
    "timestamp" : 1406986967732,
    "uptime_in_millis" : 521977,
    "load_average" : [ 1.86767578125, 2.47509765625,
2.654296875 ],
        "cpu" : {
            "sys" : 3,
            "user" : 6,
            "idle" : 90,
            "usage" : 9,
            "stolen" : 0
        } …truncated …
    },
```

❑ Statistics related to the current ElasticSearch process:

```
"process" : {
    "timestamp" : 1406986967734,
    "open_file_descriptors" : 335,
    "cpu" : {
        "percent" : 0,
        "sys_in_millis" : 39191,
        "user_in_millis" : 56729,
        "total_in_millis" : 95920
    },
    "mem" : {
        "resident_in_bytes" : 28397568,
        "share_in_bytes" : -1,
        "total_virtual_in_bytes" : 5241270272
    }
},
```

❑ Statistics related to the current JVM:

```
"jvm" : {
    "timestamp" : 1406986967735,
    "uptime_in_millis" : 23418803,
    "mem" : {
        "heap_used_in_bytes" : 127469232,
        "heap_used_percent" : 12,
        "heap_committed_in_bytes" : 387448832,
        "heap_max_in_bytes" : 1037959168,
        "non_heap_used_in_bytes" : 71069104,
        "non_heap_committed_in_bytes" : 72007680,
        … truncated …
```

```
        }
      },… truncated …
   },
```

❏   Statistics related to the thread pools:

```
"thread_pool" : {
  "percolate" : {
    "threads" : 0,
    "queue" : 0,
    "active" : 0,
    "rejected" : 0,
    "largest" : 0,
    "completed" : 0
  },…truncated….
},
```

❏   Statistics related to networking:

```
"network" : {
  "tcp" : {
    "active_opens" : 99763,
    "passive_opens" : 6171,
    "curr_estab" : 141,
    "in_segs" : 33811027,
    "out_segs" : 82198446,
    "retrans_segs" : 29297,
    "estab_resets" : 2588,
    "attempt_fails" : 12666,
    "in_errs" : 3083,
    "out_rsts" : -1
  }
},
```

❏   Node filesystem statistics:

```
"fs" : {
  "timestamp" : 1406986967741,
  "total" : {
    "total_in_bytes" : 499418030080,
    "free_in_bytes" : 80559509504,
    "available_in_bytes" : 80297365504,
    "disk_reads" : 14903973,
    "disk_writes" : 6280386,
    "disk_io_op" : 21184359,
    "disk_read_size_in_bytes" : 334106572288,
    "disk_write_size_in_bytes" : 287922098688,
```

```
         "disk_io_size_in_bytes" : 622028670976
       } ...truncated...]
     },
```

❑ Statistics related to communications between nodes:

```
"transport" : {
  "server_open" : 13,
  "rx_count" : 5742,
  "rx_size_in_bytes" : 934442,
  "tx_count" : 5743,
  "tx_size_in_bytes" : 1093207
},
```

❑ Statistics related to HTTP connections:

```
"http" : {
  "current_open" : 1,
  "total_opened" : 1019
},
```

❑ Statistics related to field data caches:

```
"fielddata_breaker" : {
  "maximum_size_in_bytes" : 622775500,
  "maximum_size" : "593.9mb",
  "estimated_size_in_bytes" : 0,
  "estimated_size" : "0b",
  "overhead" : 1.03,
  "tripped" : 0
    }
   }
  }
 }
}
```

How it works...

Every ElasticSearch node, during execution, collects statistics about several aspects of node management. These statistics are accessible via the statistics API call.

In the following recipes, we will see some examples of monitoring applications that use this information to provide real-time statistics of a node or a cluster.

The main statistics collected by this API are as follows:

▶ fs: This section contains statistics about the filesystem, such as the free space on devices, mount points, reads, and writes.

- ► `http`: This gives the number of current open sockets and their maximum number.
- ► `indices`: This contains statistics of several indexing aspects such as:
  - ❑ Usage of fields and caches
  - ❑ Statistics about operations such as GET, indexing, flush, merges, refresh, and warmer
- ► `jvm`: This section provides statistics about buffer, pools, garbage collector (creation/destruction of objects and their memory management), memory (used memory, heap, pools), threads, and uptime.
- ► `network`: This section provides statistics about the TCP traffic, such as open connections, closed connections, and data I/O.
- ► `os`: This section collects statistics about the operating system such as:
  - ❑ CPU usage
  - ❑ Node load
  - ❑ Memory and swap
  - ❑ System uptime
- ► `process`: This section contains statistics of the CPU resource used by ElasticSearch, memory, and open file descriptors.

> It's very important to monitor the open file descriptors because, if you run out of them, the indices can get corrupted.

- ► `thread_pool`: This section monitors all the thread pools available in ElasticSearch. It's important in the case of low performance, for example, to control whether there are pools that have an excessive overhead. Some of them can be configured to a new max limit value.
- ► `transport`: This section contains statistics about the transport layer, mainly about the bytes read and transmitted.

There's more...

The response is large, and it's possible to limit this by requesting only needed content. To do this, you need to pass a call query parameter to the API, specifying the following desired sections:

- ► `fs`
- ► `http`
- ► `indices`

- ▸ jvm
- ▸ network
- ▸ os
- ▸ thread_pool
- ▸ transport

For example, to only request os and http statistics, the call is:

```
curl -XGET 'http://localhost:9200/_nodes/stats?os,http'
```

See also

- ▸ The *Using the native protocol*, *Using the HTTP protocol*, and *Using the Thrift protocol* recipes in *Chapter 1, Getting Started*
- ▸ The *Setting up networking* recipe in *Chapter 2, Downloading and Setting Up*

Managing repositories

ElasticSearch provides a built-in system to quickly snapshot and restore your data. When working with live data, it's difficult to have a backup because of the large number of concurrency problems.

An ElasticSearch snapshot allows us to create snapshots of individual indices (or aliases), or an entire cluster, in a remote repository.

Before starting to execute a snapshot, a repository must be created.

Getting ready

You need a working ElasticSearch cluster.

How to do it...

To manage a repository, we will perform the following steps:

1. To create a repository called my_backup, the HTTP method is PUT and the curl command is:

```
curl -XPUT 'http://localhost:9200/_snapshot/my_backup' -d '{
  "type": "fs",
  "settings": {
    "location": "/tmp/my_backup",
    "compress": true
```

```
      }
   }'
```

The result will be:

```
{"acknowledged":true}
```

If you check on your filesystem, the directory /tmp/my_backup is created.

2. To retrieve the repository information, the HTTP method is GET and the curl command is:

```
curl -XGET 'http://localhost:9200/_snapshot/my_backup'
```

The result will be:

```
{
   "my_backup" : {
      "type" : "fs",
      "settings" : {
         "compress" : "true",
         "location" : "/tmp/my_backup"
      }
   }
}
```

3. To delete a repository, the HTTP method is DELETE and the curl command is:

```
curl -XDELETE 'http://localhost:9200/_snapshot/my_backup'
```

The result will be:

```
{"acknowledged":true}
```

How it works...

Before you start snapshotting the data, you must create a repository. The parameters that can be used to create a repository are as follows:

- ▶ type (generally, fs): This is used to define the type of the shared filesystem repository
- ▶ settings: These are the options required to set up the shared filesystem repository

If you use the fs type, the settings are as follows:

- ▶ location: This is the location on the filesystem to store the snapshots.
- ▶ compress (by default, true): This turns on compression on snapshot files. Compression is applied only to metadata files (index mapping and settings); data files are not compressed.

- `chunk_size` (by default, disabled): This defines the chunk size of the files during snapshotting. The chunk size can be specified in bytes or by using the size value notation (for example 1 g, 10 m, 5 k).

- `verify` (by default, `true`): This flag enables verification of the repository on creation.

- `max_restore_bytes_per_sec` (by default, `20mb`): This allows us to control the throttle per node restore rate.

- `max_snapshot_bytes_per_sec` (by default, `20mb`): This allows us to control the throttle per node snapshot rate.

> It is possible to return all the defined repositories by executing a GET method without giving the repository name:
> ```
> curl -XGET 'http://localhost:9200/_snapshot'
> ```

There's more...

The most common `type` for a repository backend is the `fs` (filesystem) type, but there are other official repository backends such as the following:

- AWS Cloud (`https://github.com/elasticsearch/elasticsearch-cloud-aws`) for S3 repositories

- HDFS (`https://github.com/elasticsearch/elasticsearch-hadoop/tree/master/repository-hdfs`) for Hadoop environments

- Azure Cloud (`https://github.com/elasticsearch/elasticsearch-cloud-azure`) for Azure storage repositories

When a repository is created, it is immediately verified on all data nodes to be sure that it's functional.

ElasticSearch provides a manual way to verify the node status of the repository. It is useful to check the status of cloud repository storages. The command to manually verify a repository is as follows:

```
curl -XPOST 'http://localhost:9200/_snapshot/my_backup/_verify'
```

See also

- The official ElasticSearch documentation at: `http://www.elasticsearch.org/guide/en/elasticsearch/reference/current/modules-snapshots.html`

Executing a snapshot

In the previous recipe, we defined a repository. Now you can create snapshots of indices. For every repository, it's possible to define multiple snapshots.

Getting ready

You need a working ElasticSearch cluster and the repository created in the previous recipe.

How to do it...

To manage a snapshot, we will perform the following:

▶ To create a snapshot called `snap_1` for the indices `test` and `test1`, the HTTP method is PUT and the curl command is:

```
curl -XPUT "localhost:9200/_snapshot/my_backup/snap_1?wait_for_
completion=true" -d '{
  "indices": " test-index,test-2",
  "ignore_unavailable": "true",
  "include_global_state": false
}'
```

The result will be as follows:

```
{
  "snapshot" : {
    "snapshot" : "snap_1",
    "indices" : [ "test-index" ],
    "state" : "SUCCESS",
    "start_time" : "2014-11-13T21:40:45.406Z",
    "start_time_in_millis" : 1415914845406,
    "end_time" : "2014-11-13T21:40:46.692Z",
    "end_time_in_millis" : 1415914846692,
    "duration_in_millis" : 1286,
    "failures" : [ ],
    "shards" : {
      "total" : 5,
      "failed" : 0,
      "successful" : 5
    }
  }
}
```

If you check on your filesystem, the directory `/tmp/my_backup` is populated with some files /folders such as `index` (a directory that contains your data), `metadata-snap_1`, and `snapshot-snap_1`. The following are the commands to retrieve and delete a snapshot:

1. To retrieve information about a snapshot, the HTTP method is `GET` and the curl command is:

   ```
   curl -XGET 'http://localhost:9200/_snapshot/my_backup/
   snap_1?pretty'
   ```

   The result will be similar to creating a snapshot.

2. To delete a snapshot, the HTTP method is `DELETE` and the curl command is:

   ```
   curl -XDELETE 'http://localhost:9200/_snapshot/my_backup/snap_1'
   ```

   The result will be as follows:

   ```
   {"acknowledged":true}
   ```

How it works...

The minimum configuration required to create a snapshot is the name of the repository and the name of the snapshot (for example, `snap_1`). If no other parameters are given, the snapshot command will dump all of the cluster data.

To control the snapshot process, some parameters are available:

- `indices` (a comma-delimited list of indices; wildcards are accepted): This controls the indices that must be dumped.
- `ignore_unavailable` (by default, `false`): This prevents the snapshot from failing if some indices are missing.
- `include_global_state` (by default, `true`; available values are `true/false/partial`): This allows us to store the global state in the snapshot. If a primary shard is not available, the snapshot will fail.

The query argument `wait_for_completion`, also used in the example, allows us to stop the snapshot from ending before returning the call. This is very useful if you want to automate your snapshot script to sequentially backup indices.

If the `wait_for_completion` is not set, then, in order to check the snapshot status, a user must monitor it via the snapshot `GET` call.

Snapshots are incremental, so only changed files are copied between two snapshots of the same index. This approach reduces both time and disk usage during snapshots.

ElasticSearch takes care of everything during a snapshot; this includes preventing data from being written on the files that are in the process of snapshotting and managing the cluster events (shard relocating, failures, and so on).

> To retrieve all the available snapshots for a repository, the command is as follows:
>
> ```
> curl -XGET 'http://localhost:9200/_
> snapshot/my_backup/_all'
> ```

There's more...

The snapshot process can be monitored via the _status end point that provides a complete overview of the snapshot status.

For the current example, the snapshot _status API call will be as follows:

```
curl -XGET "localhost:9200/_snapshot/my_backup/snap_1/_status?pretty"
```

The result is very long and composed of the following sections:

- Information about the snapshot:

  ```
  {
    "snapshots" : [ {
      "snapshot" : "snap_1",
      "repository" : "my_backup",
      "state" : "SUCCESS",
  ```

- Global shard statistics:

  ```
  "shards_stats" : {
    "initializing" : 0,
    "started" : 0,
    "finalizing" : 0,
    "done" : 5,
    "failed" : 0,
    "total" : 5
  },
  ```

- Snapshot global statistics:

  ```
  "stats" : {
    "number_of_files" : 125,
    "processed_files" : 125,
    "total_size_in_bytes" : 1497330,
    "processed_size_in_bytes" : 1497330,
    "start_time_in_millis" : 1415914845427,
    "time_in_millis" : 1254
  },
  ```

▸ A drill-down of snapshot index statistics:

```
"indices" : {
  "test-index" : {
    "shards_stats" : {
      "initializing" : 0,
      "started" : 0,
      "finalizing" : 0,
      "done" : 5,
      "failed" : 0,
      "total" : 5
    },
    "stats" : {
      "number_of_files" : 125,
      "processed_files" : 125,
      "total_size_in_bytes" : 1497330,
      "processed_size_in_bytes" : 1497330,
      "start_time_in_millis" : 1415914845427,
      "time_in_millis" : 1254
    },
```

▸ Statistics per index per shard:

```
"shards" : {
  "0" : {
    "stage" : "DONE",
    "stats" : {
      "number_of_files" : 25,
      "processed_files" : 25,
      "total_size_in_bytes" : 304773,
      "processed_size_in_bytes" : 304773,
      "start_time_in_millis" : 1415914845427,
      "time_in_millis" : 813
    }
  },… truncated…
```

Restoring a snapshot

After you have taken snapshots of your data, they can be restored. The restoration process is often very fast; the indexed data is copied on the nodes and then activated.

Getting ready

You need a working ElasticSearch cluster and the snapshot created in the previous recipe.

How to do it...

To restore a snapshot, we will perform the following step:

▶ To restore a snapshot called `snap_1` for the index `test` and `test2`, the HTTP method is `PUT`, and the curl command is:

```
curl -XPOST "localhost:9200/_snapshot/my_backup/snap_1/_
restore?pretty" -d '{
  "indices": "test-index,test-2",
  "ignore_unavailable": "true",
  "include_global_state": false,
  "rename_pattern": "test-(.+)",
  "rename_replacement": "copy_$1"
}'
```

The result will be as follows:

```
{
  "accepted" : true
}
```

The restoration is finished when the cluster state turns from red to yellow or green.

How it works...

The restoration process is very fast. It is internally composed of the following steps:

▶ The data is copied on the primary shard of the restored index. During this step the cluster is in the red state.

▶ The primary shards are *recovered*. During this step the cluster status turns from `red` to `yellow/green`.

▶ If a replica is set, the primary shards are copied into other nodes.

It's possible to control the restore process via parameters such as the following:

▶ `indices` (a comma-delimited list of indices; wildcards are accepted): This controls the indices that must be restored. If not defined, all indices in the snapshot are restored.

▶ `ignore_unavailable` (by default, `false`): This prevents the restore from failing if some indices are missing.

▶ `include_global_state` (by default, `true`; the available values are `true/false`): This allows us to restore the global state from the snapshot.

▶ `rename_pattern` and `rename_replacement`: The `rename_pattern` is a pattern that must be matched; the `rename_replacement` parameter uses the regular expression, `replacement`, to define a new index name.

▶ `partial` (by default, `false`). If it is set to true, it allows us to restore indices with missing shards.

Installing and using BigDesk

BigDesk is a wonderful web app developed by Lukáš Vlček, installable as an ElasticSearch plugin that allows us to monitor and analyze real-time cluster status.

With this application, it's possible to monitor both clusters and nodes in which ElasticSearch is running.

It's a modern HTML5 application and only requires a modern browser.

Getting ready

You need a working ElasticSearch cluster.

How to do it...

To install the BigDesk plugin, we will perform the following steps:

1. BigDesk plugin is a site plugin type, a plugin composed only of HTML, CSS, images, and JavaScript. It can be installed using the following command:

   ```
   bin/plugin -install lukas-vlcek/bigdesk
   ```

2. Check in your `config/elasticsearch.yml` configuration file whether JSONP is active (by default it is disabled for security reasons):

   ```
   http.jsonp.enable: true
   ```

3. After a node restart, if everything is alright it should appear in the site's list.

   ```
   [INFO ] [node] [Cassidy, Theresa] version[0.90.3], pid[37214],
   build[5c38d60/2013-08-06T13:18:31Z]
   [INFO ] [node] [Cassidy, Theresa] initializing ...
   [INFO ] [plugins] [Cassidy, Theresa] loaded [], sites [bigdesk]
   [INFO ] [node] [Cassidy, Theresa] initialized
   [INFO ] [node] [Cassidy, Theresa] starting ...
   ```

4. Now look at the interface; you need to navigate to it with your browser by using the following URL:

   ```
   http://es_address:9200/_plugin/bigdesk/
   ```

If you don't see the cluster statistics, put your node address on the left and click on **connect**.

How it works...

When the browser points to the plugin address, the web interface for BigDesk is loaded.

It's composed of three main blocks:

▶ The BigDesk Endpoint settings bar: This lets a user set the server address, the refresh time, the history size, and the connect/disconnect button

▶ The node or cluster view: This lets the user choose either monitoring nodes or the cluster data view

▶ The main view: This contains the data and graphics related to the node status

The node view is the main and the most important one, because it allows us to monitor all node aspects.

The following is the node view; as the page is very long, it has been split into three parts:

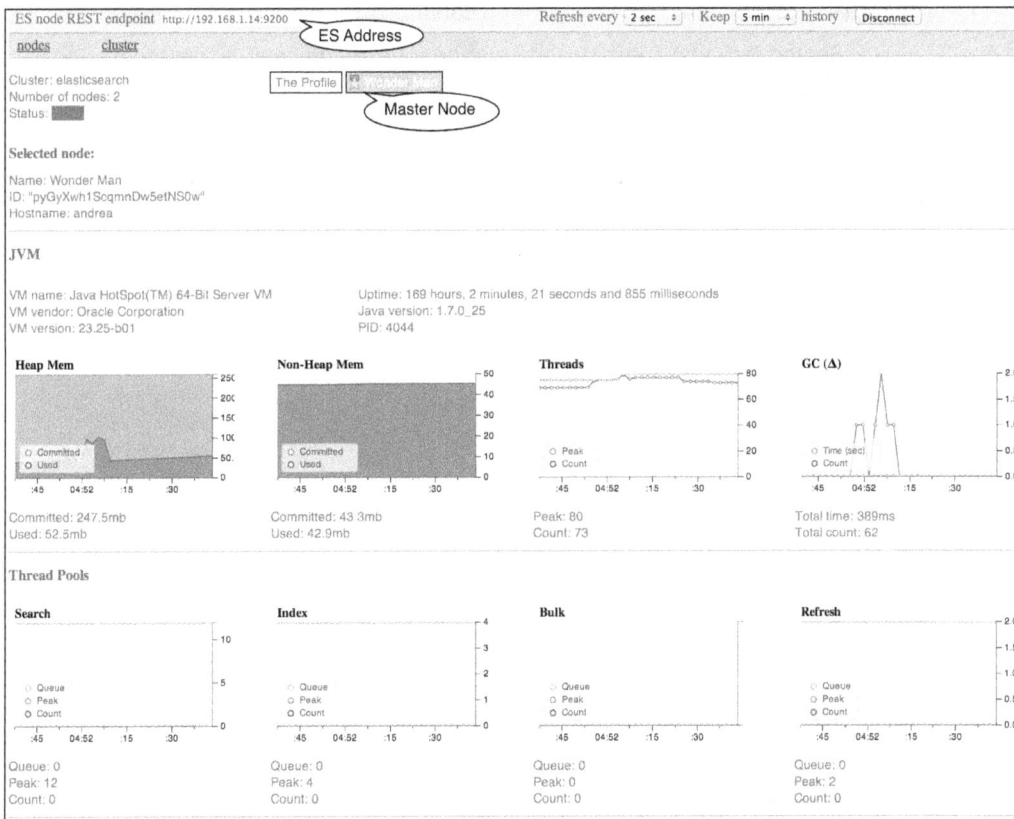

In this first part of the view, we can look at the following information:

- The names of nodes: The master node name is marked with a medal. Clicking on a node name switches the interface to monitor node statistics.

- JVM information, composed of:
    - The information about the JVM itself: This gives you the JVM name, vendor, version, and uptime.
    - The heap memory used: This must be monitored. If a JVM is out of heap memory, it is usually because of a core dump; it then shuts itself down because it is no longer able to allocate objects.
    - Non-heap memory: This is other used memory, and not the actual heap memory.
    - Threads: A JVM is not able to use a high number of threads. If the number of threads is too high, the application freezes or exists with some errors.
    - Garbage collector: This allows monitoring of how often the objects are created and destructed, and the memory released.

- The thread pool section: This is where you can monitor the following objects:
    - Search threads: These are the number of threads used in a search
    - Index threads: These are the number of threads used in indexing
    - Bulk threads: These are the number of threads used in bulk actions
    - Refresh threads: These are the number of threads used to refresh the Lucene index; they allow us to update searches to work on new indexed data

The following screenshot shows you the fragmented information of a node:

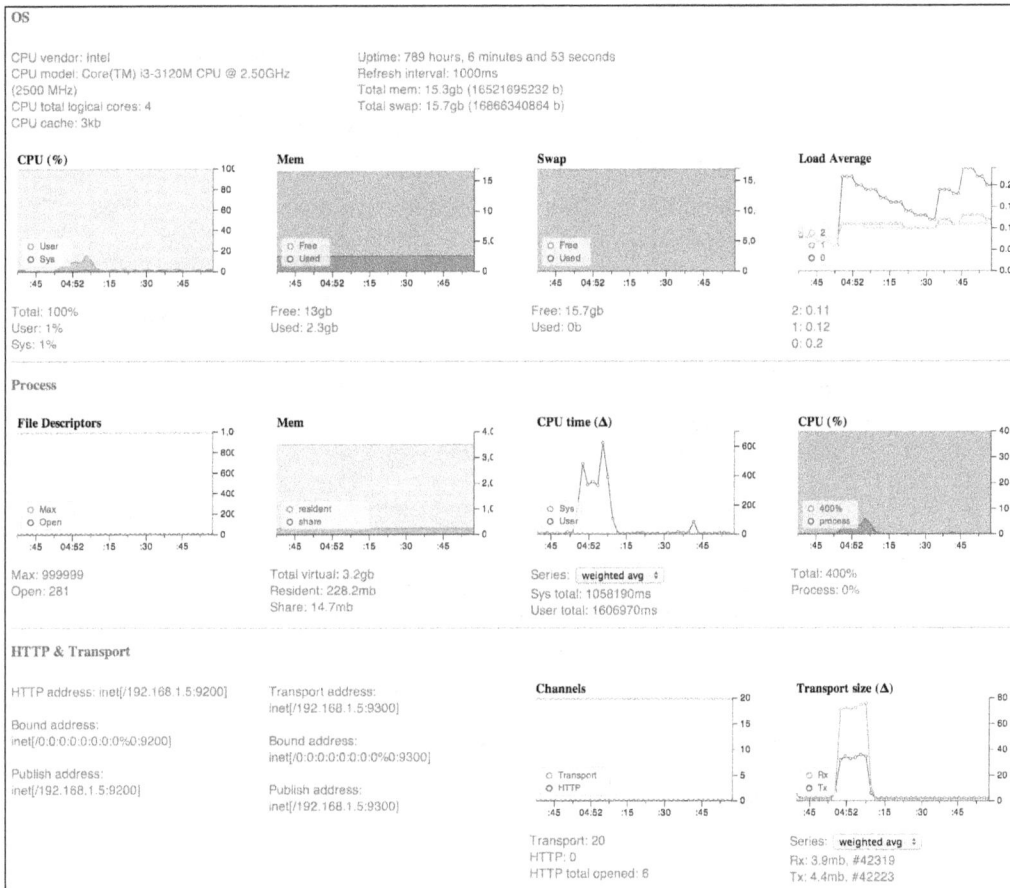

In the earlier screenshot, we see the following information:

- Operating system information:
  - Type of CPU hardware, uptime, memory: These show you a detailed inspection on the CPU type, the system uptime, and the memory available.
  - Real-time CPU usage: These show you the amount of CPU time utilized by a node in real time.
  - Real-time memory usage: If your node uses all the memory, you need to increase the memory or add a new cluster node to balance the load.
  - Real-time swap usage: If you are using swap memory, your server needs more of the main memory. Using swap memory can make the system unresponsive.
  - Real-time load (average): This shows you the amount of load on the server. If all the values are near 1.0, your server is on high load. In such cases, try to put a new node in the cluster to reduce the work load.

- The process block has information about the ElasticSearch process, such as the following:
  - File Description: These are the number of open files in the process. When ElasticSearch is out of files, Lucene indices might be corrupted and you might lose your data.
  - Memory used by the ElasticSearch process.
  - The CPUs resource used by the ElasticSearch process.

- The HTTP & Transport layer information block contains the following:
  - IP and Port address: This gives information about the IP and port addresses of several protocols.
  - Channels monitor: This allows you to control the number of HTTP connections. If the number of HTTP connections is too high because of a bad client configuration, the connections could then be dropped and your applications might have unexpected errors due to lack of connection.
  - Transport size: This allows you to monitor the bytes received and sent by ElasticSearch.

The following screenshot shows you the third fragment view:

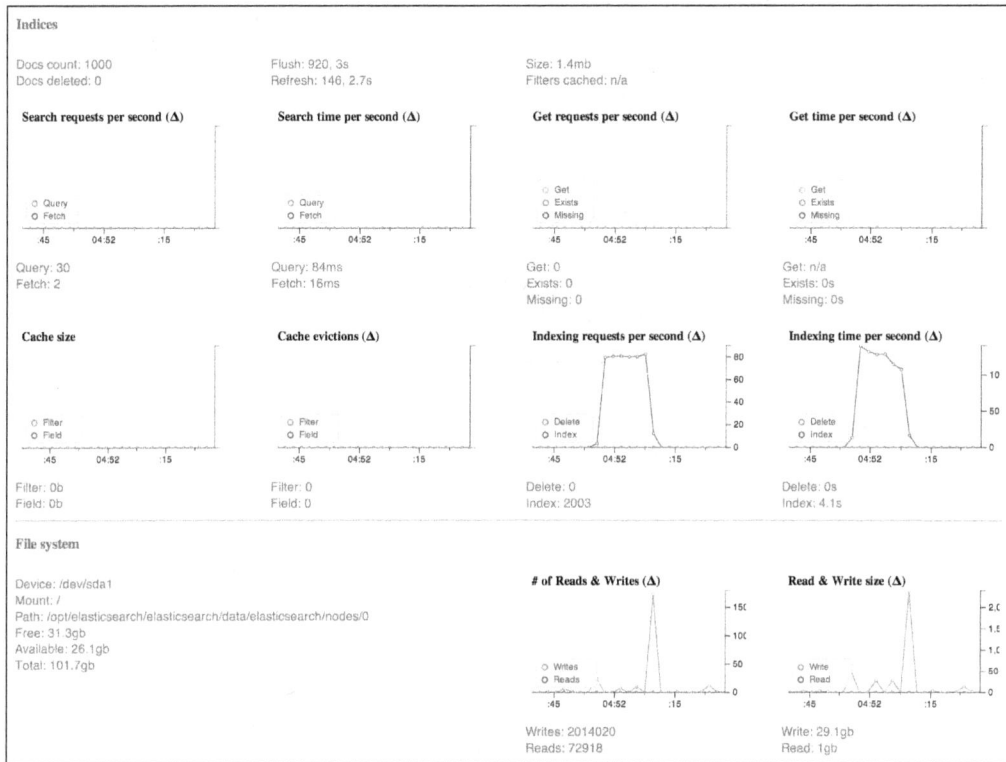

In the screenshot, there are two blocks related to the following:

- Index/search performances with details about the following:
  - Present and deleted documents
  - Flush and refresh of indices
  - Search time per second
  - GET time per second
  - Cached filters
  - Cache size and hits
  - Index requests and indexing time in seconds

- ▶ Disk I/O in which the main parameters to consider are as follows:
    - ❑ Free space on the disk.
    - ❑ Read and write sizes. If these values hit the maximum disk I/O operation for many seconds, you need to add more nodes to balance the I/O load.

There's more...

BigDesk makes it possible to understand how your cluster is working and to monitor measures that might reduce the performance of your ElasticSearch cluster. BigDesk also provides a cluster view, experimental, that can help you to graphically understand which of the available shards is the largest and which ones use the most disk space.

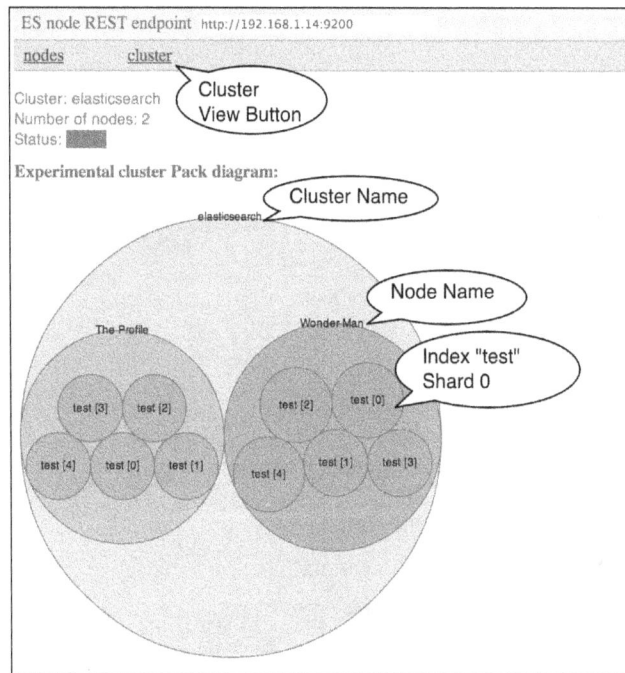

Installing and using ElasticSearch Head

The previous plugin allows us to monitor all cluster/node statistics. **ElasticSearch Head** by Ben Birch mainly focuses on data management of your cluster. It allows you to manage your data and the shards of your cluster via a nice web interface; using it is way faster than using the curl command.

Getting ready

You need a working ElasticSearch cluster and a modern HTML5 browser.

How to do it...

To install the Head plugin, we will perform the following steps:

1. The ElasticSearch Head plugin is a type of site plugin; it is composed only of HTML, CSS, images, and JavaScript. It can be installed by using the following command:

    ```
    bin/plugin -install mobz/elasticsearch-head
    ```

2. After a node restart, if everything goes well, it should appear in the sites list, as follows:

    ```
    [INFO ][node] [Cassidy, Theresa] version[0.90.3], pid[37214],
    build[5c38d60/2013-08-08T12:28:31Z]
    [INFO ][node] [Cassidy, Theresa] initializing ...
    [INFO ][plugins] [Cassidy, Theresa] loaded [], sites [head]
    [INFO ][node] [Cassidy, Theresa] initialized
    [INFO ][node] [Cassidy, Theresa] starting …
    ```

3. Now, to use the web interface, you need to navigate with your browser to the following address:

    ```
    http://es_address:9200/_plugin/head/
    ```

    If you don't see the cluster statistics, put your node address to the left and click on the **connect** button.

How it works...

ElasticSearch Head has a multiple-tab interface. Every tab has a special purpose; some of them are as follows:

▶ **Overview**: This tab shows the topology of your cluster and allows you to perform indexing and node-level operations

▶ **Indices**: This tab allows you to analyze index statistics

▶ **Browser**: This tab allows you to navigate through your data by index, type, or a simple field match

▶ **Structured Query**: This tab allows you to build queries via a customizable query builder

▶ **Any Request**: This tab allows you to execute custom requests

The following screenshot shows an example of the tabbed ElasticSearch Head web interface:

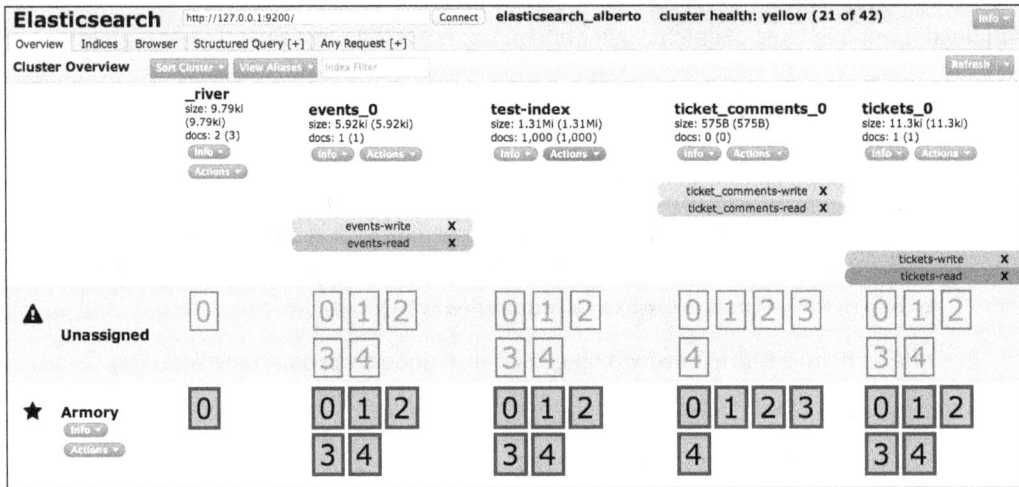

Outside the tabbed content, after connecting to a cluster, a lot of information and actions are available, such as the following:

- ▸ Cluster name and status (the information in the screenshot highlighted in yellow)
- ▸ Information about the cluster (the drop-down button on the left-hand side of the screenshot) allows you to view the following information:
  - ❑ The ElasticSearch server version
  - ❑ Status of indices
  - ❑ Node statistics
  - ❑ Cluster nodes
  - ❑ Installed plugins
  - ❑ Cluster status
  - ❑ Cluster health
  - ❑ Templates

The **Overview** tab allows you to execute a lot of cluster/node/index operations. It's a grid layout with nodes to the left and indices in columns. In the index columns, the shards distribution shows the location of the shards; you can know whether the shard is a primary or a secondary shard by clicking on it.

Under the node name, there are two buttons:

- ▸ **Info**: This button allows you to get information about the running node.
- ▸ **Actions**: This button allows you to execute commands on the node such as shutting it down.

The following details are under the index name:

▶ The index size gives you information about the size it occupies on the hard drive. The numbers in the parentheses give you its size, including replicas.

▶ This section gives you information about the number of documents that are in the index. In parentheses, it shows the exact number of records, including deleted records.

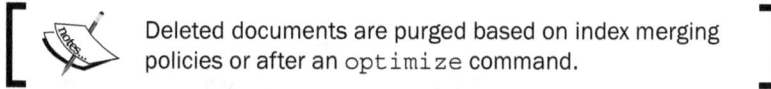

> Deleted documents are purged based on index merging policies or after an `optimize` command.

▶ The **Info** button collects status and metadata information.

▶ The **Actions** button collects several operations that can be executed on an index, which are listed as follows:

  ❑ **New Alias**: This adds an alias to the current index

  ❑ **Refresh**: This calls the refresh API

  ❑ **Flush**: This calls the flush API

  ❑ **Gateway Snapshot**: This allows you to dump index content on a gateway

  ❑ **Test Analyzer**: This allows you to view an analyzer-produced token

  ❑ **Open/Close**: This allows you to open or close an index

  ❑ **Delete**: This allows you to drop an index and delete all the mappings and their data

Under the **Indices** tab, the defined aliases are shown as follows.

Elasticsearch	http://127.0.0.1:9200/		Connect
Overview	Indices	Browser	Structured Query [+]	Any Request [+]

Indices Overview New Index

	Size	Docs
test-index	1.31Mi/1.31Mi	1.00k
_river	9.79ki/9.79ki	2
ticket_comments_0	575B/575B	0
tickets_0	11.3ki/11.3ki	1
events_0	5.92ki/5.92ki	1

The **Indices** tab is very handy for having a quick look at the space occupied by the indices. From this view, you can detect empty indices or those that are too large.

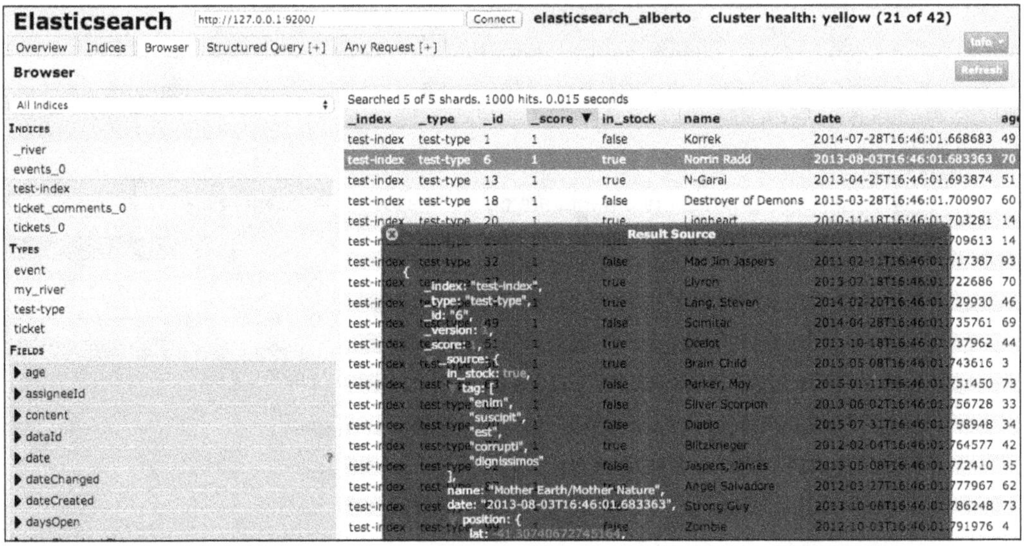

The **Browser** tab is useful for the analysis of data in your cluster. On the left-hand side, you can filter your choice by indices and types. If some data is indexed, you can also put values in the fields and the documents can use these values.

The results are represented in a table but, if you click on a result, you can see the original JSON record (if the source was stored at the time of indexing). These views are very useful for analyzing the records available in your index and to check whether the record was correctly saved.

The following screenshot shows the **Any Request[+]** tab:

The **Any Request[+]** tab allows you to execute a custom query. On the left-hand side, the following options exist:

- The history of executed commands
- The query to be executed is composed of the following:
  - URL
  - Rest entry point
  - REST method (GET, POST, PUT, DELETE)
  - The body to be sent
  - The **Validate** button, to check whether the body is a valid JSON code
  - Pretty check to **pretty-print** the JSON code
  - The **Request** button to execute the query
- **Result Transform** allows you to define the JavaScript code to postprocess the results
- **Repeat Request** allows you to execute the requests as per the scheduled time

▶ **Display Options** provide the following:

  ❏ **Show Raw JSON** (default): This is the JSON as returned by ElasticSearch

  ❏ **Graph Results**: These show a graph of results (the results must be in a list)

  ❏ **Show Search Results Table**: This shows the results similar to a table in a browser tab

There's more...

The Head plugin allows the monitoring of shard distribution and data manipulation via a simple web interface. Many actions can be taken via a web interface without the need to execute curl shell commands.

There are other good ElasticSearch GUIs, similar to Head, that are available mainly on GitHub. The most famous ones are the following:

▶ Elastic HQ (`http://www.elastichq.org/`): Elastic HQ gives you complete control over your ElasticSearch clusters, nodes, indexes, and mappings. This sleek, intuitive UI gives you all the power of the ElasticSearch Admin API, without having to tangle with REST and large cumbersome JSON requests and responses.

▶ Sense (`https://chrome.google.com/webstore/detail/sense-beta/lhjgkmllcaadmopgmanpapmpjgmfcfig?hl=en`): This is a Chrome plugin that allows only JSON manipulation and query execution, but it doesn't have monitoring capabilities.

▶ Marvel (`http://www.elasticsearch.org/overview/marvel/`): This will be discussed at the end of the chapter.

The choice of GUI tool depends on user preferences and requirements.

Installing and using SemaText SPM

The previous plugins allow real-time monitoring and analysis of your cluster status; if you need to monitor your cluster for a long time, you need tools that will collect your logs and perform analysis on them.

Sematext offers a paid service that allows remote collection and processing of your ElasticSearch activities.

Getting ready

You need a working ElasticSearch cluster and a modern HTML5 browser.

How to do it...

To install the SemaText SPM plugin, we will perform the following steps:

1. To use the SPM monitor, you need to register an account at the Sematext website (`https://apps.sematext.com/users-web/register.do`) for a trial period. For every account, an application key is generated; this key is required to download and install the client application.

2. The SPM monitor is composed of a client application, which must be installed on your server, and a web frontend managed by Sematext Cloud.

   SemaText provides native installers for the following:

   - Centos
   - Amazon Linux
   - RedHat
   - Suse
   - Debian
   - Ubuntu
   - Binaries for other Intel Linux 64

3. For common Linux distributions, the installation process is very simple; it is enough to add a binary repository and use the standard tool to install the application (`yum install`, `rpm -i`, `apt-get install`, and so on).

How it works...

After having installed and started the client on the server, this application sends your node and cluster activities to the Sematext Cloud.

SemaText Cloud stores your activities to provide you with analysis over time depending on the support plan. It allows you to monitor and compare behaviors for up to a year.

The output is displayed in an interface similar to the following screenshot:

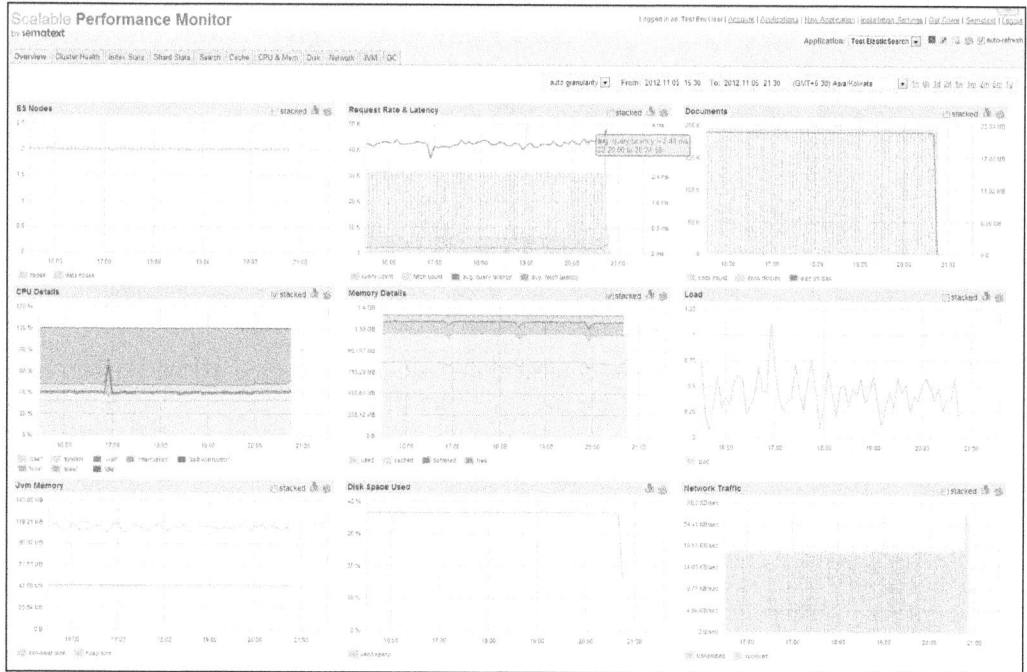

> As SPM uses the `node.name` properties to identify the nodes, it is good practice to fix the node names in the `elasticsearch.yml` file to uniquely identify nodes in the logs.

The SPM from Sematext provides a practical and commercial solution to monitor ElasticSearch's performance during long usage, without requiring to set up any infrastructure to collect, store, and monitor data.

An alternative to this service is to set up a Nagios server (`http://www.nagios.org/`) and use the Nagios plugin for ElasticSearch (available at `https://github.com/saj/nagios-plugin-elasticsearch`).

See also

- For more details on SPM go to `http://sematext.com/spm/elasticsearch-performance-monitoring/index.html`
- The Nagios plugin is available at `https://github.com/saj/nagios-plugin-elasticsearch`

Installing and using Marvel

Similar to Sematext SPM, Marvel is a commercial product (freely available for development) built by ElasticSearch to monitor and manage an ElasticSearch cluster.

Getting ready

You need a working ElasticSearch cluster.

How to do it...

To install the Marvel plugin, we will perform the following steps:

1. The plugin is composed of a native component (JAR) and a site component (HTML, CSS, images, and JavaScript). It can be installed using the following command:

   ```
   bin/plugin -i elasticsearch/marvel/latest
   ```

2. After a node restart, if everything goes well, it should appear in the sites list.

   ```
   [INFO ][node         ] [ESCookbookNode] version[1.3.1], pid[62763],
   build[2de6dc5/2014-07-28T14:45:15Z]
   [INFO ][node         ] [ESCookbookNode] initializing ...
   [INFO ][plugins      ] [ESCookbookNode] loaded [marvel], sites
   [marvel, bigdesk, head, HQ]
   [INFO ][node         ] [ESCookbookNode] initialized
   [INFO ][node         ] [ESCookbookNode] starting ...
   [INFO ][transport    ] [ESCookbookNode] bound_address
   {inet[/127.0.0.1:9300]}, publish_address {inet[/127.0.0.1:9300]}
   [INFO ][discovery    ] [ESCookbookNode]
   escookbook/TUYpmiFVTU6hY7DtjsmC3w
   ```

3. Now, to go to the interface, you need to navigate your browser to the following URL:

   ```
   http://es_address:9200/_plugin/marvel/
   ```

> The dark interface color can be changed to a lighter one in the **Configure dashboard** section (the wheel icon).

How it works...

Marvel is a commercial product developed by ElasticSearch. At the time of writing, the cost was $500 per year to monitor your first five nodes and $3,000 per year thereafter for each five-node cluster; however, it is free for development purposes.

Marvel is composed of two components:

- The native JAR is responsible for monitoring all cluster and node events, and for storing them in an index called `marvel-<<YEAR>>.<<MONTH>>.<<DAY>>` created for a particular day. Its purpose is to collect node and cluster data.

- The UI front-end, accessible at `http://es_address:9200/_plugin/marvel/`, is based on Kibana to show and analyze the data.

The Marvel plugin must be installed in every node of the cluster, so it can correctly collect the data.

The collecting part of the process stores the cluster and node data in the same ElasticSearch cluster, but it can be configured to use an external cluster for monitoring purposes.

Configurations for this part of the plugin are, as usual, in the `elasticsearch.yml` file. The most important properties are as follows:

- `marvel.agent.exporter.es.hosts` (by default, `["localhost:9200"]`): This denotes a list of hosts in the `hostname:port` format to which the statistics and events will be sent.

- `marvel.agent.enabled` (by default, `true`): This can be set to `false` to disable all data export.

- `marvel.agent.indices` (by default, `*`): This allows us to control which indices to export data for. It is a comma-separated list of names that can also be wildcards. For example, `+test*` and `-test1`.

- `marvel.agent.interval` (by default, `10s`): This controls the interval between data samples. It is set to `-1` to temporarily disable data export.

The insight part is in the frontend, based on Kibana (`http://www.elasticsearch.org/overview/kibana/`), that allows a powerful customization of the interface to provide advanced analysis.

The following screenshot shows the Marvel home page:

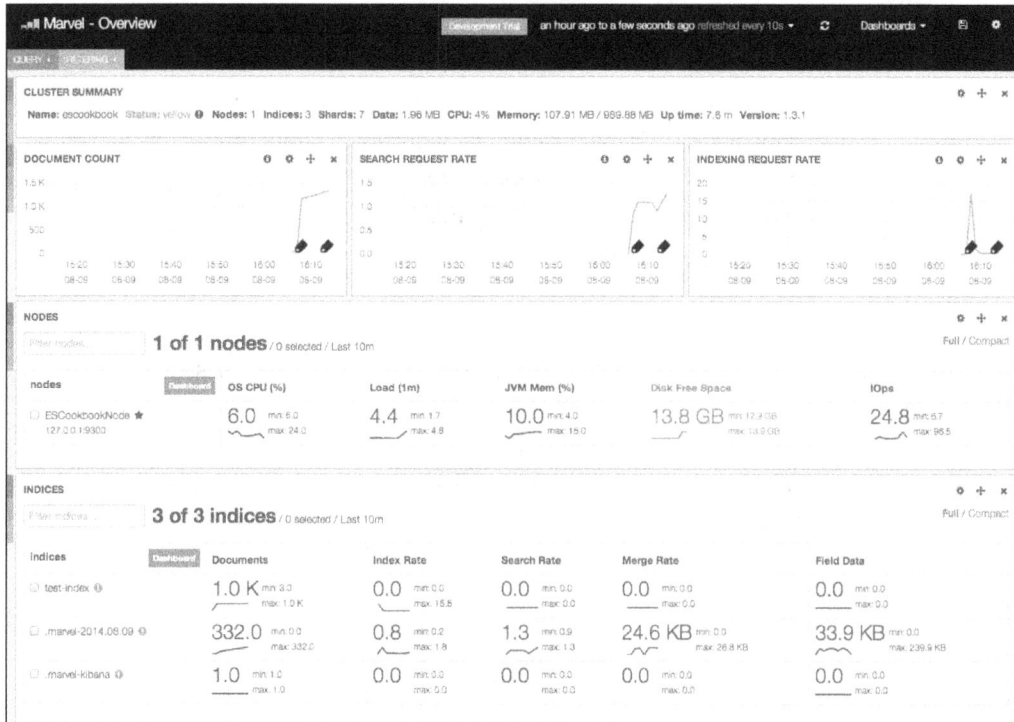

The home page gives an overview about the most important part of the cluster. The header provides settings for all the pages of the Marvel interface, listed as follows:

- The name of the Marvel cluster (in our example, **Marvel – Overview**) can be changed in the **Configure dashboard** section.

- **Development Trial** is shown because this Marvel version is running on trial mode.

- The interval that must be shown in the interface (such as, **an hour ago** to **few minutes**). Clicking on it results in the dashboard providing a common preset.

- The interface refresh interval (such as **refreshed every 10s**). When you click on it, the dashboard provides a common preset.

- The **Force refresh** icon.

- The **Dashboards** menu provides predefined dashboards such as the following:

  - **Cluster Pulse**: This is very useful in the analysis of cluster events such as index creation, node connection/disconnections, and metadata changes.

- ❑ **Shard Allocation**: This tracks shard allocation events and allows you to replay them to analyze problems or evolution in time.
- ❑ **Sense**: This is an interface for the execution of queries (as explained earlier in the chapter).
- ❑ **Node Statistics**: This allows you to analyze all node statistics, such as memory usage, and file descriptors. It shows the data that we discussed in the *Getting node statistics via the API* recipe in this chapter.
- ❑ **Index Statistics**: This allows us to analyze all index statistics.

- ▸ The **save** icon allows you to save the changes to the current dashboard.
- ▸ The settings icon allows you to change dashboard settings.

The main dashboard page provides a global cluster overview. The interface is very simple to understand, and common issues are marked in red to gain the user's attention.

Marvel is probably the most complete and available solution for monitoring an ElasticSearch cluster that is easy to use and fully customizable. Explaining all the Kibana functionalities is outside the scope of this book.

See also

- ▸ To know more about Marvel's licensing and to get an overview, go to `http://www.elasticsearch.com/marvel/`
- ▸ Marvel documentation available at `http://www.elasticsearch.org/guide/en/marvel/current/`
- ▸ To learn more about Kibana, go to `http://www.elasticsearch.org/overview/kibana/`

10
Java Integration

In this chapter we will cover the following recipes:

- ▸ Creating an HTTP client
- ▸ Creating a native client
- ▸ Managing indices with the native client
- ▸ Managing mappings
- ▸ Managing documents
- ▸ Managing bulk actions
- ▸ Building a query
- ▸ Executing a standard search
- ▸ Executing a search with aggregations
- ▸ Executing a scroll/scan search

Introduction

ElasticSearch functionalities can be easily integrated in any Java application in several ways, both via the REST API and native ones.

With the use of Java it's easy to call a REST HTTP interface with one of the many libraries available, such as Apache HttpComponents Client (`http://hc.apache.org/`). In this field there's no such thing as a *most-used library*; typically developers choose the library that suits their preferences the best or that they know very well.

Each JVM language can also use the native protocol to integrate ElasticSearch with their applications. The native protocol, discussed in *Chapter 1, Getting Started*, is one of the faster protocols available to communicate with ElasticSearch due to many factors, such as its binary nature, the fast native serializer/deserializer of data, the asynchronous approach for communicating, and the hop reduction (native client nodes are able to communicate directly with the node that contains the data without executing the double hop needed in REST calls).

The main disadvantage of using native protocol is that it evolves during the development life cycle of ElasticSearch and there is no guarantee of compatibility between versions. For example, if a field of a request or a response changes, their binary serialization changes, generating incompatibilities between client and server with different versions.

The ElasticSearch community tries not to change often but, in every version, some parts of ElasticSearch are improved, and these changes often modify the native API call signature, thus breaking the applications. It is recommended to use the REST API when integrating with ElasticSearch as it is much more stable between versions.

In this chapter, we will see how to initialize different clients and how to execute the commands that we have seen in the previous chapters. We will not go into every call in depth as we have already described the REST API ones.

ElasticSearch uses the native protocol and API internally, so these are the most tested ones compared to REST calls, due to unit and integration tests available in the ElasticSearch code base. The official documentation for the native Java API is available at `http://www.elasticsearch.org/guide/en/elasticsearch/client/java-api/current/`, but it doesn't cover all the API calls.

If you want a complete set of examples, they are available in the `src/test` directory.

As we have already discussed in *Chapter 1, Getting Started*, the ElasticSearch community recommends using the REST calls when integrating, as they are more stable between releases and well documented.

All the code presented in these recipes is available in the book code repository and can be built with Maven.

Creating an HTTP client

An HTTP client is one of the easiest clients to create. It's very handy because it allows calling not only internal methods as the native protocol does, but also third-party calls implemented in plugins that can be called only via HTTP.

Getting ready

You will need a working ElasticSearch cluster and Maven installed. The code of this recipe is in the `chapter_10/http_client` directory, present in the code bundle available on the Packt website and on GitHub (`https://github.com/aparo/elasticsearch-cookbook-second-edition`).

How to do it...

To create an HTTP client, we will perform the following steps:

1. For these examples, we have chosen the Apache HttpComponents, one of the most widely used libraries for executing HTTP calls. This library is available in the main Maven repository `search.maven.org`. To enable compilation in your Maven `pom.xml` project, just add:

```
<dependency>
    <groupId>org.apache.httpcomponents</groupId>
    <artifactId>httpclient</artifactId>
    <version>4.3.5</version>
</dependency>
```

2. If we want to instantiate a client and fetch a document with a `get` method, the code will look like this:

```
import org.apache.http.*;
import
org.apache.http.client.methods.CloseableHttpResponse;
import org.apache.http.client.methods.HttpGet;
import org.apache.http.impl.client.CloseableHttpClient;
import org.apache.http.impl.client.HttpClients;
import org.apache.http.util.EntityUtils;
import java.io.*;
public class App {
  private static String wsUrl = "http://127.0.0.1:9200";
  public static void main(String[] args) {
    CloseableHttpClient client = HttpClients.custom()
    .setRetryHandler(new
    MyRequestRetryHandler()).build();
    HttpGet method = new HttpGet(wsUrl+"/test-
    index/test-type/1");
    // Execute the method.
    try {
      CloseableHttpResponse response =
      client.execute(method);
```

```
        if (response.getStatusLine().getStatusCode() !=
        HttpStatus.SC_OK) {
          System.err.println("Method failed: " +
          response.getStatusLine());
        }else{
          HttpEntity entity = response.getEntity();
          String responseBody =
          EntityUtils.toString(entity);
          System.out.println(responseBody);

        }
      } catch (IOException e) {
        System.err.println("Fatal transport error: "
        + e.getMessage());
        e.printStackTrace();
      } finally {
        // Release the connection.
        method.releaseConnection();
      }
    }
  }
```

The result, if the document is available, will be:

```
{"_index":"test-index","_type":
"test-type","_id":"1","_version":1,"exists":true, "_source"
: {…}}
```

How it works...

We performed the preceding steps to create and use an HTTP client.

The first step is to initialize the HTTP client object. In the previous code this is done using the following:

```
CloseableHttpClient client = HttpClients.custom()
    .setRetryHandler(new
MyRequestRetryHandler()).build();
```

Before using the client, it is a good practice to customize it. In general, the client can be modified to provide extra functionalities such as retry support. Retry support is very important for designing robust applications. For example, the IP network protocol is never 100 percent reliable, so automatically retrying an action if something goes wrong (http connection closed, server overhead, and so on), is a good practice.

In the previous code, we have defined an `HttpRequestRetryHandler` method that monitors the execution and repeats it three times before raising an error.

After having set up the client, we can define the method call. In the previous example, if we want to execute the GET REST call, the used method will be `HttpGet` and the URL will be `item index/type/id` (similar to the curl example in the *Getting a document* recipe in *Chapter 4, Basic Operations*). To initialize this method the code is as follows:

```
HttpGet method = new HttpGet(wsUrl+"/test-index/test-type/1");
```

To improve the quality of our REST call it's a good practice to add extra controls to the method such as authentication and custom headers.

The ElasticSearch server by default doesn't require authentication, so we need to provide a security layer at the top of our architecture. A typical scenario is using your HTTP client with the Jetty plugin, (`https://github.com/sonian/elasticsearch-jetty`) that allows extending ElasticSearch REST with authentication and SSL. After the plugin is installed and configured on the server, the following code adds a host entry that allows providing credentials only if context calls are targeting that host. The authentication is simply `basic auth`, but it works very well for non-complex deployment.

```
HttpHost targetHost = new HttpHost("localhost", 9200, "http");
CredentialsProvider credsProvider = new
BasicCredentialsProvider();
credsProvider.setCredentials(
  new AuthScope(targetHost.getHostName(),
  targetHost.getPort()),
  new UsernamePasswordCredentials("username", "password"));
// Create AuthCache instance
AuthCache authCache = new BasicAuthCache();
// Generate BASIC scheme object and add it to the local auth cache
BasicScheme basicAuth = new BasicScheme();
authCache.put(targetHost, basicAuth);
// Add AuthCache to the execution context
HttpClientContext context = HttpClientContext.create();
context.setCredentialsProvider(credsProvider);
```

The create context must be used in executing the call as follows:

```
response = client.execute(method, context);
```

Custom headers allow passing extra information to the server for executing a call. Some examples could be API key or hints about supported formats. A typical example is using gzip data compression over HTTP to reduce bandwidth usage. To do that, we can add a custom header to the call, informing the server that our client accepts encoding `Accept-Encoding` using Gzip:

```
request.addHeader("Accept-Encoding", "gzip");
```

After having configured the call with all the parameters, we can fire up the request as follows:

```
response = client.execute(method, context);
```

Every response object must be validated on its return status. If the call is OK, the return status should be 200. In the preceding code the check is done in the `if` statement as follows:

```
if (response.getStatusLine().getStatusCode() != HttpStatus.SC_OK)
```

If the call was OK—and the status code of the response is 200—we can read the answer:

```
HttpEntity entity = response.getEntity();
String responseBody = EntityUtils.toString(entity);
```

The response is wrapped in `HttpEntity`, which is a stream. HTTP client library provides a helper method `EntityUtils.toString` that reads all the content of `HttpEntity` as a string. Otherwise we need to create some code to read from the string and build the string.

Obviously all the read part of the call is wrapped in a `try/catch` block to collect all the possible errors due to networking.

There's more...

Apache HttpComponents is one of the most used libraries in the Java world to write a REST API client. It provides a lot of out-of-the-box advanced features such as cookies, authentication, and transport layers.

> There isn't any recommended client for HTTP REST calls in the ElasticSearch community. One of the Java libraries written to resolve this problem is Jest (`https://github.com/searchbox-io/Jest`) but, at the time of writing this book, it is not a complete feature.

See also

- The Apache HttpComponents on `http://hc.apache.org/`
- The Jetty plugin to provide authenticated ElasticSearch access on `https://github.com/sonian/elasticsearch-jetty`
- Jest on `https://github.com/searchbox-io/Jest`
- The *Using the HTTP protocol* recipe in *Chapter 1, Getting started*
- The *Getting a document* recipe in *Chapter 4, Basic Operations*

Creating a native client

There are two ways to create a native client in order to communicate with an ElasticSearch server:

- ▸ Creating a client node (a node that doesn't contain data, but works as an arbiter) and getting the client from it. This node will appear in the cluster state nodes and it's able to use the discovery capabilities of ElasticSearch to join the cluster (so no node address is required to connect to a cluster). This client is able to reduce node routing due to its knowledge of cluster topology.

- ▸ Creating a transport client, which is a standard client that requires the address and port of nodes to connect.

In this recipe we will see how to create these clients.

Getting ready

You will need a working ElasticSearch cluster and a working copy of Maven.

The code of this recipe is in `chapter_10/nativeclient` in the code bundle available on Packt's website and on GitHub (`https://github.com/aparo/elasticsearch-cookbook-second-edition`).

How to do it...

To create a native client, we will perform the following steps:

1. Before starting, make sure that Maven loads the `elasticsearch.jar` and adds it to `pom.xml` as follows:

   ```
   <dependency>
       <groupId>org.elasticsearch</groupId>
       <artifactId>elasticsearch</artifactId>
       <version>1.4.0</version>
   </dependency>
   ```

> I always suggest using the latest available release of ElasticSearch or, in the case of connection to a specific cluster, the same version of ElasticSearch as the cluster.
>
> Native clients only work if the client and the server have the same ElasticSearch version.

2. Now to create a client, we have two ways:

❑ Using a node:

```
import static org.elasticsearch.node.NodeBuilder.*;
// on startup
Node node =
nodeBuilder().clusterName("elasticsearch").client(true).
node();
Client client = node.client();
// on shutdown
node.close();
```

❑ Using the transport protocol:

```
final Settings settings =
ImmutableSettings.settingsBuilder()
.put("client.transport.sniff", true)
.put("cluster.name", "elasticsearch").build();
Client client = new TransportClient(settings)
.addTransportAddress(new
InetSocketTransportAddress("127.0.0.1", 9300));
```

How it works...

The first action to create a native client is to create a node. We set it as a client node and we retrieve the client from it. The steps are:

1. Import the `NodeBuilder` class:

```
import static org.elasticsearch.node.NodeBuilder.*;
```

2. Initializie an ElasticSearch node by passing `cluster.name` and indicating that it's a client one (otherwise, it can be considered as a standard node; after joining the cluster, it fetches data from shards to load-balance the cluster):

```
Node node =
nodeBuilder().clusterName("elasticsearch").client(true).
node();
```

3. We can now retrieve a client from the node using the following line of code:

```
Client client = node.client();
```

4. If the client is retrieved from an embedded node, before closing the application, we need to free the resource needed by the node. This can be done by calling the `close` method on the node:

```
node.close();
```

The second way to create a native client is to create a transport client.

The steps to create a transport client are:

1. Create the settings required to configure the client. Typically they hold the cluster name and some other options that we'll discuss later:

```
final Settings settings = ImmutableSettings.settingsBuilder()
.put("client.transport.sniff", true)
.put("cluster.name", "elasticsearch").build();
```

2. Now we can create the client by passing it settings, addresses, and the port of our cluster as follows:

```
new TransportClient(settings)
.addTransportAddress(new
InetSocketTransportAddress("127.0.0.1", 9300));
```

The `addTransportAddress` method can be called several times until all the required addresses and ports are set.

Using any of these approaches, the result is the same—that is, a working client that allows you to execute native calls on an ElasticSearch server.

In both approaches, it is important to correctly define the name of the cluster; otherwise there will be problems in node joining or the transport client will give you warning of invalid names.

The client node is a complete ElasticSearch client node, so pay attention to defining that. It must be considered as a client node.

There's more...

There are several settings that can be passed when creating a transport client. They are listed as follows:

- `client.transport.sniff`: This is by default `false`. If activated, the client retrieves the other node addresses after the first connection, reading them by the cluster state and reconstructing the cluster topology.

- `client.transport.ignore_cluster_name`: This is by default `false`. If you set it to `true`, cluster name validation of connected nodes is ignored. This prevents printing a warning if the client cluster name is different from the connected cluster name.

- `client.transport.ping_timeout`: This is by default set to `5s`. Every client pings the node to check its state. This value defines how much time a client should wait before a timeout.

▸ `client.transport.nodes_sampler_interval`: This is also by default set to 5s. This interval defines how often to sample/ping the nodes listed and connected. These pings reduce failures if a node is down and allows balancing the requests with the available node.

See also

▸ The *Setting up for Linux systems* recipe in *Chapter 2, Downloading and Setting Up*

▸ The *Using the native protocol* recipe in *Chapter 1, Getting Started*

Managing indices with the native client

In the previous recipe we saw how to initialize a client to send calls to an ElasticSearch cluster. In this recipe, we will see how to manage indices via client calls.

Getting ready

You will need a working ElasticSearch cluster and a working copy of Maven.

The code of this recipe is in `chapter_10/nativeclient` in the code bundle, which can be downloaded from Packt's website, and on GitHub (`https://github.com/aparo/elasticsearch-cookbook-second-edition`). The referred class is `IndicesOperations`.

How to do it...

The ElasticSearch client maps all index operations under the `admin.indices` object of the client. Here, all the index operations are listed, such as create, delete, exists, open, close, optimize, and so on.

The following steps show how to retrieve a client and execute the main operations on indices:

1. The first step is importing the required classes:

```
import
org.elasticsearch.action.admin.indices.exists.indices.
IndicesExistsResponse;
import org.elasticsearch.client.Client;
```

2. Then we define an `IndicesOperations` class that manages the index operations:

```
public class IndicesOperations {
  private final Client client;
  public IndicesOperations(Client client) {
```

```
        this.client = client;
    }
```

3. We define a function used to check the index's existence:

```
    public boolean checkIndexExists(String name){
        IndicesExistsResponse
        response=client.admin().indices().prepareExists(name).
        execute().actionGet();
        return response.isExists();
    }
```

4. We define a function used to create an index:

```
    public void createIndex(String name){
        client.admin().indices().prepareCreate(name).execute().
        actionGet();
    }
```

5. We define a function used to delete an index:

```
    public void deleteIndex(String name){
        client.admin().indices().prepareDelete(name).execute().
        actionGet();
    }
```

6. We define a function used to close an index:

```
    public void closeIndex(String name){
        client.admin().indices().prepareClose(name).execute().
        actionGet();
    }
```

7. We define a function used to open an index:

```
    public void openIndex(String name){
        client.admin().indices().prepareOpen(name).execute().
        actionGet();
    }
```

8. We test all the previously defined functions:

```
    public static void main( String[] args ) throws
    InterruptedException {
        Client client
        =NativeClient.createTransportClient();
        IndicesOperations io=new IndicesOperations(client);
        String myIndex = "test";
        if(io.checkIndexExists(myIndex))
        io.deleteIndex(myIndex);
        io.createIndex(myIndex);
```

```
        Thread.sleep(1000);
        io.closeIndex(myIndex);
        io.openIndex(myIndex);
        io.deleteIndex(myIndex);
    }
}
```

How it works...

Before executing any index operation, a client must be available (we have seen how to create one in the previous recipe).

The client has a lot of methods grouped by functionalities as follows:

- In the root (`client.*`), we have record operations such as index, delete records, search, and update
- Under `admin.indices.*`, we have index-related methods such as creating an index, deleting an index, and so on
- Under `admin.cluster.*`, we have cluster-related methods such as state and health

The client methods usually follow some conventions. They are listed as follows:

- Methods starting from `prepare*` (that is, `prepareCreate`) return a request builder that can be executed with the `execute` method
- Methods that start with a verb (that is, `create`) require a build request and an optional action listener

After having built the request, it can be executed with an `actionGet` method that can receive an optional timeout, and a response is returned.

In the previous example we have seen several index calls:

- To check the existence of an index the method call is `prepareExists` and it returns an `IndicesExistsResponse` object that tells you if the index exists or not:

  ```
  IndicesExistsResponse
  response=client.admin().indices().prepareExists(name).
  execute().actionGet();
  return response.isExists();
  ```

- To create an index with the `prepareCreate` call:

  ```
  client.admin().indices().prepareCreate(name).execute().
  actionGet();
  ```

- To close an index with the `prepareClose` call:

  ```
  client.admin().indices().prepareClose(name).execute().actionGet();
  ```

▶ To open an index with the `prepareOpen` call:

```
client.admin().indices().prepareOpen(name).execute().actionGet();
```

▶ To delete an index with the `prepareDelete` call:

```
client.admin().indices().prepareDelete(name).execute().
actionGet();
```

> In the code we have put a delay of 1 second (`Thread.wait(1000)`) to prevent fast actions on indices, because their shard allocations are asynchronous and they require some milliseconds to be ready. The best practice is not to have a similar hack, but to poll an index's state before performing further operations and to perform those operations only when it goes green.

See also

▶ The *Creating an index*, *Deleting an index*, and *Opening/closing an index* recipes in *Chapter 4, Basic Operations*

Managing mappings

After creating an index, the next step is to add some mapping to it. We have already seen how to apply a mapping via the REST API in *Chapter 4, Basic Operations*. In this recipe, we will see how to manage mappings via a native client.

Getting ready

You will need a working ElasticSearch cluster and a working copy of Maven.

The code of this recipe is in `chapter_10/nativeclient` in the code bundle of this book, available on Packt's website, and on GitHub (`https://github.com/aparo/elasticsearch-cookbook-second-edition`). The referred class is `MappingOperations`.

How to do it...

The following steps show how to add a `mytype` mapping to a `myindex` index via a native client:

1. We import the required classes:

```
import
org.elasticsearch.action.admin.indices.mapping.put.
PutMappingResponse;
```

```
import org.elasticsearch.client.Client;
import org.elasticsearch.common.xcontent.XContentBuilder;
import java.io.IOException;
import static org.elasticsearch.common.xcontent.XContentFactory.
jsonBuilder;
```

2. We define a class to contain our code and to initialize the client and the index:

```
public class MappingOperations {
    public static void main( String[] args )
    {
      String index="mytest";
      String type="mytype";
      Client client
      =NativeClient.createTransportClient();
      IndicesOperations io=new IndicesOperations(client);
      if(io.checkIndexExists(index))
      io.deleteIndex(index);
      io.createIndex(index);
```

3. We prepare the JSON mapping to put in the index:

```
        XContentBuilder builder = null;
        try {
          builder = jsonBuilder().
startObject().
field("type1").
startObject().
field("properties").
startObject().
field("nested1").
startObject().
field("type").
value("nested").
endObject().endObject().endObject().
endObject();
```

4. We put the mapping in the index:

```
PutMappingResponse
response=client.admin().indices().preparePutMapping(index).
setType(type).setSource(builder).execute().actionGet();
if(!response.isAcknowledged()){
            System.out.println("Something strange
            happens");
          }
        } catch (IOException e) {
```

```
        ex.printStackTrace();
        System.out.println("Unable to create
        mapping");
    }
```

5. We delete the mapping in the index and remove the index:

```
client.admin().indices().prepareDeleteMapping(index).
setType(type).execute().actionGet();
        io.deleteIndex(index);
    }
}
```

How it works...

Before executing a mapping operation, a client must be available and the index must be created. In the previous example, if the index exists, it's deleted and recreated as a new one, so we are sure to start from scratch:

```
Client client =NativeClient.createTransportClient();
IndicesOperations io=new IndicesOperations(client);
if(io.checkIndexExists(index)) io.deleteIndex(index);
io.createIndex(index);
```

Now that we have a fresh index to put the mapping in, we need to create a mapping. As every standard object in ElasticSearch is a JSON object, ElasticSearch provides a convenient way to create a JSON object programmatically via XContentBuilder.jsonBuilder. For using them, you need to add the following imports to your Java file:

```
import org.elasticsearch.common.xcontent.XContentBuilder;
import static
org.elasticsearch.common.xcontent.XContentFactory.jsonBuilder;
```

The XContentBuilder.jsonBuilder object allows building JSON programmatically. It is a Swiss-knife of JSON generation in ElasticSearch and, due to its ability to be chained, it has a lot of methods. These methods always return a builder so they can be easily chained. The most important ones are:

▸ startObject() and startObject(name): Here name is the name of the JSON object. It defines a JSON object. The object must be closed with endObject().

▸ field(name) or field(name, value): Here name must always be a string, and value must be a valid value that can be converted to JSON. It's used to define a field in the JSON object.

▸ value(value): Here value must be a valid value that can be converted to JSON. It defines a single value in a field.

▸ startArray() and startArray(name): Here name is the name of the JSON array. It defines a JSON array that must be ended with an endArray().

Generally in ElasticSearch every method that accepts a JSON object as a parameter also accepts a JSON builder.

Now that we have the mapping in the builder, we need to call the putmapping API. This API is in the `client.admin().indices()` namespace and you need to define the index, the type, and the mapping to execute this call as follows:

```
PutMappingResponse response=client.admin().indices().
preparePutMapping(index).setType(type).setSource(builder).execute().
actionGet();
```

If everything is ok, you can check the status in `response.isAcknowledged()`; it must be `true`. Otherwise an error is raised.

If you need to update a mapping, you need to execute the same call, but in the mapping put only the fields that you need to add.

To delete a mapping, you need to call the delete mapping API. It requires the index and the type to be deleted. In the previous example, the previously created mapping is deleted using the following code:

```
client.admin().indices().prepareDeleteMapping(index).setType(type).
execute().actionGet();
```

There's more...

There is another important call used in managing the mapping called the get mapping API. The call is similar to a delete call, and returns a `GetMappingResponse` object:

```
GetMappingResponse  response=client.admin().indices().
prepareGetMapping(index).setType(type).execute().actionGet();
```

The response contains the mapping information. The data returned is structured as in an index map that contains mapping mapped as name `MappingMetaData`.

The `MappingMetaData` is an object that contains all the mapping information and all the sections that we discussed in *Chapter 4, Basic Operations*.

See also

> ▸   The *Putting a mapping in an index, Getting a mapping*, and *Deleting a mapping* recipes in *Chapter 4, Basic Operations*

Managing documents

The native APIs for managing documents (index, delete, and update) are the most important after the search ones. In this recipe, we will see how to use them. In the next recipe we will proceed to bulk actions to improve performance.

Getting ready

You will need a working ElasticSearch cluster and a working copy of Maven.

The code of this recipe is in `chapter_10/nativeclient` in the code bundle of this chapter, present on Packt's website, and on GitHub (`https://github.com/aparo/elasticsearch-cookbook-second-edition`). The referred class is `DocumentOperations`.

How to do it...

For managing documents, we will perform the following operations:

> ▶ We'll execute all the document's CRUD operations (Create, Update, Delete) via a native client using the following code:

```
import org.elasticsearch.action.delete.DeleteResponse;
import org.elasticsearch.action.get.GetResponse;
import org.elasticsearch.action.index.IndexResponse;
import org.elasticsearch.action.update.UpdateResponse;
import org.elasticsearch.client.Client;
import org.elasticsearch.common.xcontent.XContentFactory;
import java.io.IOException;
public class DocumentOperations {
  public static void main( String[] args )
  {
    String index="mytest";
    String type="mytype";
    Client client =NativeClient.createTransportClient();
    IndicesOperations io=new IndicesOperations(client);
    if(io.checkIndexExists(index))
    io.deleteIndex(index);
    try {
      client.admin().indices().prepareCreate(index)
      .addMapping(type, XContentFactory.jsonBuilder()
      .startObject()
      .startObject(type)
```

```
            .startObject("_timestamp").field("enabled",
            true).field("store", "yes").endObject()
            .startObject("_ttl").field("enabled",
            true).field("store", "yes").endObject()
            .endObject()
            .endObject())
            .execute().actionGet();
        } catch (IOException e) {
          System.out.println("Unable to create mapping");
        }
        // We index a document
        IndexResponse ir=client.prepareIndex(index, type,
        "2").setSource("text","unicorn").execute().actionGet();
        System.out.println("Version: "+ir.getVersion());
        // We get a document
        GetResponse gr=client.prepareGet(index, type,
        "2").execute().actionGet();
        System.out.println("Version: "+gr.getVersion());
        // We update a document
        UpdateResponse ur = client.prepareUpdate(index,
        type, "2").setScript("ctx._source.text =
        'v2'" , ScriptService.ScriptType.INLINE).execute().
        actionGet();
        System.out.println("Version: "+ur.getVersion());
        // We delete a document
        DeleteResponse dr = client.prepareDelete(index,
        type, "2").execute().actionGet();
        io.deleteIndex(index);
    }
}
```

▶ The result will be:

```
Aug 24, 2014 13:58:21 PM org.elasticsearch.plugins
INFO: [Masked Rose] loaded [], sites []
Version: 1
Version: 1
Version: 2
```

The document version is always incremented by 1 after an update action is performed or if the document is re-indexed with the new changes.

How it works...

Before executing a document action, a client and the index must be available and a document mapping should be created (the mapping is optional, because it can be inferred from the indexed document).

To index a document via a native client, the method `prepareIndex` is created. It requires the index and the type to be passed as arguments. If an ID is provided, it will be used; otherwise a new one will be created. In the previous example, we have put the source in the form of (key, value), but many forms are available to pass as a source. They are:

- A JSON string: `"{field:value}"`
- A string and a value (from 1 to 4 couples): `field1, value1, field2, value2, field3, value3, field4, value4`
- A builder: `jsonBuilder().startObject().field(field,value).endObject()`
- A byte array

Obviously it's possible to add all the parameters that we have seen in the *Indexing a document* recipe in *Chapter 4, Basic Operations,* such as parent, routing, and so on. In the previous example, the call was:

```
IndexResponse ir=client.prepareIndex(index, type,
"2").setSource("text", "unicorn").execute().actionGet();
```

The return value (`IndexReponse`) can be used in several ways:

- Checking if the index was successfully added or not
- Getting the ID of the indexed document, if it was not provided during the index action
- Retrieving the document version

To retrieve a document, you need to know the index, type, and ID, and the client method is `prepareGet`. It requires the usual triplet (index, type, ID), but a lot of other methods are also available to control the routing (such as souring and parent) or fields, as we have seen in the *Getting a document* recipe in *Chapter 4, Basic Operations*. In the previous example, the call was:

```
GetResponse gr=client.prepareGet(index, type,
"2").execute().actionGet();
```

The return type (`GetResponse`) contains all the request (if the document exists) and document information (source, version, index, type, ID).

To update a document, it's required to know the index, type, and ID, and provide a script or a document to be used for the update. The client method is `prepareUpdate`. In the previous example, the code was:

```
UpdateResponse ur = client.prepareUpdate(index, type,
"2").setScript("ctx._source.text = 'v2'" ,
ScriptService.ScriptType.INLINE).execute().actionGet();
```

The script code must be a string. If the script language is not defined, the default (Groovy) is used.

The returned response contains information about the execution and the new version value to manage concurrency.

To delete a document (without needing to execute a query), we must know the index, type, and ID, and we can use the client method `prepareDelete` to create a delete request. In the previous code, we have used:

```
DeleteResponse dr = client.prepareDelete("test", "type",
"2").execute().actionGet();
```

The delete request allows passing all the parameters that we have seen in the *Deleting a document* recipe in *Chapter 4, Basic Operations* to control routing and the version.

See also

▶ The *Indexing a document, Getting a document, Deleting a document,* and *Updating a document* recipes in *Chapter 4, Basic Operations*

Managing bulk actions

Executing atomic operation on items via single call is often a bottleneck if you need to index or delete thousands/millions of records. The best practice in this case is to execute a bulk action. We have discussed bulk action via the REST API in the *Speeding up atomic operations (bulk operations)* recipe in *Chapter 4, Basic Operations*.

Getting ready

You will need a working ElasticSearch cluster and Maven installed.

The code of this recipe is in `chapter_10/nativeclient` in the code bundle of this chapter, which is available on Packt's website, and on GitHub (`https://github.com/aparo/elasticsearch-cookbook-second-edition`). The referred class is `BulkOperations`.

How to do it...

To manage a bulk action, we will perform the following actions:

▶ We'll execute a bulk action adding 1,000 documents, updating them and deleting them as follows:

```
import org.elasticsearch.action.bulk.BulkRequestBuilder;
import org.elasticsearch.client.Client;
import org.elasticsearch.common.xcontent.XContentFactory;
import java.io.IOException;
```

```java
public class BulkOperations {
  public static void main( String[] args )
  {
    String index="mytest";
    String type="mytype";
    Client client =NativeClient.createTransportClient();
    IndicesOperations io=new IndicesOperations(client);
    if(io.checkIndexExists(index))
    io.deleteIndex(index);
    try {
      client.admin().indices().prepareCreate(index)
      .addMapping(type, XContentFactory.jsonBuilder()
      .startObject()
      .startObject(type)
      .startObject("_timestamp").field("enabled",
      true).field("store", "yes").endObject()
      .startObject("_ttl").field("enabled",
      true).field("store", "yes").endObject()
      .endObject()
      .endObject())
      .execute().actionGet();
    } catch (IOException e) {
      System.out.println("Unable to create mapping");
    }
    BulkRequestBuilder bulker=client.prepareBulk();
    for (Integer i=1; i<=1000; i++){
      bulker.add(client.prepareIndex(index, type,
      i.toString()).setSource("position", i.toString()));
    }
    System.out.println("Number of action: " +
    bulker.numberOfActions());
    bulker.execute().actionGet();
    System.out.println("Number of actions for index: "
    + bulker.numberOfActions());
    bulker.execute().actionGet();
    bulker=client.prepareBulk();
    for (Integer i=1; i<=1000; i++){
      bulker.add(client.prepareUpdate(index, type,
      i.toString()).setScript("ctx._source.position
      += 2" , ScriptService.ScriptType.INLINE));
    }
    System.out.println("Number of actions for update: "
    + bulker.numberOfActions());
    bulker.execute().actionGet();
    bulker=client.prepareBulk();
    for (Integer i=1; i<=1000; i++){
      bulker.add(client.prepareDelete(index, type,
      i.toString()));
    }
```

```
        System.out.println("Number of actions  for delete:
        " + bulker.numberOfActions());
        bulker.execute().actionGet();
        io.deleteIndex(index);
    }
}
```

▶ The result will be:

```
Number of actions for index: 1000
Number of actions for udpate: 1000
Number of actions for delete: 1000
```

How it works...

Before executing these bulk actions, a client must be available and the index and document mapping must be created (the mapping is optional).

We can consider `bulkBuilder` as a collector of different actions:

▶ `IndexRequest` or `IndexRequestBuilder`

▶ `UpdateRequest` or `UpdateRequestBuilder`

▶ `DeleteRequest` or `DeleteRequestBuilder`

▶ A bulk formatted array of bytes.

Generally when used in a code, we can consider it as a "List" in which we add actions of the supported types.

To initialize `bulkBuilder` we use:

```
BulkRequestBuilder bulker=client.prepareBulk();
```

In the previous example we have added 1,000 index actions (the `IndexBuilder` is similar to the previous recipe):

```
        for (Integer i=1; i<=1000; i++){
          bulker.add(client.prepareIndex(index, type,
          i.toString()).setSource("position", i.toString()));
        }
```

After having added all the actions, we can print the number of actions and then execute them:

```
        System.out.println("Number of action: " +
        bulker.numberOfActions());
        bulker.execute().actionGet();
```

After having executed `bulkBuilder`, the bulker is empty. We have populated the bulk with 1,000 update actions:

```
for (Integer i=1; i<=1000; i++){
  bulker.add(client.prepareUpdate(index, type,
  i.toString()).setScript("ctx._source.position += 2" ,
  ScriptService.ScriptType.INLINE));
}
```

After having added all the update actions, we can execute them in a bulk as follows:

```
bulker.execute().actionGet();
After, the same step is done with the delete action:
for (Integer i=1; i<=1000; i++){
  ulker.add(client.prepareDelete(index, type,
  i.toString()));
}
```

To commit the delete operation, we need to execute the bulk.

> In this example, to simplify a bulk operation, I have created a bulk with the same type of actions but, as described previously, you can put up any supported type of action in the same bulk operation.

See also

▸ The *Speeding up atomic operations (bulk operations)* recipe in *Chapter 4, Basic Operations*

Building a query

Before a search, a query must be built and ElasticSearch provides several ways to build these queries. In this recipe, we will see how to create a query object via `QueryBuilder` and via simple strings.

Getting ready

You will need a working ElasticSearch cluster and a working copy of Maven. The code of this recipe is in `chapter_10/nativeclient` in the code bundle available on Packt's website, and on GitHub (`https://github.com/aparo/elasticsearch-cookbook-second-edition`). The referred class is `QueryCreation`.

How to do it...

To create a query, we will perform the following steps:

1. There are several ways to define a query in ElasticSearch and they are interchangeable. Generally a query can be defined as a combination of the following components:

   ❑ QueryBuilder: This is a helper to build a query.

   ❑ XContentBuilder: This is a helper to create JSON code. We have discussed it in the *Managing mappings* recipe in this chapter. The JSON code to be generated is similar to the previous REST, but converted in programmatic code.

   ❑ **Array of bytes or string**: In this case, it's usually the JSON to be executed as we have seen in REST calls.

   ❑ Map: It contains the query and the value of the query.

2. We'll create a query using QueryBuilder and execute a search (searching via a native API will be discussed in the next recipe):

```
...truncated ...
import org.elasticsearch.common.xcontent.XContentFactory;
import org.elasticsearch.index.query.BoolQueryBuilder;
import org.elasticsearch.index.query.QueryBuilder;
import org.elasticsearch.index.query.RangeQueryBuilder;
import org.elasticsearch.index.query.TermFilterBuilder;
import java.io.IOException;
import static org.elasticsearch.index.query.QueryBuilders.*;
import static org.elasticsearch.index.query.FilterBuilders.*;
public class QueryCreation {
  public static void main( String[] args )
  {
    String index="mytest";
    ... truncated ...
    BulkRequestBuilder bulker=client.prepareBulk();
    for (Integer i=1; i<1000; i++){
      bulker.add(client.prepareIndex(index, type,
        i.toString()).setSource("text", i.toString(),
        "number1", i+1, "number2", i%2));
    }
    bulker.execute().actionGet();
    client.admin().indices().prepareRefresh(index).execute().ac
    tionGet();
    TermFilterBuilder filter = termFilter("number2", 1);
```

```
RangeQueryBuilder range =
rangeQuery("number1").gt(500);
BoolQueryBuilder bool = boolQuery().must(range);
QueryBuilder query = filteredQuery(bool, filter);
SearchResponse
response=client.prepareSearch(index).setTypes(type).setQuer
y(query).execute().actionGet();
System.out.println("Matched records of elements: "
+ response.getHits().getTotalHits());
io.deleteIndex(index);
    }
}
```

I have removed the redundant parts that are similar to the example in the previous recipe.

3. The result will be:

    ```
    Matched records of elements:250
    ```

How it works...

In the preceding example, we created a query via `QueryBuilder`. The first step is to import the query builder from the namespace:

```
import static org.elasticsearch.index.query.QueryBuilders.*;
```

But we also need the field builders and, to import them, use the following line of code:

```
import static org.elasticsearch.index.query.FilterBuilders.*;
```

The query used in the example is a filtered query composed by `BooleanQuery` and a term filter. The goal of the example is to show how to mix several query/filter types for creating a complex query.

The Boolean query contains a `must` clause with a `range` query. Use the following code to create the `range` query:

```
RangeQueryBuilder range = rangeQuery("number1").gte(500);
```

This range query matches the `number1` field to all the values greater than or equal to `gte (500)`.

After having created the range query, we can add it to a Boolean query in the `must` block:

```
BoolQueryBuilder bool = boolQuery().must(range);
```

In real-world complex queries, you can have a lot of nested queries in a Boolean query or filter.

To build our filtered query, we need to define a filter. In this case we have used a term filter, which is one of the most used filters:

```
TermFilterBuilder filter = termFilter("number2", 1);
```

The `termFilter` method accepts a field name and a value, which must be a valid ElasticSearch type. The preceding code is similar to the JSON or REST {term: {number2:1}.

Now, we can build the final filtered query that we can execute in the search:

```
QueryBuilder query = filteredQuery(bool, filter);
```

> Before executing a query and to be sure not to miss any results, the index must be refreshed. In the example, it's done with the help of the following code: `client.admin().indices().prepareRefresh(index).execute().actionGet();`

There's more...

The possible native queries/filters are the same as the REST ones and have the same parameters but the only difference is that they are accessible via builder methods.

The most common query builders are:

- `matchAllQuery`: This allows matching of all the documents.
- `matchQuery` and `matchPhraseQuery`: These are used to match against text strings.
- `termQuery` and `termsQuery`: These are used to match term value(s) against a specific field.
- `boolQuery`: This is used to aggregate other queries with Boolean logic.
- `idsQuery`: This is used to match a list of ids.
- `fieldQuery`: This is used to match a field with a text.
- `wildcardQuery`: This is used to match terms with wildcards (*,?).
- `regexpQuery`: This is used to match terms via a regular expression.
- **Span query family** (`spanTermsQuery`, `spanTermQuery`, `spanORQuery`, `spanNotQuery`, `spanFirstQuery`, and so on): These are a few examples of the span query family. They are used in building a span query.
- `filteredQuery`: In this, the query is combined with a filter where the filter applies first.
- `constantScoreQuery`: This accepts a query or a filter and all the matched documents are set with the same score.

- ► `moreLikeThisQuery` and `fuzzyLikeThisQuery`: These are used to retrieve similar documents.
- ► `hasChildQuery`, `hasParentQuery`, and `nestedQuery`: These are used in managing related documents.

The preceding list is not complete, because it is evolving during the life of ElasticSearch. New query types are added to cover new search cases or they are occasionally renamed such as `Text Query` to `Match Query`.

Similar to the query builders, there are a lot of query filters, explained as follows:

- ► `matchAllFilter`: This matches all the documents
- ► `termFilter` and `termsFilter`: These are used to filter given value(s)
- ► `idsFilter`: This is used to filter a list of ids
- ► `typeFilter`: This is used to filter all the documents of the same type
- ► `andFilter`, `orFilter`, and `notFilter`: These are used to build Boolean filters
- ► `wildcardFilter`: This is used to filter terms with wildcards (*,?)
- ► `regexpFilter`: This is used to filter terms via a regular expression
- ► `rangeFilter`: This is used to filter using a range
- ► `scriptFilter`: This is used to filter documents using the scripting engine
- ► `geoDistanceFilter`, `geoBoundingBoxFilter`, and other `geo` filters: These provide geo filtering of documents
- ► `boolFilter`: This is used to create a Boolean filter that aggregates other filters

See also

- ► The *Querying/filtering for a single term* recipe in *Chapter 5, Search, Queries, and Filters*

Executing a standard search

In the previous recipe, we saw how to build a query. In this recipe we can execute this query to retrieve some documents.

Getting ready

You will need a working ElasticSearch cluster and a working copy of Maven.

The code of this recipe is in `chapter_10/nativeclient`, in the code bundle placed on Packt's website, and on GitHub (`https://github.com/aparo/elasticsearch-cookbook-second-edition`). The referred class is `QueryExample`.

How to do it...

To execute a standard query, we will perform the following steps:

1. After having created a query, it is enough to use the `prepareQuery` call in order to execute it and pass it your query object. Here is a complete example:

```java
import org.elasticsearch.action.search.SearchResponse;
import org.elasticsearch.client.Client;
import org.elasticsearch.index.query.QueryBuilder;
import org.elasticsearch.search.SearchHit;
import static org.elasticsearch.index.query.FilterBuilders.*;
import static org.elasticsearch.index.query.QueryBuilders.*;
public class QueryExample {
  public static void main(String[] args) {
  String index = "mytest";
    String type = "mytype";
    QueryHelper qh = new QueryHelper();
    qh.populateData(index, type);
    Client client=qh.getClient();
    QueryBuilder query =
    filteredQuery(boolQuery().must(rangeQuery("number1").gte(50
    0)), termFilter("number2", 1));
    SearchResponse response =
    client.prepareSearch(index).setTypes(type)
    .setQuery(query).addHighlightedField("name")
    .execute().actionGet();
    if(response.status().getStatus()==200){
      System.out.println("Matched number of
      documents: " + response.getHits().totalHits());
      System.out.println("Maximum score: " +
      response.getHits().maxScore());
      for(SearchHit hit:
      response.getHits().getHits()){
        System.out.println("hit:
        "+hit.getIndex()+":"+hit.getType()+":"
        +hit.getId());
      }
    }
    qh.dropIndex(index);
  }
}
```

2. The result should be similar to this one:

```
Matched number of documents: 251
Maximum score: 1.0
hit: mytest:mytype:505
```

```
hit: mytest:mytype:517
hit: mytest:mytype:529
hit: mytest:mytype:531
hit: mytest:mytype:543
hit: mytest:mytype:555
hit: mytest:mytype:567
hit: mytest:mytype:579
hit: mytest:mytype:581
hit: mytest:mytype:593
```

How it works...

The call to execute a search is `prepareSearch` and it returns `SearchResponse`:

```
import org.elasticsearch.action.search.SearchResponse;
....
SearchResponse response = client.prepareSearch(index).setTypes(type).
setQuery(query).execute().actionGet();
```

The search call has a lot of methods to allow setting all the parameters that we have already seen in the *Executing a search* recipe in *Chapter 5, Search, Queries, and Filters*. The most used methods are:

- ▶ `setIndices`: This allows defining the indices to be used.

- ▶ `setTypes`: This allows defining the document types to be used.

- ▶ `setQuery`: This allows setting the query to be executed.

- ▶ `addField(s)`: This allows setting fields to be returned (used to reduce the bandwidth by returning only the needed fields).

- ▶ `addAggregation`: This allows adding aggregations to be computed.

- ▶ `addFacet` (Deprecated): This allows adding facets to be computed.

- ▶ `addHighlighting`: This allows highlighting results to be returned. The simple case is to highlight a field `name` as follows:

  ```
  .addHighlightedField("name")
  ```

- ▶ `addScriptField`: This allows returning a scripted field. A scripted field is a field computed by server-side scripting using one of the available scripting languages. For example :

  ```
  Map<String, Object> params = MapBuilder.<String,
  Object>newMapBuilder().put("factor", 2.0).map();
  .addScriptField("sNum1", "doc['num1'].value * factor",
  params)
  ```

After having executed a search, a response object is returned.

It's good practice to check if the search is successful or not, by checking the returned status and, optionally, the number of hits. If the search was executed correctly, then the return status is 200.

```
if(response.status().getStatus()==200)
```

The response object contains a lot of sections that we have analyzed in the *Executing a Search* recipe in *Chapter 5, Search, Queries, and Filters*. The most important one is the `hits` section that contains our results. The main methods that access this section are:

- `totalHits`: This allows obtaining the total number of results:

  ```
  System.out.println("Matched number of documents: " + response.
  getHits().totalHits());
  ```

- `maxScore`: This gives the maximum score of the documents. It is the same score value of the first `SearchHit` method:

  ```
  System.out.println("Maximum score: " + response.getHits().
  maxScore());
  ```

- `hits`: This is `SearchHit` array that contains the results, if available.

The `SearchHit` is the result object. It has a lot of methods, of which the most important ones are:

- `index()`:This is the index that contains the document.
- `type()`: This is the type of the document.
- `id()`: This is the ID of the document.
- `score()`: This is the query score of this document, if available.
- `version()`: This is the version of the document, if available.
- `source()`, `sourceAsString()`, `sourceAsMap()`, and so on: These return the source of the document in different forms, if available.
- `explanation()`: If available (required in the search), it contains the query explanation.
- `fields, field(String name)`: These return the fields requested if fields are passed to search the object.
- `sortValues()`: This is the value/values used to sort the record. It's only available if sort is specified during the search phase.
- `shard()`: This is the shard of the search hit. This value is very important in the case of custom routing.

In the following example, we have printed only the index, type, and ID of each hit.

```
for(SearchHit hit: response.getHits().getHits()){
System.out.println("hit:
"+hit.getIndex()+":"+hit.getType()+":"+hit.getId());
}
```

> The number of returned hits, if not defined, is limited to 10.
> To retrieve more hits you need to define a larger value in the
> `size` method or paginate using the `from` method.

See also

▶ The *Executing a search* recipe in *Chapter 5, Search, Queries, and Filters*

Executing a search with aggregations

The previous recipe can be extended to support aggregations and to retrieve analytics on indexed data.

Getting ready

You will need a working ElasticSearch cluster and a working copy of Maven.

The code of this recipe is in `chapter_10/nativeclient` folder in the code bundle of this chapter available on Packt's website, and on GitHub (`https://github.com/aparo/elasticsearch-cookbook-second-edition`). The referred class is `AggregationExample`.

How to do it...

To execute a search with aggregations, we will perform the following steps:

1. We'll calculate two different aggregations (terms and extended statistics) as follows:

    ```
    import org.elasticsearch.action.search.SearchResponse;
    import org.elasticsearch.client.Client;
    import
    org.elasticsearch.search.aggregations.AggregationBuilder;
    import
    org.elasticsearch.search.aggregations.bucket.terms.Terms;
    import
    org.elasticsearch.search.aggregations.metrics.stats.extended.
    ExtendedStats;
    ```

```
import
org.elasticsearch.search.aggregations.metrics.stats.extended.
ExtendedStatsBuilder;
import static
org.elasticsearch.index.query.QueryBuilders.matchAllQuery;
import static
org.elasticsearch.search.aggregations.AggregationBuilders.*;
public class AggregationExample {
  public static void main(String[] args){
    String index = "mytest";
    String type = "mytype";
    QueryHelper qh = new QueryHelper();
    qh.populateData(index, type);
    Client client = qh.getClient();
    AggregationBuilder aggsBuilder =
    terms("tag").field("tag");
    ExtendedStatsBuilder aggsBuilder2 =
    extendedStats("number1").field("number1");
    SearchResponse response =
    client.prepareSearch(index).setTypes(type)
    .setQuery(matchAllQuery()).addAggregation(aggsBuilder).
    addAggregation(aggsBuilder2)
    .execute().actionGet();
    if (response.status().getStatus() == 200) {
      System.out.println("Matched number of documents: " +
      response.getHits().totalHits());
      Terms termsAggs =
      response.getAggregations().get("tag");
      System.out.println("Aggregation name: " +
      termsAggs.getName());
      System.out.println("Aggregation total: " +
      termsAggs.getBuckets().size());
      for (Terms.Bucket entry : termsAggs.getBuckets()) {
        System.out.println(" - " + entry.getKey() +
        " " + entry.getDocCount());
      }
      ExtendedStats extStats =
      response.getAggregations().get("number1");
      System.out.println("Aggregation name: " +
      extStats.getName());
      System.out.println("Count: " + extStats.getCount());
      System.out.println("Min: " + extStats.getMin());
      System.out.println("Max: " + extStats.getMax());
      System.out.println("Standard Deviation: " +
      extStats.getStdDeviation());
```

```
            System.out.println("Sum of Squares: " +
            extStats.getSumOfSquares());
            System.out.println("Variance: " +
            extStats.getVariance());
        }
        qh.dropIndex(index);
    }
}
```

2. The result should be similar to this:

```
Aug 24, 2014 4:07:43 PM org.elasticsearch.plugins
INFO: [Legion] loaded [], sites []
Matched number of documents: 1000
Aggregation name: tag
Aggregation total: 4
  - nice 264
  - bad 257
  - amazing 247
  - cool 232
Aggregation name: number1
Count: 1000
Min: 2.0
Max: 1001.0
Standard Deviation: 288.6749902572095
Sum of Squares: 3.348355E8
Variance: 83333.25
```

How it works...

The search part is similar to the previous example. In this case we have used a `matchAllQuery`, which matches all the documents. To execute an aggregation, first you need to create it. There are three ways to do so:

- Using a string that maps a JSON object
- Using `XContentBuilder` that will be used to produce a JSON
- Using `AggregationBuilder`

The first two ways are trivial; the third one requires the builders to be imported:

```
import static org.elasticsearch.search.aggregations.
AggregationBuilders.*;
```

There are several types of aggregation, as we have already seen in *Chapter 6, Aggregations*. The first one, which we have created with `AggregationBuilder`, is a `Terms` one that collects and counts all terms occurrences in buckets:

```
AggregationBuilder aggsBuilder = terms("tag").field("tag");
```

The required value for every aggregation is the name passed in the builder constructor. In the case of a terms aggregation, the field is required to be able to process the request. (There are a lot of other parameters, see the *Executing the terms aggregation* recipe in *Chapter 6, Aggregations* for full details).

The second `aggregationBuilder` that we have created is an extended statistical one based on the `number1` numeric field:

```
ExtendedStatsBuilder aggsBuilder2 = extendedStats("number1").
field("number1");
```

Now that we have created `aggregationBuilders`, we can add them on a search method via the `addAggregation` method:

```
SearchResponse response = client.prepareSearch(index).setTypes(type)
                .setQuery(matchAllQuery()).addAggregation(aggsBuilder)
                addAggregation(aggsBuilder2)
                .execute().actionGet();
```

Now the response holds information about our aggregations. To access them we need to use the `getAggregations` method of the response.

The aggregations results are contained in a hash-like structure and you can retrieve them with the names that you have previously defined in the request.

To retrieve the first aggregation results we need to execute the following code:

```
Terms termsAggs = response.getAggregations().get("tag");
```

Now that we have an aggregation result of type `Terms` (see the *Executing the terms aggregations* recipe in *Chapter 6, Aggregations*), we can get the aggregation properties and iterate on buckets:

```
System.out.println("Aggregation name: " + termsAggs.getName());
System.out.println("Aggregation total: " + termsAggs.getBuckets().
size());
for (Terms.Bucket entry : termsAggs.getBuckets()) {
   System.out.println(" - " + entry.getKey() + " " + entry.
getDocCount());
}
```

To retrieve the second aggregation result, because the result is of type `ExtendedStats`, you need to cast to it as follows:

```
ExtendedStats extStats = response.getAggregations().get("number1");
```

Now you can access the result properties of this kind of aggregation:

```
System.out.println("Aggregation name: " + extStats.getName());
System.out.println("Count: " + extStats.getCount());
System.out.println("Min: " + extStats.getMin());
System.out.println("Max: " + extStats.getMax());
System.out.println("Standard Deviation: " + extStats.
getStdDeviation());
System.out.println("Sum of Squares: " + extStats.getSumOfSquares());
System.out.println("Variance: " + extStats.getVariance());
```

Using aggregations with a native client is quite easy; you only need to pay attention to the returned aggregation type to execute the correct type cast to access your results.

See also

> ▸ The *Executing the terms aggregations* and *Executing the stats aggregations* recipes in *Chapter 6, Aggregations*

Executing a scroll/scan search

Pagination with a standard query works very well if you are matching documents that do not change too often; otherwise, doing pagination with live data returns unpredictable results. To bypass this problem, ElasticSearch provides an extra parameter in the query called **scroll**.

Getting ready

You will need a working ElasticSearch cluster and a working copy of Maven.

The code of this recipe is in `chapter_10/nativeclient` in the code bundle, present on Packt's website and on GitHub (`https://github.com/aparo/elasticsearch-cookbook-second-edition`). The referred class is `ScrollScanQueryExample`.

How to do it...

The search is done in the same way as in the previous recipe. The main difference is a `setScroll` timeout that allows storing the result's ids for a query for a defined timeout in memory.

We can change the code of the previous recipe to use scroll in the following way:

```java
import org.elasticsearch.action.search.SearchResponse;
import org.elasticsearch.action.search.SearchType;
import org.elasticsearch.client.Client;
import org.elasticsearch.common.unit.TimeValue;
import org.elasticsearch.index.query.QueryBuilder;
import static org.elasticsearch.index.query.FilterBuilders.termFilter;
import static org.elasticsearch.index.query.QueryBuilders.*;
public class ScrollScanQueryExample {
  public static void main(String[] args) {
    String index = "mytest";
    String type = "mytype";
    QueryHelper qh = new QueryHelper();
    qh.populateData(index, type);
    Client client=qh.getClient();
    QueryBuilder query =
    filteredQuery(boolQuery().must(rangeQuery("number1").gte(500)),
termFilter("number2", 1));
    SearchResponse response =
    client.prepareSearch(index).setTypes(type)
    .setQuery(query).setScroll(TimeValue.timeValueMinutes(2))
    .execute().actionGet();
    // do something with searchResponse.getHits()
    while(response.getHits().hits().length!=0){
      // do something with searchResponse.getHits()
      //your code here
      //next scroll
      response =
      client.prepareSearchScroll(response.getScrollId()).
setScroll(TimeV
      alue.timeValueMinutes(2)).execute().actionGet();
    }
    SearchResponse searchResponse = client.prepareSearch()
    .setSearchType(SearchType.SCAN)
    .setQuery(matchAllQuery())
    .setSize(100)
    .setScroll(TimeValue.timeValueMinutes(2))
    .execute().actionGet();
    while (true) {
      searchResponse =
      client.prepareSearchScroll(searchResponse.getScrollId()).
setScroll
      (TimeValue.timeValueMinutes(2)).execute().actionGet();
      // do something with searchResponse.getHits() if any
```

```
            if (searchResponse.getHits().hits().length == 0) {
              break;
            }
          }
        }
      qh.dropIndex(index);
    }
}
```

To use the result of scrolling, it's enough to add the `setScroll` method with a timeout to the method call. When using scrolling some behaviors must be considered:

▸ The timeout defines the time slice for which an ElasticSearch server stores the results. Asking for a scroll, after the timeout, will result in the server returning an error. So you must be careful with short timeouts.

▸ The scroll consumes memory until the scroll ends or a timeout is raised. Setting a large timeout period without consuming the data will result in unnecessary memory occupation. Using a large number of open scrollers consumes a lot of memory proportional to the number of ids and their related data (score, order, and so on) in the results.

▸ Scrolling, it's not possible to paginate the documents, as there is no *start* to it. The scrolling is designed to fetch consecutives results.

So a standard search is changed to a scroll in this way:

```
SearchResponse response = client.prepareSearch(index).setTypes(type).
setQuery(query).setScroll(TimeValue.timeValueMinutes(2)).execute().
actionGet();
```

The response contains the results that consist of a standard search plus a scroll ID that is required to fetch the next results.

To execute the scroll you need to call the `prepareSearchScroll` client method with a scroll ID and a new timeout. In the following example, we process all the result documents:

```
while(response.getHits().hits().length!=0){
    // do something with searchResponse.getHits()
    //your code here
    //next scroll
    response =
    client.prepareSearchScroll(response.getScrollId()).setScroll(TimeV
    alue.timeValueMinutes(2)).execute().actionGet();
}
```

To make sure that we are at the end of the scroll, we can check that no results are returned.

There are a lot of scenarios in which scroll is very important. For example, working on big data solutions where the result number is very huge, it's very easy to hit the timeout. In these scenarios it is important to have a good architecture in which you can fetch the results as fast as possible and, also, you don't have to process the results iteratively in the loop; however, it defers the result manipulation in a distributed way.

There's more...

Scroll call is used in conjunction with scan queries (see the *Executing a scan query* recipe in *Chapter 5, Search, Queries, and Filters*). Scan queries allow you to execute a query and provide results in a scroll for fast performance.

The scan query consumes less memory than a standard scroll query because of the following reasons:

- It doesn't compute score and doesn't return it
- It doesn't allow sorting, so it is not necessary to store the order value(s) in memory
- It doesn't allow computing facets or aggregations
- It doesn't allow execution of a child query or nested query, which in turn reduces memory usage

The scan method collects the results and iterates them. It stores only the ids of the scan method and hence it is very useful when you need to return all the documents that match a query if the result set is very huge.

To execute a scan query, the search type value must be passed to the search call as follows:

```
SearchResponse searchResponse = client.prepareSearch()
            .setSearchType(SearchType.SCAN)
            .setQuery(matchAllQuery())
            .setSize(100)
            .setScroll(TimeValue.timeValueMinutes(2))
            .execute().actionGet();
```

A big difference in using scan rather than the scroll is that the first call doesn't return hits but only the scroll id; thus, to get the first result you have to execute a new scroll query.

In the preceding code, the loop iterates until no results are available:

```
while (true) {
   searchResponse = client.prepareSearchScroll(searchResponse.
getScrollId()).setScroll(TimeValue.timeValueMinutes(2)).execute().
actionGet();
   // do something with searchResponse.getHits() if any
   if (searchResponse.getHits().hits().length == 0) {
   break;
   }
}
```

See also

- ▶ The *Executing a scan query* recipe in *Chapter 5*: *Search, Queries, and Filters*

11
Python Integration

In this chapter, we will cover the following recipes:

- ▶ Creating a client
- ▶ Managing indices
- ▶ Managing mappings
- ▶ Managing documents
- ▶ Executing a standard search
- ▶ Executing a search with aggregations

Introduction

In the previous chapter, we saw how we can use a native client to access the ElasticSearch server with a Java implementation. This chapter is dedicated to the Python language and managing common tasks via its clients.

Apart from Java, the ElasticSearch team supports official clients for **Perl**, **PHP**, **Python**, **.Net**, and **Ruby** (see the announcement post on the ElasticSearch blog at `http://www.elasticsearch.org/blog/unleash-the-clients-ruby-python-php-perl/.`). This is pretty new as the initial public release was in September 2013. These clients have a lot of advantages against other implementations. A few of them are mentioned here:

- ▶ The clients are strongly tied to the ElasticSearch API, as defined here:

    All of the ElasticSearch APIs provided by these clients are direct translations of the native ElasticSearch REST interface. There should be no guessing required.

    -The ElasticSearch team

- They handle dynamic node detection and failover: they are built with a strong networking base to communicate with the cluster.

- They have a full coverage of the REST API. They share the same application approach for every language in which they are available, so switching from one language to another can be done quickly.

- They provide transport abstraction so that a user can plug in to different backends.

- They are easily extensible.

The Python client works well with other Python frameworks such as **Django**, **web2py**, and **Pyramid**. It allows very fast access to documents, indices, and clusters.

In this chapter, besides the standard ElasticSearch client, we will discuss the **PyES** client developed by me and other contributors since 2010. PyES extends the standard client with a lot of functionalities and helpers, as follows:

- The automatic management of common conversion between types.

- An object-oriented approach to common ElasticSearch elements. The standard client only considers the use of the Python dictionary as a standard element.

- It has helpers for a search, such as advanced iterators on the results and Django-like querysets.

In this chapter, I'll try to describe the most important functionalities of ElasticSearch's official Python client and PyES (`https://github.com/aparo/pyes`). For additional examples and in-depth references, I suggest that you take a look at the online GitHub repository at `https://github.com/elasticsearch/elasticsearch-py` and the documentation.

Creating a client

The official ElasticSearch clients are designed to support several transport layers. They allow you to use HTTP, Thrift, or the Memcached protocol without changing your application code.

The Thrift and Memcached protocols are binary ones and, due to their structures, they are generally a bit faster than the HTTP one. They are wrapped in the REST API and share the same behavior, so switching between these protocols is easy.

In this recipe, we'll see how to instantiate a client with the different protocols.

Getting ready

You need a working ElasticSearch cluster and plugins for extra protocols. The full code of this recipe is in the `chapter_11/client_creation.py` file, available in the code bundle of this book and on GitHub (`https://github.com/aparo/elasticsearch-cookbook-second-edition`).

How to do it...

In order to create a client, perform the following steps:

1. Before using the Python client, you need to install it (possibly in a Python virtual environment). The client is officially hosted on PyPi (http://pypi.python.org/) and it's easy to install the client with the pip command:

```
pip install elasticsearch
```

This standard installation only provides the HTTP protocol.

2. To install the Thrift protocol, you need to install the plugin on the ElasticSearch server:

```
bin/plugin -install elasticsearch/elasticsearch-transport-
thrift/2.3.0
```

On the client side, you need to install the Thrift support for Python, available in the Thrift package (https://pypi.python.org/pypi/thrift/), installable using the pip command:

```
pip install thrift
```

3. To install the Memcached protocol, you need to install the plugin on the ElasticSearch server:

```
bin/plugin -install elasticsearch/elasticsearch-transport-
memcached/2.3.0
```

After having installed a plugin, remember to restart your server to load it.

On the client side, we need to install Memcached support for Python provided by the pylibmc package, which is installable via the pip command:

```
pip install pylibmc
```

> To compile this library, the libmemcache API must be installed. On Mac OS X, you can install it via a brew install libmemcached, on Linux via the libmemcache-dev package in Debian.

4. After having installed the server and the required libraries to use the protocol, you can instantiate the client. It resides in Python's elasticsearch package and must be imported to instantiate the client, as follows:

```
import elasticsearch
```

If you don't pass arguments to the ElasticSearch class, it instantiates a client that connects to a localhost and port 9200 (the default ElasticSearch HTTP port):

```
es = elasticsearch.Elasticsearch()
```

5. If your cluster is composed of more than one node, you can pass the list of nodes as a *round-robin* connection between nodes, and distribute the HTTP load, with the following configuration:

```
es = elasticsearch.Elasticsearch(["search1:9200",
"search2:9200"])
```

6. Often, the complete topology of the cluster is unknown. If you know at least the IP of a node, you can use the option sniff_on_start=True. This option activates the client's ability to detect other nodes in the cluster:

```
es = elasticsearch.Elasticsearch(["search1:9200"],
sniff_on_start=True)
```

7. The default transport is the **Urllib3** HttpConnection but, if you want to use the HTTP requests transport, you need to override the connection_class class by passing a RequestsHttpConnection class:

```
from elasticsearch.connection import RequestsHttpConnection
es = elasticsearch.Elasticsearch( sniff_on_start=True,
connection_class= RequestsHttpConnection)
```

8. If you want to use **Thrift** as a transport layer, you should import the ThriftConnection class and pass it to the client:

```
from elasticsearch.connection import ThriftConnection
es = elasticsearch.Elasticsearch(["search1:9500"],
sniff_on_start=True, connection_class= ThriftConnection)
```

9. If you want to use **Memcached** as a transport layer, you should import the MemcachedConnection class and pass it to the client:

```
from elasticsearch import Elasticsearch, MemcachedConnection
es = elasticsearch.Elasticsearch(["search1:11211"], sniff_on_
start=True, connection_class=MemcachedConnection)
```

How it works...

In order to communicate with an ElasticSearch cluster, a client is required.

The client manages all the communication layers from your application to an ElasticSearch server, using the specified protocol. The standard protocol for REST calls is the HTTP protocol.

The ElasticSearch Python client allows you to use one of the following protocols:

▶ **HTTP**: This provides two implementations based on **requests** (https://pypi.python.org/pypi/requests) and one on **urllib3** (https://pypi.python.org/pypi/urllib3).

▶ **Thrift**: This is one of the fastest protocols available. To use it, Thrift libraries on both the server and client sides must be installed.

▶ **Memcached**: This allows you to communicate with ElasticSearch, as if it was a MemCached server. To use it, memcache libraries must be installed on the server and the client.

For general usage, the HTTP protocol is very good and it's the de facto standard. The other protocols too work well because, often, they reuse the same client object so that you don't have to reinstantiate the connections too often. (For more information, in *Chapter 1, Getting Started*, there is a comparison of the different protocols available).

The ElasticSearch Python client requires a server to connect to. If it is not defined, it tries to use one on the local machine (localhost). If you have more than one node, you can pass a list of servers to connect to.

> The client automatically tries to balance the operations on all the cluster nodes. This is a very powerful functionality provided by the ElasticSearch client.

To improve the list of available nodes, it is possible to set the client to autodiscover new nodes. I suggest that you use this feature, because it is common to have a cluster with a lot of nodes and you might need to shut down some of them for maintenance. The following options can be passed to the client in order to control the discovery:

▶ `sniff_on_start` (by default, `False`): This allows you to obtain the list of nodes from the cluser at startup time

▶ `sniffer_timeout` (by default, `None`): This is the number of seconds between the automatic sniffing of the cluster nodes

▶ `sniff_on_connection_fail` (by default, `False`): This senses whether a connection failure will trigger a sniff on the cluster nodes

The default client configuration uses the HTTP protocol via the urllib3 library. If you want to use other transport protocols, you need to pass the type of the transport class to the `transport_class` variable. These are the currently implemented classes:

▶ `Urllib3HttpConnection` (default): This class uses HTTP (usually on port 9200)

▶ `RequestsHttpConnection`: This is an alternative to the `Urllib3HttpConnection` class, based on the requests library

▶ `ThriftConnection`: This uses the Thrift protocol (usually on port 9500)

▶ `MemcachedConnection`: This uses the Memcached protocol (usually on port 11211)

There's more...

If you need more high-level functionalities than the official client, PyES gives you a more *Pythonic* (following the Python approach) and object-oriented approach to work with ElasticSearch. PyES is easily installable via the `pip` command (the more recent version is available on GitHub):

```
pip install pyes
```

To initialize a client, you need to import the `ES` object and instantiate it:

```
from pyes import ES
es = ES()
```

The protocol is detected by the URL of the servers' list passed to the constructor. If no server parameter is passed to the constructor, the localhost on port 9200 is used.

The PyES client offers the same connection functionalities as the official client, as described in the previous paragraphs, because it internally uses the official ElasticSearch client.

See also

- ▸ PyES on GitHub at `https://github.com/aparo/pyes` and on PyPI at `https://pypi.python.org/pypi/pyes`
- ▸ The PyES online documentation at `http://pythonhosted.org/pyes/`
- ▸ The Python Thrift library at `https://pypi.python.org/pypi/thrift/`
- ▸ The ElasticSearch Thrift plugin at `https://github.com/elasticsearch/elasticsearch-transport-thrift`
- ▸ ElasticSearch Transport Memcached at `https://github.com/elasticsearch/elasticsearch-transport-memcached`
- ▸ The Python Memcached library at `http://pypi.python.org/pypi/pylibmc/1.2.3`

Managing indices

In the previous recipe, we saw how to initialize a client in order to send calls to an ElasticSearch cluster. In this recipe, we will see how to manage indices via client calls.

Getting ready

You need a working ElasticSearch cluster and the packages in the *Creating a client* recipe of this chapter.

The full code of this recipe is in the `chapter_11/indices_management.py` file, available in the code bundle of this book and on GitHub (`https://github.com/aparo/elasticsearch-cookbook-second-edition`).

How to do it...

In Python, managing the life cycle of your indices is easy. Perform the following steps:

1. First, initialize a client, as follows:

```
import elasticsearch
es = elasticsearch.Elasticsearch()
index_name = "my_index"
```

2. All the indices' methods are available in the `client.indices` namespace. You can create and wait for (delay) the creation of an index:

```
es.indices.create(index_name)
es.cluster.health(wait_for_status="yellow")
```

3. You can close/open an index, as follows:

```
es.indices.close(index_name)
es.indices.open(index_name)
es.cluster.health(wait_for_status="yellow")
```

4. You can optimize an index, as shown here:

```
es.indices.optimize(index_name)
```

5. You can delete an index:

```
es.indices.delete(index_name)
```

How it works...

The ElasticSearch Python client has two special managers: one for indices (`<client>.indices`) and one for clusters (`<client>.cluster`).

For every operation that needs to work with indices, the first value is generally the name of the index. If you need to execute an action on several indices in one go, the indices must be concatenated with a comma (for example, `index1, index2, indexN`). It's also possible to use glob patterns to define multiple indexes, such as `index*`.

In PyES, the concatenation is automatically managed.

To create an index, the call requires the index name (`index_name`); use the following the code:

```
es.indices.create(index_name)
```

Other optional parameters are also required, such as index settings and mappings; you will see this advanced feature in the next recipe.

Index creation can take some time (from a few milliseconds to seconds); it is an asynchronous operation and it depends on the complexity of the cluster, the speed of the disk, the network congestion, and so on. To be sure that this action has completed, you need to check whether the cluster's health turns to `yellow` or `green`, as follows:

```
es.cluster.health(wait_for_status="yellow")
```

> It's a good practice to wait till the cluster status is yellow (at least) after operations that involve the creation and opening of indices, because these actions are asynchronous.

To close an index, the method is `<client>.indices.close`, which gives the name of the index to be closed:

```
es.indices.close(index_name)
```

To open an index, the method is `<client>.indices.open`, which gives the name of the index to be opened:

```
es.indices.open(index_name)
es.cluster.health(wait_for_status="yellow")
```

Similar to index creation, after an index is open, it is a good practice to wait until the index is fully open before you execute an operation on the index. This action is done by checking the cluster's health.

To improve the performance of an index, ElasticSearch allows you to optimize it by removing deleted documents (documents are marked as deleted, but not purged from the segments' index for performance reasons) and reducing the number of segments. To optimize an index, the `<client>.indices.optimize` method must be called on the index to be optimized:

```
es.indices.optimize(index_name)
```

Finally, if you want to delete the index, call the `<client>.indices.delete` function and give the name of the index to remove it. Remember that deleting an index removes everything related to it, including all the data, and this action cannot be reverted.

The PyES indices management code is the same as the official client code.

See also

- The *Creating an index* recipe in *Chapter 4, Basic Operations*
- The *Deleting an index* recipe in *Chapter 4, Basic Operations*
- The *Opening/closing an index* recipe in *Chapter 4, Basic Operations*

Managing mappings

After creating an index, the next step is to add some type mappings to it. We saw how to put a mapping via the REST API in *Chapter 4, Basic Operations*. In this recipe, we will see how to manage mappings via the official Python client and PyES.

Getting ready

You need a working ElasticSearch cluster and the required packages that are used in the *Creating a client* recipe in this chapter.

The code of this recipe is present in `chapter_11/mapping_management.py` and `chapter_11/mapping_management_pyes.py` file, which is available in the code bundle of this book and on GitHub (`https://github.com/aparo/elasticsearch-cookbook-second-edition`).

How to do it...

After you have initialized a client and created an index, the following actions are available in order to manage the indices:

- Creating a mapping
- Retrieving a mapping
- Deleting a mapping

These steps can be easily managed with the following code:

1. Use the following code to initialize the client:

   ```
   import elasticsearch
   es = elasticsearch.Elasticsearch()
   ```

2. You can create an index as follows:

   ```
   index_name = "my_index"
   type_name = "my_type"
   es.indices.create(index_name)
   es.cluster.health(wait_for_status="yellow")
   ```

3. In order to put a mapping, use the following code:

   ```
   es.indices.put_mapping(index=index_name, doc_type=type_name,
   body={type_name:{"_type": {"store": "yes"}, "properties": {{
       "uuid": {"index": "not_analyzed", "type": "string", "store":
   "yes"},
   ```

```
       "title": {"index": "analyzed", "type": "string", "store":
"yes", "term_vector": "with_positions_offsets"},
       "parsedtext": {"index": "analyzed", "type": "string", "store":
"yes", "term_vector": "with_positions_offsets"},
    … truncated…}}})
```

4. You can retrieve the mapping, as shown here:

    ```
    mappings = es.indices.get_mapping(index_name, type_name)
    ```

5. The mapping can be deleted, as follows:

    ```
    es.indices.delete_mapping(index_name, type_name)
    ```

6. To delete an index, use the following code:

    ```
    es.indices.delete(index_name)
    ```

How it works...

We saw the initialization of the client and index creation in the previous recipe. In order to create a mapping, the call method is `<client>.indices.create_mapping`, giving the index name, type name, and mapping. Creating a mapping is fully covered in *Chapter 3, Managing Mapping*. It is easy to convert the standard Python types to JSON and vice versa:

```
es.indices.put_mapping(index_name, type_name, {…})
```

If an error is generated in the mapping process, an exception is raised. The `put_mapping` API has two behaviors: create and update.

> In ElasticSearch, you cannot remove a property from a mapping. The schema manipulation allows you to only enter new properties with the PUT mapping call.

To retrieve a mapping with the GET mapping API, use the `<client>.indices.get_mapping` method by providing the index name and type name:

```
mappings = es.indices.get_mapping(index_name, type_name)
```

The returned object is obviously the dictionary that describes the mapping.

To remove a mapping, the method is `<client>.indices.delete_mapping`; it requires the index name and the type name, as shown here:

```
es.indices.delete_mapping(index_name, type_name)
```

> Deleting a mapping is a destructive operation: it removes the mapping and all the documents of this type.

There's more...

Creating a mapping using the official ElasticSearch client requires a lot of attention when building the dictionary that defines the mapping.

PyES also provides an object-oriented approach to creating a mapping, reducing the probability of errors in defining the mapping and adding a typed field with useful presets. The previous mapping can be converted in PyES in this way:

```
from pyes.mappings import *
docmapping = DocumentObjectField(name=mapping_name)
docmapping.add_property(
        StringField(name="parsedtext", store=True, term_vector="with_
positions_offsets", index="analyzed"))
docmapping.add_property(
        StringField(name="name", store=True, term_vector="with_
positions_offsets", index="analyzed"))
docmapping.add_property(
        StringField(name="title", store=True, term_vector="with_
positions_offsets", index="analyzed"))
docmapping.add_property(IntegerField(name="position", store=True))
docmapping.add_property(DateField(name="date", store=True))
docmapping.add_property(StringField(name="uuid", store=True,
index="not_analyzed"))
nested_object = NestedObject(name="nested")
nested_object.add_property(StringField(name="name", store=True))
nested_object.add_property(StringField(name="value", store=True))
nested_object.add_property(IntegerField(name="num", store=True))
docmapping.add_property(nested_object)
```

The following is a list of the main fields:

- ▸ `DocumentObjectField`: This is a document mapping that contains the object properties
- ▸ `StringField`, `DateField`, `IntegerField`, `LongField`, `BooleanField`: These are the fields that map the respective field type
- ▸ `ObjectField`: This field allows you to map an embedded object field
- ▸ `NestedObject`: This field allows you to map a nested object
- ▸ `AttachmentField`: This field allows you to map the attachment field
- ▸ `IPField`: This field maps the IP field

The object definition of the mapping enforces that, if the types are correctly defined, all the mapping properties are valid.

The PyES GET mapping API does not return a Python dictionary but returns a `DocumentObjectField` object of the specified mapping, which automatically manages the transformation from dictionary to objects for easy parsing and editing.

See also

- ▸ The *Putting a mapping in an index* recipe in *Chapter 4, Basic Operations*
- ▸ The *Getting a mapping* recipe in *Chapter 4, Basic Operations*
- ▸ The *Deleting a mapping* recipe in *Chapter 4, Basic Operations*

Managing documents

The APIs for managing documents (indexing, updating, and deleting) are the most important APIs after the search ones. In this recipe, we will see how to use them in a standard way and in bulk actions to improve performance.

Getting ready

You need a working ElasticSearch cluster and the packages used in the *Creating a client* recipe of this chapter.

The full code of this recipe is in the `chapter_11/document_management.py` and `chapter_11/document_management_pyes.py` files, available in the code bundle of this book and on GitHub (`https://github.com/aparo/elasticsearch-cookbook-second-edition`).

How to do it...

There are three main operations to manage documents, as follows:

- ▸ `index`: This stores a document in ElasticSearch. It is mapped on the Index API call.
- ▸ `update`: This allows you to update some values in a document. This operation is composed internally (via Lucene) by deleting the previous documents and reindexing the document with new values. It is mapped to the Update API call.
- ▸ `delete`: This deletes a document from the index. It is mapped to the Delete API call.

With the ElasticSearch Python client, the index, update, and delete operations can be performed using the following steps:

1. First, initialize a client and create an index with the mapping:

```
import elasticsearch
from datetime import datetime
```

```
es = elasticsearch.Elasticsearch()

index_name = "my_index"
type_name = "my_type"

from utils import create_and_add_mapping
create_and_add_mapping(es, index_name, type_name)
```

2. Then, index a document, as follows:

```
es.index(index=index_name, doc_type=type_name, id=1,
        body={"name": "Joe Tester", "parsedtext": "Joe Testere
nice guy", "uuid": "11111", "position": 1,
            "date": datetime(2013, 12, 8)})
... truncated...
```

3. Next, update a document as shown here:

```
es.update(index=index_name, doc_type=type_name, id=1
body={"script": 'ctx._source.position += 1', "lang":
"groovy"})
```

4. Use the following code to delete a document:

```
es.delete(index=index_name, doc_type=type_name, id=1)
```

5. You can insert some documents in bulk, as follows:

```
from elasticsearch.helpers import bulk_index
bulk_index(es, [{"name": "Joe Tester", "parsedtext": "Joe Testere
nice guy", "uuid": "11111", "position": 1,
            "date": datetime(2013, 12, 8), "_index":index_name,
"_type":type_name, "_id":"1"},
            {"name": "Bill Baloney", "parsedtext": "Bill
Testere nice guy", "uuid": "22222", "position": 2,
            "date": datetime(2013, 12, 8)}
])
```

6. Lastly, remove the index:

```
es.indices.delete(index_name)
```

How it works...

In order to simplify the example, after having instantiated the client, a function of the `utils` package, which sets up the index and puts the mapping, is called:

```
from utils import create_and_add_mapping
create_and_add_mapping(es, index_name, type_name)
```

This function contains the code used to create the mapping explained in the previous recipe.

To index a document, the method is `<client>.index`; it needs the name of the index, the type of the document, and the body of the document (if the ID is not provided, it will be autogenerated):

```
es.index(index=index_name, doc_type=type_name, id=1,
         body={"name": "Joe Tester", "parsedtext": "Joe Testere nice
guy", "uuid": "11111", "position": 1,
              "date": datetime(2013, 12, 8)})
```

It also accepts all the parameters that we have seen in the REST Index API call in the *Indexing a document* recipe in *Chapter 4, Basic Operations*. These are the most common parameters passed to this function:

- ▶ `id`: This provides an ID to be used in order to index the document
- ▶ `routing`: This provides a shard routing to index the document in the specified shard
- ▶ `parent`: This provides a parent ID to be used in order to put the child document in the correct shard

To update a document, the method used is `<client>.update`, and it requires the following parameters:

- ▶ The index name
- ▶ The type name
- ▶ The ID of the document
- ▶ The script or document that is to be updated
- ▶ The language to be used (usually, `groovy`)

The following is the code to update a document:

```
es.update(index=index_name, doc_type=type_name, id=2,
body={"script": 'ctx._source.position += 1', "lang":
"groovy"})
```

Here, the call accepts all the parameters that we have discussed in the *Updating a document* recipe in *Chapter 4, Basic Operations*.

To delete a document, the method used is `<client>.delete`, and it requires the following parameters:

- ▶ Index name
- ▶ Type name
- ▶ ID of the document

You can use the following code to delete a document:

```
es.delete(index=index_name, doc_type=type_name, id=3)
```

> Remember that all the ElasticSearch actions that work on a document are never seen instantly in a search. If you want to search without having to wait for the automatic refresh (every second), you need to manually call the Refresh API on the index.

To execute bulk indexing, the ElasticSearch client provides a helper function, which accepts a connection, an iterable list of documents, and the bulk size. The bulk size (by default, 500) defines the number of actions to be sent via a single bulk call. The parameters that must be passed to correctly control the indexing of the document are put in the document with the _ prefix. Generally, these are the special fields:

- _index: This is the name of the index that must be used to store the document
- _type: This is the document type
- _id: This is the ID of the document

The following is the code used to index a document in bulk:

```
from elasticsearch.helpers import bulk_index
bulk_index(es, [{"name": "Joe Tester", "parsedtext": "Joe Testere nice
guy", "uuid": "11111", "position": 1,
            "date": datetime(2013, 12, 8), "_index":index_name, "_
type":type_name, "_id":"1"},
            {"name": "Bill Baloney", "parsedtext": "Bill Testere
nice guy", "uuid": "22222", "position": 2,
            "date": datetime(2013, 12, 8)}])
```

There's more...

The previous code can be executed in PyES using the following code:

```
from pyes import ES

es = ES()

index_name = "my_index"
type_name = "my_type"

from utils_pyes import create_and_add_mapping

create_and_add_mapping(es, index_name, type_name)
```

```
es.index(doc={"name": "Joe Tester", "parsedtext": "Joe Testere nice
guy", "uuid": "11111", "position": 1},
        index=index_name, doc_type=type_name, id=1)
es.index(doc={"name": "data1", "value": "value1"}, index=index_name,
doc_type=type_name + "2", id=1, parent=1)
es.index(doc={"name": "Bill Baloney", "parsedtext": "Bill Testere nice
guy", "uuid": "22222", "position": 2},
        index=index_name, doc_type=type_name, id=2, bulk=True)
... truncated...

es.force_bulk()

es.update(index=index_name, doc_type=type_name, id=2, script='ctx._
source.position += 1')
es.update(index=index_name, doc_type=type_name, id=2, script='ctx._
source.position += 1', bulk=True)

es.delete(index=index_name, doc_type=type_name, id=1, bulk=True)
es.delete(index=index_name, doc_type=type_name, id=3)

es.force_bulk()
es.indices.refresh(index_name)

es.indices.delete_index(index_name)
```

The PyES `index`/`update`/`delete` methods are similar to the ElasticSearch official client, with the exception that the document must be put in the `doc` variable.

In PyES, to execute an action as bulk, the `bulk=True` parameter must be passed to the `index`/`update`/`create` method. Using the bulk parameter, the body of the action is stored in a `ListBulker` object that collects elements of all the bulk actions until it is full. When the bulk basket is full (the size is defined during the ES client initialization), the actions are sent to the server and the basket is emptied, ready to accept new documents.

To force the bulk (even if it is not full), you can call the `<client>.force_bulk` method or you can execute a refresh or flush an index.

See also

- ▸ The *Indexing a document* recipe in *Chapter 4, Basic Operations*
- ▸ The *Getting a document* recipe in *Chapter 4, Basic Operations*
- ▸ The *Deleting a document* recipe in *Chapter 4, Basic Operations*
- ▸ The *Updating a document* recipe in *Chapter 4, Basic Operations*
- ▸ The *Speeding up atomic operations (bulk operations)* recipe in *Chapter 4, Basic Operations*

Executing a standard search

After you have inserted documents, the most commonly executed action in ElasticSearch is the search. The official ElasticSearch client APIs that are used to search are similar to the REST API.

Getting ready

You need a working ElasticSearch cluster and the packages used in the *Creating a client* recipe in this chapter.

The code of this recipe is present in the `chapter_11/searching.py` and `chapter_11/searching_pyes.py` files, available in the code bundle of this book and on GitHub (`https://github.com/aparo/elasticsearch-cookbook-second-edition`).

How to do it...

To execute a standard query, the `search` client method must be called by passing the query parameters, as shown in *Chapter 5, Search, Queries, and Filters*. The required parameters are the index name, type name, and query DSL. In this example, you will see how to call a `match_all` query, a `term` query, and a `filter` query. To do this, perform the following steps:

1. First, initialize the client and populate the index:

    ```
    import elasticsearch
    from pprint import pprint

    es = elasticsearch.Elasticsearch()
    index_name = "my_index"
    type_name = "my_type"

    from utils import create_and_add_mapping, populate

    create_and_add_mapping(es, index_name, type_name)
    populate(es, index_name, type_name)
    ```

2. Then, execute a search with a `match_all` query and print the results:

    ```
    results = es.search(index_name, type_name, {"query": {"match_all":
    {}}})
    pprint(results)
    ```

3. Next, execute a search with a term query and print the results:

    ```
    results = es.search(index_name, type_name, {
        "query": {
    ```

```
            "query": {
                "term": {"name": {"boost": 3.0, "value": "joe"}}}
    }})
pprint(results)
```

4. You then need to execute a search with a filtered query and print the results:

```
results = es.search(index_name, type_name, {"query": {
    "filtered": {
        "filter": {
            "or": [
                {"term": {"position": 1}},
                {"term": {"position": 2}}]
        },
        "query": {"match_all": {}}}}})
pprint(results)
```

5. Lastly, remove the index, as follows:

```
es.indices.delete(index_name)
```

How it works...

The idea behind ElasticSearch official clients is that they should offer a common API that is more similar to REST calls. In Python, it is easy to use the query DSL as it provides an easy mapping from the Python dictionary to JSON objects and vice versa.

In the earlier example, before calling the search, we need to initialize the index and put some data in it. This is done using the two helpers available in the `utils` package, available in the `chapter_11` directory.

The two helpers are as follows:

▶ `create_and_add_mapping(es, index_name, type_name)`: This initializes the index and puts the correct mapping to perform the search. The code of this function is taken from the *Managing mappings* recipe in this chapter.

▶ `populate(es, index_name, type_name)`: This populates the index with data. The code of this function is taken from the previous recipe.

After having initialized some data, we can execute queries against it. To execute a search, the method that must be called is the `search` on the client. This method accepts all the parameters described for REST calls in the *Executing a search* recipe in *Chapter 5, Search, Queries, and Filters*.

This is the actual method signature for the search method:

```
    @query_params('analyze_wildcard', 'analyzer', 'default_operator',
'df', 'explain', 'fields', 'ignore_indices', 'indices_boost',
'lenient', 'lowercase_expanded_terms', 'offset', 'preference', 'q',
'routing', 'scroll', 'search_type', 'size', 'sort', 'source', 'stats',
'suggest_field', 'suggest_mode', 'suggest_size', 'suggest_text',
'timeout', 'version')
    def search(self, index=None, doc_type=None, body=None,
params=None):
```

The following can be the `index` values:

- ▶ An index name or an alias name
- ▶ A list of index (or alias) names as a string, separated by a comma (for example, `index1`, `index2`, `indexN`)
- ▶ The `_all` special keyword, which indicates all the indices

The `type` value can be the following:

- ▶ A type name
- ▶ A list of type names as a string, separated by a comma (for example, `type1`, `type2`, `typeN`)
- ▶ `None`, which indicates all the types

The body is the search DSL, as we have seen in *Chapter 5, Search, Queries, and Filters*. In the preceding example, we have the following queries:

- ▶ A `match_all` query (see the *Matching all the documents* recipe of *Chapter 5, Search, Queries, and Filters*) to match all the index type documents;

  ```
  results = es.search(index_name, type_name, {"query":{"match_all":
  {}}})
  ```

- ▶ A `term` query that matches the term `joe` with a boost of `3.0`:

  ```
  results = es.search(index_name, type_name, {
      "query": {
          "query": {
              "term": {"name": {"boost": 3.0, "value": "joe"}}}
      }})
  ```

- ▶ A `filter` query with a `match_all` query and an OR filter with two term filters that match `position` 1 and 2, as shown here:

  ```
  results = es.search(index_name, type_name, {"query": {
      "filtered": {
          "filter": {
  ```

```
            "or": [
                {"term": {"position": 1}},
                {"term": {"position": 2}}]
        },
        "query": {"match_all": {}}}}})
```

The returned result is a JSON dictionary that we have discussed in *Chapter 5, Search, Queries, and Filters*.

If some hits match, they are returned to the hits field. The standard number of results returned is 10. To return more results, you need to paginate the results with the `from` and `start` parameters.

In *Chapter 5, Search, Queries, and Filters*, there is a definition of all the parameters used in the search.

There's more...

If you are using PyES, you can execute the previous code in a more object-oriented way using queries and filter objects. These objects wrap the low-level code that is normally used to process a query, generating the JSON and validating it during generation. The previous example can be rewritten in PyES with the following code:

```
... truncated...

from.query import *
from pyes.filters import *

results = es.search(MatchAllQuery(), indices=index_name, doc_
types=type_name)

print "total:", results.total
for r in results:
    print r

print "first element: ", results[0]
print "slice elements: ", results[1:4]

results = es.search(TermQuery("name", "joe", 3), indices=index_name,
doc_types=type_name)
... truncated...
```

For access to query objects, you need to import the `query` and `filters` namespaces:

```
from pyes.query import *
from pyes.filters import *
```

To execute a `match_all` query, use the `search` client method with the same parameters as the ElasticSearch official client. The main difference is that the `body` parameter is mapped as a `query` object in PyES. The following code is used to execute such a `match_all` query:

```
results = es.search(MatchAllQuery(), indices=index_name, doc_
types=type_name)
```

The PyES search method accepts several type of values as a query, as follows:

- A dictionary as the official client
- A query object or a derived class
- A search object that wraps a query and adds additional functionalities related to the search, such as highlighting, suggestting, aggregating, and explaining

The main difference from the official ElasticSearch client is that the returned result is a special `ResultSet` object that can be iterated. The `ResultSet` object is a useful helper because of the following reasons:

- It's lazy, so the query is fired only when the results need to be evaluated/iterated.
- It is iterable, so you can traverse all the records automatically by fetching new ones when required. Otherwise, you need to manage the pagination manually. If the size is not defined, you can traverse all the results. If you define the size, you can traverse only the size of object.
- It automatically manages scrolling and scanning queries using a special `ResultSet` iterator.
- It tries to cache a result range, in order to reduce server usage.
- It can process other extra result manipulations, such as automatic conversion from `string` to `datetime`.

For further details on query/filter objects, I suggest that you take a look at the online documentation at `http://pythonhosted.org/pyes/`.

See also

- The *Executing a search* recipe in *Chapter 5, Search, Queries, and Filters*
- The *Matching all the documents* recipe in *Chapter 5, Search, Queries, and Filters*
- The PyES online documentation at `http://pythonhosted.org/pyes/`

Executing a search with aggregations

Searching for results is obviously the main activity of a search engine; thus, aggregations are very important because they often help to augment the results.

Aggregations are executed along with the search by doing an analysis on the searched results.

Getting ready

You need a working ElasticSearch cluster and the packages used in the *Creating a client* recipe in this chapter.

The code of this recipe is in the `chapter_11/aggregation.py` and `chapter_11/aggregation_pyes.py` files, available in the code bundle of this book and on GitHub (`https://github.com/aparo/elasticsearch-cookbook-second-edition`).

How to do it...

In order to extend a query with aggregations, you need to define an aggregation section similar to what you saw in *Chapter 6, Aggregations*. In the case of the official ElasticSearch client, you can add the aggregation DSL to the search dictionary in order to provide aggregations results. To do this, perform the following steps:

1. Initialize the client and populate the index, as follows:

```
import elasticsearch
from pprint import pprint

es = elasticsearch.Elasticsearch()
index_name = "my_index"
type_name = "my_type"

from utils import create_and_add_mapping, populate

create_and_add_mapping(es, index_name, type_name)
populate(es, index_name, type_name)
```

2. Execute a search with a `terms` aggregation:

```
results = es.search(index_name, type_name,
    {
        "query": {"match_all": {}},
        "aggs": {
            "pterms": {"terms": {"field": "parsedtext", "size":
10}}
```

```
            }
        })
    pprint(results)
```

3. Execute a search with a `date_histogram` aggregation, as shown here:

```
    results = es.search(index_name, type_name,
        {
            "query": {"match_all": {}},
            "aggs": {
                "date_histo": {"date_histogram": {"field": "date",
    "interval": "month"}}
            }
        })
    pprint(results)

    es.indices.delete(index_name)
```

How it works...

As described in *Chapter 6*, *Aggregations*, you can calculate aggregations during the search in a distributed way. When you send a query to ElasticSearch with defined aggregations, it adds an additional step in the query processing, allowing aggregation computation.

In the earlier example, there are two kinds of aggregations: the term aggregation and the date histogram aggregation.

The first one is used to count terms, and it is often seen in sites that provide facet filtering on the term aggregations of results, such as producers, geographic locations, and so on, as shown here:

```
    results = es.search(index_name, type_name,
        {
            "query": {"match_all": {}},
            "aggs": {
                "pterms": {"terms": {"field": "parsedtext", "size": 10}}
            }
        })
```

The term aggregation requires a field to count on. The default number of buckets for a field that is returned is 10; this value can be changed when defining the `size` parameter.

The second kind of aggregation that is calculated is the date histogram, which provides hits based on a datetime field. This aggregation requires at least two parameters—that is, the datetime field to be used as the source and the interval to be used for the computation, as shown here:

```
results = es.search(index_name, type_name,
    {
        "query": {"match_all": {}},
        "aggs": {
            "date_histo": {"date_histogram": {"field": "date",
    "interval": "month"}}
        }
    })
```

The search results are standard search responses that we have already seen in *Chapter 6, Aggregations*.

There's more...

This is how the preceding code can be rewritten in PyES:

```
...
from pyes.query import *
from pyes.aggs import *

q = MatchAllQuery()
search = q.search()
search.get_agg_factory().add(TermsAgg('pterms', field="parsedtext"))

results = es.search(search, indices=index_name, doc_types=type_name)

q = MatchAllQuery()
search = q.search()
search.get_agg_factory().add(DateHistogramAgg('date_add',
    field='date',
    interval='month'))

results = es.search(search, indices=index_name, doc_types=type_name)  ...
```

In this case, the code is much more readable. Similar to queries and filters classes, PyES provides aggregation objects that are available in the pyes.aggs namespace.

Because aggregation is a search property and not a query (remember that queries can also be used for delete and count calls), we need to define the aggregation in a search object.

Every query can be converted to a Search object using the `.search()` method:

```
q = MatchAllQuery()
search = q.search()
```

The search object provides a lot of helpers to improve their search experience, as follows:

- `AggregationFactory`: This is accessible via the `agg` property to easily build aggregations
- `Highlighter`: This is accessible via the `highlight` property to easily build highlight fields
- `Sorted`: This is accessible via the `sort` property to add sort fields to a search
- `ScriptFields`: This is accessible via the `script_fields` property to add script fields

The `AggregationFactory` helper easily defines several types of aggregations, as follows:

- `add_term`: This defines a term aggregation. For example, in the preceding code, we have used the `add_term` function:

  ```
  search.agg.add_term ('tag')
  ```

- `add_date`: This defines a date histogram aggregation
- `add_geo`: This defines a geo distance aggregation
- `add`: This allows you to add to the aggregation definition for every aggregated object:

  ```
  search.add.add(DateHistogramAgg('date_agg',
      field='date',
      interval='month'))
  ```

After you have executed the query, in the `ResultSet` response there are calculated aggregations contained in the `aggs` field (such as, `results.aggs`).

See also

- The *Executing the terms aggregation* recipe in *Chapter 6, Aggregations*
- The *Executing the stats aggregation* recipe in *Chapter 6, Aggregations*

12
Plugin Development

In this chapter, we will cover the following recipes:

- ▶ Creating a site plugin
- ▶ Creating a native plugin
- ▶ Creating a REST plugin
- ▶ Creating a cluster action
- ▶ Creating an analyzer plugin
- ▶ Creating a river plugin

Introduction

ElasticSearch can be extended with plugins to improve its capabilities. In the previous chapters, we have installed and used many of these plugins, such as transport, river, and scripting.

Plugins are application extensions that can add many features to ElasticSearch. They have several usages, as follows:

- ▶ Adding a new transport layer (the thrift and memcached plugins are examples of this type)
- ▶ Adding a new scripting language (such as Python and JavaScript plugins)
- ▶ Extending Lucene-supported analyzers and tokenizers
- ▶ Using native scripting to speed up the computation of scores, filters, and field manipulation
- ▶ Extending node capabilities, for example, creating a node plugin that can execute your logic
- ▶ Adding a new river to support new sources
- ▶ Monitoring and administering the cluster

ElasticSearch plugins are of two kinds such as site and native plugins.

A **site** plugin is generally a standard HTML5 web application, while a **native** plugin has some Java content that defines a plugin's endpoints and implements plugin functionalities.

In this chapter, we will use the Java language to develop the native plugin, but it is possible to use any JVM language that generates JAR files.

Creating a site plugin

Site plugins do not add internal functionalities to ElasticSearch. They are HTML-based web applications that work on top of ElasticSearch. They generally provide frontend functionalities, such as monitoring and administration. In *Chapter 9, Cluster and Node Monitoring*, we saw the use of several site plugins such as ElasticSearch Head and BigDesk.

Getting ready

You will need a working ElasticSearch node, a web browser, and your preferred HTML editor.

How to do it...

In order to create a site plugin, perform the following steps:

1. The site plugin is one of the most easy plugins to develop. It is mainly a standard web application composed of only HTML, JavaScript, and images.The simplest plugin is composed of a single `index.html` page, as shown here:

```
<!DOCTYPE html>
<html>
  <head>
    <title>Simple site plugin</title>
    <meta name="viewport" content="width=device-width,
      initial-scale=1.0">
    <link href="http://netdna.bootstrapcdn.com/twitter-
      bootstrap/2.3.0/css/bootstrap-combined.min.css"
      rel="stylesheet">
  </head>
  <body>
    <h1>Hello, from the site plugin!</h1>
    <script src="http://code.jquery.com/jquery.js"></script>
    <script src="http://netdna.bootstrapcdn.com/twitter-
bootstrap/2.3.0/js/bootstrap.min.js"></script>
  </body>
</html>
```

2. The HTML file and the resources must be put in the `_site` directory under the `plugin` directory.

How it works...

When ElasticSearch starts, it analyzes the plugin's directory. If a `_site` directory is present in the `plugin` directory, it loads the plugin as a site plugin; otherwise, the plugin is considered as a native plugin.

Site plugins have static contents. When the browser is pointed to the server address of the plugin (that is, `http://localhost:9200/_plugins/<plugin_name>/`), ElasticSearch serves as the resource for a traditional web application. It generally searches for an `index.html` file and serves it and its related resources.

> While writing a plugin and loading resources (that is, images, JavaScript, or CSS), make sure that every resource is specified relative to the `index.html` file or has an absolute URL, in order to prevent errors.

Site plugins work very well to package a small web application that executes some focused tasks, as follows:

▸ Displaying information regarding status and data aggregation, and a quick view of some important aspects of your ElasticSearch cluster or indices.

▸ Administration and sending commands via a web interface is easier than via curl commands or the programming API. A user can aggregate his administrative pipeline (index creation, data manipulation, and custom commands) and use it to manage its custom data.

> To easily develop your plugin, I suggest you develop it outside ElasticSearch and to pack it in a ZIP file for distribution.

Site plugins allow the use of every HTML5 web application framework available for the client's site development. It's quite normal that the currently available site plugins will use different JavaScript frameworks, such as JQuery (including, Bootstrap), AngularJS, and Ember.js.

There's more...

Many of the interfaces used to manage an ElasticSearch cluster are generally developed as site plugins. These are the most popular ones:

▸ The BigDesk plugin

▸ The ElasticSearch-head plugin

▸ Elastic HQ

We have already seen many of plugins in *Chapter 9, Cluster and Node Monitoring.*

See also

▸ You can get more information on ElasticSearch plugins at
`http://www.elasticsearch.org/guide/en/elasticsearch/`
`reference/current/modules-plugins.html#_plugins`

Creating a native plugin

In the previous recipe, we saw the site plugin. ElasticSearch also allows you to create a more powerful type of plugin, the: native JAR plugins.

Native plugins allow you to extend several aspects of the ElasticSearch server, but this requires a good knowledge of Java. Because these plugins are compiled through the JVM bytecode, they are generally very fast. In this recipe, we will see how to set up a working environment in order to develop native plugins.

Getting ready

You will need a working ElasticSearch node, a Maven build tool, and optionally a Java IDE. The code of this recipe is available in the `chapter12/simple_plugin` directory, kept in the code bundle of the chapter on the Packt Publishing website.

How to do it...

Generally, ElasticSearch plugins are developed in Java using the Maven build tool and deployed as a ZIP file. In order to create a simple JAR plugin, perform the following steps:

1. To correctly build and serve a plugin, the following files must be defined:

   ❑ `pom.xml`: This file is used to define the build configuration for Maven.

   ❑ `es-plugin`: This states the properties that define the namespace of the plugin class that must be loaded.

   ❑ `<name>plugin`: In Java, this is the main plugin class; it is loaded at start up and initializes the plugin *action*.

   ❑ `plugin.xml`: These assemblies define how to execute the assembly steps of Maven. It is used to build the ZIP file to deliver the plugin.

2. A standard `pom.xml` file used to create a plugin contains the following code:

   ❏ This is how a Maven `pom.xml` header will look:

```xml
<?xml version="1.0" encoding="UTF-8"?>
<project xmlns="http://maven.apache.org/POM/4.0.0"
  xmlns:xsi="http://www.w3.org/2001/XMLSchema-
  instance"
  xsi:schemaLocation="http://maven.apache.org/POM/4.0.0
  http://maven.apache.org/xsd/maven-4.0.0.xsd">
    <name>elasticsearch-simple-plugin</name>
    <modelVersion>4.0.0</modelVersion>
    <groupId>com.packtpub</groupId>
    <artifactId>simple-plugin</artifactId>
    <version>0.0.1-SNAPSHOT</version>
    <packaging>jar</packaging>
    <description>A simple plugin for
    ElasticSearch</description>
    <inceptionYear>2013</inceptionYear>
    <licenses>…    </licenses>
```

   ❏ This is the parent `pom.xml` file used to derive common properties or settings:

```xml
<parent>
  <groupId>org.sonatype.oss</groupId>
  <artifactId>oss-parent</artifactId>
  <version>7</version>
</parent>
```

   ❏ Some properties mainly used to simplify the dependencies are given as follows:

```xml
<properties>

<elasticsearch.version>1.4.0</elasticsearch.version>
  </properties>
```

   ❏ A list of JAR dependencies:

```xml
<dependencies>
  <dependency>
    <groupId>org.elasticsearch</groupId>
    <artifactId>elasticsearch</artifactId>
    <version>${elasticsearch.version}</version>
    <scope>compile</scope>
  </dependency>
    <dependency>
    <groupId>log4j</groupId>
```

```
            <artifactId>log4j</artifactId>
            <version>1.2.17</version>
            <scope>runtime</scope>
        </dependency>
      <!- test dependencies -->
    </dependencies>
```

❑ A list of Maven plugins required to build and deploy the artifact; the following is the code for enabling the Maven plugin:

```
<build>
    <plugins>
        <plugin>
            <!- for compiling -->
            <groupId>org.apache.maven.plugins</groupId>
            <artifactId>maven-compiler-
          plugin</artifactId>
            <version>3.1</version>
            <configuration>
                <source>1.7</source>
                <target>1.7</target>
            </configuration>
        </plugin>
        <plugin>
            <!- optional for executing tests -->
            <groupId>org.apache.maven.plugins</groupId>
            <artifactId>maven-surefire- plugin</artifactId>
            <version>2.12.3</version>
            <configuration>
                <includes>
                    <include>**/*Tests.java</include>
                </includes>
            </configuration>
        </plugin>
        <plugin>
            <!- optional for publishing the source
    -->
            <groupId>org.apache.maven.plugins</groupId>
            <artifactId>maven-source- plugin</artifactId>
            <version>2.3</version>
            <executions>
                <execution>
                    <id>attach-sources</id>
                    <goals>
```

```
                        <goal>jar</goal>
                    </goals>
                </execution>
            </executions>
        </plugin>
        <plugin>>
            <!- for packaging the plugin -->
            <artifactId>maven-assembly-
                plugin</artifactId>
            <version>2.3</version>
            <configuration>
                <appendAssemblyId>false</appendAssemblyId>
                <outputDirectory>${project.build.directory}/
releases/
</outputDirectory>
                <descriptors>
                    <descriptor>${basedir}/src/main/
assemblies/plugin.xml
</descriptor>
                </descriptors>
            </configuration>
            <executions>
                <execution>
                    <phase>package</phase>
                    <goals>
                        <goal>single</goal>
                    </goals>
                </execution>
            </executions>
        </plugin>
    </plugins>
</build>undefined</project>
```

❑ In JAR, there must be a `src/main/resources/es-plugin.properties` file that defines the entry point class that must be loaded during plugin initialization. This file must be embedded in the final jar, as it is usually put in the `src/main/resources` directory of the Maven project. It generally contains a single line of code:

```
plugin=org.elasticsearch.plugin.simple.SimplePlugin
```

3. Optionally, in the `src/main/resources/es-plugin.properties` file, a version of the plugin can be provided, as follows:

```
version=0.1
```

4. The `src/main/java/org/elasticsearch/plugin/simple/SimplePlugin.java` class is an example of the minimum code that needs to be compiled in order to execute a plugin:

```java
package org.elasticsearch.plugin.simple;
import org.elasticsearch.plugins.AbstractPlugin;
public class SimplePlugin extends AbstractPlugin{
    @Override
    public String name() {
        return "simple-plugin";
    }
    @Override
    public String description() {
        return "A simple plugin implementation";
    }
}
```

5. To complete the compilation and deployment of the workflow, you need to define a `src/main/assemblies/plugin.xml` file used in the Maven assembly step. This file defines the resources that must be packaged into the final ZIP archive:

```xml
<?xml version="1.0"?>
<assembly>
    <id>plugin</id>
    <formats>
      <format>zip</format>
    </formats>
    <includeBaseDirectory>false</includeBaseDirectory>
    <dependencySets>
      <dependencySet>
        <outputDirectory>/</outputDirectory>
        <useProjectArtifact>true</useProjectArtifact>
        <useTransitiveFiltering>true</useTransitiveFiltering>
        <excludes>
          <exclude>org.elasticsearch:elasticsearch</exclude>
        </excludes>
      </dependencySet>
    </dependencySets>
</assembly>
```

How it works...

Several parts comprise the development life cycle of a plugin—for example, designing, coding, building, and deploying. To speed up the building and deployment steps, common to all plugins, you need to create a Maven `pom.xml` file.

The previously explained `pom.xml` file is a standard for developing ElasticSearch plugins. This file is composed of the following parts:

- Several section entries used to set up the current Maven project. In detail, we have the following sections:

  - The name of the plugin (that is, `elasticsearch-simple-plugin`):

    ```
    <name>elasticsearch-simple-plugin</name>
    ```

  - The `groupId` and `artifactId` parameters are used to define the plugin's artifact name:

    ```
    <groupId>com.packtpub</groupId>
    <artifactId>simple-plugin</artifactId>
    ```

  - The plugin version:

    ```
    <version>0.0.1-SNAPSHOT</version>
    ```

  - The type of packaging:

    ```
    <packaging>jar</packaging>
    ```

  - A project description with the start year:

    ```
    <description>A simple plugin for
    ElasticSearch</description>
    <inceptionYear>2013</inceptionYear>
    ```

- An optional license section is also provided in which you can define the license for the plugin. For the standard Apache, the license should look as follows:

  ```
  <licenses>
    <license>
      <name>The Apache Software License, Version 2.0</name>
      <url>http://www.apache.org/licenses/LICENSE-
      2.0.txt</url>
      <distribution>repo</distribution>
    </license>
  </licenses>
  ```

- A parent POM is used to inherit common properties. Generally, for plugins, it is useful to inherit from the Sonatype POM file:

  ```
  <parent>
    <groupId>org.sonatype.oss</groupId>
    <artifactId>oss-parent</artifactId>
    <version>7</version>
  </parent>
  ```

▶ The global variables are set. Typically, in this section, the ElasticSearch version and other library versions are set:

```
<properties>
    <elasticsearch.version>1.4.0</elasticsearch.version>
</properties>
```

> It's very important that the ElasticSearch JAR version matches the ElasticSearch cluster version in order to prevent issues that occur due to changes between releases.

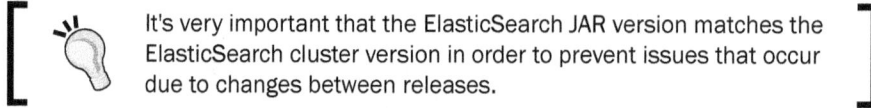

▶ A list of dependencies is provided. In order to compile a plugin, the ElasticSearch jar and the `log4j` library are required during the compilation phase:

```
<dependency>
  <groupId>org.elasticsearch</groupId>
  <artifactId>elasticsearch</artifactId>
  <version>${elasticsearch.version}</version>
  <scope>compile</scope>
</dependency>
<dependency>
  <groupId>log4j</groupId>
  <artifactId>log4j</artifactId>
  <version>1.2.17</version>
    <scope>runtime</scope>
</dependency>
```

▶ The Maven plugin section contains a list of the Maven plugins that execute several build steps, as follows:

  ❑ **Compiler section**: This requires a source compilation. The Java version is fixed to 1.7:

```
<plugin>
    <groupId>org.apache.maven.plugins</groupId>
    <artifactId>maven-compiler-plugin</artifactId>
    <version>3.1</version>
    <configuration>
        <source>1.7</source>
        <target>1.7</target>
    </configuration>
</plugin>
```

  ❑ **Source section**: This enables the creation of source packages to be released with the binary output (useful for debugging):

```
<plugin>
    <groupId>org.apache.maven.plugins</groupId>
```

```
        <artifactId>maven-source-plugin</artifactId>
        <version>2.3</version>
        <executions>
            <execution>
                <id>attach-sources</id>
                <goals>
                    <goal>jar</goal>
                </goals>
            </execution>
        </executions>
</plugin>
```

❑ **Assembly section**: This builds a ZIP file using a configuration file (`plugin. xml`) and puts the output in the `releases` directory, as shown here:

```
<plugin>
        <artifactId>maven-assembly-plugin</artifactId>
        <version>2.3</version>
        <configuration>
          <appendAssemblyId>false</appendAssemblyId>
<outputDirectory>${project.build.directory}/releases/
</outputDirectory>
        <descriptors>
<descriptor>${basedir}/src/main/assemblies/plugin.xml
</descriptor>
        </descriptors>
        </configuration>
        <executions>
          <execution>
            <phase>package</phase>
            <goals><goal>single</goal></goals>
          </execution>
        </executions>
</plugin>
```

Related to `pom.xml`, we have the `plugin.xml` file that describes how to assemble the final ZIP file. This file is usually contained in the `/src/main/assemblies/` directory of the project.

The following are the most important sections of this file:

▶ `formats`: In this section, the destination format is defined:

```
<formats><format>zip</format></formats>
```

▶ `excludes`: This is set in the `dependencySet`. It contains the artifacts to be excluded from the package. Generally, we exclude ElasticSearch jar, as it's already provided in the server installation:

```
<dependencySet>
    <outputDirectory>/</outputDirectory>
```

```
<useProjectArtifact>true</useProjectArtifact>
<useTransitiveFiltering>true</useTransitiveFiltering>
<excludes>
    <exclude>org.elasticsearch:elasticsearch</exclude>
</excludes>
</dependencySet>
```

- ▸ includes: This is set in dependencySet. It contains the artifacts to be included in the package. These are mainly the jars required to run the plugin:

```
<dependencySet>
    <outputDirectory>/</outputDirectory>
    <useProjectArtifact>true</useProjectArtifact>
    <useTransitiveFiltering>true</useTransitiveFiltering>
    <includes>… truncated …</includes>
</dependencySet>
```

During plugin packaging, the include and exclude rules are verified and only those files that are allowed to be distributed are put in the ZIP file. After having configured Maven, we can start to write the main plugin class. Every plugin class must be derived from the AbstractPlugin one and it must be public; otherwise it cannot be loaded dynamically from the jar:

```
import org.elasticsearch.plugins.AbstractPlugin;
public class SimplePlugin extends AbstractPlugin {
```

The AbstractPlugin class needs two methods to be defined: name and description. The name method must return a string and it's usually a short name. This value is shown in the plugin's loading log:

```
@Override
public String name() {
    return "simple-plugin";
}
```

The description method must also return a string. It is mainly a long description of the plugin:

```
@Override
    public String description() {
        return "A simple plugin implementation";
    }
```

After having defined the required files to generate a ZIP release of our plugin, it is enough to invoke the Maven package command. This command will compile the code and create a ZIP package in the target or releases directory of your project. The final ZIP file can be deployed as a plugin on your ElasticSearch cluster.

In this recipe, we have configured a working environment to build, deploy, and test plugins. In the following recipes, we will reuse this environment to develop several plugin types.

There's more...

Compiling and packaging the plugin is not enough to define a good life cycle of your plugin. For this, you need to add a test phase.Testing the plugin functionalities with test cases reduces the number of bugs that can affect the plugin when it is released.

It is possible to add a test phase in the Maven build `pom.xml`. In order to do this, we first need to add the required package dependencies to test ElasticSearch and Lucene. These dependencies must be added for testing:

```
<dependency>
    <groupId>org.apache.lucene</groupId>
    <artifactId>lucene-test-framework</artifactId>
    <version>${lucene.version}</version>
    <scope>test</scope>
</dependency>
<dependency>
    <groupId>org.elasticsearch</groupId>
    <artifactId>elasticsearch</artifactId>
    <version>${elasticsearch.version}</version>
    <type>test-jar</type>
    <scope>test</scope>
</dependency>
```

The order is very important, so make sure to put `lucene-test-framework` at the top of your dependencies; otherwise, problems with loading and executing tests might occur.

For unit and integration testing, the ElasticSearch community mainly uses the Hamcrest library (`https://code.google.com/p/hamcrest/`). To use the library, you need to add its dependencies in the `dependency` section of the `pom.xml` file, as follows:

```
<dependency>
    <groupId>org.hamcrest</groupId>
    <artifactId>hamcrest-core</artifactId>
    <version>1.3.RC2</version>
    <scope>test</scope>
</dependency>

<dependency>
    <groupId>org.hamcrest</groupId>
    <artifactId>hamcrest-library</artifactId>
    <version>1.3.RC2</version>
```

```
        <scope>test</scope>
    </dependency>
```

> Note that the compiling scope is `test`, which means that these dependencies are applicable only during the test phase.

To complete the `test` part, we need to add a Maven plugin that executes the tests:

```
<plugin>
    <groupId>org.apache.maven.plugins</groupId>
    <artifactId>maven-surefire-plugin</artifactId>
    <version>2.12.3</version>
    <configuration>
        <includes><include>**/*Tests.java</include></includes>
    </configuration>
</plugin>
```

The `includes` section lists all the possible classes that contain `test` via the glob expression.

Creating a REST plugin

The previous recipe described how to set up a working environment and the steps required to build a native plugin. In this recipe, we will see how to create one of the most common ElasticSearch plugins: the REST plugin.

This kind of plugin allows you to extend the standard REST calls with custom ones to easily improve the capabilities of ElasticSearch.

In this recipe, we will see how to define a REST entry point and create its action. In the next recipe, we will see how to execute this action and distribute it in shards.

Getting ready

You will need a working ElasticSearch node, a Maven build tool, and an optional Java IDE. The code of this recipe is available in the `chapter12/rest_plugin` directory in the code bundle of the same chapter, which can be downloaded from the Packt Publishing website.

How to do it...

To create a REST entry point, we first need to create the action and then register it in the plugin. Perform the following steps:

1. Create a REST simple action (`RestSimpleAction.java`):

```java
public class RestSimpleAction extends BaseRestHandler {
  @Inject
  public RestSimpleAction(Settings settings, Client
  client, RestController controller) {
    super(settings, controller, client);
    controller.registerHandler(POST, "/_simple", this);
    controller.registerHandler(POST, "/{index}/_simple",
    this);
    controller.registerHandler(POST,
    "/_simple/{field}", this);
    controller.registerHandler(GET, "/_simple", this);
    controller.registerHandler(GET, "/{index}/_simple",
    this);
    controller.registerHandler(GET, "/_simple/{field}",
    this);
  }
  @Override
  protected void handleRequest(final RestRequest request,
  final  RestChannel channel, final  Client client) throws
  Exception {
    final SimpleRequest simpleRequest = new
    SimpleRequest(Strings.splitStringByCommaToArray
    (request.param("index")));
    simpleRequest.setField(request.param("field"));
    client.execute(SimpleAction.INSTANCE, simpleRequest,
    new ActionListener<SimpleResponse>() {
    @Override
      public void onResponse(SimpleResponse response) {
      try {
        XContentBuilder builder =
        channel.newBuilder();
        builder.startObject();
        builder.field("ok", true);
        buildBroadcastShardsHeader(builder, response);
        builder.array("terms",
        response.getSimple().toArray());
        builder.endObject();
        channel.sendResponse(new
        BytesRestResponse(OK, builder));
```

```
        } catch (Exception e) {
            onFailure(e);
        }
    }
    @Override
    public void onFailure(Throwable e) {
        try {
            channel.sendResponse(new
            BytesRestResponse(channel, e));
        } catch (IOException e1) {
            logger.error("Failed to send failure
            response", e1);
        }
    }
});
}
```

2. Also, we need to register the entry point in the plugin using the following lines of code:

```
public class RestPlugin extends AbstractPlugin {
    @Override
    public String name() {
        return "simple-plugin";
    }
    @Override
    public String description() {
        return "A simple plugin implementation";
    }
    public void onModule(RestModule module) {
        module.addRestAction(RestSimpleAction.class);
    }
}
```

How it works...

Adding a REST action is very easy. We just need to create a `RestXXXAction` class that handles the calls. The REST action is derived from the `BaseRestHandler` class and needs to implement the `handleRequest` method. The constructor is very important, as shown here:

```
@Inject
public RestSimpleAction(Settings settings, Client client,
RestController controller)
```

The consturctor's signature is usually injected via **Guice**, which is a lightweight dependency injection framework and very popular in the Java ecosystem. For more details on Guice, refer to the library's home page at `https://github.com/google/guice`. The REST action has the following parameters:

- `Settings`: This can be used to load custom settings for your REST action
- `Client`: This will be used to communicate with the cluster (see *Chapter 10, Java Integration*)
- `RestController`: This is used to register the REST action to the controller

In the constructor of the REST action (`RestController`), the list of actions that must be handled registered, as follows:

```
controller.registerHandler(POST, "/_simple", this);
```

To register an action, the following parameters must be passed to the controller:

- The REST method (`GET/POST/PUT/DELETE/HEAD/OPTIONS`)
- The URL entry point
- The `RestHandler` class, usually the same class that must answer the call

After having defined the constructor, if an action is fired, the `handleRequest` class method is called in the following manner:

```
@Override
protected void handleRequest(final RestRequest request, final
RestChannel channel, final  Client client) throws Exception {
```

This method is the core of the REST action. It processes the request and sends the response back. These parameters are passed to the method:

- `RestRequest`: This is the REST request that hits the ElasticSearch server
- `RestChannel`: This is the channel used to send back the response
- `Client`: This is the client used to communicate in the cluster

A `handleRequest` method is usually composed of the following phases:

- Processing the REST request and building an inner ElasticSearch request object
- Calling the client with the ElasticSearch request
- If this is ok, processing the ElasticSearch response and building the JSON result
- If there are errors, sending the JSON error response back

In the following example, it shows how to create `SimpleRequest` by processing the request:

```
final SimpleRequest simpleRequest = new SimpleRequest(Strings.
splitStringByCommaToArray
(request.param("index")));
simpleRequest.setField(request.param("field"));
```

The request accepts a list of indices (we split the classic comma-separated list of indices via the `Strings.splitStringByCommaToArray` helper), and we have the `field` parameter, if available. We will discuss `SimpleRequest` thoroughly in the next recipe.

Now that we have `SimpleRequest`, we can send it to the cluster and get back a `SimpleResponse` response:

```
client.execute(SimpleAction.INSTANCE, simpleRequest, new
ActionListener<SimpleResponse>() {
```

The `client.execute` method accepts an action, a request, and an `ActionListener` class that maps a future response. We can have two kinds of responses, as follows:

▸ `onResponse`: This is obtained if everything is all right

▸ `onFailure`: This is obtained if something goes wrong

The `onFailure` function is usually the propagation via a REST error:

```
@Override
public void onFailure(Throwable e) {
    try {
      channel.sendResponse(new BytesRestResponse(channel, e));
    } catch (IOException e1) {
      logger.error("Failed to send failure response", e1);
    }
}
```

The `onResponse` method receives a `Response` object that must be converted into a JSON result:

```
@Override public void onResponse(SimpleResponse response)
```

To build the JSON response, a builder helper is used:

```
XContentBuilder builder = channel.newBuilder();
```

The builder is a standard JSON `XContentBuilder`, which we have already seen in *Chapter 10, Java Integration*. After having processed the cluster response and built the JSON, it can be sent via the following channel:

```
channel.sendResponse(new BytesRestResponse(OK, builder));
```

Obviously, if something goes wrong during JSON creation, an exception must be raised:

```
try {/* JSON building*/
} catch (Exception e) {
    onFailure(e);
}
```

There's more...

To test the plugin, you can compile and assemble it with an `mvn` package. Then, you need to deploy the resulting unzipped file in an ElasticSearch server, in the `plugins` directory. After having restarted the server, the name of the plugin should pop up in the list of installed ones:

```
[...] [INFO ] [node    ] [Amalgam] initializing ...
[...] [INFO ] [plugins ] [Amalgam] loaded [river-twitter, transport-
thrift, jdbc-river, rest-plugin], sites [HQ]
```

If everything is all right, we can test the plugin as follows:

```
curl -XPOST http://127.0.0.1:9200/_simple
```

This is how the response will look:

```
{"ok":true,"_shards":{"total":15,"successful":15,"failed":0},"terms":[
"null_4","null_1","null_0","null_3","null_2"]}
```

You can also test it using the following line of code:

```
curl -XPOST http://127.0.0.1:9200/_simple/goofy
```

Here, this is how the response will look:

```
{"ok":true,"_shards":{"total":15,"successful":15,"failed":0},"terms":[
"goofy_1","goofy_2","goofy_3","goofy_4","goofy_0"]}
```

To fully understand the response, the next recipe will show you how the action is executed at cluster level.

See also

► You can find more information about Google Guice, used for dependency injection, at `https://code.google.com/p/google-guice/`

Creating a cluster action

In the previous recipe, we saw how to create a REST entry point but, to execute the action at cluster level, we need to create a cluster action.

An ElasticSearch action is generally executed and distributed in the cluster; in this recipe, we will see how to implement this kind of action. The cluster's action will be a bare minimum; we will send a string with a value for every shard, and the shards echo a resultant string, which is a concatenation of the string with the shard number.

Getting ready

You need a working ElasticSearch node, a Maven build tool, and an optional Java IDE. The code of this recipe is available in the `chapter12/rest_plugin` directory.

How to do it...

In this recipe, we will see that a REST call is converted to an internal cluster action. To execute an internal cluster action, the following classes are required:

- The `Request` and `Response` classes to communicate with the cluster.
- A `RequestBuilder` class used to execute a request to the cluster.
- An `Action` class used to register the action and bind it to `Request`, `Response`, and `RequestBuilder`.
- A `Transport*Action` class to bind the request and the response to `ShardRequest` and `ShardResponse`, respectively. It manages the `reduce` part of the query.
- The `ShardRequest` and `ShardResponse` classes to manage a shard query.

To convert a REST call into a cluster action, we will perform the following steps:

1. Write a `SimpleRequest` class, as follows:

```
public class SimpleRequest extends BroadcastOperationRequest<Simpl
eRequest> {
  private String field;
  SimpleRequest() {}
  public SimpleRequest(String... indices) {
    super(indices);
  }
  public void setField(String field) {
    this.field = field;
  }
```

```
   public String getField() {
     return field;
   }
   @Override
   public void readFrom(StreamInput in) throws
   IOException {
     super.readFrom(in);
     field = in.readString();
   }
   @Override
   public void writeTo(StreamOutput out) throws
   IOException {
     super.writeTo(out);
     out.writeString(field);
   }
 }
```

2. The `SimpleResponse` class is very similar to the `SimpleRequest` class. To bind the request and the response, an action (`SimpleAction`) is required, as follows:

```
public class SimpleAction extends ClientAction<SimpleRequest,
SimpleResponse, SimpleRequestBuilder> {
   public static final SimpleAction INSTANCE = new
   SimpleAction();
   public static final String NAME = "indices/simple";
   private SimpleAction() {
     super(NAME);
   }
   @Override
   public SimpleResponse newResponse() {
     return new SimpleResponse();
   }
   @Override
   public SimpleRequestBuilder newRequestBuilder(Client client) {
     return new SimpleRequestBuilder(client);
   }
 }
```

3. The `Transport` class is the core of the action. The code for this class is quite long, so we will present only the important parts, as follows:

```
public class TransportSimpleAction extends TransportBroadcastOpera
tionAction<SimpleRequest,
SimpleResponse, ShardSimpleRequest, ShardSimpleResponse> {
   @Override
```

```
protected SimpleResponse newResponse(SimpleRequest
request, AtomicReferenceArray shardsResponses,
ClusterState clusterState) {
  int successfulShards = 0;
  int failedShards = 0;
  List<ShardOperationFailedException> shardFailures =
  null;
  Set<String> simple = new HashSet<String>();
  for (int i = 0; i < shardsResponses.length(); i++)
  {
    Object shardResponse = shardsResponses.get(i);
    if (shardResponse == null) {
    // a non active shard, ignore...
  }
  else if (shardResponse instanceof
  BroadcastShardOperationFailedException) {
    failedShards++;
    if (shardFailures == null) {
      shardFailures = newArrayList();
    }
    shardFailures.add(new
    DefaultShardOperationFailedException((
    BroadcastShardOperationFailedException)
    shardResponse));
  } else {
    successfulShards++;
    if (shardResponse instanceof
    ShardSimpleResponse) {
      ShardSimpleResponse resp =
      (ShardSimpleResponse) shardResponse;
      simple.addAll(resp.getTermList());
    }
  }
}
  return new SimpleResponse(shardsResponses.length(),
  successfulShards, failedShards, shardFailures,
  simple);
}
@Override
protected ShardSimpleResponse
shardOperation(ShardSimpleRequest request) {
  synchronized (simpleMutex) {
    InternalIndexShard indexShard =
    (InternalIndexShard)
    indicesService.indexServiceSafe(request.
    index()).shardSafe(request.shardId().id);
```

```
        indexShard.store().directory();
        Set<String> set = new HashSet<String>();
        set.add(request.getField() + "_" +
        request.shardId());
        return new
        ShardSimpleResponse(request.shardId(), set);
    }
}
```

How it works...

As you saw, in order to execute a cluster action, the following classes are required:

- A couple of `Request/Response` classes to interact with the cluster
- A task action at the cluster level
- A couple of `Request/Response` classes to interact with the shards
- A `Transport` class to manage the map/reduce shard part that must be invoked by the REST call

These classes must extend one of the supported kinds of action available, as follows:

- `BroadcastOperationRequest/Response`: This is used for actions that must be spread across all the clusters.
- `MasterNodeOperationRequest/Response`: This is used for actions that must be executed only by the master node (such as index and mapping configuration). In order to get a simple acknowledgement on the master, there are `AcknowledgedRequest/Response` actions available.
- `NodeOperationRequest`: This is used for actions that must be executed by every node (that is, for all the node statistic actions).
- `IndexReplicationOperationRequest`: This is used for an action that must be executed at an index level (that is, deleted by query operation).
- `SingleCustomOperationRequest`: This is used for an action that must be executed only by a node (that is, analyze actions).
- `InstanceShardOperationRequest`: This is used for an action that must be executed on every shard instance (that is, bulk shard operations).
- `SingleShardOperationRequest`: This is used for an action that must be executed only in a shard (that is, the get action).

In our example, we defined an action that will be broadcast to every shard:

```
public class SimpleRequest extends BroadcastOperationRequest<SimpleRe
quest>
```

All the `Request/Response` classes extend a `Streamable` class; thus, for serializing their content, the following two methods must be provided:

▸ The `readFrom` method that reads from a `StreamInput` class, a class that encapsulates common input stream operations. This method allows you to deserialize the data that you transmit on the wire. In the previous example, we read a string with the following code:

```
@Override
public void readFrom(StreamInput in) throws IOException {
    super.readFrom(in);
    field = in.readString();
}
```

▸ The `writeTo` method writes the contents of the class to be sent via a network. The `StreamOutput` class provides convenient methods to process the output. In the preceding example, we have serialized a string, as follows:

```
@Override
public void writeTo(StreamOutput out) throws IOException {
    super.writeTo(out);
    out.writeString(field);
}
```

In both the actions, the super must be called to allow the correct serialization of the parent classes.

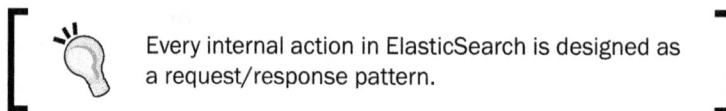

> Every internal action in ElasticSearch is designed as a request/response pattern.

To complete the `request/response` action, we must define an action that binds the request to the correct response and a builder to construct it. To do so, we need to define an `Action` class, as follows:

```
public class SimpleAction extends ClientAction<SimpleRequest,
SimpleResponse, SimpleRequestBuilder>
```

This `Action` object is a singleton object. We can obtain it by creating a default static instance and private constructors, as follows:

```
public static final SimpleAction INSTANCE = new SimpleAction();
public static final String NAME = "indices/simple";
private SimpleAction() {super(NAME);}
```

The static string `NAME` is used to uniquely identify the action at the cluster level. To complete the `Action` definition, the following two methods must be defined:

- The `newResponse` method, which is used to create a new empty response:

```
@Override public SimpleResponse newResponse() {
    return new SimpleResponse();
}
```

- The `newRequestBuilder` method, which is used to return a new request builder for the current action type:

```
@Override
public SimpleRequestBuilder newRequestBuilder(Client client) {
    return new SimpleRequestBuilder(client);
}
```

When the action is executed, the request and the response are serialized and sent to the cluster. To execute your custom code at the cluster level, a `Transport` action is required. Transport actions are usually defined as **map** and **reduce** jobs. The map part consists of executing the action on several shards (via the `ShardRequest` and `ShardResponse` methods), and the reduce part consists of collecting all the results from the shards in a response that must be sent back to the requester.

The `Transport` action is a long class with many methods, but the most important ones are the `ShardOperation` (the map part) and `newResponse` (the reduce part) methods. The original request is converted into a distributed `ShardRequest` method that is processed by the `shardOperation` method:

```
@Override protected ShardSimpleResponse shardOperation(ShardSimpleReq
uest request){
```

It is a good design principle to execute the shard operation using a lock to prevent the problem of concurrency:

```
synchronized (simpleMutex) {…}
```

To obtain the internal shard, we need to ask the `IndexService` method to return a shard based on a required index. The shard request contains the index and the ID of the shard that must be used to execute the action:

```
InternalIndexShard indexShard = (InternalIndexShard) indicesService.
indexServiceSafe(request.index()).shardSafe(request.shardId().id());
```

The `InternalIndexShard` object allows you to execute every possible shard operation (search, get, index, and many others). In this method, you can execute every data shard manipulation that you want.

> Custom shard actions can execute an application's business operation in a distributed and fast way.

In the following example, we have created a simple set of values:

```
Set<String> set = new HashSet<String>();

set.add(request.getField() + "_" + request.shardId());
```

The final step of our shard operation is to create a response to be sent back to the reduce step. In order to create the shard response, we need to return the result plus information about the index and the shard that executed the action:

```
return new ShardSimpleResponse(request.shardId(), set);
```

The distributed shard operations are collected in the reduce step (the `newResponse` method). This step aggregates all the shard results and sends back the result to the original action:

```
@Override protected SimpleResponse newResponse(SimpleRequest request,
AtomicReferenceArray shardsResponses, ClusterState clusterState){
```

Apart from the result, we also need to collect information about the shard's execution (if there are failed shard executions). This information is usually collected in three values: `successfulShards`, `failedShards`, and `shardFailures`:

```
int successfulShards = 0;
int failedShards = 0;
List<ShardOperationFailedException> shardFailures = null;
```

The request result is a set of collected strings, as shown here:

```
Set<String> simple = new HashSet<String>();
```

To collect the results, we need to iterate over the shard responses:

```
for (int i = 0; i < shardsResponses.length(); i++) {
    Object shardResponse = shardsResponses.get(i);
```

We need to skip the null `shardResponse`, mainly due to inactive shards:

```
if (shardResponse == null) {}
```

If an exception is raised, we also need to collect information about them to inform the caller:

```
else if (shardResponse instanceof
BroadcastShardOperationFailedException) {
    failedShards++;
```

```
   if (shardFailures == null) {
     shardFailures = newArrayList();
   }
   shardFailures.add(new
```

```
efaultShardOperationFailedException((BroadcastShardOperation
FailedException) shardResponse));
```

At last, we can aggregate the valid results:

```
} else {
  successfulShards++;
    if (shardResponse instanceof ShardSimpleResponse) {
      ShardSimpleResponse resp = (ShardSimpleResponse) shardResponse;
      simple.addAll(resp.getTermList());
    }
  }
```

The final step is to create the response, collected during the previous result, and check the response status using the following code:

```
return new SimpleResponse(shardsResponses.length(), successfulShards,
failedShards, shardFailures, simple);
```

Creating a cluster action is required when there are low-level operations that you want to execute very fast, such as a special facet or a complex manipulation. These operations require too principle ElasticSearch calls to be executed, but these can be easily written as a cluster action.

See also

 ▸   The *Creating a REST plugin* recipe in this chapter

Creating an analyzer plugin

ElasticSearch provides, out-of-the-box, a large set of analyzers and tokenizers to cover general needs. Sometimes, we need to extend the capabilities of ElasticSearch to add new analyzers. Typically, you need to create an analyzer plugin when you need to do the following:

 ▸   Adding standard Lucene analyzers/tokenizers, which are not provided by ElasticSearch

 ▸   Integrating third party analyzers

 ▸   Adding a custom analyzer

In this recipe, we will add a new custom English analyzer similar to the one provided by ElasticSearch.

Getting ready

You will need a working ElasticSearch node, a Maven build tool, and optionally a Java IDE. The code of this recipe is available in the `chapter12/analysis_plugin` directory.

How to do it...

An analyzer plugin is generally composed of the following three classes:

- A plugin class that registers the `BinderProcessor` class
- A `BinderProcessor` class that registers one or more `AnalyzerProviders` class
- An `AnalyzerProviders` class that provides an analyzer plugin

To create an analyzer plugin, perform the following steps:

1. The plugin class is the same as the one used in the previous recipes, plus a binder registration method:

   ```
   @Override
   public void processModule(Module module){
     if (module instanceof AnalysisModule){
       AnalysisModule analysisModule = (AnalysisModule)
       module;
       analysisModule.addProcessor(new
       CustomEnglishBinderProcessor());
     }
   }
   ```

2. The `BinderProcess` method registers the analysis module and one or more analyzer providers:

   ```
   public class CustomEnglishBinderProcessor extends AnalysisModule.
   AnalysisBinderProcessor {
        @Override
   public void processAnalyzers(AnalyzersBindings
   analyzersBindings){

   analyzersBindings.processAnalyzer(CustomEnglishAnalyzerProv
   ider.NAME, CustomEnglishAnalyzerProvider.class);
        }
   }
   ```

3. The `analyzer provider` class initializes our analyzer by passing the parameters provided in the settings:

   ```
   import org.apache.lucene.analysis.en.EnglishAnalyzer;
   import org.apache.lucene.analysis.util.CharArraySet;
   ```

```
import org.elasticsearch.common.inject.Inject;
import org.elasticsearch.common.inject.assistedinject.Assisted;
import org.elasticsearch.common.settings.Settings;
import org.elasticsearch.env.Environment;
import org.elasticsearch.index.Index;
import org.elasticsearch.index.settings.IndexSettings;
public class CustomEnglishAnalyzerProvider extends
AbstractIndexAnalyzerProvider<EnglishAnalyzer>{
  public static String NAME="custom_english";
  private final EnglishAnalyzer analyzer;
  @Inject
  public CustomEnglishAnalyzerProvider(Index index,
  @IndexSettings Settings indexSettings, Environment
  env, @Assisted String name, @Assisted Settings
  settings){
    super(index, indexSettings, name, settings);
    analyzer = new EnglishAnalyzer(version,
    Analysis.parseStopWords(env, settings,
    EnglishAnalyzer.getDefaultStopSet(),
    version),
    Analysis.parseStemExclusion(settings,
    CharArraySet.EMPTY_SET, version));
  }
  @Override
  public EnglishAnalyzer get(){
    return this.analyzer;
  }
}
```

After having built the plugin and installed it on the ElasticSearch server, our analyzer is accessible just like any native ElasticSearch analyzer.

How it works...

Creating an analyzer plugin is quite simple. This is the general workflow:

1. Wrap the analyzer initialization in a provider.
2. Register the analyzer provider in the binder so that the analyzer is accessible via the analysis module level.
3. Register the binder in the plugin.

In the previous example, we registered a `CustomEnglishAnalyzerProvider` class that extends `EnglishAnalyzer`:

```
public class CustomEnglishAnalyzerProvider extends AbstractIndexAnalyz
erProvider<EnglishAnalyzer>
```

We need to provide a name to the analyzer:

```
public static String NAME="custom_english";
```

We instantiate a private scope Lucene analyzer, provided on request with the `get` method:

```
    private final EnglishAnalyzer analyzer;
```

The `CustomEnglishAnalyzerProvider` constructor can be injected via Google Guice with settings that can be used to provide cluster defaults via index settings or `elasticsearch.yml`:

```
@Inject
public CustomEnglishAnalyzerProvider(Index index, @IndexSettings
Settings indexSettings, Environment env, @Assisted String name, @
Assisted Settings settings){
```

For our analyzer to work correctly, we need to set up the parent constructor via the `super` call:

```
super(index, indexSettings, name, settings);
```

Now, we can initialize the internal analyzer that must be returned by the `get` method:

```
analyzer = new
EnglishAnalyzer(version,Analysis.parseStopWords(env, settings,
EnglishAnalyzer.getDefaultStopSet(), version),
Analysis.parseStemExclusion(settings,
CharArraySet.EMPTY_SET, version));
```

This analyzer accepts the following:

- ▶ The Lucene version
- ▶ A list of stopwords that can be loaded by setting them or set by the default ones
- ▶ A list of words that must be excluded by the stemming step

After having created a provider for our analyzer, we need to create another class `CustomEnglishBinderProcessor` that registers our provider in the analyzer module:

```
public class CustomEnglishBinderProcessor extends AnalysisModule.
AnalysisBinderProcessor{
```

To register our analyzer in the binder, we need to override the `processAnalyzers` method. Then, we add our analyzer by defining the name (referred in the REST calls) and the class of our provider:

```
@Override public void processAnalyzers(AnalyzersBindings
analyzersBindings){
    analyzersBindings.processAnalyzer(CustomEnglishAnalyzerProvider.
NAME, CustomEnglishAnalyzerProvider.class);
  }
}
```

Finally, we need to register our binding in the plugin, hooking with `processModule` to check whether the module is an `AnalysisModule`:

```
@Override
public void processModule(Module module){
    if (module instanceof AnalysisModule){
```

The analysis module allows you to register one or more bind processors that will be initialized during the analysis module service initialization via the `addProcessor` method:

```
AnalysisModule analysisModule = (AnalysisModule) module;
analysisModule.addProcessor(new CustomEnglishBinderProcessor());
```

Creating a river plugin

In *Chapter 8, Rivers*, we saw how powerful the river plugins are. They allow you to populate an ElasticSearch cluster from different sources (DBMS, NoSQL system, streams, and so on). Creating a custom river is necessary if you need to do the following:

- Add a new NoSQL data source that is not supported by the already existing plugins
- Add a new stream type
- Add a custom business logic to import data in ElasticSearch, such as field modification, data aggregation, and, in general, a data brewery

In this recipe, we will implement a simple river that generates documents with a field that contains an incremental value and ingests them in ElasticSearch.

Getting ready

You will need a working ElasticSearch node, a Maven build tool, and optionally a Java IDE. The code of this recipe is available in the `chapter12/river_plugin` directory.

How to do it...

To create a river plugin, we need the following three classes at least:

- ▸ The plugin that registers a river module
- ▸ A river module that registers our river
- ▸ The river that executes our business logic

Perform the following steps to create a river plugin:

1. This part of the plugin class is similar to the previous one:

   ```
   ...
   public void onModule(RiversModule module){
       module.registerRiver("simple", SimpleRiverModule.class);
   }
   ...
   ```

   (The common plugin part is omitted, as it is similar to the previous one.)

2. The river module registers the river class as a singleton:

   ```
   public class SimpleRiverModule extends AbstractModule{
     @Override
     protected void configure(){

   bind(River.class).to(SimpleRiver.class).asEagerSingleton();
     }
   }
   ```

3. Now, we can write the river core. This code section is very long, so I have split it into several parts, as follows:

   - ❑ This is the code for the class definition:

     ```
     ... truncated ...
     public class SimpleRiver extends AbstractRiverComponent
     implements River {
     ... truncated ...
     ```

   - ❑ The following code is the constructor definition, in which you set up the river and collect user settings;

     ```
     @SuppressWarnings({"unchecked"})
     @Inject
     Public SimpleRiver(RiverName riverName, RiverSettings
     settings, Client client, ThreadPool threadPool) {
         super(riverName, settings);
         this.client = client;
     ```

```
    if (settings.settings().containsKey("simple")) {
      Map<String, Object> simpleSettings =
      (Map<String, Object>)
      settings.settings().get("simple");
      simpleNumber =
      XContentMapValues.nodeIntegerValue(
      simpleSettings.get("number"), 100);
      fieldName =
      XContentMapValues.nodeStringValue(
      simpleSettings.get("field"), "test");
      poll =
      XContentMapValues.nodeTimeValue(
      simpleSettings.get("poll"),
      TimeValue.timeValueMinutes(60));
    }
    logger.info("creating simple stream river for
    [{} numbers] with field [{}]", simpleNumber,
    fieldName);
    if (settings.settings().containsKey("index"))
    {
      Map<String, Object> indexSettings =
      (Map<String, Object>)
      settings.settings().get("index");
      indexName =
      XContentMapValues.nodeStringValue(
      indexSettings.get("index"), riverName.name());
      typeName =
      XContentMapValues.nodeStringValue(
      indexSettings.get("type"), "simple_type");
      bulkSize =
      XContentMapValues.nodeIntegerValue(
      indexSettings.get("bulk_size"), 100);
      bulkThreshold =
      XContentMapValues.nodeIntegerValue(
      indexSettings.get("bulk_threshold"), 10);
    } else {
      indexName = riverName.name();
      typeName = "simple_type";
      bulkSize = 100;
      bulkThreshold = 10;
    }
  }
```

❑ This is the code for the `start` function that manages the start of the river and initializes the bulk processor:

```
@Override
public void start(){
```

```
logger.info("starting simple stream");
bulkProcessor = BulkProcessor.builder(client,
new BulkProcessor.Listener() {…truncated…
}).setBulkActions(bulkSize).
setFlushInterval(TimeValue.timeValueMinutes(5))
.setConcurrentRequests(bulkThreshold).build();
thread =
EsExecutors.daemonThreadFactory(
settings.globalSettings(), "Simple
processor").newThread(new SimpleConnector());
.start();
}
```

❏ The following code is used for the `close` function, which cleans up internal states before exiting:

```
@Override
public void close() {
    logger.info("closing simple stream river");
    bulkProcessor.close();
    this.closed = true;
    thread.interrupt();
}
```

❏ This code shows a `wait` function used to reduce the throughtput:

```
private void delay() {
    if (poll.millis() > 0L) {
    logger.info("next run waiting for {}", poll);
    try {
      Thread.sleep(poll.millis());
    } catch (InterruptedException e) {
      logger.error("Error during waiting.", e,
      (Object) null);
    }
  }
}
```

❏ This is the code for a producer class that yields the item to be executed in bulk:

```
private class SimpleConnector implements Runnable {
  @Override
  public void run() {
    while (!closed) {
    try {
      for (int i = 0; i < simpleNumber; i++) {
```

```
            XContentBuilder builder =
            XContentFactory.jsonBuilder();
            builder.startObject();
            builder.field(fieldName, i);
            builder.endObject();

        bulkProcessor.add(Requests.indexRequest(indexName)
        .type(typeName).id(UUID.randomUUID().toString())
        .create(true).source(builder));
            }
            //in this case we force the bulking, but it should
        seldom be done
            bulkProcessor.flush();
            delay();
        } catch (Exception e) {
            logger.error(e.getMessage(), e,
            (Object) null);
            closed = true;
        }
        if (closed) {
            return;
            }
        }
    }
}
```

4. After having deployed the river plugin in an ElasticSearch cluster, we can activate it with a similar call, as shown here:

```
curl -XPUT localhost:9200/_river/simple_river/_meta -d '
{
  "type" : "simple",
  "simple" : {
    "field" : "myfield",
    "number" : 1000
  },
  "index" : {
    "index" : "simple_data",
    "type" : "simple_type",
    "bulk_size" : 10,
    "bulk_threshold" : 50
  }
}
```

How it works...

The river core is quite long but it covers a lot of interesting parts that are useful not only for the river, as follows:

- ▶ Processing the settings passed to a river
- ▶ Initializing a thread that populates the data (consumer) and its status management
- ▶ Executing a *safe* bulk index

A custom river class must extend the `AbstractRiverComponent` class and implement the interfaces defined in the `River` interface:

```
public class SimpleRiver extends AbstractRiverComponent implements
River {
```

The river constructor accepts the following parameters:

- ▶ The `RiverName` object that contains the name defined in the /_river/<river_ name>/_meta call.
- ▶ The river settings that are the settings passed as JSON.
- ▶ A client to send/receive data. For example, the native client of the previous chapter.
- ▶ A thread pool to control the thread allocation:

```
@Inject
    public SimpleRiver(RiverName riverName, RiverSettings settings,
    Client client, ThreadPool threadPool) {
```

We need to pass the river's name and settings to the parent constructor in order to initialize it:

```
        super(riverName, settings);
```

Then, we need to store the client for future bulk operations:

```
        this.client = client;
```

Now, we can check whether our river settings are available (the `simple` section in JSON):

```
    if (settings.settings().containsKey("simple")) {
```

Next, we can extract the number of items to be created and populate the fields:

```
    Map<String, Object> simpleSettings = (Map<String, Object>) settings.
    settings().get("simple");
    simpleNumber = XContentMapValues.nodeIntegerValue(simpleSettings.
    get("number"), 100);
    fieldName = XContentMapValues.nodeStringValue(simpleSettings.
    get("field"), "test");
    }
```

The ElasticSearch content parser gives you a lot of useful functionalities to pass this kind of data. Usually, some index settings are specified to define the index that must be used to store the data, the type that must be used, and the parameters to control the following bulk operation:

```
if (settings.settings().containsKey("index")) {
    Map<String, Object> indexSettings = (Map<String, Object>)
settings.settings().get("index");
    indexName =
XContentMapValues.nodeStringValue(indexSettings
.get("index"), riverName.name());
    typeName =
XContentMapValues.nodeStringValue(indexSettings
.get("type"), "simple_type");
    bulkSize =
XContentMapValues.nodeIntegerValue(indexSettings
.get("bulk_size"), 100);
    bulkThreshold =
XContentMapValues.nodeIntegerValue(indexSettings
.get("bulk_threshold"), 10);
```

It is good practice to provide default index names if they are not provided, as follows:

```
indexName = riverName.name();
typeName = "simple_type";
bulkSize = 100;
bulkThreshold = 10;
```

A river is internally seen as a service, so we need to provide the start and close methods. The start method initializes a bulk processor and starts the producer thread called SimpleConnector:

```
@Override
public void start() {
    logger.info("starting simple stream");
    bulkProcessor = BulkProcessor.builder(client, new
    BulkProcessor.Listener()
  {}) .setBulkActions(bulkSize).setFlushInterval(TimeValue
  .timeValueMinutes(5))
.setConcurrentRequests(bulkThreshold).build();
    thread =
EsExecutors.daemonThreadFactory(settings.globalSettings(),
"Simple processor").newThread(new SimpleConnector());
    thread.start();
}
```

The `BulkProcessor` APIs are convenient APIs introduced in the latest ElasticSearch versions to manage bulk jobs. They allow you to define the following:

- The maximum number of bulk actions via `setBulkActions`
- A concurrent bulk limit via `setConcurrentRequests`
- A flush interval via `setFlushInterval`

The `close` method usually sets the status to `closed` and stops the producer thread:

```
@Override
public void close() {
    logger.info("closing simple stream river");
    bulkProcessor.close(); // it must be closed to flush the
    contained actions
    this.closed = true;
    thread.interrupt();
}
```

In the preceding code, a `delay` method is present; it is used to delay the producer thread in order to prevent the overloading of the ElasticSearch cluster. The plugin is generally composed of a producer thread, which produces data to be indexed, and a consumer thread (in this case, we have simplified this to a single bulk function), which consumes the data in bulk actions.

The core of the river is the producer thread that generates index actions to be executed in bulk. This object is a thread and implements the methods of the `Runnable` class:

```
private class SimpleConnector implements Runnable {
```

Obviously, the main method of this class is `run`:

```
@Override
public void run() {
```

When executing the `run` part in the thread, check whether the thread is active or closed (stopped):

```
while (!closed) {
```

The main part of the `run` method generates documents with the builder (as we have seen in the previous chapter) and then adds them to the bulk processor.

There's more...

Creating a river for the first time can be a bit long and complicated, but the base skeleton is reusable (it changes very little from river to river). While developing a river, the maximum time is spent in designing and parsing the settings and in developing the `run` function of the producer thread. The others parts are often reused in a lot of rivers.

If you want to improve your knowledge of how to write rivers, some good examples are available on GitHub, and we have already seen some of them in *Chapter 8, Rivers*.

See also

- ▸ To learn more about rivers, see *Chapter 8, Rivers*
- ▸ The official ElasticSearch page that lists the most common rivers at `http://www.elasticsearch.org/guide/en/elasticsearch/reference/current/modules-plugins.html#riverS`

Index

X

Y

[PACKT] open source*
PUBLISHING   community experience distilled

Thank you for buying
ElasticSearch Cookbook
Second Edition

About Packt Publishing

Packt, pronounced 'packed', published its first book, *Mastering phpMyAdmin for Effective MySQL Management*, in April 2004, and subsequently continued to specialize in publishing highly focused books on specific technologies and solutions.

Our books and publications share the experiences of your fellow IT professionals in adapting and customizing today's systems, applications, and frameworks. Our solution-based books give you the knowledge and power to customize the software and technologies you're using to get the job done. Packt books are more specific and less general than the IT books you have seen in the past. Our unique business model allows us to bring you more focused information, giving you more of what you need to know, and less of what you don't.

Packt is a modern yet unique publishing company that focuses on producing quality, cutting-edge books for communities of developers, administrators, and newbies alike. For more information, please visit our website at www.packtpub.com.

About Packt Open Source

In 2010, Packt launched two new brands, Packt Open Source and Packt Enterprise, in order to continue its focus on specialization. This book is part of the Packt open source brand, home to books published on software built around open source licenses, and offering information to anybody from advanced developers to budding web designers. The Open Source brand also runs Packt's open source Royalty Scheme, by which Packt gives a royalty to each open source project about whose software a book is sold.

Writing for Packt

We welcome all inquiries from people who are interested in authoring. Book proposals should be sent to author@packtpub.com. If your book idea is still at an early stage and you would like to discuss it first before writing a formal book proposal, then please contact us; one of our commissioning editors will get in touch with you.

We're not just looking for published authors; if you have strong technical skills but no writing experience, our experienced editors can help you develop a writing career, or simply get some additional reward for your expertise.

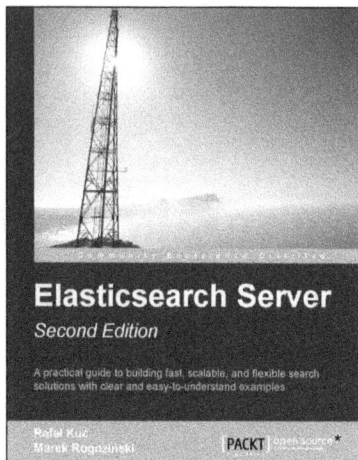

Elasticsearch Server

Second Edition

ISBN: 978-1-78398-052-9   Paperback: 428 pages

A practical guide to building fast, scalable, and flexible search solutions with clear and easy-to-understand examples

1. Learn about the fascinating functionality of Elasticsearch such as data indexing, data analysis, and dynamic mapping.

2. Fine-tune Elasticsearch and understand its metrics using its API and available tools, and see how it behaves in complex searches.

3. A hands-on tutorial that walks you through all the features of Elasticsearch in an easy-to-understand way, with examples that will help you become an expert in no time.

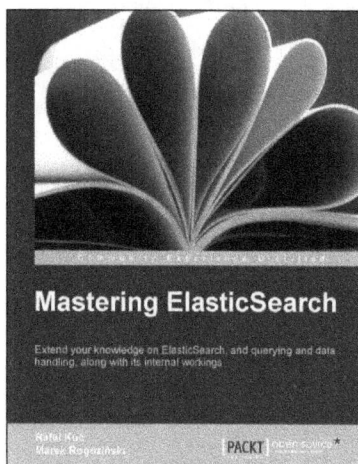

Mastering ElasticSearch

ISBN: 978-1-78328-143-5   Paperback: 386 pages

Extend your knowledge on ElasticSearch, and querying and data handling, along with its internal workings

1. Learn about Apache Lucene and ElasticSearch design and architecture to fully understand how this great search engine works.

2. Design, configure, and distribute your index, coupled with a deep understanding of the workings behind it.

3. Learn about the advanced features in an easy-to-read book with detailed examples that will help you understand and use the sophisticated features of ElasticSearch.

Please check **www.PacktPub.com** for information on our titles

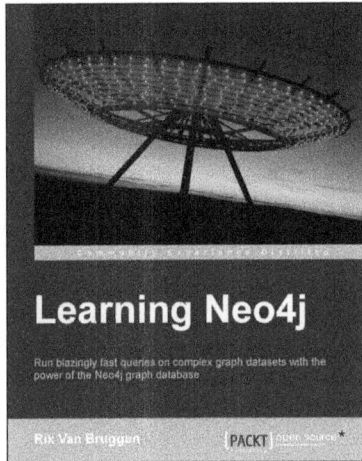

Learning Neo4j

ISBN: 978-1-84951-716-4   Paperback: 222 pages

Run blazingly fast queries on complex graph datasets with the power of the Neo4j graph database

1. Get acquainted with graph database systems and apply them in real-world use cases.

2. Get started with Neo4j, a unique NoSQL database system that focuses on tackling data complexity.

3. A practical guide filled with sample queries, installation procedures, and useful pointers to other information sources.

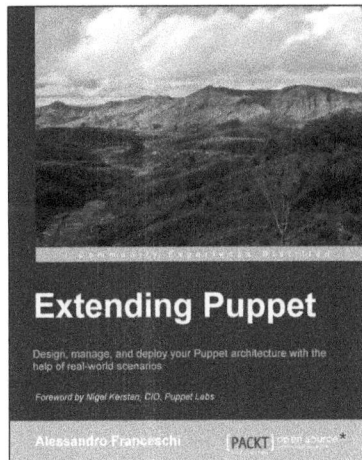

Extending Puppet

ISBN: 978-1-78398-144-1   Paperback: 328 pages

Design, manage, and deploy your Puppet architecture with the help of real-world scenarios

1. Plan, test, and execute your Puppet deployments.

2. Write reusable and maintainable Puppet code.

3. Handle challenges that might arise in upcoming versions of Puppet.

4. Explore the Puppet ecosystem in-depth, through a hands-on, example-driven approach.

Please check **www.PacktPub.com** for information on our titles

www.ingramcontent.com/pod-product-compliance
Lightning Source LLC
Chambersburg PA
CBHW080129220326
41598CB00032B/5002